The Controlled D[emolition of the]

American [Empire]

From the Founding of the Federal Reserve, to 9/11, to the Coronavirus Panic

by Jeff Berwick with Charlie Robinson

This book is dedicated to my wife, Kena, my daughter, Naomi, my son Leonardo, my seven dogs, Lucy, Bruce Lee, Lara, Jerry, Rango, Polo and Coco.

It is also with big thanks to all the team at The Dollar Vigilante including Mari-Louise Kaplan for editing, and a big thanks to Charlie Robinson for helping put together an almost incalculable amount of information into a readable format!

- Jeff Berwick

Table of Contents

PUSHING DOWN THE PLUNGER

CLEARING THE DEBRIS

Jeff asked me to write a foreword to this book because we share the same concerns about what's happening in the world today.

I've been saying for some time that Western Civilization, and the US in particular, are at a major turning point. And that they're clearly turning in the wrong direction—at least if you value the things that made them great. But then I thought more about this book's title. It's accurate. The West is no longer experiencing just decline. It's undergoing a controlled demolition.

One of the few laws I believe in is the Second Law of Thermodynamics. It basically states that, barring outsides inputs, everything falls apart over time. The phenomenon is called entropy—it's why nothing lasts forever.

That includes great civilizations. Ancient Sumer and Egypt are long gone. So are Greece and Rome. But they left a legacy of philosophy, science, art, and literature that are still with us today. They culminated in Western Civilization—the crowning achievement of human history.

Let's talk about what that means. I've listed twelve things below that are unique to the West. They're characteristics we may not think about, but they're responsible for most of what we consider good and noble in our society. Their benefits aren't automatic, or even usual to humanity, however. They all have to be actively defended and maintained, or they'll disappear.

The factors I've listed arose with Western civilization, and the US in particular, and are what made them special and different. Incidentally, I said the US-- not America-- because America doesn't really exist anymore in the US. America is an idea, a set of values, that took root in a certain piece of geography. Unfortunately, the idea of America, as well as a lot of names and statues that represent it, is now subject to controlled demolition.

America is being replaced by the US, which is just another of 200 nation-states that cover the face of the planet like a skin disease.

So what are the 12 things that made America and Western civilization different from all the others?

First, free speech. The right to say what you want to who you wish. It's enshrined in the First Amendment, but like the rest of the Bill of Rights, it's becoming a dead letter. We now live in a world where even innocent opinions are labeled hate speech, and trigger warnings are considered necessary. The meanings of words today are constantly being twisted today, and the right to use many is vanishing. As Orwell pointed out in *1984*, if you can control speech, you control thought.

Two, free thought. Controlling speech makes it much easier to control thought; they image each other. You've got to double-think these days for fear of committing a thought crime. You can forget about free minds and the concept of being a free thinker. The peasants, workers, and other drones don't need to think. Besides, it's hard work...

Three, free markets. The right to buy and sell any commodity without regulation. We have remnants of free markets and capitalism under our current regime of economic fascism, but the State taxes and regulates everything. Which mainly benefits government cronies. Now enemies of liberty are looking to enforce overt socialism, the silly notion that everyone can live at the expense of everyone else.

Four, the concept of limited government. Destroyers love the State, and they love it not despite the fact it's congealed and concentrated force, but because that's what it is. If you want to "get things done" and "move forward", as the politicos say, you need a strong government. We're moving towards a busybody society of unlimited government, a kind of dictatorship of the proletariat, where the worst people—the kind who go into government—control everything.

Five, the concept of individualism. The rugged individual, the lone Western hero, has been replaced by the collective, and identity politics. Today you're no longer supposed to view yourself as an individual, but a member of a race, sex, gender, religion, party, or some other group.

Six, rationality. That's the ability to think logically and coherently, using the faculty of reason. It's being replaced by political correctness, a secular religion, which is also replacing science. Political correctness runs on superstition and groupthink.

Seven, the concept of individual liberty. It's now considered dangerous because free people can't be easily controlled. In a free society, someone might offend, or do better, than someone else. Safety is now preferred over liberty.

Eight, the concept of progress. The idea that things can get better through hard work, savings, and innovation is a peculiarly Western idea. But you can't have real progress in a static world where nothing changes. The enemy hates progress, because some people will progress more than others, and some are left behind.

Nine, the right to privacy. Privacy doesn't exist in primitive, or collectivist, societies. In the West, privacy is being replaced by transparency, the idea that everyone has a right better to monitor and watch everyone else. Minding your own business is considered anti-social. The Chinese Social Credit System is coming to the US and will be considered a good thing.

Ten, property rights. Your primary possession is your own body, although the State believes it owns that as well. But neither do you have a real right to anything else—your income, your savings, or your home. Outright slavery has been abolished, but Americans are being transformed into serfs. We're moving towards a world based on need, not virtue. Property rights are being replaced by poverty rights.

Eleven, the Rule of Law. The West invented the idea that the law should be simple and knowable—basically do all you say you'll do, and don't impinge on others or their property. It applied to everyone, regardless of their birth, wealth, race, or anything else. The concept is being replaced with thousands of micromanaging rules, enforced arbitrarily.

Twelve, the importance of Industry and Entrepreneurship. Today industrialists are seen as "robber barons" and despoilers of nature. Entrepreneurs and developers are seen as exploiters.

It's not an all-inclusive list. But the West is unique in making all of these points part of its essence. Read them carefully. Other parts of the world have them only because they were imported from the West. Without them, men are reduced to the level of serfs or savages.

It's accurate—but very politically incorrect—to say that Western civilization is the only civilization in the world's history that's actually human. From the viewpoint of the average man, his personal freedom, and his standard of living, all the others are worthless by comparison-- with some mild exceptions. For all its charms, China's main gifts to the world have been Taoism, martial arts, and Chinese cuisine. India came up with yoga—but not much else. There's nothing from at all from Africa or the pre-Colombian Americas.

Yes, I'm being harsh. But nothing is even in the same class as Western civilization, which is responsible for almost all the good things that we have in the world today. But it's dying—being murdered really.

Western civilization is in collapse, and it's being replaced by an unnamed system, but let's call it political correctness. So what is political correctness? When I first heard the term, it was on Saturday Night Live early in the eighties. I thought it was a punchline in a skit, where a comedian acting PC was the butt of a joke. But it was completely serious, and the PC meme has now conquered Western society. The concept of political correctness should be considered perverted, degraded, and antihuman, akin to the related Soviet notion of being "politically unreliable". But now they're not only accepted but even praised. They're completely antithetical to Western civilization and its values.

In conclusion, I might cavil about a few points Jeff makes in this book. But, overall, he's spot on. The US and the West are the objects of controlled demolition. If they fall, we could be in for a new Dark Age.

- Doug Casey, Casey Research

Introduction By Jeff Berwick

Apocalypse (ἀποκάλυψις) is a Greek word that means "revelation", or "an unveiling or unfolding of things not previously known and which could not be known apart from the unveiling".

Without a doubt, the year 2020 has openly unveiled the power of governments and their rulers to remove all rights, liberty, and equality at will. The controlled demolition of freedom has been a gradual process, starting with the "Founding Fathers", linked by the US Federal Reserve, and leading up to the greatest false flag event the world has ever seen: The 9/11 terror attacks.

Some, like myself, have recognized and understood the truth long before Those Who Would Rule The World openly removed their masks with the unleashing of the Coronavirus & "planned-demic".

You see, the exact blueprint of the COVID-19 plandemic was provided by Bill Gates' Event 201 exercise in November 2019, planning for a complete shutdown of the world economic and financial system, bringing financial collapse and enslavement, impoverishment and, the "final solution", mass forced vaccinations and tracking of everyone on Earth.

It is with incredible surrealness that I release this book during the events that are unfolding around us. Yet, bizarrely, the book predicted much of what is currently ongoing at the time of this writing. In fact, I wrote the following extract from Chapter 1 in 2019, pre-Coronavirus:

In 2015, Deagel – a mysterious defense-oriented website – published predictions for a US population of just 65-million people in 2025, a decrease of over 245-million people![1]

It listed two reasons for its prediction of an American collapse by 2025:
1) a pandemic like Ebola; and
2) financial collapse.

The leadup to a financial crisis is actually pretty easy to imagine, especially in light of what everyone saw during the 2008 meltdown. There will be lies, lies, and more lies told by the banks, the media, and politicians, leading up to the crisis, and especially during it. Much like when Ben Bernanke came out and told

---

[1] Deagel, "List of Countries Forecast 2025".

the world that the fundamentals of the housing market were strong immediately before the housing market collapsed, the level and amount of lies one should be expecting is massive.

When they come out and make a huge point of telling the people that everything is fine, that is the cue that everything is NOT fine, and it is coming.

The Ebola part of their prediction is much less obvious because it could come from a variety of directions, but the one thing that is for certain is that the event, or the trigger, will be intentional and deliberate, not some fluke like the movie Outbreak where a wayward monkey accidentally infects the country. It will be portrayed as being an accident, or caused by some rogue nation as an act of international biological terrorism.

What will America look like in the grips of a viral pandemic crisis? It will not be pretty and everyone can kiss civility goodbye. Americans cannot control themselves on Black Friday when they are elbowing old ladies to get a $2 salad mixer, how are they going to act restrained when they think that their neighbor might kill them just by accidentally breathing on them?

Forced vaccinations?

Almost certainly.

Indiscriminate quarantines?

Yes.

Panic fueled by the media?

Yes, like the world has never seen before.

Lies by the CDC?

Of course. They do that already.

The Greatest Depression in human history?

That, unfortunately, is already baked in the cake.

Bizarre. Surreal. Only, it is not actually that bizarre, or surreal, because the very foundation of the book rests on connecting the dots of a centuries-long agenda to destroy the Western world and bring in a "new world order" – long before our brave "new normal".

In the book, we use the metaphor of a building, from its planning and foundation phases, to laying the first bricks creating support columns – only to be demolished, once it has served its purpose, to make space for a new formation – Ground Zero if you will.

And now that it is clear that the final charge, in the shape of a manufactured viral outbreak, has been laid in the controlled demolition of the American Dream – I suddenly find myself writing about world-changing history in real-time.

"The American Empire is coming to an end, that is undeniable, but what may surprise many is that when it happens, it is not an accident and it will not be left to random chance."
– The Controlled Demolition of the American Empire

What is This Book About?

If you are new to my work then much of this book will shock you.
To put it plainly, everything you have ever been told by governments, the mainstream media, Hollywood movies, and the government indoctrination (school) system has been mostly all lies.

If that shocks you then take a deep breath and read slowly. Like they said in the movie, The Matrix, once you take the red pill (truth) you can never go back to the way you were before.

For those of you who have been following my work at The Dollar Vigilante since we began in June 2010 with the tagline, "Surviving and Prospering, During and After the Dollar Collapse", you will be a lot more prepared for what is in this box as I have spoken about most of these topics over the last ten years.

I have never connected all the dots in one succinct, all-encompassing book with all the evidence clearly laid out.

The way things are going, though, there might soon need to be an addendum, or even an entirely new book, looking back on how the US and all of Western society collapsed.

However, the story has not been fully written yet. If enough people can become aware of the contents of this book we can stave off our Brave New World, Orwellian "new normal" future.

And so, if you enjoy this book, please share it and its contents with as many people as possible.

Our future depends on it.

- Jeff Berwick

Symptoms of A Dying Empire

All empires fall.

The history books will clearly show that America was an Empire.

Was. Past tense.

They might not call it such, but for a long time, the United States has demonstrated all the characteristics of a modern empire, including a centralized government, a strong military, a dominant position in the global political theatre, and American imperialism – extending political, economic, and cultural influence and control over areas beyond its boundaries. (Also referred to as economic colonization)

It is tempting to assume that empire-building was really only a distant part of human history or a relic of an almost forgotten time, but the reality is that most people have been living through the gradual destruction of the largest Empire history has ever known, the British Empire, as well as the massive expansion of the American Empire.

Some people will be able to say that during their lifetime they were witness to the end of both...

Empires, governments, and countries rise and fall for the same reason: The thirst for power.

If the love of power is the root of all evil, then greed is the seed. Most emperors believe they are the gods of men. Their arrogance and hunger for wealth and power are the reason they rise and progress, getting stronger and ever more powerful. That arrogance is part of the fuel that transforms a relatively normal, but growing, civilization into one with empirical aspirations: the whole-hearted belief that they will remain relevant and in charge of the world prevents them from being objective in their analysis of their strengths and weaknesses.

History shows that there are many common symptoms forewarning the end of an empire. Significantly, the following signs preceded the fall of the Roman Empire:

Subjugation: During the early parts of the Roman Empire, as many as one-third of the people in Rome were slaves. Slaves were people of all races, ages, and genders mostly brought to the Roman Empire from the new lands its mighty war machine had conquered. Other slaves were bought from slave traders and pirates who captured people from foreign lands and brought them to Rome.

Children of slaves also became slaves. And sometimes criminals were sold into slavery. A few people even sold themselves into slavery in order to pay their debts. When Rome's oppressed slave labor finally woke to the power within their numbers, the empire was rocked by a labor deficit.

Aggression: The Ancient Romans fought many battles and wars in order to expand and protect their empire. The regime became obsessed with power and as such, would strive for dominance over their neighbors and promoting fear over their enemies. This over-involvement in the world constantly involved more and more corruption money going towards military control of its territorial possessions. There were also civil wars where Romans fought Romans in a ruthless power struggle for control and its most influential wars may have been the ones it fought against itself.

Importantly, the slaves of Rome banded together and rebelled several times during the history of Ancient Rome. With many enemies rising up against the State, Rome struggled to marshal enough troops and resources to defend its frontiers from three major slave rebellions called the "Servile Wars." Perhaps the most famous of these was the Third Servile War led by the gladiator Spartacus.

Extortion: Even as Rome was under attack from outside forces, it was also crumbling from within thanks to a severe financial crisis. Monetary policy's first aim is and always has been to serve the needs of the rulers, not the ruled. In Imperial Rome, constant wars and overspending had significantly lightened the treasury's coffers, and oppressive taxation and inflation had widened the gap between rich and poor. In the hope of avoiding the taxman, which levied taxes against land, homes, and other real estate, slaves, animals, personal items, and monetary wealth, many members of the wealthy classes had even fled to the countryside and set up independent fiefdoms. Price controls and quotas and extortion fees became increasingly burdensome and trade began to collapse, causing desperate food shortages.

Diversion: The last days of the Roman empire were marked by its moral decline, but in reality, it was the "bread-and-circuses" used by corrupt governments to placate a population that brought about the fall of the empire.

"Give them bread and circuses and they will never revolt." – Juvenal, a poet in Ancient Rome.

People became, and were encouraged to become, more interested in "being happy" than in education and training or being confronted with inconvenient truths that would force them out of their comfort coma. Their primary need was amusement, and they were entirely satisfied to blindly follow whoever gave them a sense of protection and safety and played into their pleasure and wants regardless of the consequences.

Sound familiar?

Modern scholars like to proclaim that the Roman Empire did not "fall", but instead refer to it as a "transformation". Call it whatever people want, but the modern Portuguese, Chinese, Spanish, Russian and British empires all have many of the same things in common:

• They all collapsed over a period of time.

• They all had scapegoats for their kingdoms' collapse, from natural disasters to disease epidemics, peasant revolt against a corrupt ruling class, constant warfare among states and nations, economic troubles, or some combination thereof.

• None of their destruction was intentional or planned.

So what is it that distinguishes the current crumbling of the American Empire from all its predecessors?

America is Burning. All Signs Point to Arson

One crucial detail: The American Empire is not dying naturally of manmade causes like most of the empires which went before. America has been rigged for demolition and the evidence is everywhere – from its internal crumbling due to a manipulated financial crisis, to external attack because of the rise of the Eastern Empire.

Its intentional destruction can be seen in the purposeful breakdown of the population's mental and physical health through mercury and aluminum filled vaccines, hard street drugs, Big Pharma drugs, cigarettes and alcohol, silent EMF pollution, toxic chemtrails, fluoride in the drinking water, poisonous GMO food, radioactive body scanners at the airports, poor nutrition, emotional stress, financial instability, political uncertainty, and societal disconnection.

It is carefully hidden behind a constant barrage of disinformation aimed at disguising the Machiavellian false reality manufactured to create a culture of helplessness, hopelessness, ambivalence, and blind acceptance.

Basically, they are feeding people bullshit and the people are swallowing with a smile.

The term "Rome is burning" refers to the Great Fire of Rome on the night of 19 July 64 AD. This often goes hand in hand with "Fiddling while Rome burns" which means to take little to no productive action during a crisis. The phrase refers to the legend of the Roman Emperor Nero playing the lyre as Rome burned down.

Speaking of classic history, interestingly, the word "praetor" in Latin doubles as moneylender or judge, while the Praetorian Guard (Latin: *cohortes praetoriae*) was an elite unit of the Imperial Roman army whose members served as personal bodyguards and intelligence for the Roman emperors.

In modern English, "praetorian" means degenerate or evil...

Yet, even Rome, with its cast of evil *praetors* and *praetorians*, emperors, philosophers, slaves, and gladiators, could not dream up the intent to carefully originate three of the most devastating Big Lies the world has ever seen:

- On 11 September 2001, the 9/11 terror attack became a real-life test for the "five exercise hijack events" which North American Aerospace Defense Command's (NORAD) practiced between November 1999 and October 2000 – all of which included "a suicide crash into a high-value target". The results were perfect, with no questions asked about the preceding identical-coincidental "scenario-planning exercises".

- On 7 July 2005, the 7/7 London bombings perfectly mirrored the simulation of "simultaneous attacks on an underground and mainline station" and "bombs going off precisely at the railway stations" at which the actual bombings occurred.

- On 15 April 2013, the Boston Marathon Bombing almost perfectly matched the role-play exercise called Urban Shield, in which investigators had to track down footage of the bombers caught by street surveillance cameras and the phones of "witnesses" – eerily similar to the police investigation that led to the capture of the alleged Boston Marathon bombers.

"The real thing happened before we were able to execute", said a law enforcement official with direct knowledge of the planned exercise. *"We've already been tested".*

All in the name of practice for the Biggest Lie Of All: The 2020 Plandemic that would start world destruction.

A lie so big that the human mind cannot comprehend its enormity and therefore refuse to.

Hitler said it clearly: *"It would never come into their heads to fabricate colossal untruths, and they would not believe that others could have the impudence to distort the truth so infamously. Even though the facts which prove this to be so may be brought clearly to their minds, they will still doubt and waver and will continue to think that there may be some other explanation. For the grossly impudent lie always leaves traces behind it, even after it has been nailed down, a fact which is known to all expert liars in this world and to all who conspire together in the art of lying."* — Adolf Hitler, Mein Kampf, vol. I, ch. X

However, for the Biggest Lie to work, the structure of the American Empire had to be hollowed out from the inside by the rats and parasites until all it took to cave in the structure was one good kick to the front door for the whole place to come down.

So that is what they did: repeatedly weaken the structure with a great, big wrecking ball that destroyed, swing by swing, the Economy (swing), Education (swing), Health (swing), and Freedom (swing, swing, swing).

But, importantly, the United States government did not do it alone. And they did not do it over the course of ten or twenty or fifty years.

The Roman Empire ruled for close to 1500 years. The United States of America is less than 250 years old – yet its current rotten political landscape and festering problems have been orchestrated almost from the very beginning – right from that great moment in history when the Declaration of Independence was signed in 1776.

So if a planned functional obsolescence of the American Empire is true, what does it say about the people running the show, and what are the implications for the future of the nation?

The Secret Order of Power and Profit

Or if one is looking for something a bit more familiar – the New World Order...

One of the signs of an Empire that is due for destruction is government corruption. And who is ultimately the Masters of All Beings everywhere in the world? They typically operate under the guise of your friendly neighborhood Senate or Parliament, but in reality, the true Ruling Party is a combination of oligarchs, plutocrats, and kleptocrats taking control of the government. In plain language – the Illuminated old Elite and new Billionaires, who control and operate the united nations of the world, the central banks, the military, and the corporations – and have been doing so for hundreds of years.

People need to get really honest with themselves about who is running the show in America, and virtually every other country in the world:

It is not the federal government, or parliament, or House of Whatever (although they all have a role to play).

It is not Donald Trump, though he fantasizes about leading the charge on a white horse that really brings out the orange in his skin.

The real stars of the show are the Corporations and the Military-Information-Terror complex, and they are driving the world off a cliff like they were Thelma and Louise in a red convertible. They are in the UN, the Church, and the WHO. They sit on thrones and boards and wait for their rings to be kissed in homage and awe.

Some call them the Controllers.

These Controllers have used the old system of election processes to get a foothold in governments all over the world, then financed the candidates that could rig the system from the inside. For instance, America's Citizens United that allowed the internal mechanism to be permanently rewired in a way that benefits the companies with enough money to buy a voice. The more money, the louder the voice.

To refresh one's memory of the definition of bribery: the act of offering someone money or something valuable in order to persuade them to do something for you.

They are not the front-office politicians, but they have reset the rules of the election game to favor themselves – creating a feedback loop that uses the money to finance candidates with the ability to change laws. The changes to these laws then create more power, which in turn, allows for even more money to be made.

Take America as an example.

Much like the housing market in a city like Los Angeles, at some point, the home prices rise to a level that creates a major separation and people are either in as owners, or they are out as renters, for good.

The same has happened in Washington, District of Criminals (D.C.), where those with money have rigged the system in a way that locks out the vast majority of the American people. They no longer have a say in what happens in their government, leaving them in a position of hoping that someone with money happens to want the same thing they want, and has financed a candidate in their district to try and make that happen.

They have essentially been relegated to wishing for good luck.

That is the state of America these days. The rest of the world is not looking much better.

The multinational corporations and the Military-Information-Terror complex boast about the coming digital age that will bring the world together, while they re-key the locks so that the American people will be forever outside of their government, looking in the window while trying to wiggle their old key in the door and wondering why it no longer fits.

America has lit the fuse on its own destruction through the arrangements it has built linking the federal government with these two destructive entities and their funding mechanism, the private Federal Reserve central bank.

Wake up! Humanity is being shackled to the Slave Masters by their own indebtedness. When people have used up all their Monopoly money from their stimulus checks and business rescue and mortgage deferrals THEY WILL HAVE TO PAY IT BACK! And when they cannnot do so, they will be a debt slave – forever bound to their liege lord in the labor bondage contract they signed when they accepted their totalitarian control over their body, their mind, and their freedom.

"Brace yourself. The American empire is over. And the descent is going to be horrifying." – Chris Hedges, Pulitzer Prize-winning journalist, *The World As It Is*.

Crash!

Famously, at a UN dinner in 1994, David Rockefeller said, *"We are on the verge of a global transformation. All we need is the right major crisis".*

It is easy to imagine these masters of men, the most powerful and richest people in the world, plotting "The Day That Changed America" over a soupçon of rich French cognac and fat Cuban cigars.

It all started with the Department of Offense, slyly named the Department of Defense. As with all things today, Orwellian doublespeak is everywhere.

As far as the United States is concerned, foreign countries must submit themselves fully to Washington if they wish for their governmental structure to remain intact. Some have described this as a sort of vassal state, or a country that gives the appearance of retaining their independence while actually functioning as a captured satellite of the American Empire.

The terms of this arrangement are rather clear and to the point: do what the Empire demands, vote the way they tell the country to vote, and allow for all sorts of one-sided concessions, or else the country will be painted as an emerging world political problem through the control and manipulation of their corporate media and dealt with accordingly.

Rogue states, from the point of view of the American Empire, that make it through the gauntlet of bad publicity, verbal attacks, criminal accusations, and blatant lies than face the next phase which features physical control through the destabilization of their economy, the intentional dismantling of their established political structure, and the omnipotent threat and the eventual emergence of a West-backed political rival. The message is clear: bow to Washington's demands or you will be replaced; bend to their will or be broken in two.

For those considering the Devil's Bargain, they must come to understand that they can either do it the easy way or the hard way, with an almost unlimited variety of hard ways on the drawing board.

In South America, they have a term for this sort of deal: Plata O Plomo, Silver or Lead.

Take the bribe or they take your life. It is really that simple, and a failure to comprehend the lengths that the American government will go to in order to maintain their failing grip on world power is done so at one's own risk.

Author John Perkins explained the game in which he stepped in on behalf of his corporate bosses to offer the silver in exchange for their cooperation. He also explained what happened when those in positions of power turned their backs on the bribes, and how the jackals went about delivering the lead in the form of very messy plane crashes involving General Torrijos in Panama, as well as the former president of Ecuador, Jaime Roldos, two leaders that were dismissive of the demands of the corporatocracy and met similar fates over the course of a few months in 1981.[2]

The goal is empire building, the cover had always been "spreading democracy", but the new term is "humanitarian interventions". E1very time the term "humanitarian intervention" is pushed through the controlled media, what they really mean is "empire building".

The corporate media latches on to a particular story involving a country that is experiencing major hardship, usually in the form of bombs raining down on their country, targeted killings of political members, chemical attacks against civilians, drinking water, and food shortages, and a rogue terrorist group responsible for all of the carnage. The aftermath is shown across televisions in the Western world with the blame placed directly on the terrorist group, and the push towards a "humanitarian intervention" begins. What is not mentioned to the viewer is that the terrorist group responsible for these events is 100% funded by the West, usually the CIA, in order to stir up trouble and provide them with the pretext for getting involved in a country that does not want them.

Order Out of Chaos, That Is the Strategy

---

[2] John Perkins, *Confessions of an Economic Hitman*.

They create the problem, then step up to offer the solution to the problem that they just created. That is the truth about the foreign policy decisions made by the American Empire. They intend to get involved in every situation happening on Earth so that they can manipulate it in a way that benefits them, all the while pretending that they are there to save the day.

The problem that the American Empire now has is that the word is out about who they really are and what they are actually up to. They cannot sneak up on anybody any longer, and they have been running the same play for so long that countries know what to expect, as evidenced with what happened, or more accurately, what did not happen, in the Syrian province of Idlib in the fall of 2018 once the word of an impending false flag attack was leaked by Putin in advance in order to disrupt the event.

Neocon psychopath and former United Nations representative, Nikki Haley, was in charge of the set up for the event during her fake outburst at the U.N. when she told the delegation that:

"The world has seen a clear military escalation from Assad and his allies, whose militaries have conducted over 100 airstrikes in the Syrian province of Idlib. If Assad, Russia, and Iran continue down the path they are on, the consequences will be dire. I also want to reiterate what I said last week to the Assad regime and anyone else contemplating the use of chemical weapons in Syria. The United States followed through when we said that we would respond to the use of chemical weapons."

The Russian government said that there was going to be footage of the White Helmets, a fully-financed arm of Western intelligence agencies, treating supposed victims of a staged chemical weapon attack by Damascus against their own people. Video footage meant to prove that the Syrian government had conducted a chemical weapon attack in Idlib would be provided to global news outlets.

Multiple Middle East TV channels and even a US news channel had been sent to Jisr al-Shughur to produce the footage needed for the staged event, according to the Russian Center for Syrian Reconciliation. It stated that the intelligence came from local residents of Jisr al-Shughur.[3]

Russia had repeatedly warned that another false flag chemical weapon attack was being prepared in Idlib, with the hope of giving the American Empire the justification to attack the Syrian government, which is what they were desperate

---

[3] RT, *Filming of Staged Chemical Attack in Idlib, Syria Begins - Russian MoD.*

for. American officials had threatened Assad with retaliation if he used chemical weapons in Idlib and even preemptively assigned the blame for any such attack to him, which made it pretty obvious that they were planning to use a false flag attack and blame it on Assad. What they did not want was for a country like Russia to announce their plans in advance, thus removing the element of surprise and creating a difficult explanation for an event that would unfold exactly as Russia said it would.

With their trick exposed and the Globalists caught completely off guard, the staged chemical attack did not happen, thanks to Russia. Of course, that was not something that the American people would ever hear about on their nightly news, and nobody ever gets credit for a non-event, but Russia threw a big red monkey wrench in the American War Machine and probably saved Syria from a full-blown invasion by the West.

The push for wars in Syria and Iran fulfills multiple agendas. The Neocon Globalists that are loyal to Israel are determined to redraw the map in the Middle East, on behalf of their partners in Tel Aviv. They want the oil that is under the ground, and they want the people destroyed that are above ground. A destabilized Middle East is what Israel is focused on bringing about because it allows them to control the region, an impressive feat for such a small nation. This is part of the Yinon Plan for a Greater Israel.[4]

These wars are extremely profitable for the arms manufacturers that sell their products to the military. These companies cannot sell new products until the ones they sold last year get used, so they will always push for more wars as a business model. Any war will do, but preferably the ones that last a very long time and turn into quagmires, like Vietnam, Afghanistan, and Iraq.

Smokescreen of Chaos

Another reason for these wars is that they are a form of distraction for the American people. One would think that after 19+ years of wars in the Middle East the last thing the American people would want is another war, but the media sees things much differently. If the topic of conversation can be steered towards discussing the finer points of dropping bombs on people, then there is less time on the nightly news to expose the very real economic issues caused by the debasing of the dollar, and the whereabouts of the money that has disappeared down the governmental rat holes.

---

[4] Michel Chossudovsky, *Greater Israel: The Zionist Plan for the Middle East.*

The corporate media have been playing the demonization card with Iran for years, but Syria has been the immediate focus. They are pushing for wars every single day, and the reason for this is because they are the mouthpiece for the CIA and they want chaos all over the planet – just so they can provide a "miracle" solution!

The push towards escalating the war in Syria and instigating a war with Iran is not some haphazard endeavor that sprung up from nowhere. It has been planned for years and is right on schedule. Think that sounds a bit fanciful? Remember what General Wesley Clark said to Amy Goodman on Democracy Now!:

"This is a memo that describes how we're going to take out seven countries in five years, starting with Iraq, and then Syria, Lebanon, Libya, Somalia, Sudan and, finishing off, Iran."

This is not an accident. This is not a reaction to an event, it is the intention of those in control, and if people actually stop to listen to what these maniacs are telling the people they will understand the plan. General Wesley Clark knows what the plan is and he has told the world. If the world chooses to pretend that he is a kook and dismiss his claims then it is up to the rest of the people that are awake to sound the alarm bells about what is coming.

A war with Iran would be catastrophic for both sides, and it would have the added implication of drawing Russia into the fight, just the way they want it. So what started the mess in the Middle East that got the American Empire involved in the first place? The Tale of 9/11 is a story so outrageous and scary that nobody in their right mind could ever make it up, so it must be true. Something so harmful to the nation that anyone who denies its truth puts the very country at risk through their lack of patriotism and willingness to expose the country to the potential division of the public.

The First Big Lie

The official story of 9/11 that the corporate media sold to the public was a conspiracy theory, to borrow an overused term of theirs.

The United States government and their lackeys in the corporate media put forth a version of the events of September 11th, 2001 that are laughable, disjointed, and totally impossible. Scientifically impossible. Criminally impossible. Physically impossible.

Some might not understand what 9/11 has to do with the final collapse of the American Empire, or how something that happened two decades earlier was used to lay the foundation for the destruction of the country? It was more about what came as a direct result of 9/11 in the way of federal regulations and laws that were enacted after that event happened. An understanding that the events surrounding 9/11 were actually false flag events is paramount to uncovering why it happened.

The reason why 9/11 had to happen, as seen through the eyes of the Globalist cabal running the world, was to use the event as the pretext to unveil a control grid and reduction of personal rights that Orwell would be shocked by, while also creating the cover story to justify launching the "War on Terror" in order to destroy the powerful countries that challenged the Project for a New American Century's vision for the Middle East.[5]

The story of Muslim hijackers was a lie designed to give America a reason to get involved in a military conflict that would destroy the Middle East, make the arms companies richer than they already were, control the oil in Iraq and prevent Saddam Hussein from selling it for anything other than the dollar, allow the CIA to control the $15 trillion in minerals and set up their opium growing and distribution operation in Afghanistan to fund their black projects, make sure none of the regional countries were allowed to challenge Israel's control of the region, allow trillions of dollars to be diverted into the intelligence agencies, replace foreign leaders with ones of PNAC's choosing, remove a couple of million Muslims from the planet, create a culture of fear within America, and drain the wealth from the United States in order to weaken the country so that it can be brought down later.

The fake story of 9/11 also had another unintended consequence: it galvanized a nation under one flag, it made questioning the official story tantamount to treason, and it normalized blatant racism against Muslims as the new reality in a post-9/11 America.

In order for the official story to be true, the laws of physics would have had to have been suspended on that day, especially when reviewing the 9/11 Commission Report, more accurately known as the 9/11 Omission Report, which may as well have been written with crayons to reflect the total lack of anything

---

[5] The Project for a New American Century: *Rebuilding America's Defenses*, September 2000.

resembling science, truth, or seriousness.

Those that have taken a deeper look found the controlled demolition of Building 7 to be an insurmountable hurdle that defies logic, explanation, and science, not to mention the fact that the American corporate media never acknowledged that the building even fell. The BBC did, actually, report that it collapsed, however, they did so 26 minutes before it actually happened, making them either psychics, liars, or collaborators.

The media, with a straight face, told the world a story about a hijacker's magical paper passport that somehow flew out of an exploding airplane, through the giant fireball, around a pulverized building then somehow landed safely blocks away at the foot of an FBI agent who was able to realize that it was from Satam Muhammed Abdel Rahman al-Suqami, one of the hijackers of American Flight 11.[6]

The media spoke of how Mohammad Atta, the mastermind of the operation, left his suicide note and confession letter inside his luggage that he checked into the very plane that he intended to crash into the World Trade Center an hour later, but coincidentally that one piece of luggage was lost by United Airlines and found by, wait for it, an FBI agent that opened the suitcase, found the confession letter plus a fake prayer, and solved the case in less than an afternoon.[7]

But if someone questions the official story of 9/11 that makes them a "conspiracy theorist"?

Stop it. Just stop it.

Most people are not aware that these things actually happened on 9/11, or in the aftermath of the event, but they most certainly did. Those unaware of the scope of the crimes that were committed on that day in 2001, or that only sought their information about 9/11 from the corporate media, might initially find the following disturbing, disrespectful to the victims, blasphemous, crazy, inaccurate, or maybe even treasonous. None of those terms makes this list any less true, and the understanding of what happened on that day is fundamental to comprehend what those that perpetrated 9/11, and we are not talking about 19 Arabs with box cutters, have planned to finish the job that they started and that is to finally destroy America.

---

[6] CNN, Garrick Utley, September 2001.
[7] Bob Woodward, Washington Post, *"In Hijacker's Bag, A Call To Planning, Prayer, and Death."* 2007.

This is not meant to be a complete list, just a collection of interesting facts that went unreported or underreported pertaining to the events of that day.

• Three buildings fell on 9/11, not two.

• Larry Silverstein bought the leases for the complex for $115 million just weeks before the event and specifically insured the buildings against terrorist events, though he had been running the half-empty buildings that were filled with asbestos for decades.

• Silverstein, who admits that he speaks on the phone to Israeli Prime Minister Netanyahu every Sunday, cashed out $4.55 billion from his insurance settlement.[8]

• Benjamin Netanyahu wrote a book in 1995 in which he predicted that the World Trade Center would be brought down by "militant Islam".

• Silverstein admitted on a PBS documentary that he gave the order to "pull it", then watched as WTC 7 came down at free-fall speed at 5:25 pm on the afternoon of September 11th, 2001.

• Larry Silverstein and his family members skipped their normal daily routine of having breakfast at Windows on the World on the 107th floor of WTC Tower 1 because of a dermatologist appointment.

• Four men were arrested in New Jersey after police were called on the morning of September 11th, 2001 due to their suspicious activities. They were filming the destruction of the Twin Towers from a tripod-mounted video camera on the roof of a moving van from a Mossad front company called Urban Moving Systems that had a picture of a plane crashing into two buildings, and the men were all dancing in celebration.[9]

• An FBI alert, known as a BOLO or "Be on the Lookout," was sent out at 3:31 p.m. on September 11th, 2001. It read: "Vehicle possibly related to New York terrorist attack. White, 2000 Chevrolet van with New Jersey registration with 'Urban Moving Systems' sign on back seen at Liberty State Park, Jersey City, NJ, at the time of the first impact of the jetliner into the World Trade Center. Three individuals with vans were seen celebrating after the initial impact and subsequent explosion. FBI Newark Field Office requests that, if the van is

---

[8] Anemona Hartocollis, New York Times, *"Developer Sues to Win $12.3 Billion in 9/11"*.
[9] Greg Fernandez, Jr., 21st Century Wire, *"9/11 Revisited: Declassified FBI Files Reveal New Details About 'The Five Israelis'"*.

located, hold for prints and detain individuals".[10]

• The van left the scene but was later stopped near the George Washington Bridge and was packed with explosives.

• Later the FBI searched the offices of Urban Moving Systems and questioned owner Dominik Suter, causing him to flee to Israel before he could be questioned further. Eventually, Suter's name appeared on the May 2002 FBI Suspect List, along with the 19 hijackers.[11]

• The four men, known as the "Dancing Israeli's" were all Israeli citizens, and were deported after two months back to Israel at the direction of Michael Chertoff, a dual U.S./Israeli citizen himself. They were not prosecuted.[12]

• The Dancing Israeli's went on national television in Israel and admitted that they "were there to document the event".[13]

• On June 22, 2001, Urban Moving Systems received a one-time payment of $498,750 from the Federal Government Assistance Program.[14]

• Odigo, an Israeli instant messaging service, said that two of its workers received messages two hours before the Twin Towers attack on September 11 predicting the attack would happen.[15]

• The American Think Tank "The Project For a New American Century" (PNAC) published a paper just 12 months before the event claiming that in order for their proposal to get the type of support they believed they would require, they would need "some catastrophic and catalyzing event – like a new Pearl Harbor".

• Half of the members of PNAC are dual U.S./Israeli citizens.[16]

• There was a hurricane that was churning towards the coast of New York in the three days leading up to the event, but the corporate news forgot to mention that to the citizens. It turned the opposite direction on the morning of September

---

[10] East Rutherford Police Department CSRR# 014157, Reported by Sgt. Dennis Rivelli, General report filed by PO De-Carlo.
[11] Christopher Bollyn, July 31, 2002, "Terror Suspect Hiding in Israel".
[12] Mark Gaffney, "9/11: The FBI Report and The Dancing Israelis Standing Truth On Its Ear".
[13] Oded Ellner, National Israeli television.
[14] FedSpending.org/faads, via the Way Back Machine, as the entry has been removed.
[15] Haaretz, July 16, 2004, "Odigo Says Workers Were Warned of Attack".
[16] Christopher Bollyn, *The War on Terror: The Plot To Rule the Middle East.*

11th, immediately following the event.[17]

• The Twin Towers were pulverized and turned into a fine powder, a physical impossibility if the destruction was actually due to jet fuel and a pancaking of the floors.[18]

• Multiple bombs were reported exploding in the basement and sub-basement levels in WTC 1 & 2 before the planes hit the two buildings. These explosions were reported by workers, firemen, police, and can be heard on multiple private videos of the event.[19]

• There were no bodies found in the Shanksville crash site.[20]

• There are massive cancer-related deaths of first-responders that worked on the site in the days after 9/11.

• Not only did AA 11 and UA 175 both fly over Stewart International Airport in New Windsor, NY, but they both flew over it at the same time and switched off their transponders at the same moment.

• Stewart International Airport became the first U.S. commercial airport to be privatized when United Kingdom-based National Express Group was awarded a 99-year lease on the airport, under Governor Nelson Rockefeller. It was used as a hub for the importation of illicit drugs, using American military assets as cover, and also was the airport used when the American hostages returned from Iran.

• A large dump truck was found under Building 6, stuck on a fallen steel beam, and was filled with gold bars. The vault in the basement level of the building was empty and the door was left wide open.[21]

• There were multiple war games being conducted at the same exact time, in the same area, simulating 29 different hijackings of airplanes scenarios.[22]

• George H.W. Bush was having a meeting with Osama Bin Laden's father in Washington D.C. at the moment that the 9/11 event was happening.[23]

---

[17] Jon Erdman, Weather.com, "The 9/11 Hurricane That Missed New York City".
[18] Dr. Judy Woods, *Where Did The Towers Go?*
[19] Dylan Avery, *Loose Change.*
[20] Wallace Miller, Coroner, Somerset County, Pennsylvania.
[21] Nicholas Wapshott, Times Online, "Crushed Towers Give Up Cache of Gold Ingots".
[22] James Corbett, The Corbett Report, *9/11 War Games.*
[23] Michel Chossudovsky, Global Research, March 2015.

- The Bin Laden family was allowed to leave the United States in a private jet while the rest of the country's airplanes were grounded by the FAA.[24]

- The Securities and Exchange Commission declared a national emergency and invoked its emergency powers to ease regulatory restrictions for clearing and settling security trades for the next 15 days. These changes allowed an estimated $240 billion in covert government securities to be cleared upon maturity without the standard regulatory controls around identification of ownership.[25]

- Despite being the most secure building in the world, there were no videos released to the public showing an airplane hitting the Pentagon, only three frames of film that only show an explosion but no cause.

- Several television shows were aired before 9/11 and featured plots showing hijacked airplanes being flown into the Twin Towers and blamed on terrorists when it was actually their own government.[26]

- On September 10th, 2001, a number of top Pentagon brass suddenly cancel travel plans for the next morning, apparently because of security concerns.[27]

- President Bush said he was opposed to establishing an independent commission to probe 9/11, and Vice President Cheney also opposed any public hearings on 9/11.[28]

- When pushed to open an investigation by the "Jersey Girls", Bush named Henry Kissinger to lead an independent investigation into the 9/11 terrorist attacks. That decision lasted two weeks until public pressure was so great that Kissinger was forced to resign.

- The White House refused to increase the $3 million in funding for the 9/11 Commission's investigation into the worst terror attack ever.[29]

- A book by 9/11 Commission chairmen Hamilton and Kean outlined multiple

---

[24] Patrick Tyler, The New York Times, September 30, 2001, "A Nation Challenged: The Family; Fearing Harm, Bin Laden Kin Fled From the U.S.".
[25] Fred Burks, American Herald Tribune, "Evidence 9/11 Used to Launder $240 Billion in Covert Securities in a Covert Economic War".
[26] Fox Network, Lone Gunman Files: Pilot Episode.
[27] Newsweek, September 13, 2001.
[28] Pete Brush, CBS, May 15, 2002, "Bush Opposes 9/11 Query Panel".
[29] Timothy J. Burger, Time, March 6, 2003, "9/11 Commission Funding Woes".

deceptions by the FAA & the Pentagon, including the timelines of Flights 77 and 93.

- *"I truly am not that concerned about him,"* said George Bush about Bin Laden. Military chief Myers stated that "the goal has never been to get bin Laden."

- The 9/11 collapse of the 47-story WTC building 7 was the first time a modern, steel-reinforced high-rise in the US has ever collapsed in a fire.[30]

- The SEC was storing files related to numerous Wall Street investigations including Citigroup and the WorldCom bankruptcy in Building 7. The files for approximately 3,000 to 4,000 cases were destroyed.[31]

- FBI Director Robert Mueller, who took over the FBI one week before 9/11, said that Flight 77's data recorder provided altitude, speed, headings, and other information, but the voice recorder contained "nothing useful".[32]

- A recording of six air traffic controllers who dealt with two of the hijacked airliners described the events within hours of the attacks, but the tape was never given to the FBI and was instead illegally destroyed by a supervisor without anyone listening to it.[33]

- The large American bases that were built during the Afghan war are in the same location as the route of the projected oil pipeline.

These are only some of the unusual events that happened on 9/11 and not meant to be a comprehensive or exhaustive list by any means, but rather to illustrate how many important aspects of the event, interesting happenings to be sure, never ended up on the controlled corporate media to interfere with the official version of events. The public never heard about the planes switching off their transponders over Stewart Air Force base, not because it was not true or was not interesting, but because it was too much of a coincidence that might have received unwanted attention. They were already having a rough time trying to explain how a paper passport survived the exploding plane, the last thing they wanted to do was have some inflatable news anchor try to explain why these planes flew over an American military base at the exact same time without being

---

[30] Architects & Engineers For 9/11 Truth, "Building 7 Implosion: The Smoking Gun of 9/11".
[31] Margaret Cronin Fisk, National Law Journal, "SEC and EEOC: Attack Delays Investigations".
[32] Brian Dakss, CBS, February 25, 2002.
[33] Sara Kehaulani Goo, The Washington Post, "Controllers' 9/11 Tape Destroyed, Report Says".

shot down.

Think the American government would not lie to its citizens? There have been 9,795 first-responders, downtown workers, and students that have been diagnosed with 9/11-related cancer, according to the World Trade Center Health Program, with the figures for other illnesses not related to cancer being astronomical as well. They rushed into the contaminated area in part because Environmental Protection Agency Administrator Christine Todd Whitman assured the public as early as just one day after the event, and on at least 30 different occasions, that both the air and water quality was safe, a statement that she knew was a flat-out lie but repeated anyway under the cover of claiming to not be a scientist and relying on their reports.[34]

So with all of this blood on her hands was Whitman dragged in front of a judge and handed a 20-year sentence in Rikers Island? Of course not, she became the Governor of New Jersey instead as her reward for keeping her mouth shut on orders from the White House about the toxic waste site known as "ground zero". Honesty is punished; corruption is rewarded. A core principle of a dying empire, and certainly not limited to the events surrounding 9/11 and the "War of Terror".

The lies of 9/11 would fill multiple books, but an understanding of the level of criminality is essential when painting the picture of the lengths that government psychopaths will go to in order to put their plans in motion.

Boom!

Still, despite all the evidence that debunks the 9/11 "terror attack" big lie, some people refuse to believe that these facts are anything but conspiracy theories.

The Oxford English Dictionary defines conspiracy theory as "the theory that an event or phenomenon occurs as a result of a conspiracy between interested parties; or a belief that some covert but influential agency (typically political in motivation and oppressive in intent) is responsible for an unexplained event". Basically, conspiracy believers perceive a governmental threat to individual rights. For this, they are ridiculed and called "misguided", despite the fact that actual conspiracies occur quite regularly.

So-called "truthers" have exposed many secret and not-so-secret political

---

[34] Joanna Walters, The Guardian, "Former EPA Head Admits She Was Wrong to Tell New Yorkers Post-9/11 Air Was Safe".

assassinations, scandals and cover-ups, terrorist attacks, and a lot of everyday government activity involving genuine plots and collusion between multiples of people. The biggest reason for this is because conspiracies rarely work out according to plan. Collusion on a grand scale involves many players – individuals and organizations with competing (and often concealed) goals and agendas. Between herding angry cats and managing contingencies, it is impossible to entirely prevent cock-ups, errors, and betrayals.

COVID-19: Conspiracy Lies! Lies! Lies!

So what do people call it when conspiracy theories become conspiracy facts?

This is important because the 2020 Designer "Pandemic" is the product of a longstanding pattern of events and behaviors – turning virtually every "conspiracy theory" into fact, with corroborating evidence!

COVID-19 has brought it all together.

- The global power elite plotting to impose a totalitarian New World Order.

- Implementation of an authoritarian world government controlled by the United Nations and a global central bank.

- Political power through the financialization of the economy.

- Widespread use of state terrorism.

- Mass surveillance.

- Forced vaccinations.

- Mind control.

- Restriction of speech through the concentration of media ownership.

These are just some of the conspiracy "myths" that have been proven since the onset of the Coronavirus. From mind control to population control, crowd control, and exchange control – if people do not see a pattern here, they may beyond help.

But first, it is important to have a look at the Coronavirus Plandemic and the events of 2020 that made the world go boom!

Virus X

- Pneumonia of unknown cause detected in Wuhan, China was first reported to the WHO Country Office in China on 31 December 2019.

- The outbreak was declared a Public Health Emergency of International Concern on 30 January 2020.

- On 11 February 2020, WHO announced a name for the new coronavirus disease: COVID-19. 'CO' stands for corona, 'VI' for the virus, and 'D' for the disease. The 19 is for 2019.

Sounds plausible enough, right? The Plague, Spanish Flu, SARS, MERS, Ebola, Swine Flu – humanity has seen them all. Many of them were essentially lies as well. But, outbreaks happen, people get infected, some die, life goes on, the disease goes away. No vaccine was necessary. The world economy was not put on hold.

SARS (Severe Acute Respiratory Syndrome), caused by a coronavirus, is an epidemic disease that seemed on the brink of a pandemic in the early 2000s. It spread rapidly from its origin in Asia in 2002-2003 to Europe and the Americas before it just disappeared. It faded away in 2004, and since then no new cases have been reported.

So what makes COVID-19 so different?

First, allegedly, it is more contagious, more deadly, and easier to contract than all those other viruses. Miraculously, despite all these extremities, this will be the one disease that they can cure by the vaccine. This claim comes despite the fact that even the plain, old, garden variety Coronavirus that causes common household flu and colds, cannot be prevented by a single vaccine, because the strains mutate every season.

Second, for the first time in history, the world has been "forced" to adopt severe tactics to slow the spread of COVID-19: social distancing, shutdowns, closures, and cancellations. In the US alone, 40 million people have been laid off, small businesses have been forcibly shut down and those businesses who have managed to survive were then forced to implement costly new health measures.

People see the word "forced" stick out its ugly head everywhere, and with good reason. It is no secret that the current agenda on the table is to use Coronavirus prevention as a cover for the digital fascism of a totalitarian society.

COVID-19 shut down the world and all the people in it, holding seven billion people for ransom. And the price to be paid for freedom? Volunteer to be vaccinated and tracked for the rest of your life.

The more one studies this virus, the more they find the same name: Bill Gates.

- He is the 2nd largest funder of the WHO.

- He is building 7 vaccine labs.

- He basically controls global health policy through his grants.

- His plan is to use forced vaccines to digitally track humanity's every move.

- He suppresses negative attention by funding dozens of media organizations.

On 18 March 2020, Bill Gates called for a "Digital Certificate" to identify who received the COVID-19 vaccine.

The following day, a website called Biohackinfo.com posted a story with the headline: "Bill Gates will use microchip implants to fight coronavirus."

The Gates Foundation:

- DENIED its plan to use vaccines to track people and thereby control the global health policy.

- DENIED Gates' effort to help develop a vaccine is some kind of nefarious attempt to control, follow, or depopulate the world's population via a "microchip" of some sort.

- DENIED developing trackable vaccine data and "implanting everybody with a global ID".

They then justified their diabolical plans to enslave humanity as a whole by saying:

"It's about creating digital certificates that would expand home-based, self-administered testing for COVID-19. The microchip assertion is unrelated. We're just proposing keeping a record of vaccination on a patient's skin. That's why we tested an invisible dye that could last up to five years and be read with a specially adapted smartphone."

Right.

The truth is a funny thing. It is slippery, it is not always self-evident, it can seem implausible, and it can even be inconvenient.

Digitally tracking people's every move has been a dream of the globalists for years. This health crisis is the perfect vehicle for them to push this.

The media and its masters have heavily mocked and sneered at "conspiracy" predictions from those who have been predicting that the elite are just waiting for the right moment to roll out their "mark of the beast" technology to remotely identify and control every single human being on the planet, thus sealing their plans for a one-world government.

Here is an example of how those "theories" can be changed into evidence.

- FACT: On 4 April 2020 Bill Gates states that mass public gatherings will not come back "at all" until they have mass vaccination.

- FACT: MIT is working on a "quantum tattoo" that will mark people with an invisible identifier while also delivering a vaccine...at Bill Gates' direction and funded first and foremost by the Bill and Melinda Gates Foundation.

- FACT: In the Book of Revelation [13:16-17], written about 2000 years ago, the Bible warned about being branded with an ID code: *"And he causeth all, both small and great, rich and poor, free and bond, to receive a mark in their right hand, or in their foreheads: And that no man might buy or sell, save he that had the mark".*

- FACT: Microsoft owns International patent #060606 (#666) which is a cryptocurrency system using humans who have been chipped as the "Miners".

Surveillance capitalism is of course in line with *1984* – a George Orwell hit written 71 years ago which should have prepared the public for the reality of a Big Brother dystopia, but clearly did not. Especially if one looks at the ease with which the Coronavirus has, seemingly overnight, enabled governments all over the world to implement mass totalitarian surveillance under the auspice of creating weapons against disease.

The inhabitants are kept safe from harm in the surveillance state as long as they obey Big Brother. They have near-absolute safety, but no freedom.

Here are a few current-day examples:

- Russia – 100,000 facial recognition cameras are watching Moscow's quarantine through a network of sophisticated state surveillance the city rolled just before the epidemic reached Russia. Police have logged their locked-in citizen's details and warned them that sneaking out could lead to a five-year jail term or deportation for foreigners.

- Hong Kong – Hong Kong has introduced mandatory wristbands for those in quarantine so they can be tracked.

- Taiwan – Taiwan has a monitoring system known as "the electronic fence" where those who are meant to be in isolation will be visited by the authorities if they turn off their mobiles.

- South Korea – In South Korea, the government gathers huge amounts of data from phone records, CCTV images, and credit cards to help track citizens during the COVID crisis.

- Singapore – In Singapore, phone users are encouraged to download the "TraceTogether" app which keeps a record of all the other numbers that have been in close proximity to the smartphone.

- China – China is boasting that it is building the "world's largest camera surveillance network".

However, those are all foreign countries, one might say. It has nothing to do with everyone else in their comfortable house arrest in front of their big screen TV. The United States will never become a surveillance state...the constitution says so.

Wrong.

The constitutional right to freedom went out the window when the signing of the Patriot Act "normalized the US government's mass surveillance powers". The only difference between the US's mass surveillance and those other countries mentioned, is that the US is doing a pretty good imitation of the Invasion of the Body Snatchers while they are at it.

What once was considered inalienable, fundamental "rights" are now mere privileges to be taken away on government bureauRATS' say-so. This is because governments the world over have learned a few lessons they will not ever forget:

- At the first sign of danger, people will gladly give up their freedom in exchange for safety, or the perception of safety.

- People will readily deliver their friends and neighbors to the authorities for daring to walk their dogs.

- Soldiers and police will be welcomed with open arms to patrol the streets looking for drifters like some sort of dystopian movie.

- People will anxiously wait to line up for their chip, willing to do just about anything to get some sense of normalcy back in their lives.

The Coronavirus lockdowns have shown that people are ready to report each other for the slightest transgressions by justifying that "the government told me it's the right thing to do".

How Could All of This Have Happened?

"Jeff, I've been watching some of your walk and talk videos, doing everything possible to wake people up in a world gone mad. Some people are shocked by the events of today, but this has been done before. Criminals and tyrants invaded, this land, bringing disease to the Native Americans by giving them smallpox infected blankets, then quarantine them, giving them free food, and supplies, keeping them suppressed, asleep and obedient, while the natives watched their land being raped and pillage front of them. Having been brainwashed, broken, and diseased they gladly submitted, giving up their freedom and lives to their new slave owners.

I'm not shocked by the events of today themselves...but by the mass submission of sheepeople the world over!!" – A Fan

Everything people see in the media and on television is specifically crafted to put them in a trance and in a state of fear. It is true, not some random speculation.

Think of the flickering effect sometimes seen on TV. Whether people see it or not, it is there, and it tells a different story to the images they are consciously seeing. The minds of humans react to it by going into a hypnotic trance and switching from Beta brain waves to Alpha waves – which is exactly what it is engineered to do. And what happens when a person is hypnotized? They react the way their mind is controlled to do, every time they receive the right trigger.

Zen Gardner, author of *You Are The Awakening*, said:

"Hypnagogia is the experience of the transitional state between wakefulness and sleep in humans: the hypnagogic state of consciousness, during the onset of sleep. Mental phenomena that occur during this "threshold consciousness" phase include lucid thought, lucid dreaming, hallucinations, and sleep paralysis."

That is a pretty apt description of the mass human condition, manifested most predominantly in the vast majority refusing to see the true state of affairs on this planet. Sleepwalking.

As George Carlin famously said. *"It's called the American dream – because you have to be asleep to believe it."*

Bang!

Because of worldwide Coronavirus lockdowns, millions of people have been forced out of their jobs and their businesses – over 40 million in the US alone! Small businesses have been buried already, large businesses are starting to stink and economies are flailing helplessly.

In March 2020, the world's seven key western economies, Canada, France, Germany, Italy, Japan, the UK, and the US, pledged to fight off a world-wide Great Depression by standing united against the Coronavirus economic meltdown.

It is a beautiful thing all this love and trust and cooperation. Almost unprecedented. United we stand; Divided we fall. Just follow the plan, really.

The FED, which has the most practice in the money printing business, is leading the way by showing the rest of the G7 what it looks like to "do anything necessary to address a glaring shortage of dollars across the world economy."

Just print more. It is the right thing to do.

The stock markets feeling blue? Print some money!

People losing jobs? Print some money!

The Federal Reserve has been running off dollars hot off the printing press since 1913, but never before has anyone seen this level of money printing.

Printing the Final Demolition Notice

The official national debt of the United States of America in 2019 was $22 trillion and growing. That figure grew by a trillion dollars just in 2019 alone, and times were supposed to be good economically. This official number is actually much lower than the real figure, like most governmental numbers that are massaged, inflated, deflated, ignored, or just plain false. One should add another zero to the end of the government's $22 trillion figure to find the real level of debt and liabilities accumulated.

What will happen when things get bad and the Fed decides that they need to restart quantitative easing for the fifth time, or as it should be called, money printing and debasing the currency?

If a thousand billion dollars needed to be spent by the federal government over and above the listed budget, and things are "good", then how much more will they add when the stock market, the housing market, jobs market, and bond market all go into the toilet? Two trillion more? Ten trillion more? What will this crazy money printing do to the value of the dollars that currently exist? The answer is pretty obvious that the value of anything denominated in U.S. dollars would skyrocket due to a massive oversupply in dollars.

Everyone is going to see the effect very soon, especially because during the Coronavirus crisis, the US government and the Fed have authorized the printing of another ten trillion dollars!

People thought that spending tons of money on the military was crazy because by 2023 the interest payments on the debt alone will exceed what is spent yearly on the armed forces. The Federal Reserve bank will be paid back more money than the cost of the entire military budget for the year, just because they loaned money that did not exist into existence at interest, and that interest is paid back to the Fed before anyone else gets any of their money.

By 2023, almost a trillion dollars in interest payments will be due annually, easily outpacing spending on several other social programs.[35]

This is ONLY for the military budget.

How can this system continue to go on once the word gets out about how the banking system actually works, and why do some people still have this blind faith that the government will save people when they are $31 trillion in debt? This is delusional.

There is also the very real probability that this money printing will lead to hyperinflation like that witnessed in Venezuela and Zimbabwe. When $21 trillion cannot solve a nation's problem, governments always print even more money in order to solve their problems, like struggling to get out of quicksand, it has the same deadly effect.

The Hype is Real

For hyperinflation to become a reality, very bad things have to happen: 1) the Government has to completely lose control, or/and 2) the people have to completely lose faith in the monetary system.

So what is going to happen to people who choose to stick with the system?

A few things, and none of them are good:

• Banks will close.

• Money will be worthless.

---

[35] New York Times, "As Debt Rises, The Government Will Soon Spend More On Interest Than On The Military".

- Stocks will be a mess.

- Will lose most of their mutual funds.

- Exchange Traded Funds will be gone (including gold & silver ETFs).

They have taken people's jobs, their businesses, their freedom of speech, and freedom of movement. Now they are coming for their social security, their pension, and their house.

It is up to the people whether they let them.

Sounding the Alarm For the Death of the Dollar

No country on earth has the kind of massive printing press that the Federal Reserve and the Treasury of the United States have to manufacture United States dollars either physically through the printing of sheets of currency that is sliced into rectangles in order to fit nicely in everyone's wallet or to digitally print currency in online ledgers that the Fed then loans into existence with the attachment of interest in order to perpetuate the Ponzi scheme that is the American monetary policy.

The American Empire has been slowly debasing their own currency for decades, but they have a nice and normalized term for this kind of theft of purchasing power stolen from the people. They call it inflation, as in the inflation of the money supply and subsequent deflation of the value. This is the money printers' oldest trick in the book and one they learned from previous corrupt regimes that made a habit of debasing their own currency.

Some of the things the Roman Empire did to debase their currency included coin clipping, which is to actually clip off a small piece of the coin and collect all of the scraps together to make another coin, as well as the removal of precious metals from the coins and the inclusion of base metals as a replacement.

Basically, they committed fraud against the general public in order to try to hide that they were manipulating the money supply. If the Romans had had a money printing machine like the Federal Reserve has or a decent color copier, they would have been printing as much fake money as they possibly could. That is not a societal flaw limited to the Romans or the Fed, but rather everybody that ever comes across the ability to print money ends up abusing it to the point where they debase their own currency and kill their "golden goose". They just cannot help themselves, especially if they believe that they are much smarter than everyone else, or if they feel that nobody will ever notice.

At some point, people always notice.

The financial alchemists at the Federal Reserve are really nothing more than coin debasers in nice suits, chipping away at the edges of their coins to try and take as much from the people before being exposed as the common criminals that they really are.

Destroying the value of the United States dollar by printing too many of them is one way to slowly depress the worth of all dollars, but this process can be manipulated and hidden by lying about how many dollars have actually been created. As long as not all of them are currently in circulation, it is pretty hard to tell how many are being stashed away and out of the view of prying eyes. Without an accurate number, the public is left to speculate as to how many total dollars are floating around making up the supply of money, but after decades and decades of the same scam, it becomes obvious that even though the public may never get an accurate number as to the total number of U.S. dollars that exist, everyone knows that the reality is that they have already created WAY too many to justify the current valuation.

The dollar is not worth nearly as much as people perceive it to be, in part because of the excessive money printing, but that is not the biggest problem that it faces these days, and it is not the only reason for the difference between the perceived value of the dollar and its actual value.

The removal of the Petrodollar as the world's reserve currency will mean that countries around the world will no longer be forced to purchase all of the oil that they require in U.S. Dollars exclusively. When these dollars are no longer needed, they will return back to whence they came, which is the United States. As they begin to pile up inside America, their value will fall, and this removal as the world's reserve currency will be the event that destroys the American Empire, financially at first, then socially only weeks later.

America will do what all flailing empires do when faced with their own mortality: they will pretend that this time is different and that those empires that have crumbled before them were either weak militarily, lacking in fiscal creativity, or morally inferior, but none of this will matter because in the end all empires crumble under the weight of their own greed and arrogance, and no amount of propping up by their bought-off accomplices in the corporate media will help to break their fall.

And the fall will be unlike anything the world has ever seen.

Of course, the United States government is not the first, and will not be the last, to play the game of manipulating the supply and value of money while lying to their citizens and the rest of the world about the true nature, value, and amount of their currency.

Many countries these days do not even have their own currency to debase, even if they wanted to. Several countries have joined forces to set aside their old currency, like the Italian lira, the Spanish peseta, the Greek drachma, and the French franc, to be a part of a basket of currencies known as the Euro. Of course, that currency gets debased plenty by those running the European Union, but the individual countries no longer have the control of the money supply that they once had so that they could print money to infinity to finance their hair-brained ideas and countless wars.

A rudimentary understanding of economics shows that the more of a supply a market has for a certain item, be it apples, horses, or dollars, the less the value should be. In a world where apples grow on trees, it becomes difficult to charge a person very much for an apple if all they have to do is reach into their own tree and pick one for themselves. Likewise, when a country floods the markets with its own currency, how much value could it really retain? There comes a point where the country's money kind of grows on trees too.

What corrupt countries have been trying to do for ages is to find that magical point where they can create a ton of money that they can circulate throughout the land, while not creating so much that all of their money loses its value.

They always cross that threshold at some point, without fail, whether they are an average country just trying to find that line, an up-and-coming country testing out the boundaries of their currency, or a decrepit and corrupt empire on its last leg.

For every country that has been delisted as the world's reserve currency, they have been immediately plunged into a decade's long depression featuring a string of wars and bloody revolutions on the streets. These currency situations are not built to be sustainable, and they are not, lasting usually about a century under the best of circumstances. Like a metropolis built on a fault line, the question is not "if" the big one is coming, but "when"?

- Portugal (1450-1530) 80 years.

- Spain (1530-1640) 110 years.

- Netherlands (1640-1720) 80 years.

- France (1720-1815) 95 years.

- Brittan (1815-1945) 130 years.

- United States (1945-2020+) 75 years.

Officially the U.S. dollar has only been the world's reserve currency for a little over 75 years, but the dollar has been used to settle trades since 1920 and has been used in world finance for purposes like world wars and the like. The Federal Reserve started their scheme in 1913 and instituted the Internal Revenue Service as the funding mechanism, so the dollar has been in its current iteration for over 100 years, maybe not as the reserve currency the entire time, but definitely globally manipulated since the beginning, and recognized by most nations as the dominant currency.

Britain ruled for over a century after the Napoleonic Wars bled France dry, and France was able to rise to the top of the pyramid after the Dutch spread their spice businesses and military empires too thin during the Anglo-Dutch Wars. The dollar had been backed by gold until 1971 when Nixon took the nation off of the gold standard to combat the speculators, a flat-out lie of epic proportions that was meant to allow the bankers to re-peg the dollar to oil instead. A case can be made that these days the United States dollar is actually backed by the United States military. One look at what happened to Iraq in 2003 and Libya in 2011 when they decided to announce their plans to sell their oil in exchange for something other than the dollar should clear up what the Globalists do to countries that mess with their system.

Fifty years under the Petrodollar paradigm is a very long time to keep up appearances as a stable currency, but the cracks and age of the foundation are beginning to show for those that are looking. So what are the signs of impending collapse?

It might be easier to envision America as a person that has gotten themselves into a very dangerous situation due to their own foolish and reckless behavior, like a lost hiker that forgot to pack their common sense.

When an Empire Dies it Starts First at the Extremities

If someone hiking Mt. Everest fails to recognize or understand the coming blizzard, and they march up the mountain because all they see is clear skies in front of them, the results of their ignorance may include frostbite and even death. When the coming storm rolls in, and the path back down the mountain becomes invisible, that hiker then realizes that it is too late and they must pay the price for their lack of vision and arrogance, plus their lack of preparation. When a person is freezing to death the blood retreats away from the fingers and condenses into the most important region, like closer to the heart. Getting caught out in the blizzard leaves the hiker with extreme frostbite and the loss of parts of their body, in the best-case scenario, or if the issues are ignored and they decide to just hope the sun will come out again, then death.

What is happening across the globe is the death of the economic extremities in places like Venezuela, Greece, Argentina, and Turkey that are at the very ends of the American hegemony, and from there the necrosis moves inward toward the important body parts until it kills the patient.

The blood of the American Empire is the U.S. Dollar, and as the countries around the world wake up to the fraud and criminality that the United States has been perpetrating on them for decades, and the Petrodollar paradigm falls apart, these countries will flood the United States with all of the dollars that they had been forced to hold for things like purchasing oil. As these dollars come flooding home, the massive influx will kill the value of the dollar and plunge the United States into a 3rd World country almost immediately. With no one forcing foreign governments to hold dollars specifically to buy oil, they will choose an alternative method that better fits the needs of their countries such as a different currency, a basket of currencies, gold, silver, or possibly cryptocurrencies.

Besides the financial reasons for ditching the dollar, governments around the world will take that opportunity to give the United States a taste of their own medicine by turning their back on them and helping to destroy the dollar as payback for all of the times they have done it to other countries. Fringe countries that have been pushed around for decades will find themselves with leverage that they never had before, and decisions to vote the United States' way on U.N. Resolutions will no longer become a given, while deciding to sell their own oil in exchange for something like the Chinese Yuan or silver will become a no-brainer.

Much like the high school bully that had been making everybody's life hell for as long as they can remember, these formerly captured countries will join forces with all of the kids that have been tormented and had their lunch money stolen over the years and collectively humiliate America by stuffing them in a locker and giving that government what they deserve.

America can prop up the dollar through the use of its military for only so long before it becomes an exercise in futility. There are over seven billion people living on the planet, so guns and bombs cannot control everyone, and at some point, it is going to become clear that the game is over. The only real question will be how many people have to die before everyone comes to understand this?

Once the dollar is exposed as being unstable, it will have a cascading effect. Wall Street will disintegrate as people rush to try and dump their holdings onto a market missing any buyers. Margin calls will automatically kick in, forcing a tidal wave of losses. Without a way to accurately place valuations on their financial instruments, the bond market will fail.

As the dollar continues to fall, the real estate market will implode and drag the rest of the country down as equity vanishes literally overnight, and pension funds that hold trillions of dollars of Americans' life savings will be wiped out over the course of a week. Hyperinflation will kick in as dollars search for the real price discovery of goods and services. The pendulum will probably swing a bit too far in the hyperinflation direction before settling down a bit, but it will not matter as the damage will already be done.

How do markets collapse?

Slowly, then all at once.

The Debt Trap

The Federal Reserve and the federal government of the United States have long been co-conspirators in a massive fraud that has destroyed the purchasing power of the people by over 96% in the past century.

In 2020, they went one step further: literally destroying people's purchasing power by refusing them access to their places of employment – then printing more money to hand out their "stimulus" pity checks. A stimulus to what? Feed the economy? Feed a family? How long does $1,200 last?

People have praised governments all over the world for "deferring" mortgages, rents, and bills. Does the public know what that means? They have to pay when the time is up. With the money they have not been earning because they have no job!

This is yet another devastating symptom of the Coronavirus, and possibly the worst – it's paralyzing effect on millions, if not billions of people's personal debt. People who have been hard-working, tax-paying proles all their lives suddenly find themselves without an income – having to rely on family, "stimulus" scraps, and maxed out credit cards. Direct debits are bouncing and car and mortgage payments are almost last in line for being deferred. Right before gas and phone bills.

150 years ago, people did not have to ask the government for permission to own a property, start a business, build a home, own a gun, sell or buy food, protest, or even prospect for gold.

The thing with losing freedom and self-autonomy – and money – is that it rarely happens suddenly. If a frog is placed into a pot of boiling water it will immediately try to jump out; but if it is placed into a pot of cool water that is gradually heated until boiling, it will stay put and never try to jump out.

Many (most) people do not even realize they are bankrupt until they already are, and then once it has happened they are overwhelmed and powerless to stop it or change it.

That is exactly how freedoms have been eroding over the past few decades in so-called free societies like Canada and the US. At the start of 2020 people made plans to travel, to retire, to buy property, to be promoted. Suddenly they had no freedom of movement and were not allowed to leave their homes. They are forbidden to meet with family or get together with friends. They are not permitted to spend their money as they wish. They are forbidden to work and earn the money they need to survive. They are told their job is not essential. They may not assemble; they may not share the truth about what is really happening on mainstream social media and criticism will soon be forbidden and punished.

• Suddenly, without any violent struggle or contest, they have given up their fundamental human rights to freedom of movement, opinion, expression, and assembly.

- Suddenly, they are told they must submit their own and their children's bodies to experimental tracking chips and vaccines – or lose these rights forever.

- Suddenly, and completely out of the blue, they find themselves living in a bizarre, fantastical world where they, the previously sovereign individual, are locked up like a sheep, while governments around the world mindlessly shut down their economies.

However, it is not suddenly at all. It has been planned for over a decade and there have been a lot of warning signals if one were alert to the masses and masses of propaganda and mind control that has been exercised openly and blatantly in the media, movies, TV, events – all of it. Contemptuously one might say.

When the psychopathic ex-Chief of Staff for Obama, Rahm Emanuel, says that they never want to let a good crisis go to waste, what he means is that while the population is distracted by their own survival, the government will cram through laws to remove freedom from the people.

But what freedoms are left to remove? The public have already seen how easy it is for them to lock everyone up and take away their jobs and businesses. The citizens have already heard that it is only a question of time before they will have to submit to a "vaccination" that will track their every movement.

What is left to take?

Think property, stocks, pensions.

It is all about stealing everyone's money, and knowing they can get away with it because most people are pre-programmed to believe that politicians are appointed to protect and serve their rights; and that government is always right.

However, it is all part of a bigger scheme. A distracting crisis, say, like a pandemic, is the perfect opportunity for the 0.1% to consolidate their control over resources and assets that they do not already have access to. It is the old Rothschild saying about buying while there is blood in the streets. These groups do not just sit around and wait for the next crisis to occur organically, they manufacture these events so that they do not have to sit around and hope that something bad happens. This is why false flags happen. They create a crisis that will provide them with the justification to do what they have been wanting to do but just do not have the peoples' support.

In the wake of the financial meltdown of 2008, every country running massive budget deficits, like the United States, was threatened with becoming "the next Greece", unless they immediately began raising taxes while simultaneously cutting their spending. This push for austerity was seen as the responsible thing to do in light of the mess that Wall Street had created, and the people would need to pull their weight, suffer this burden, and show their patriotism by going without so that the country would survive. This would, in turn, fuel businesses to invest more in America and kickstart the economy once again.

All of this was a bunch of lies dressed up to look like an urgent and necessary step toward fiscal sanity. The banks were not going to be kicking in any money to help out the economy, in fact, they were sitting on all of what they received during TARP and refusing to lend it out to small businesses, instead opting to loan it to other banks. They could have saved the economy themselves, but they were not interested in taking that risk, even with other people's money.

Even before the onset of the panic pandemic, America has been in terrible shape financially, with over $21 billion of acknowledged debt and likely multiples more hidden in the shadows.

That number has likely skyrocketed since January 2020 and the bankers will not forgive or forget. They will come for their money once the country defaults on the debt. And the way the United States government will choose to repay this debt will be with We The People's money, selling it to the public through their co-conspirators in the corporate media as: "Americans need to pull their weight and buckle down through austerity programs!"

Sounds good? First, they masked everyone and locked them up, next they are going to tell them what they are allowed to wear, where they are allowed to go and how much they are allowed to spend, and on what.

Stand up or get out. Because the "new normal" is looking austere and if people think this is an exaggeration, just ask the Greeks.

Do people like being part of that world? Where they decide what the people may and may not hear, and say? Do people like a world where the government and the central bank manipulate their money's worth? Where they can track their every move and every transaction? Is this the world people want their children to inherit?

The people are in control. The people make their own choices. The people decide what dreams and stories they do and do not buy – going right back to the Original Sins.

Original Sins

The American Empire has already been quietly dismantled well in advance so as not to raise the alarm bells that could wake sleeping dogs. Think a decline in morals and values, urban decay, government transparency, and most pervasively, the gradual removal of freedom.

The most logical question is "why"? Why must the American Empire fall?

The answer is relatively simple.

The people in charge are going to bring this beast down on purpose to destroy the citizens that they have no respect for, to reset their fraudulent central banking system that has come to the end of its functional lifespan, and to hide their numerous and horrendous crimes against humanity... and then offer their solution. A one-world government, a one-world central bank, and a one-world digital, trackable fiat currency.

But where does it all start, and how long has demolition been the end goal?

"Begin at the beginning," the King said, very gravely, "and go on till you come to the end." – Lewis Caroll, *Through the Looking Glass*

A ROTTING FOUNDATION

America, Land of Opportunity Built On Lies

Most people have heard the story of the founding of America by those looking to escape the overbearing nature and criminal behavior of the British Empire.

Oh, the irony.

When people feel that their personal liberties are being infringed upon, sometimes they pack up and move to a different place that sees the relationship between the State and the citizens in a better and more healthy way.

Despite what kids these days might think, Christopher Columbus did not discover the "New World", and for the record, he was not from England. There were plenty of people already living in North America back when the Pilgrims landed on Plymouth Rock, and they did not have a big Thanksgiving dinner with their new Indian buddies a couple of hundred years ago. People conflate these two very different stories.

Christopher Columbus preceded the Pilgrims by a century and a half and was actually Italian, though financed by the Spanish.

This is where the lies of HIStory begin for American students as they are forced in the government indoctrination camps (schools) to learn a warped and incorrect version of history that paints their so-called and cultish sounding "founding fathers" as intrepid adventurers, and not as the invading force that they actually were.

To leave England because of the rampant fraud and persecution, and then move to a new location where they immediately begin to persecute the locals, set the tone for the hypocrisy that America would later become known for. They did not escape from England because of racism and religious persecution, they exported it to the New World and picked right up where the British left off.

The first American settlers also brought with them the power structure that had shaped their society back across the Atlantic, though this time they did their best to hide it from the rest of the inhabitants of their newest franchise.

Freemasons Built America

America was formed as a colony of the British Empire which brought with it the organized formation of Freemasonry straight from the Grand Lodge of England in 1717. Only thirteen years later, the first American Mason lodge was established in Philadelphia in 1730, and future revolutionary leader Benjamin Franklin was a founding member.

What few people know is that many of America's founding fathers were Freemasons. Some of the more notable were: George Washington, the first president of the United States of America, Ben Franklin who led the Pennsylvania chapter, Paul Revere who led a Massachusetts chapter, John Hancock, and Chief Justice John Marshall who greatly influenced the shaping of the Supreme Court. Altogether it is believed that about nine of the fifty-six men that signed the Declaration of Independence were Masons, and about thirteen of the thirty-nine that signed the US Constitution were also Masons.

According to Wikipedia, there are hundreds of conspiracy theories involving Freemasonry, usually involving allegations of control of governments and creating a New World Order; and theories that focus on the embedding of symbols in otherwise ordinary items, such as street patterns, national seals, corporate logos, etc.

Aaaah, those conspiracy theories again...

There is plenty of evidence to turn conspiracy *theories* into "just conspiracies".

Symbology Will Be Their Downfall

The best-known practices of the occult sciences include numerology, symbols, rituals, buildings, and monuments.

To be initiated as a Freemason, a prospective candidate has to declare a belief in a "Supreme Being". This is according to the Masons' Book of Constitution. Who and what the "supreme being" needs to be is a mystery and privilege only known to members – and they ain't telling.

Symbology is their language. They use mathematics to encode language into structures in order to convey messages to one another over the centuries. Billboards crumble and fade away, but monuments will stand for centuries, the layout of an entire city will be kept in place for generations, their messages will remain for as long as the nation stands.

In the current direction that the country is headed, that will not be for very much longer.

Washington D.C.'s urban layout clearly shows a star like the one used by the *Order of the Eastern Star*. What makes it unique is that it features a pentagon in the center of the star, with five lines of equal length, creating five isosceles triangles connected to the center. The Masons see this as a visual representation of the mathematical concept of the Golden Ratio.

The street layout makes a square and compass as if to show that they built Washington D.C., probably in more ways than one. The architecture of Washington D.C.'s streets is completely Masonic as well, adding another layer to the visual depiction of their control of the city.

It might seem a bit of a stretch to think that the construction of roads and city blocks were laid out in a manner to show a particular image from above, especially considering they were designed before airplanes and the like were even on the drawing board. One must remember that just because most people would not find this to be important, it does not mean that they did not place major significance on things such as the number of city blocks between important locations, the number of feet an obelisk stands, the number of interlocking streets within a central core, or other mathematical oddities surrounding the particular layout of the Freemason's most important project in the New World.

It is almost impossible to read too much into the hidden meanings of the structures put in place by the Freemasons because they were masters of steganography or the art of hiding pictures inside of other pictures. The locations were selected for a specific reason, perhaps due to longitude or latitude. The distance away from other structures was not a product of chance but by design. The number of steps from one level to the next usually contained a number with significance to their order.

Of course, the Pentagon shape comes back into play much later in the United States in the form of the largest building in the world that just so happens to be the epicenter for the destruction of the planet. The design of the United States military's Pentagon building, which some call the Pentagram, is clearly not an accident. It was created by the Freemasons that are still very much in charge of aspects of the government that are entrenched in positions of power, that have decision making capability on spending vast sums of stolen (taxed) dollars on wars and foreign conquest, and feel no accountability to the people they profess to defend.

The Freemasons found a way to visually hijack many symbols that have come to be known as American beacons of freedom, like the Statue of Liberty and the Washington Monument.

"Liberty Enlightening the World" is the official name for the Statue of Liberty that stands in New York harbor, created by French engineer Gustave Eiffel and sculptor Bartholdi, and it has come to be the most recognizable symbol of the United States of America. It was a gift from the French Grand Orient Temple Masons to the Masons of the United States in 1884, and she is holding the Masonic "Torch of Enlightenment" or the "Flaming Torch of Reason". Though it has come to symbolize liberty for America, it was really presented to the American Masons to mark the 100 years of the first Masonic Republic.

Freemasonic Influence in Washington D.C.

- Washington has 36 lodges of the Grand Lodge of Free and Accepted Masons.

- Many of the Founding Fathers were Masons, including George Washington, Benjamin Franklin, and James Monroe.

- The Architects who designed the White House, the US Capitol, and the Washington Monument, were all Masons, like James Hoban, Benjamin Latrobe, and Robert Mills.

- Cornerstones for all the important structures were laid after Masonic parades and dedication ceremonies.

- The House of the Temple, north of the White House on 18th Street.

- George Washington Masonic National Memorial.

- The L'Enfant Street Plan.

- The statue of Albert Pike.

- There are Freemasonic symbols found printed on American currency.

Freemason lodges are still found everywhere throughout America, but they seem to be rather nondescript and fly well below the radar, much like the imprint they put on the governmental structure of the United States.

The Start of Democracy

Almost a third of the US presidents have been Freemasons...that the public knows about.

Masonic influences came into play at Washington's first inauguration with George Washington swearing his oath on a Bible from St. John's Masonic Lodge No. 1 in New York. So, what drew a grand total of 14 chief executives (15 counting LBJ, who was initiated but never raised) to become Masons?

And where did a secret society that existed from the 1500s and included some of the most powerful men in America disappear to?

Robert Cooper, the curator of the Grand Lodge of Scotland and author of the book *Cracking the Freemason's Code*, denies that it is a secret society.

"If we're a secret society, how do you know about us? This is a public building; we've got a website, a Facebook page, Twitter. We even advertise things in the press. But we're still a 'secret society' running the world! A real secret society is the Mafia, the Chinese triads. They are real secret societies. They don't have a public library. They don't have a museum you can wander into."

(Hey, the Rockefellers founded the Museum of Modern Art [MOMA], and David Rockefeller admitted to his family being part of a New World Order, so no secrets there...)

The Dawn of American Democracy

The role of Freemasonry and individual Masons prior to and through the American Revolution was that of the destruction of the traditional social and political order based on an authoritarian philosophy and characterized by inequality and privilege.

With the victorious end of the American Revolution, Masonic philosophy had, for the first time in history, an opportunity to play a constructive role in the erection of political and social order. It is generally accepted that the founding fathers were responsible for the start of the great American democracy – but what did democracy really mean? The freedom to labor? Or free labor?

Thousands of years earlier, the Greek philosopher Plato used the "democratic man" to represent democracy. The democratic man is the son of the oligarchic man. Unlike his father, the democratic man is consumed with unnecessary desires. Plato describes the necessary desires as desires that we have out of instinct or desires that we have to survive. Unnecessary desires are desires people can teach themselves to resist, such as the desire for riches. The democratic man takes great interest in all the things he can buy with his money. Plato believes that the democratic man is more concerned with his money over how he can help the people. He does whatever he wants whenever he wants to do it. As long as he has free labor.

Two centuries ago, at the dawn of the American Empire, democracy was necessitated by forests to be cleared, mines to be worked, fields to be plowed, things to be made. It was difficult to find more excuses not to abolish slavery and the wealthy needed workers.

By today's standards, the founding fathers were racist, sexist, elitists who also envisioned a western expansion of the nation but made no reasonably humane provisions to mitigate the impact that would have on the Native Americans. One could argue that this all happened almost 250 years ago – in a society that did not hold the same contemporary attitudes about democracy.

The population's expectations of democracy might have changed, but the people who direct and control our freedom, have not. They are exactly the same people, with exactly the same motivation: free labor and wealth. Remove the fields in which a man can labor or the rewards of his labor, and democracy will disappear. It will be named despotism, and it will degenerate into tyranny, with tyrants stealing and conquering to satiate their desires.

Morals, Laws and the Constitution

America has become a society that is managed by moral relativity, meaning that the morals that govern the conduct of people are subject to change and interpretation by the conductor of the action.

Mark Passio's Natural Law is *"a set of universal, inherent, objective, non-man-made, eternal and immutable conditions which govern the consequences of behaviors of beings with the capacity for understanding the difference between harmful and non-harmful behavior."*

The Natural Law that Mark Passio speaks about has no relationship to Darwin's "Survival of the Fittest", the "Law of the Jungle", or "Natural Order".

The more a person drifts from an understanding of this, the easier they are to be picked off by the State and coerced into committing unspeakable crimes in the name of peace, justice, or the "American Way".

It goes back to the hypocrisy of the State where a person that kills another person gets put in a cage, unless they were wearing a soldier costume, in which case they will be given a medal because their murderous ways are sanctioned by the State and encouraged, provided they are conducting this murder on behalf of the government. According to the sales pitch of the American military, as long as they were committing this crime while wearing a uniform they are covered in a legal sense by their government. Whether they are absolved of any eternal damnation by whoever they think makes the call on these sorts of issues relating to their soul is up for debate.

This strongly links to one of the characteristics of the fall of the Roman empire mentioned earlier in this book. With so many enemies rising up against the State, including its oppressed slave labor who were finally waking up to the power within their numbers, Rome struggled to marshal enough troops and resources to defend its frontiers from local rebellions. Because they could not recruit enough soldiers from the Roman citizenry, the emperors began hiring foreign mercenaries to prop up their armies. The ranks of the legions eventually swelled with Germanic Goths and other barbarians, so much so that Romans began using the Latin word "barbarus" in place of "soldier".

Back to today, US laws, regulations, morals, and ethics have all become relative – with no greater example than the Constitution of the United States, which is (supposed to be) the foundation of our American Government. The Constitution, written in 1787, is the "supreme law of the land" because no law may be passed that contradicts its principles. No person or government is exempt from following it.

Except this is not true.

Take the example of the Corona plandemic which has seen an abject disregard of the First Amendment of the United States Constitution. The "outbreak" has conveniently provided the perfect opportunity for the State to wholly disregard and actively demolish the American people's "rights" to freedom of expression, assembly, and right to petition.

One example of this has been the deliberate and government-sanctioned censorship of any news, videos, and social posts that do not agree with the official agenda and story; despite this grossly contravening the First Amendment Act that guarantees freedom of expression by prohibiting Congress from restricting the press or the rights of individuals to speak freely.

Another example of laws being "qualified" at will and whim, is of course when the signing of the Patriot Act normalized the US government's mass surveillance powers – directly violating the Fourth Amendment which says the government cannot conduct a search without obtaining a warrant and showing probable cause to believe that the person has committed or will commit a crime.

Scared yet?

The Constitution is out of date and out of time. The word "democracy" appears nowhere in the Constitution. And when it pops up in comments of the Framers of the Constitution, it is almost always a reference to the importance of guarding the new republic against the dangers of too much democracy.

Executive Power

The greatest structural problem of the Constitution is the control exerted by a small elite class, which bends policy in the elite's favor at the expense of the majority.

Elite control was built into the Constitution from the start. Its first act? Ensuring the survival of slavery through the power reserved to the slave states. It took the Civil War to end it, and the Thirteenth, Fourteenth, and Fifteenth Amendments to overrule the three-fifths compromise.

The biggest advantage of a democratic republic over monarchy/aristocracy is that the rulers would resemble the public and thus make decisions appropriate for the populace. The solution? Build in the two-party system which is designed to perpetuate a status quo benefiting a small plutocracy. No matter who the voters choose, the elitists win, because the election system has only two "states", both of which are constructed by and acceptable to the plutocrats.

The 5 principles of today's democracy could be considered the consent of the governed, representative government, individual rights, the rule of law, and a system of checks and balances.

If a person believes these principles can all be checked, they should stop reading immediately! Their mind has already been altered, and their brain has been eaten. They should watch some TV instead.

Founding of The Federal Reserve

People might have wondered about where these Controllers get all their money?

Well, there is *your* money of course, and then there is stolen old money, and crooked new money – popularly referred to as Foundations, Estates, and Trusts.

But mostly, when talking about the globalists and their funding machine, people are referring to the US Federal Reserve – the biggest printing press in the world.

If one goes all the way back to the founding of the Federal Reserve in 1913, and the very first money that was created, it becomes clear that the system is designed to fail.

If the first $100 is created by the Fed and loaned to ACME Bank at 6% interest for the year, ACME Bank will be required to pay the Fed back $106 after the year concludes. Where are they going to get the extra $6 that they need to pay for the interest if there is only a total of $100 in the system?

They will not be able to find the extra money because it does not exist. The only solution is to borrow the $6 from the bank, but what happens at the end of the next year? They have to borrow the $.36 of interest for the additional $6 that they borrowed the year before.

This is known as the fiat currency system, and it is designed to force the central bank to constantly create more and more money in order for it to work. As more money is created and injected into the system, the value of the money shrinks a little bit each time because the supply is increased. This is how citizens lose 96.1% of the value of the United States dollar over a century.

People can also classify this system as a Ponzi scheme, or a pyramid scheme because new money is always needed to pay off the previous investors. Once the flow of new money stops, the pyramid collapses.

Once the Federal Reserve stops printing money, the value of the money outstanding stops devaluing. If they remove money from the system then the value of the outstanding money actually goes up because the supply is being reduced, which is a good thing, unless one has borrowed a ton of money at a certain interest rate. What happens in this scenario is that the borrower is still required to pay their loan back plus interest, but the value of the money is now worth more, so the loan is even more expensive than just the rate of interest.

In the end, the best way to picture this is to think about the standard formula of supply and demand where the more the supply of a product, the less value will be because it is theoretically easier to find the product. A reduction of the supply will increase the value because the product is harder to find.

The banking system mechanics can be intimidating and confusing, but at the core, it is just a simple concept of measuring the value of something based on the supply.

The FED and the IRS: Mutually Parasitic Relationship

Most people do not know very much about central banks, in part because they never interact with them. A person cannot borrow money from a central bank the way they can with a traditional retail bank like Bank of America or Wells Fargo. Central banks only deal with governments and retail banks, not individuals.

One of the reasons for this is because when dealing with the government, the dollar amounts that are being loaned out are astronomical, and thus the profits are enormous.

Another reason is that the government can repay their debts to the central bank because of their ability to impose and collect taxes.

The mechanism for the United States government to finance these loans is through taxation, so is it any surprise to learn that the Internal Revenue Service was also founded in 1913, the same year that the Federal Reserve was born?

Is this just a random coincidence?

No, it was done by design in order to put the payment burden on the taxpayer instead of the government.

The 16th Amendment to the U.S. Constitution was ratified on February 3rd,1913. Later that year, the United States Revenue Act of 1913 imposed a personal income tax on the American people.

The Federal Reserve and the IRS have a mutually parasitic relationship, and they have been used together to control the United States for over 100 years. The Fed loans the money to the American government, then the IRS collects the money through government taxation like a loan shark with a baseball bat looking to collect an unpaid debt.

This is one of the biggest hidden truths that create the world that we live in. It is important to note that all of this tax money that the American people pay each year actually goes toward repaying the debt that the Federal Reserve created, not the services Americans assume the money is being spent on.

Taxing Your Way To Prosperity

Federal taxes, state taxes, city taxes, county taxes, sales taxes, usage taxes, property taxes, licensing fees...where does it ever end?

There was a time when there were no taxes in America and the world still managed to keep on turning. In fact, it was the most prosperous time in American history.

It is no secret why people hate the idea of taxes, but they hate the process of doing taxes as well. For starters, there are 10.1 million words written in the tax code, which might explain the inefficiencies of a system that made over 5,000 different changes from 2001-2012.76 The 1040 tax form has 100 pages of instructions, and the estimates are that each year Americans spend 8.9 billion hours trying to comply with federal tax laws, time that could be put to better use doing just about anything else, including sleeping.

Income taxes were set up by the American government at the behest of the big banks to work as a feeder mechanism for repaying the debt that was created when the Federal Reserve was formed in 1910 and came into power in 1913, the same year that the Internal Revenue Service was born.

Not a coincidence.

The debt that was created when the Fed brought their form of money into existence and attached an interest payment to it was paid for with the money that was stolen from the people by the introduction of the federal income tax. The United States government borrowed the money from the Federal Reserve, at interest, and the American people have been paying that money back with their taxes every year for the past century, but that pile of debt keeps growing.

That is the scam of central banking and taxation boiled down to one paragraph. The American government treats its citizens like cows that they may milk at random, whenever they choose, for as long as they want. When they can no longer extract the milk that they desire, they turn their cows into hamburger meat and move on to the next cow.

What is the first rule when owning cows? Do not ever name them or else it makes it harder to turn them into dinner. The Globalists have a term that they use to describe Americans: useless eaters. They certainly see the public as a bunch of cows, and since they control the government, is it really a stretch to think that the government itself feels the same way about the public?

Once people come to understand how they are actually viewed by the controllers, the tax system makes a whole lot more sense. They want to milk the population for all they are worth, then slaughter them.

Pretty simple.

Although the politicians in Washington would never admit this, the reality is that taxes are not for everyone, just the middle class and the working poor.

The way the tax laws are structured, those with a smart tax attorney can see gaping loopholes that the majority of Americans simply cannot. All sorts of legal maneuvering through tax shelters, trusts, and corporate structuring can shave large percentages off of the bill. Tax havens like the Cayman Islands, Bermuda, and Jersey are simply not options for the general public if they even know where they are and what they do in the first place.

The data demonstrate that the U.S. individual income tax continues to be very progressive, according to the government. These are some of their tax figures from 2015:

• There were 141.2 million taxpayers that reported total earnings of $10.14 trillion in adjusted gross income and paid $1.45 trillion in individual income taxes.

• The share of reported income earned by the top 1% of taxpayers rose to 20.7%, while their share of federal individual income taxes fell slightly, to 39%.

• The top half of all taxpayers paid 97.2% of all individual income taxes, while the bottom half paid the rest.

• The top 1% paid a greater share of individual income taxes (39%) than the bottom 90% combined (29.4%).

• The top 1% of taxpayers paid a 27.1% individual income tax rate, which is more than seven times higher than taxpayers in the bottom half (3.6%).

What these figures do not show is that the bottom half of the population pays a much greater percentage of their income towards things like licensing fees, usage taxes, sales tax, their mortgage, mortgage insurance, and property taxes (if they even own a home), or their monthly rent (if they do not).

The Bureau of Labor Statistic shows that in 2017 "consumer units", which is defined as families, financially independent individuals, and people living in a single household who share expenses, spent 70% more on federal, state, and local taxes ($16,749) than on food and clothing ($9,562). For anyone searching for a reason why consumer spending on retail is way down in America these days, the reason might just be because far too much of their money is going out the door in the form of taxes to a bloated and out of control government.

The government likes to paint the picture that the rich do all of the paying of taxes and that is simply not the case. The poor pay a disproportionate amount of court fines, parking tickets, legal penalties, predatory interest rates, medical bills due to lack of insurance, and a variety of other forms of taxation that amounts to death by a thousand paper cuts, and it is designed in a way to lock people out of ever having a chance to rise up out of poverty.

A speeding ticket that costs a driver $300 has a much bigger impact on a person making $24,000 a year than one making $150k, even though the fines are the exact same amount. These fees and fines add up to destroy the poor in the form of a type of regressive tax on the uneducated, where the idea of saving up in a 401k is replaced with buying lottery tickets as a financial planning strategy.

Sure the rich pay more taxes, but the poor pay a larger percentage of their income when all forms of taxation are factored into the calculation. There is not much talk of the effective tax rate, a figure that is always considerably lower for the rich once all the tax avoidance schemes are implemented.

According to the U.S. Census Bureau, Americans in the "Land of the Free" pay a ton of money each year in a variety of taxes and fees.

- $2.4 trillion is paid yearly in income taxes.

- $1.5 trillion is collected from social insurance taxes.

- $1.6 trillion flows into the government for ad valorem taxes, working out to...

- $4,950 paid by each person, including children.

- $730 billion is paid each year on property taxes for the privilege of owning a home.

- $600 billion for fees and charges are collected yearly by the American government.

- $375 billion is generated from general sales tax, which calculates to about...

- $1,160 paid by each American, including children.

Crazy amounts of money flow into the American government, but it is so poorly managed by unaccountable bureauRATS. It is almost impossible to imagine how different the country and the world would be if this money was actually retained by the people instead of being squandered by the political establishment that hands out free cash to countries, companies, and buddies for a variety of unjustifiable reasons.

Is the Government Trying To Kill You?

First, in 1973, an MIT computer predicted the end of the world would start in 2020, then Deagel jumped on board in projecting the death of millions in America by 2025.

Deagel is a company that provides studies for military equipment and civil aviation, and their chart shows that the population of the United States would fall from 327 million in 2017 down to 99.5 million by 2025. The company, whose clients include the National Security Agency, North Atlantic Treaty Organization (NATO), Organisation for Economic Co-operation and Development (OECD), Russian Defense Procurement Agency, The World Bank, and the United Nations (UN), offer two possible reasons for this mass exodus or mass die-off by 2025:

1. A pandemic like Ebola that will get out of control due to a healthcare system that becomes overwhelmed.

2. A financial system collapse of stock and financial markets, and pension systems – wiping out most Americans and reversing migration patterns, sending people out of the United States in search of stability and a sound financial system.

But way before that, in 1973, came the simulation by Massachusetts Institute of Technology's (MIT's) computer program called "World One", which eerily echoes Deagel's sentiments about an upcoming collapse. This simulation, which was financed by the Club of Rome, a Globalist think tank, predicts the collapse of civilization by 2040. But the first catastrophic milestone set by the algorithm was an abrupt drop in the standard of living – in 2020.

Unlike the Deagel prognosis that sounded horrifying but reasonable, the MIT program results listed two different reasons for the collapse that are very much in line with the agenda of the Globalists: Overpopulation and global warming will be the causes that take down the planet, so to their logic, the only way to save the planet is to depopulate and institute carbon taxes. This has always seemed unlikely because the Globalists finance studies like these in order to scare the hell out of the public – pushing the public sentiment towards supporting their agenda for killing the "useless eaters" and stealing the money from whoever is left through a fraudulent carbon tax scam.

Hey, if the weather doesn't kill people the Banksters will.

Deagel's proposal, on the other hand, proposed the collapse of the United States through the implosion of the financial markets and the destruction of the medical system, two areas that could be seen as not just possible but probable. A dark analysis and one few people took seriously – until January 2020 revealed the Wuhan bats and rats virus, and the world went crazy.

Arguably, the onset of the Coronavirus pandemic has announced the beginning of the end of the American Empire, as well as the Old Word Order. The public have been so brainwashed with Zombie Apocalypse preprogramming through television and movies that it is the end of the world as we know it but we feel fine.

Move along everyone, nothing to see here.

The Club of Rome, the Rockefeller and Alexander King depopulation Think Tank, could not ask for a better situation than this to thin out the herd, forcing mandatory medical poisonous injections into the public, destroying civil society, and creating order out of chaos.

Order out of chaos, now where has that been mentioned before? Oh yeah, everywhere the New World Order puppets speak, and in all of their writings.

Eric Pianka, a controversial pro-population controller said, *"War and famine would not do. Instead, disease offered the most efficient and fastest way to kill the billions that must soon die if the population crisis is to be solved. AIDS is not an efficient killer because it is too slow. My favorite candidate for eliminating 90% of the world's population is airborne Ebola (Ebola Reston) because it is both highly lethal and it kills in days, instead of years. We've got airborne diseases with 90 percent mortality in humans. Killing humans. Think about that. You know, the bird flu's good, too. For everyone who survives, he will have to bury nine."* – Dr. Eric Pianka, University of Texas evolutionary ecologist and eugenicist.

The depopulation agenda is a real thing, born out of the Initiative for the United Nations ECO-92 EARTH CHARTER. It might sound like something out of a Netflix series or a science fiction novel, but there is a real push towards reducing the population of this amazing planet by a bunch of psychopathic men that have the capacity to actually make it happen when they want to.

The long-term plan for depopulation is shrouded in mystery and dressed up to look like a man-made disaster caused by the people, but like most of the attempts by the New World Order to control the world, it is lies upon lies forced upon the people by the corrupted corporate media.

The Dark Matter of Power

Being in control offers the types of rewards that true psychopaths seek: real power, almost endless amounts of money, fame, and everything that comes with it, a feeling of importance, the ability to make life and death decisions, and the influence to cover them up.

It is this ability to cover up and intentionally keep the "People They Serve" blind and in the dark, that gives them the ability to change laws and influence morals, safe in the knowledge that people are generally uncomfortable with revealing the rot – as long as they can pretend it is not there.

To use an astronomy analogy to explain, even though nothing put out by N.A.S.A. should be believed, due to their history of lies about everything including the moon landings.

Astronomers are sometimes able to find new stars, not by actually seeing them, but by noticing their effects on other celestial bodies near them. There is an unseen influence that has to be causing a neighboring star to act in a way that is uncharacteristic, and therefore the astronomer can determine that a new star is actually there, even though they cannot see it.

In politics, the supreme powers are also being influenced by something that the people cannot see, but know is there. It remains in the darkness, but the control that it has over the politician is easily determined by his uncharacteristic actions that expose the hidden hand of influence. In the never-ending vastness of political dark matter, one only really begins to understand what they are up against when they make the decision to illuminate the places intentionally kept in the dark.

To put it another way: Spreading mold covers more ground when the pantry door is shut, the light is turned off, and no one is watching. Sunlight is the best solution to illuminate the problem – and also to disinfect it.

Everybody knows that politics is a dirty business. But how dirty things really get is not something covered on the nightly news and never honestly debated on CSPAN.

In fact, the very concept of politics and governments are inherently immoral, evil means of mind control. It is only by shining a spotlight on the rot that is constantly spreading and causing disease that we can hope to prevent further destruction.

Illuminating the Decay

One of the major issues that plague the American Empire and undermine its credibility has always been its inconsistency in the enforcement of laws and policy, together with a focus on the least important things at the expense of some of the most important things.

As an example, the police in Portland might show up at a person's house and arrest them for collecting rainwater, but decide not to take a person that is selling heroin to minors to the police station.[36]

The city of Flint, Michigan made a deal to switch from drawing their water from Lake Michigan to instead pull it from the Flint River even though they knew the water was full of lead, but nobody was taken in for questioning for a crime pertaining to the poisoning of an entire city. This issue has not been fixed even after many years and countless public shamings, but a farmer selling unpasteurized milk is put in handcuffs and his farm is shut down.

The Coronapanic has shown everyone how easily their Rulers can decide to ignore all codes and legislation and order them to obey the rules of the minute through a show of aggressive martial force.

How can a society be expected to know how the government wants them to behave when there is one set of rules for the people with money and influence, another set of rules for those without, no rules for the multinational corporations, and the laws governing the people are written in pencil but the only ones with erasers are the powerful?

Way before the Plandemic, the American experiment had been in trouble, not from without, but from within. Americans have become fearful of their government in a way that only inner-city minorities have been over the years. They are worried about being pulled over by the police for no reason. They worry about showing up to work and being told that their services are no longer needed. Many are living paycheck-to-paycheck after being ravaged by the IRS and inflation of the Federal Reserve. Parents are worried that they cannot afford

---

[36] Kendra Alleyne, CNBC, "Oregon Man Sentenced To 30 Days In Jail For Collecting Rainwater On His Property".

to send their children to college. Some are even worried about calling someone the wrong gender pronoun.

Worry and fear are types of low-vibrational states of mind that are not ideal for making important decisions based on facts, but they are, however, perfect to make fight or flight, emotional, decisions. This is one reason why people suggest "sleeping on it" before committing to a big decision so that the brain has a chance to gather more information and a little bit of room to look at the information from an alternative point of view.

It might be that at their core, Americans feel the end approaching, and this subconscious knowing is manifesting itself as fear and worry. They may be trying to consciously connect this feeling to something more benign like the thought of losing a job when in actuality, they are beginning to feel that something major is happening.

The pessimists will call it the end, while optimists may decide to define it as a new beginning. Either way, everything is about to change.

The really frightening part is that the American people, to date, have allowed this to happen without a whimper, and those who have stood up in protest have been quashed into submission.

American Idiots

Don't wanna be an American idiot
One nation controlled by the media
Information age of hysteria
It's calling out to idiot America
Welcome to a new kind of tension
All across the alienation
Where everything isn't meant to be okay

– Green Day, *American Idiot*

Author Chris Hedges talks of a pattern that leads to the end of an Empire, and that if one can identify it soon enough, they can remove themself from the impending doom. It is a time when the respected and noble are replaced by the idiots. They take over every aspect of society and government, and their actions give them away and out them as the true idiots that they are.

It begins with the leadership at the top being taken over by someone so incompetent and narcissistic that it signals that the end is near. It is the cue that the other idiots were waiting for in order to make their move, and these will be the final days of a crumbling empire. They are unencumbered by common sense, and they see the State as a projection of their own vanity.

- Idiot generals wage endless, unwinnable wars that bankrupt the nation.

- Idiot economists call for more money printing that destroys the economy and project economic growth on the basis of a myth.

- Idiot bankers gamble on self-created financial bubbles and impose crippling debt payments on the citizens.

- Idiot journalists pretend despotism is democracy and become purely a mouthpiece for their own corrupt government.

- Idiot intelligence operatives orchestrate the overthrowing of foreign governments to create lawless enclaves that give rise to enraged fanatics.[2]

If there really is a checklist for extinction, is America in the process of ticking all the boxes?

Those empires that came before the American Empire saw their society collapse, in part, because the desires and fantasies of the idiots running the show were cemented into law.

That is how empires fall. They are hollowed out from the inside by the rats and parasites until all it takes to cave in the structure is one good kick to the front door and the whole place comes down.

Those Americans that are awake to the reality of the situation no longer blindly trust in their government, and with damn good reason.

- They feel the lack of protection from those sworn to defend them, and they recognize the conflict of interest between the media and the government.

- They are waking up to the disaster that people face with the destruction of the healthcare system.

- They know about the water in Flint, Michigan.

- They watched the video of Eric Garner being choked to death by a group of psychopathic cops. Then they watched the video of George Floyd being choked to death in exactly the same way – and being told that the cause of death was not asphyxiation.

- They look up and see the Chemtrails being sprayed on them.

- They know people that lost their houses to the banks after the crash in 2008 as they are losing their own homes now.

- They are in an ever-downward spiral of debt because of the continuous printing of dollars by the Federal Reserve Printing Press.

- Yet they see that there is always money for war. Endless amounts of money for warring with foreign nations, and with awakened American people.

And, all along the way, day by day, month by month, year by year and decade by decade the more rights and money are taken away and the more big government invades every aspect of their lives.

All Governments Are Illegal

Everything, so far, points toward the fact that all governments are immoral, evil, hypocritical, and corrupt on some level. So, what happens when the criminals that the government claims to be fighting against turn out to be the very government itself?

Hitler...Stalin... the list goes on. And on.

Crazy talk?

Hitler's concentration camps eradicated a lot of people, but nowhere near what they state in HIStory textbooks. So did Stalin's Gulags. Except that the Soviet dictator's mass system of forced labor camps was driven by economic and political greed rather than racial discrimination.

The Soviet ideology involved the large-scale purge of peasants (depopulation ring a bell?), as well as the so-called Kulaks, who were deemed capitalists by the state, and by extension enemies of socialism. The term "Kulak" became associated with anyone who opposed or even seemed unsatisfied with the Soviet government.

Scary?

Not as terrifying as the fact that what is happening in the world right now has been done before and the people did not stop it from happening again. When looking back at empires that have collapsed, it is so obvious that things are going to end badly. Think of the Romans, the Russians, the Brits; there is little sympathy for those that were harmed because the observer sees the signs clearly and assumes that the people must have been willfully ignorant to their impending doom.

The end of the American Empire has launched a long time ago. It is not an accident and it was not left to random chance.

The Coronavirus pandemic is merely the final trigger for the pre-planned explosion.

In the end, those that review how it all ended will feel the same way, have the same lack of empathy, and wonder the same things: how did they not see it coming, the signs were *everywhere* – starting with the flashing neon red arrows pointing out rogue governments all over the world.

- They do not care if the people become aware of their criminality, and they do not worry about prosecution because they know that they control the halls of (in)justice.

- They take the "bread and circuses" approach towards dealing with the general public since they do not respect them, and they treat the people as if they work for them, not the other way around.

- They conduct scientific experiments on the population without their consent and run human trafficking, organ harvesting, and weapons distribution operations.

- Though they claim to be trying to stop drug trafficking, they are actually the ones running the importation operation.

- They fund the very terrorists that they claim to be fighting against, and in some cases, they are the terrorists themselves.

- They constantly invent new reasons to extort (tax) the public to the point of near exhaustion, then sic their tax collection agencies on anyone critical of their government.

- They control the media either through disinformation, propaganda, the restriction of information, or the manufacturing of consent.

- They cover up their crimes until they are certain that they will get away with them while using intimidation and the threat of arrest to create a culture of fear of authority and self-censorship.

- They operate blackmail rings to ensnare politicians, foreign leaders, business mavens, Hollywood moguls, media spokespeople, and other powerful people.

- They pull false flag operations both nationally and internationally in order to create false narratives on things like gun control, terrorism, religion, hatred towards another country, and the division of the public.

- They grow massive armies then go looking for fights, play the "victim card" and lie about reasons to take the country to war, then demand patriotism under the threat of social ostracization.

- They use their spy agencies to keep the population in constant fear of imprisonment for thought crimes against the government, while they collect as much information about the public as they possibly can to be used against them at some later date.

- They turn the police against their own citizens by seeking out psychopathic new recruits, weaponizing them, then training them to be ultra-aggressive towards the public, while they imprison certain social, ethnic, or political groups at a disproportionate rate in order to silence dissent.

- They put their own citizens in concentration camps, and in some cases resort to mass murder.

- They take a heavy-handed approach to the state-controlled education where they intentionally dumb down the population, either slowly over time by poisoning their food, water, medicine, and education system, or quickly by rounding up the intellectuals and murdering them.

- They claim to run a democratic government but they privatize portions of the economy for themselves and those closest to them to control and pillage, they rig the financial markets for their own benefit, and then lie about the health of the economy and the infallibility of the marketplace.

Spot anything familiar?

Everyone should, because these are the governments that have taken their jobs, their businesses, their freedom of speech, and freedom of movement – all in the name of "saving lives". They are the politicians and the banksters and the Military-Information-Terror cabal. They are the people who give the public no choice. They are the ones who steal the people's money in the name of "Tax"; who force them to inject their children with poison as a smokescreen for population control and mass surveillance; and who would not stop at creating a virus, or a terror attack, or a martyr, or an organized riot – all in the name of domination.

And they have been doing it for a long, long time – easily gouging away the rotten foundation, and exposing the weak points.

Installing the Asbestos Insulation

After the collapse of the twin towers, an estimated 410,000 to 525,000 people, including more than 90,000 rescue, recovery, and cleanup workers, were exposed to a toxic plume containing 400 tons of pulverized asbestos and a host of other carcinogens.

Nineteen years later, the World Trade Center Health Program, which monitors all 9/11-related illnesses, has reported more than 14,000 cases of cancer, including malignant mesothelioma – directly linked to toxicity exposure in the aftermath of the 9/11 terrorist attack on New York City in 2001.

This number includes first responders such as police and firemen, recovery and cleanup workers and volunteers, and those who worked, lived, or went to school in the disaster area.

How did this happen?

Asbestos was the go-to insulation starting in the 1860s and lasting all the way until 1978, in large part because of the mineral's durability and fire-resistant properties. It was used for everything from building materials, steam pipes, boilers, valves, and many other products. It could be rolled in the attic of homes for traditional insulation, sprayed on walls and ceilings, and wrapped around pipes and ducts, both residential and commercially.

It was cheap to make, easy to install, available for everything, and also very toxic. They never replaced it because it would cost too much. What are a few thousand lives compared to billions of dollars, right?

Any disturbance of asbestos-filled materials in a home can release fibers into the air, which when breathed in, can cause mesothelioma and lung cancer. Millions and millions of products were sold, hundreds of millions of people, if not billions, were exposed to it for over a century, and now it is common knowledge that it is an institutional poison that has killed thousands of people already, and continues to kill more every day.[37]

It seems crazy now to consider working inside an office building that is packed with asbestos, but that is the very real situation that millions of people face, whether they realize it or not, every day.

What else are people living with right now, passed to the consumer as safe, that might turn out to kill them in a decade?

Certainly, Wi-Fi will end up on a list two decades from now, once the damage is already done. GMO crops are already on the list, but not enforced in any capacity by the bought-off FDA. Fluoride has been a lot like asbestos, but it has a much better public relations company working on its behalf. Vaccines are filling kids up with all sorts of toxins plus aborted fetal tissue.[38] Glyphosate is killing farmers in a way that asbestos could only dream of, but that information is being actively suppressed from the public by Monsanto.[39] Cell phones are probably going to end up sterilizing an entire generation of men from being kept in their front pockets. 5G is going to cook people from the inside like microwave popcorn, and smart meters are filling people with electromagnetic pollution.[40]

There is little doubt that future generations will shake their heads in dismay when they look back at this generation's willingness to be used as guinea pigs

---

[37] Cancer.gov, "Asbestos Exposure and Cancer Risk".
[38] Liz Neporent, ABC, "What Aborted Fetuses Have To Do With Vaccines".
[39] Carey Gillam, "Glyphosate: A Toxic Legacy".
[40] Lloyd Burrell, ElectricSense, "5G Radiation - 11 Reasons To Be Concerned".

the same way this generation looks at the old cigarette ads showing four out of five doctors recommending Lucky Strikes to their patients.

But can people really act surprised to find that a government that allowed asbestos to wrap every building in the country, is also wrapped in a toxic double standard that is slowly killing it as well? The American government has fostered a culture of toxicity through unchecked regulation of the actual things that are killing people, like poisonous food, a reckless medical industry that kills a quarter of a million people a year, and chemtrails, while focusing trillions of dollars on things that are not killing Americans like terrorism, Russia, and fake news.

On average, about two Americans die each year from terrorism in the United States, yet the government would have the people to believe that there were head-chopping maniacs around every corner just waiting for them to put their guard down for two seconds.[41] Where is the massive over-reaction by the government to what geoengineering is doing to the skies? There is not going to be one because they are involved in it. Where are the restrictions placed on the sale of GMO foods throughout the country? They are not coming because the agencies in place to handle something like this have been bought off by the lobbying companies hired by the Agra giants.

The real issues are ignored because the fake issues get all of the attention.

The toxic culture in America was perpetuated when government agencies like the Environmental Protection Agency turned the other way when British Petroleum blew up the Gulf of Mexico because the American Empire needs BP to continue to sell them the oil they require to keep the war machine going. Do they think that the American public did not notice this betrayal?

It is difficult to create a healthy environment, be it a physical, emotional, or spiritual, when the government that a person is living under is actively working against their best interest as the United States does against their people. Kids that grow up in a family with crazy parents usually turn out a bit crazy themselves, so is it really that much of a stretch to discover that the dysfunction of the American Empire has spread to the people in a predictable way?

Large corporations have been able to step over regulations that were put in place to protect the American people, so what develops is a society that thinks that there are regulations in place to protect them when in actuality those regulations were created by the large corporations to create monopolies and are not being

---

[41] Jennie Eastery, CNN, "More Die In Bathtubs Than Terrorism. It's Still Worth Spending Billions To Fight It".

enforced and it is leaving them vulnerable and completely exposed.

The Most Dangerous Company in the World

Most people are inherently distrustful of large, multinational corporations, and for good reason. They have shown a history of playing the corporate jurisdiction game with ruthless efficiency while ducking responsibility for their actions like their head is on a swivel. There is something to be suspicious about when a corporation's size has expanded so much that it has outgrown even its own country, and has shed its patriotic skin in exchange for a bigger shell.

A shell company, if you will.

Profits are accounted for in an Irish corporation in order to shake the avoid extortion (taxes), then funneled through a Cayman Island corporation that shares an address with 26,000 other like-minded corporations. They later feign poverty in a jurisdiction to avoid carrying their responsibility in the local community and demand further tax breaks as a condition of building their new headquarters in a particular county through the trumpeting of how many new jobs the facility will create.

This is how the game is played when a corporation owes no allegiance to any flag, and when they swear an oath of loyalty to the bottom line, not the people. Some will argue that this is the way the system has been built over the years and those smart enough to figure out the loopholes are simply playing this game to the best of their abilities. They would be doing a disservice to their shareholders if they did not explore all of the tax deferment options that were available to them.

This is not about taxes. Anyone that wants to figure out a way to not pay taxes to a corrupt government will not get any criticism here. In fact, it is a duty to evade extortion by criminals.

This is about using a corporate shell to absolve a company from responsibility for their actions; actions that negatively impact, and intentionally hurt other people. This is not to say that all corporations are evil, not at all. The problems can arise because one of the things that corporations do is transfer responsibility and blame away from the individual, and into a corporation that sprung to life only through a series of paperwork filings. This sort of talk gets Mitt Romney all hot and bothered, which is obviously a bad visual, but it is important to remember that the intent of these business vehicles depends on who is driving. Not all corporate entities are used to defraud consumers, cheat taxpayers, scam the general public, destroy the environment, poison the population, infect the sick, corrupt the judicial system, modify nature, suffocate humanity, rewire our brains, shirk responsibility, taint the food supply, and kill human beings, but when they do all of these things we call them Monsanto and Bayer.

2018 brought the marriage of two of the most despised and feared corporations in the history of the world: agri-conglomerate and Mustard Gas inventor Bayer, and the Most Hated Company in America for the last decade straight, and inventor of the humanity-ending Genetically Modified Organisms, Monsanto. The history of Bayer is as disturbing as Monsanto's, which strangely makes them a perfect fit for one another.[42]

Bayer has its roots in Germany from the mid-1800s. It was part of the infamous I.G Farben that rose to worldwide fame for the manufacturing of Zyklon B that was used in World War 2. Of course, they got their start making the chemicals that were used to manufacture a variety of poison gases that were used to kill thousands of people during World War 1, so is it really a surprise that they made a special appearance in the sequel?

Most people know them as the inventor of Aspirin, but they do not realize that they also first brought heroin to market as a non-addictive pain reliever. That first part did not work out so well for them, with the overdoses and all. They knowingly, yes, knowingly, sold HIV-infected drugs to hemophiliacs in Asia after they were caught doing it in the United States first.[43] They have sold expired vaccines and tainted GMO rice that ended up costing them $750,000,000 in lawsuits, but this is just the cost of doing business when you are one of the most dangerous companies in modern history, a company that is in the business of killing people.[44] As of 2018, Bayer was currently involved in liability lawsuits against the 32 different products that they manufacture.

Monsanto also has a checkered history of killing people in wars with their toxic products. The way Monsanto sees things, the chemical, Agent Orange, that Monsanto created and sprayed all over Vietnam to make the leaves fall off of the trees, does not mean that they are in the poison business, but rather they are in the lumber industry.

---

[42] James Corbett, The Corbett Report, *Bayer + Monsanto = A Match Made In Hell.*
[43] Suzanne Goldenberg, The Guardian, "Bayer Division 'Knowingly Sold' HIV-Infected Protein".
[44] Bloomberg News, "Bayer Settle With Farmers Over Modified Rice Seeds".

Do not forget about Dioxin and PCBs.

They dump toxic waste wherever they please in part because they stock the halls of justice with judges favorable to their cause. Supreme Court mute, Judge Clarence Thomas, worked as a corporate attorney for Monsanto in the 1970s and has voted Monsanto's way on every single ruling he has been involved with, surprising absolutely no one.

The World Health Organization has admitted that Monsanto's Roundup is "probably carcinogenic", and that glyphosate is toxic waste masquerading as a weed killer.[45] Even the Environmental Protection Agency (EPA) labeled glyphosate a carcinogen way back in 1985, only to reverse their stance six years later for some reason. Today, Roundup is the most popular weed killer in America, selling 100 million pounds per year that are sprayed on more than a billion acres, and is very much legal to purchase.

"It is commonly believed that Roundup is among the safest pesticides... Despite its reputation, Roundup was by far the most toxic among the herbicides and insecticides tested. This inconsistency between scientific fact and industrial claim may be attributed to huge economic interests, which have been found to falsify health risk assessments and delay health policy decisions." – R. Mesnage et al., Biomed Research International, Volume 2014

They have sued farmers relentlessly for decades in an effort to "protect" seed patents, and the lawsuits had led directly to the suicides of over 200,000 farmers in India alone.[46] They actively suppress scientific dissent and ruthlessly stomp out lawsuits meant to expose their utter corruption. They have been busted for bribing public officials and false advertising, among their less serious crimes against humanity.

They created Genetically Modified Organisms (GMOs) too, a time-bomb just waiting to kill off a generation of oblivious consumers that had the bad-sense to trust Monsanto's claims that their products were safe, even though they are clearly in the poison business. They have admitted that they seek to have a monopoly on the world's food supply.[47]

These two companies have merged to form a toxic conglomerate that will be responsible for 25% of the world's food, a thought that is truly frightening. And if

---

[45] The Guardian, March 21, 2015, "Roundup Weed Killer Probably Causes Cancer, Says WHO Study".
[46] SumOfUs, "Monsanto's Royalties Profit From Misery".
[47] Pete Dolack, Counterpunch, "Monsanto Seeks To Control World's Food".

anyone thinks that somehow the consolidation will stop now that the two largest have joined forces, they simply do not understand the bigger plan that is being put into place. This is the early stage of the lockdown of the planet's food supply.

This will be in conjunction with a massive spike in food prices throughout the world. The seeds and fertilizer that Monsanto sells have already increased in price 300% in just the past couple of years, so those prices are bound to explode now that the two biggest competitors have joined forces.

Perfect timing for those 15 million Americans that already cannot afford the price of food, so things are headed to a very dangerous place and are certain to get much, much worse. There is a plan that is being put in place by these Agri-giants that their former CEO openly spoke about, in which the three largest industries in the world - agriculture, food, and health - that once operated as separate businesses, would be integrated through a set of changes that would be pushed through by the American government. What he spoke about in the late 1990s has happened already, and continues to happen, through corporate mergers such as these.

If the plan is to weaken the support columns of the American Empire, a good place to start would be to poison the agriculture, food, and health industries that the population depends on.

When Monsanto's poisons started killing off large chunks of the bee population, they just bought up the independent organizations that were conducting studies to find out why all the bees were dying and took control of the information. If you can't beat them, just buy them and put them out of business.

The world should expect more of this behavior, not just from these two Agri-giants, but from all corporations whose business model is based on the consolidation of the major players, the ruthless extermination of the smaller players, and the suppression of dissent from watchdog groups keeping an eye on the direction an industry is headed and sounding the alarm on what is yet to come.

The marriage of Monsanto & Bayer might be one of the most dangerous, but it certainly will not be the biggest or the last. The merger and acquisition business makes a ton of money for those on Wall Street and the C-Level employees of the two companies, so as long as that remains the same, the world should continue to expect gigantic conglomerates to slowly take over the planet unless Monsanto and Bayer destroy it first.

An Idea So Good That It Has To Be Mandatory

The massive and blind push of vaccines onto the population is staggering and horrifying. They pretend that they work better than they actually do, and they downplay the side effects to the point that if people raise the point about actual safety they are branded as "anti-science".

This is total madness!

Some vaccines do not even make any sense, like giving the HPV vaccine to boys or the Vitamin K shot to babies. It is essential that people know that the #1 ingredient of the Vitamin K shot that is given at birth, is Polysorbate 80, a sterilization agent.[48] This is widely known and yet it is still being administered in hospitals to this day. An obvious question is why would something like this be given to anyone, let alone a brand new baby?

For those that point out the obvious flaws of some of these medical procedures and traditions, a typical question that is flipped back onto the person pointing out these glaring issues is whether or not they are a doctor, implying that only a doctor is qualified to make these types of judgments.

Does one have to be a doctor to understand that injecting aluminum into a person might have side effects or could pose a health risk? Is it possible to not have a background in medicine but still understand that mercury is a deadly substance that requires a hazardous materials team to remove it if it spills, yet it is still being injected into babies?

The argument that one must be a professional in order to question what appears to be quite obvious issues surrounding vaccines is a tactic that is used to discredit the messenger rather than to actually discuss the message. That is what a person does when they know that an honest investigation into a subject would destroy their position and expose their guilt. If this argument cannot be won through scientific facts, they believe that the next best thing is to try and attack the person and whittle away at their credibility.

The CDC has been dishonest in their handling of the MMR vaccine and their claim that it has no association with autism, even going so far as to hide the data from their own study on the MMR vaccine and autism. A whistleblower at the CDC

---

[48] Vaccine Information Network, "Vaccines Can't Prevent Diseases, But Effective In Sterilizing Children".

named Dr. William Thompson came forward to confess his involvement in fraudulently manipulating this study, after a decade of denial. He provided a reporter his documents showing what he, and others at the CDC, did to hide the data showing the MMR vaccine causes a 340% increase of autism in young, African-American boys.[49]

Once the CDC discovered that the MMR vaccine had huge problems, they did not do the things one would hope a regulatory agency would do in a situation like this. Instead of putting a stop to these vaccines and demanding more studies, they turned a blind eye and pretended that everything was fine.

This is not science, but the CDC has never really been about the science anyway. They operate more like another dysfunctional government agency than a safety valve there to protect the people. The only people that the CDC is interested in protecting are the bureaucrats inside their organization and the pharmaceutical companies that offer those very bureaucrats cushy jobs once they leave the government sector and look to cash in with the private sector.

It is not totally accurate to say that vaccines do not provide immunity, because they do provide immunity to the pharmaceutical companies that produce them thanks to a deal they pushed through Congress back in 1986 that granted those companies immunity from lawsuits filed by patients that were injured or killed by their products.[50]

Even the most basic of research into the adjuvants being used in these vaccines turn up major questions about why aluminum is so prevalent, especially considering how dangerous it is.

There are actually several different types of aluminum adjuvants that can be found in vaccines like amorphous aluminum hydroxyphosphate sulfate, aluminum phosphate, aluminum hydroxide, potassium aluminum sulfate, and "aluminum salts".

An adjuvant is added to vaccines in order to antagonize the body into fighting back against it since it is clearly not supposed to be inside a human body. The immune system is tricked into thinking that the weakened antigens in the vaccines are the cause of the disruption, not the adjuvants so that the body will create a response to those antigens and make the body better at defending itself the next time it sees these same antigens, which is where the immunity is said to

---

[49] Andrew Wakefield, *Vaxxed: From Coverup To Catastrophe.*
[50] The National Childhood Vaccine Injury Act (NCVIA) of 1986.

arise from.

The cumulative effects of aluminum injected into a child happens to be one of the neurotoxic factors many proponents of childhood vaccines either are not aware of, or intentionally ignore, and it is a big one. According to the vaccine schedule, by a year and a half, a child should have had 4,925 micrograms of aluminum injected into their bodies, bypassing the natural defense shields like the skin and the gut, and exposing the child to massive amounts of aluminum all at once.[51]

If a baby ingested the same amount of aluminum orally, the digestive process would break it down over the course of hours as it works its way through the system. If a child is unable to rid itself of this aluminum and it actually enters the bloodstream in large amounts, the results are potentially devastating, and not just in the short-term. The effects of a massive amount of different ingredients that are injected into a baby create walking science projects where the effects of these ingredients might not show up for many years, and when they do, it is hard to isolate one particular cause because of the delayed or cumulative effect that they have.

If the National Vaccine Injury Compensation Program is ever repealed, the victims of vaccine damage will try to sue vaccine manufacturers, the CDC, and probably members of the ACIP committee who recommend the vaccines. However, the CDC has already thought this out and they have created a system that makes pinning vaccine damage on a particular vaccine rather difficult.

As an example, if a child receives ten vaccines over a two year period and develops autism, from a legal standpoint it is difficult to pin the blame on any one of these vaccines without creating reasonable doubt that it could have been one of the other nine vaccines that were responsible. So in a sense, the schedule itself provides legal cover because there is never a time where only one shot is given without other shots being required within a close time frame that works to muddy the waters of culpability.

This is not by accident, it is intentional. If the legal protection that the government is providing these vaccine makers ever goes away, this clustering of shots into groups acts as a way of creating reasonable doubt in the minds of those tasked with dishing out potential punishment.

---

[51] Collective Evolution, December 9, 2017, "Scientists Prove Link Between Aluminum and Early Onset Alzheimer's Disease".

30 Billion Reasons to Keep This Train Moving

People cannot forget that this is also a business, so the ownership stake in these vaccines is very relevant for trying to understand the reason that the system is as broken as it is. With $30 billion in yearly profits, there is more than enough of an incentive to continue to expand the schedule to include more shots, not just for children, but also a huge push is being made on the elderly as well.

The CDC and some of their members own more than 50 patents connected to vaccinations, so they have a major financial stake in making sure that things do not change.[52] It makes a person stop and wonder about how an organization that sets the schedule for vaccines can also financially benefit by making one of their vaccines a part of the schedule, thus ensuring the purchase of their product throughout the country. This is the very definition of a conflict of interest because they profit every time one of their new vaccines is brought to market and forced onto the American people under penalty of not being allowed to attend school, in the case of California currently, and throughout the nation, eventually.

The direction that vaccinations are headed is also exposed through their patents. In addition to the ownership stake they hold on the vaccines, the CDC also owns multiple patents for the method of administering shots through aerosol delivery or basically spraying vaccines on the population through airplanes.

People think they hate chemtrails now, just wait until they are loaded up with vaccines and randomly rained down upon unsuspecting people in order to achieve the magical and totally fictional concept of "herd immunity".

Doctors are also compensated by Big Pharma and medical insurance companies based on their ability to maintain high levels of vaccination rates. In some cases, doctors that maintain 63% vaccination rates are rewarded with $400 for each patient, which for a standard pediatrician practice with 250 patients puts $100,000 per year into the doctor's pocket.[53] This is an incentive to push vaccines to everyone, both young and old, and to suppress evidence that conflicts with the narrative set by the CDC, the pharmaceutical companies, and the doctors themselves.

People better get their flu shots because their doctor wants a new Range Rover.

---

[52] Weltcheck, Mallahan, & Weltcheck, "CDC Members Own More Than 50 Patents Connected To Vaccinations".
[53] Children's Health Defense, "Incentivizing Pediatricians To Follow The CDC Vaccination Schedule".

This Can't Be Happening

There is cognitive dissonance happening in the medical communities where pediatricians simply will not allow themselves to ponder the possibility that the vaccines that they have been pushing on their clients are actually the problem, not the solution. They have sent so many kids down that path that to admit they were wrong at this point in their careers would be psychologically devastating for the doctors, it would open them up to legal repercussions from the families of the injured children, it would make them a target of retribution by other doctors that have no desire to make an admission such as this, and they would be shut out by Big Pharma who would instigate a public relations war against them in order to paint them as rogue doctors that are falling into some unproven area of pseudoscience. The downside for doctors that wake up to the reality of their actions is obvious and steep, so hoping for change from existing doctors is probably unrealistic.

A more likely option is to educate the next generation of doctors to the reality of the vaccine industry's dirty secret and criminal practices so that they never even go down that path in the first place. Perhaps if they learn early on about the relationship between the CDC, the vaccine manufacturers, and those in a position to profit from increases to the schedule, they might realize that at the very least there is the potential for a conflict of interest for those that make the decisions.

It is important for future doctors to also understand that there is an intentional suppression of accurate information by the manufacturers of the vaccines so that the general public can remain in the dark about the danger of the ingredients, as well as the surprising lack of real testing of vaccinated vs. unvaccinated kids, the most obvious medical test a company can commission.

Future doctors must also understand the depths of the criminal collusion between the CDC and Merck with regard to their fraudulent burying of evidence in the MMR study in which the CDC conspired to rig the results of a study on autism by shredding documents so that it would not show a 340% increase for African-American boys in Georgia, the subject of the award-winning documentary "VAXXED, From Cover-up to Catastrophe".

There is no slowdown in sight for the host of vaccines that are working their way through the approval process so that they can be added to the schedule of vaccines recommended by doctors, and in some cases, required by the State, despite major concerns about the increase in mandatory vaccines and the association with the increase in autism and other disorders.

The Costs of Doing Business

It is important to understand that there are payoffs being made for people that have been injured by vaccines. Major payoffs that rival the payoffs that have been made by the Catholic church to settle sexual abuse allegations, both in the range of about $4 billion.

There are side-effects to vaccines like there are with all medicines. The fact that the industry tries to pretend like there are not is a bright red flag being waved for anyone with the eyes to see it and the common sense to comprehend the situation. There have been 6,000 different victims compensated by the National Vaccine Injury Compensation Program, a number that is significant, especially considering how difficult it is for one to even qualify for payment through this system.[54] More than half of them are from issues arising from the flu shots that the media is constantly pushing on the public as if there is no downside risk at all.

Organizations do not generally agree to substantial financial payoffs to settle claims regarding their behavior unless by doing so it makes the public less aware of their actions, and of course, this should be alarming because it is an admission that they are responsible for harming people, otherwise they would not be paying out anything, let alone thousands of millions of dollars. Lawyers can argue about whether a company is actually liable, but it does not require a law degree to understand that companies that pay people billions of dollars are doing so because they have an involvement in hurting people on some level, and no amount of public relations is going to obscure this quite obvious connection.

It is worth mentioning that the money that is paid to injured or deceased victims does not even come from the pharmaceutical companies that make the vaccines, it comes from a $.75 tax that is paid by each of the parents that authorize the doctors to inject their children. The concept of "hitting Big Pharma where it hurts", meaning in the wallet, does not even hold up because it is not their money that is being paid out to these injured children, it is the patient's money that is collected in advance and held in accounts in order to pay out the sick kids that were able to jump through all of the hoops and navigate through the legal waters in order to receive a payment that requires them to sign a confidentiality

---

[54] Jodie Fleischer, NBC, "Half of All New Federal Vaccine Cases Allege Injury From Shots Given Incorrectly".

clause that allows the fund to claw back 10 times the payout amount if they mention their payout amount or break their legally binding silencing mechanism.

If people wonder why they have not heard about this fund, that is the reason why.

Where Is This All Going?

It is important to know that anti-vaccine Japan has the World's lowest infant mortality rate and the highest life expectancy following its ban on mandatory vaccinations. They also did away with the MMR vaccine a long time ago because it was causing far too many problems, even though they were facing a serious push by Big Pharma.

Probably just a coincidence that they are considered to be the healthiest country on the planet, in spite of their "anti-science" approach to vaccines.

The people that are informed and educated about what is going on with the obfuscation of the facts by Big Pharma are demanding full-disclosure regarding vaccine science, ingredients, the studies that have been performed, as well as which studies have not been performed. They demand fully informed medical consent and the ability to make the choice for themselves and their children to vaccinate or not, especially considering that the science has not been settled, despite what they would have the public believe.

Sounds reasonable.

One can bring up the dangers of vaccines to Big Pharma but, to many people's surprise, they do not want to hear it. They are not interested in fixing it.

Their goal is really clear: they want the removal of all non-medical exemptions for vaccines. That is what they are lobbying for, and that is what they are going to get with their lobbying money. The best investment of their careers by removing informed consent, and replacing it with mandatory compliance. The groundwork has already been laid with SB277 in California that makes vaccinations mandatory before a child can attend school, without allowing for a medical exemption or a personal-belief exemption.[55] It is no surprise that Congressman Pan who pushed the bill was heavily funded by Big Pharma, and

---

[55] National Vaccine Information Center, "California Enacts Vaccine Law That Forces Parents To Choose Between Human Rights and Civil Rights".

this strategy is set to be duplicated in the other 49 states because all someone needs to create laws is a lot of money, and they have plenty of that already.

There has also been a change in laws surrounding some federal employees and hospital workers that are required to get flu shots and vaccines as a condition of continued employment, which is nothing more than medical fascism being enforced by the government under the guise of safeguarding the public's health.

The sick truth and purpose of the whole vaccine and flu shot industry are that not only do the products not fix the problems that they claim to help, but they destroy the good health of the patient intentionally in order to create a sick person that becomes a repeat customer for the pharmaceutical companies.

A society without the right for self-determination with regards to health decisions is not a society for the people and by the people, but rather for the State and by the State, or for the Corporation by the Corporation, which can be exponentially more dangerous.

It causes one to question why their health is intentionally being compromised by the government? Is this a coincidence, or is there a secret society with a plan in place to kill a large portion of the American people?

A "club" if you will.

The Club Of Rome

If the Club of Rome does not ring a bell, that is because this organization preferred to fly under the radar when possible, and for good reason. Their goals are very Malthusian, and not exactly dinner party conversation unless they are having a dinner party at one of the Rothschild's castles like in *Eyes Wide Shut*.

The Club of Rome was founded in 1968 as an informal association of independent leading personalities from politics, business, and science, men and women who are long-term thinkers interested in contributing in a systemic interdisciplinary and holistic manner to a better world.

This is not a club that any sane and rational human being would want to be a part of because, although it sounds like a glamorous bar that you might find in Caesar's Palace in Las Vegas, it is really a front group run by megalomaniacs pushing for world government.

The aim of the Club of Rome is:

"To identify the most crucial problems which will determine the future of humanity through integrated and forward-looking analysis; to evaluate alternative scenarios for the future and to assess risks, choices and opportunities; to develop and propose practical solutions to the challenges identified; to communicate the new insights and knowledge derived from this analysis to decision-makers in the public and private sectors and also to the general public and to stimulate public debate and effective action to improve the prospects for the future." [56]

Of course, none of this sounds bad.

This is what think tanks focus on for the most part, but the problem comes when one dives deeper into the true purpose of the Club of Rome. It is naive to assume that an organization will telegraph their evil intentions for all to see through its mission statement. Those waiting for that will be sorely disappointed. They are never going to come right out and tell the world that their plan is to subjugate humanity under their rule because that would look stupid on a bumper sticker, so they employ a tried and true method for tricking people into believing something that is not true.

They let the public assume that their intentions are noble by hiding them in plain sight.

Nothing about The Club of Rome's stated goals is actually a lie.

1. They have identified crucial problems, but they see the problems as too many people living on "their" planet and not paying them enough money.

2. They do really have alternative solutions for the future, but they involve removing billions of people from the Earth under the guise of saving it.

3. They have found a very lucrative opportunity that allows them to profit immensely from their plan and it is called "Carbon Taxes".

4. Their risk assessment shows too many people standing in the way of their desire to run the world, but they have taken care of the next step by devising solutions to that problem.

---

[56] ClubofRome.org.

5. They have been communicating their new insights to the decision-makers that they control for years now, with the help of the captured corporate media.

6. The debate that they have been speaking of sparking has been a discussion about whether to put their plans into place immediately or to wait a little while longer before implementing their solution for humanity.

7. Lastly, the foundation of their plan for humanity is in place to fix the problem that they have identified: People.

One makes the assumption that their goals are about helping the people of Earth.

They are not.

Their goals are about helping themselves, and this plan becomes self-evident a few years after their creation when they introduce a term that will come to symbolize their plan: Global Warming.

The Club of Rome was founded by psychopathic mastermind David Rockefeller and Dr. Alexander King, one of the founders of NATO and the Committee of 300. King was a scientist credited with pioneering the sustainable development movement, while also being named a Commander of the Order of the British Empire. Dr. Alexander King's resume reads like a laundry list of Globalist organizations and State-funded institutions, many of which he is credited with creating.

Dr. King was also credited as one of the chief architects of the Tavistock Institute, an organization that seeks to use the field of psychology to alter human behavior for the benefit of the State. When the Club of Rome wanted to know how to go about implementing their evil plan on the public, they commissioned the Tavistock Institute to prepare the blueprint for how this could be achieved.

This whole climate change hysteria began in the early 1970s, but the concept took many years of work by the Tavistock Institute in order to infect the public and find its way into the collective consciousness. The foundation was laid and their plan was unveiled in their 1971 book. They then took it one step further and explained how they are going to do it.

"The common enemy of humanity is man. In searching for a new enemy to unite

us, we came up with the idea that pollution, the threat of global warming, water shortages, famine, and the like would fit the bill. All these dangers are caused by human intervention, and it is only through changed attitudes and behaviour that they can be overcome.

The real enemy then is humanity itself. We believe humanity requires a common motivation, namely a common adversary in order to realize world government. It does not matter if this common enemy is a real one or one invented for the purpose." – Club of Rome, 1971.[57]

This document is something that they did not want anyone outside of their circle to read.

This is their plan.

This is not an opinion of what they are doing, these are their own words. It does not matter if the enemy is not even real. It does not matter if there is climate change or not, they are going to use that as their excuse to institute a world government anyway.

This carbon tax is planned to be one of the main funding mechanisms of the world government that they are seeking to create.

The Carbon Tax Hustle

There are few terms that evoke a deep sadness about the way that humanity has let down the planet quite like "Global Warming". Skinny polar bears clinging to dwindling icebergs is the iconic image associated with the overheating of the planet due to Man's selfish ways.

How stupid can people be to trash the only home they have? How can they call this a civilized society when people destroy the very planet that they depend on for survival. What kind of suicidal culture have they developed that refuses to deal with their impending doom to instead focus on acquiring more things in order to make themselves feel better about how broken they really are?

If the plan was to make people feel guilty for their actions then it was a smashing success.

---

[57] ClubofRome.org, "Report: The Limits To Growth".

But what if what the public was told was not actually the truth? Have people ever stopped to consider the possibility that the story they were sold about the state of the planet was a lie?

It sounds preposterous to consider that. What kind of a psycho would misrepresent these facts about the planet in an attempt to manipulate humanity's emotions?

The kind of people that are behind The Club of Rome fit the bill, among others. Take two steps back, remove the emotion that global warming reflexively evokes, and think about how an evil mastermind would back the population into a plan designed to control their actions. The best way to control someone is to convince them to control themselves. If one could make this mechanism an involuntary reaction caused by guilt then they would have a system that is self-policing and reinforced through public shaming.

It is the perfect system that only requires that the belief of Global Warming continue to exist. As long as that is in place then the people will take care of the rest and the controllers will not need to force people to comply with their plan because they will do so through a combination of duty, pride, guilt, and the fear of ridicule.

It is believed that the United States has taken the lead on fixing what was once known as Global Warming, but has lately undergone an Orwellian "Doublespeak" meets New Coke rebranding to officially become known as Climate Change. The problem with the old name was that it fixed their position to a particular temperature, in this case, warming. If the temperatures across the world ever go down, as they have over the past decade in a variety of locations, it becomes harder and harder to sell a name that is not meant to be ironic.

When they made the move to the ambiguous "Climate Change", it allowed them to account for these fluctuations in temperatures because technically the climate is always changing, so they are covered, both from a perception standpoint and legally, as well.

Why would being covered "legally" be something that the pushers of Climate Change would be interested in having for their protection?

They want the legal coverage and the ambiguous name because they are selling a lie, and they know it.

But one has to admit that the rebranding is genius.

The Trillion Dollar Lie

This is a controversial point, but it is an important one that needs to be made in order to fully understand how rotten and decrepit the facade of the American Empire has become.

First, it is important to differentiate between climate change and pollution. They are not the same, not even close.

The contamination of the soil, the water, and the air by substances that are harmful to living things is pollution. There are many forms of it, both natural and unnatural, but the focus is on pollution resulting from human activity.

Human beings dispose of literally tons of toxic waste, nuclear waste, medical waste, and various other industrial waste products into the lakes, oceans, rivers, landfills, and local dumps daily. Gas-combustion engines belch microscopic particles that combine together in the atmosphere to affect the amount of sunlight that makes it to the surface of the planet to fulfill its obligation to the cycle of life on this planet.

This is pollution.

Here are a few facts about pollution in the United States:

• Almost half of the lakes in America are classified as extremely polluted and not fit for swimming or fishing.

• Over 1.5 million tons of nitrogen pollution flows down the Mississippi River and in the Gulf of Mexico yearly.[58]

• One trillion gallons of untreated sewage and industrial waste is dumped in the U.S water system annually.

• Americans purchase almost 30 million bottles of water every year, with only about 13% of these bottles recycled every year.

• Indoor air pollution is 200%-500% more toxic than the air outdoors.

[58] USGS, "Source and Transport of Nitrogen in the Mississippi River Basin".

- Americans throw away 1.8 billion diapers, 30 billion foam cups, and 220 million tires each year.[59]

- Although Americans only represent 5% of the world's population, it produces about 30% of the world's waste and uses about 25% of the world's natural resources.[60]

- 110 million Americans live in areas where pollution is classified as "harmful" by the federal government.

- America burns 1.5 million barrels of oil just to import bottled water for its consumers, at a cost 10,000 x higher than regular tap water.

- A typical American family uses 300 gallons of water every single day.

- Estimates are that 5,000 people die in Southern California alone from pollutants emanating out of diesel engine trucks each year.[61]

- It is estimated that 200,000 people die each year in America from pollutants in the air.[62]

- The United States uses 2.2 billion pounds of toxic pesticides every year.

- Americans dump 960 tons of sewage into their waters, every hour.

Pollution is obviously not limited to America, and the statistics in developing nations is frightening and totally unsustainable:

- China is among the countries with the highest air pollution in the world. Breathing air in Beijing is the equivalent of smoking 21 cigarettes every day.

- Almost 750,000 people die from air pollution in China every year. 300,000 deaths are attributed to outdoor air pollution, while 400,000 are from indoor air pollutants.[63]

---

[59] Earth Over Us, "Pollution".
[60] Scientific American, "Use It And Lose It: The Outsize Effect of U.S. Consumption on the Environment".
[61] The Center For Public Integrity, "The Fear of Dying Pervades Southern California's Oil-Polluted Enclaves".
[62] Jennifer Chu, MIT News Office, August 29, 2013, "Study: Air Pollution Causes 200,000 Early Deaths Each Year in the United States".
[63] Richard Spencer, The Telegraph, "Pollution Kills 750,000 in China Every Year".

- Globally, air pollution is the fourth largest killer, causing over 6 million deaths every year.[64]

- The Great Pacific Garbage Patch is an island of floating plastic and trash in the Pacific Ocean and is estimated to be larger than the United States.

- 14 billion pounds of garbage is dumped into the oceans each year.

- Over 80% of the waste in India is dumped directly into the Ganges River.

- Over 1 million birds and 100 million mammals die yearly from pollution.

- Over 3 million children ages five and under die due to environmental factors like pollution annually.

- There are currently 1.2 billion cars on the road today, with that number set to grow to 2 billion by 2035.[65]

- Over 1 billion people do not have access to clean drinking water, with an average of 5,000 people dying from polluted water daily.[66]

- One hundred billion plastic bags are thrown away according to the Worldwatch Institute, with less than 1% finding their way into a recycle bin. Estimates show that around 1 billion birds and mammals die each year because of eating plastic.

- Traffic and air pollution exposure account for 12% of heart attacks globally, the largest contributing factor.[67]

- The typical person has between 70 and 90 different types of chemicals and pollutants in their bloodstream alone at any given moment. The number rises to over 500 with respect to the entire body.

- There are currently over 80,000 synthetic chemicals that human being come in contact with, most of which did not exist prior to the late-1800s.[68]

Pollution is real, it is everywhere, it is what most people are really upset about,

[64] Niall McCarty, Forbes, "Air Pollution Contributed To More Than 6 Millions Deaths in 2016".
[65] John Voelcker, Green Car Reports, "1.2 Billion Vehicles on World's Roads Now, 2 billion By 2035:Report".
[66] Ashley Seager, The Guardian, "Dirty Water Kills 5,000 Children A Day".
[67] Harvard, "Traffic and Air Pollution Most Significant Triggers of Heart Attacks Worldwide".
[68] MomsRising.org, "80,000 Chemicals In Everyday Products, But Who's Counting (No One)".

and it is one of the biggest threats to humanity. When one sees people screaming about saving the environment, they are talking about the need to reduce the current levels of pollution and cleaning up the existing pollution in the air, water, land, and in our bodies.

Climate change, however, has nothing to do with pollution.

It is a scam designed to usher in a carbon tax, with this tax money flowing to those politicians and multinational corporations that are in control. It has absolutely nothing to do with science, and everything to do with an enormous transfer of wealth through a fake tax dressed up as a savior for the planet.

The two items, pollution, and climate change have been intentionally blurred in an effort to obfuscate the truth of the matter which is that they are not the same. They have taken pollution, which is a real thing, and hijacked the negative properties of it for Climate Change to use, which is not a real thing.

They then simultaneously created a push to demonize anyone who figures out this scam as "climate change deniers" as a means of discrediting by reflex action and effectively putting them in the same category as flat-earthers and Holocaust deniers. They were also forced into the same group as Big Oil pollution deniers who stand over a wrecked oil tanker or the latest offshore oil well that blew up and proudly proclaim that there is "nothing to see here".

The people that see through the scam are not denying pollution, they are just exposing the climate change concept as being a cause that has been quietly taken hostage by a group with no concern for the environment whatsoever.

Now, this is not some outrageous conspiracy "theory" that tin foil hat wearing kooks have accused the Rockefellers of conspiring in, this is part of an actual plan that the Rockefellers signed their names to in 1971, but hoped people would never find out about.[69]

This information has been, and currently still is, suppressed by those in positions of power. If this secret gets out their whole trillion-dollar scam will come undone.

So what is the secret plan? Is it kept in the vault in the basement of the Smithsonian? Is it encrypted and sealed in a motion detector-protected cleanroom?

---

[69] ClubofRome.org, "Report: The Limits To Growth".

No, the plan is in a document written in 1971 by The Club of Rome.

Climate change is designed to finance the New World Order, and the American Empire is steering the ship. They are telling the world this, directly, in their Club of Rome document. All one needs to do is read and understand their words. This is not Nostradamus and his intentionally ambiguous and confusing quatrains, this is plain English.

Here is the passage again:

"The common enemy of humanity is man. In searching for a new enemy to unite us, we came up with the idea that pollution, the threat of global warming, water shortages, famine, and the like would fit the bill. All these dangers are caused by human intervention, and it is only through changed attitudes and behaviour that they can be overcome.

The real enemy then is humanity itself. We believe humanity requires a common motivation, namely a common adversary in order to realize world government. It does not matter if this common enemy is a real one or one invented for the purpose." – Club of Rome, 1971.

This is the translation:

As a ploy to unite humanity into a one-world government, we [The Club of Rome] came up with the idea that global warming would work great because we could blame it on people, and then make them do something to fix it. The people need to be motivated to form a One World government, and it does not really matter if we make up the reason or not.

The "something" that they will say will "fix" the problem is for the people to pay for polluting. They will suggest that the payment component should be a tax to punish this sort of careless behavior, and this tax will be promoted as a punishment to the people and governments that exceed a certain threshold deemed acceptable by society, a threshold that they will determine in actuality.

The sales pitch will be that since pollution does not recognize or respect national boundaries, and because the problem is global in nature, the solution must be global and free of sovereign boundaries as well. The problem impacts the entire world and encourages mankind, hell, forces mankind, to think bigger than the current nation-state paradigm. A world pollution problem deserves a world solution: A One World Government.

A New World Order

Former Prime Minister of Britain, Gordon Brown, flat out said that a New World Order is needed to deal with the Climate Change crisis. Cass Sunstein, Obama's former head of the Office of Information & Regulatory Affairs, said that redistribution should occur through climate change policy.

Maybe everyone should listen to these people when they tell the world all about their plan?

The Club of Rome is just another branch of the Rockefeller Foundation, and if there is one thing to know about the Rockefeller family it is that they are not looking to solve the world's problems, they are the people creating them.[70] That is what the Rockefellers do, they finance many groups that push the globalist agenda. When people see their name attached to a project that is dressed up to look like a charity, they can be assured that nothing good will come from it. The Rockefeller family's mission statement is to develop new ways to destroy humanity and enslave the people, and they are very good at what they do. The Club of Rome is just another one of their deceptive creations, so their words and intentions must be scrutinized and double-checked based on a long record of greed, corruption, and utter destruction.

"The Club of Rome is focusing on its new program on the root causes of the systemic crisis by defining and communicating the need for, the vision and the elements of a new economy, which produces real wealth and wellbeing; which does not degrade our natural resources and provides meaningful jobs and sufficient income for all people." – Description from the Club of Rome website, ClubOfRome.org.

If an organization like The Club of Rome declares its intentions, interpreting its true meaning helps when the text is inverted. When they announce their intention to create real wealth and wellbeing, they plan to strip-mine the wealth out of the system and leave the host sick and hollow. If they proclaim to be the protector of the natural resources, one can bet they will slash and burn and scorch the ground. Meaningful jobs with sufficient income mean assembly line factories paying slave wages.

As if that was not enough, they also seek to reorder society in a way that fits

---

[70] Recycling Washington, "Unraveling the Club of Rome".

their goals, by weakening what they call the "moral fiber of the nation" and to demoralize workers in the labor class by creating mass unemployment as jobs dwindle due to the post-industrial zero growth policies introduced by the Club of Rome.

Welcome to the Dystopian future envisioned by The Club of Rome: working 18-hour shifts making Soylent Green in order to earn enough money to pay mandatory carbon taxes to a world government.

The Plan is Already Happening

If this sounds a bit too crazy to believe, then look no further than the policy of "Cap and Trade" to see that this plan is not just on the drawing board in some James Bond villain's subterranean bunker, this policy is already in place and in the early stages of operations.

It is happening now.

The way it works is that a Cap is set on emissions designated as "greenhouse gases" that allow companies to pollute only a specified amount, then they are penalized (taxed) if their actual emissions exceed the agreed-upon threshold.

The Trade component is that a new market is created for other companies to buy or sell allowances to offset their pollution. If a company does not pollute at a rate that exceeds their limit, they can sell that extra amount of room they have between their actual greenhouse emissions and their allowed cap amount to another company for a price if their amount exceeds their threshold. Another company can buy their leftover emission space for a price. A company can bank their excess capacity to use the next year, or they can offer it up to the highest bidder.

The government then distributes these cap amounts either without a charge, or they sell them to companies through auctions. The government imposes an artificial limit, decided by them, on something that they, in their sole discretion deem to be a problem, then they sell the solution to companies, and force them to comply with their new regulation under penalty of fine or shutting down their business.

What a scam!

This creates a marketplace for these carbon taxes to be bought and sold, so who gets involved when imaginary widgets are changing hands for billions of dollars?

Wall Street, of course.

And who is the poster child for reckless Wall Street speculation and fraud?

Enron.

And how was Enron scamming the world?

Through selling fraudulent carbon credits, and everyone knows how that turned out.

The current version of Cap & Trade is more like a dress rehearsal for what is going to be rolled out worldwide in the coming decade unless sanity is finally reintroduced back into society and the mainstream media.

Not That Kind of Green

The Green Climate Fund is a new global fund created to support the efforts of developing countries to respond to the challenge of climate change. They were pushed into a position of prominence after the Paris Agreement in 2015. GCF helps developing countries reduce their greenhouse gas emissions and adapt to "climate change". They claim to seek to promote a paradigm shift to low-emission and climate-resilient development, taking into account the needs of nations that are particularly vulnerable to climate change impacts.

It was set up by the 194 countries who are connected to the United Nations Framework Convention on Climate Change in 2010, as part of the Convention's financial mechanism. It plans to deliver equal amounts of funding to both adaptation and prevention, with an emphasis on the Least Developed Countries (LDCs), Small Island Developing States (SIDS), and the African States.

If the United Nations is involved, then it is a scam, so it is not surprising to discover that the Rockefeller family was instrumental in the creation of the United Nations. That really nice piece of property that their New York headquarters sits on was donated to the U.N. by David Rockefeller as well, so they are tightly connected.

Each year the United Nations puts out a laughable list of goals that they seek to accomplish, knowing full well that they intend to do the exact opposite.

17 Sustainable Develop Goals Each Year According to the United Nations:

- Zero hunger.

- No poverty.

- Good health and well-being.

- Quality education.

- Gender Equality.

- Clean water & sanitation.

- Affordable & clean energy.

- Decent work and economic growth.

- Industry, innovation, & infrastructure.

- Reduced inequalities.

- Sustainable cities & communities.

- Responsible consumption & production.

- Climate action.

- Life below water.

- Life on land.

- Peace, justice, & strong institutions.

- Partnerships for the goals.

If there is one thing humanity can be absolutely certain of, it is that the United Nations is not spending much of their time trying to fulfill their 17 promises.

So how much money does the United Nations' Green Climate Fund hope to raise, Robin Hood-style, by taking from the rich and giving to the poor?

$100,000,000,000 a year by 2020.[71]

One trillion dollars of government money per decade is planned to be funneled through a fund with ties to the Rockefeller family.

What could possibly go wrong?

This money will then be "invested" in poor countries to help them fix their climate change-related issues, but these countries routinely rank as the most corrupt places in the world, short of the Bank for International Settlements, the IMF headquarters, the Pentagon, Buckingham Palace, and the United Nations in New York.

This sounds a whole lot like the scam that John Perkins wrote about in *Confessions of an Economic Hitman* where the IMF and World Bank loan money to poor countries to help them modernize their infrastructure, then cripple them when the loans are not paid back in time, thus enslaving entire countries through debt. Just change the pretext of infrastructure modernization to climate change compliance and you have a slightly different trap being set (fixing climate change), with a similar justification (modernization of infrastructure), using the same bait (pre-approved loans), resulting in a similar outcome (the pilfering of the money through corporations connected to the Green Climate Fund). This is one way to launder enormous sums of money through third world countries without anyone making a big deal about it.

The only thing "green" that the Green Climate Fund cares about is money, and they plan to get their hands on a ton of it by proclaiming to save the planet.

Tim Wirth, the President of the U.N. Foundation, is on the record saying that they need to ride the global warming issue even if the theory is wrong because it is the right thing in terms of economic policy.

So are they making these decisions in order to save the planet or make a ton of money? If the President of the United Nations Foundation is not totally sold on the concept of global warming, why the hell should the rest of us?

---

[71] Timmons Roberts, Brookings Institute, "Roadmap To Where? Is the & '$100 Billion by 2020' Pledge From Copenhagen Still Realistic?".

Russia has long said they do not think carbon taxes are based on real science, and they are right. It is meant to shut down all major economies not controlled by the IMF and the World Bank. It has two purposes; neither of them has been made public.

The first part of the carbon tax scam is that the IMF and the World Bank will collect taxes from companies that create too much carbon waste. They will set an allowable limit and tax everything over the limit amount unless a company gets an exemption, like all of the oil companies will have. The general public will be forced to buy new "green" products under threat of fines, companies will be forced to retrofit their machinery or face fines, and even countries will be forced to comply with new regulations or face fines and sanctions.

Who will impose sanctions on these countries?

The United Nations will, and these draconian sanctions will destroy a country to the point where the vulture companies controlled by those connected to the U.N. & Rockefeller Foundations will swoop in and buy their industries for next to nothing.

Who will impose the fines on these companies and industries that do not comply?

The IMF and World Bank will, and a company that finds themselves on the wrong side of them will be taxed out of existence, or crippled to the point where they are bought for pennies on the dollar.

Climate change is purely a wealth confiscation scheme disguised as a mission to save the planet. The United Nations, through their banking entities, the IMF and World Bank, is using the manufactured fear of "climate change" to collect trillions of dollars in future taxes that will be used to lay the foundation for an unelected global government.

This is not a very complicated hustle to understand.

IPCC Report

The Intergovernmental Panel on Climate Change's (IPCC) Special Report is a document that was written by politically appointed diplomats, not scientists. The diplomats negotiated the Summary For Policy Makers, then that summary was used to determine the text of the supposed scientific report that the summary was supposedly summarizing.

This is insanity and totally backward. It is diplomats telling the scientists what they want to be written in their scientific reports. If diplomats write the summary, then the summary is used to determine what scientific reports are in the document, then diplomats are actually writing the document. They changed the scientific report to be in line with the admittedly political report. The science did not drive the report, the politics did. They changed the scientific report to be in line with the political document.

From the report:

"Summary: Human-induced warming has already reached about 1°C above pre-industrial levels at the time of writing of this Special Report. By the decade 2006–2015, human activity had warmed the 5 world by 0.87°C (±0.12°C) compared to pre-industrial times (1850–1900). If the current warming rate 6 continues, the world would reach human-induced global warming of 1.5°C around 2040.

The choice of pre-industrial reference period, along with the method used to calculate global average 17 temperature, can alter scientists' estimates of historical warming by a couple of tenths of a degree 18 Celsius. Such differences become important in the context of a global temperature limit just half a 19 degree above where we are now. But provided consistent definitions are used, they do not affect our 20% understanding of how human activity is influencing the climate."

In this summary, they are admitting that their margin of error for these already fake numbers are a couple of tenths of a degree, yet they are saying temperatures will be going up .5 degrees, or five-tenths of a degree, more to reach the 1.5-degree mark. So the math works out like this: they say it is going up .5 degrees, but their margin for error is at least .2 degrees, and since "a couple of tenths of a degree" could actually mean all five-tenths, at best they are running at a 40% margin of error and maybe more. There are few things less scientific than running tests with 40%+ margins of error, but when one examines the source of the figures it really should come as no surprise.

When talking about the numbers they like to tell the public that they have "high confidence" in their numbers. From this point forward, when hearing the term "high confidence" it is best to replace it with "no confidence" because it is a vague statement that locks them into absolutely nothing, and it certainly does not mean concrete proof.

The Hadlet Met Centre has been responsible for providing the data on average world temperatures for 70 years, and their data, after undergoing its first-ever audit, was found to be wildly inaccurate, with average daily temperatures for a tropical island at 0 degrees for an entire month, an average temperature of -40 degrees for a city in Romania, and a monthly average temperature of 80 degrees Celsius for a village in Brazil. These are the data the climate scientists are using to make their predictions. The United Nations then uses this info to build their reports, and in their reports, they call for Orwellian control over resources in the name of saving the planet.

From the United Nations, *"According to the IPCC's report, limiting warming to 1.5 degrees is possible, but requires unprecedented transitions in all aspects of society. To minimize future global warming, we will need to achieve zero net emissions by mid-century. This, in turn, will require us to rapidly transition the world's economy onto such a pathway. Over the next 10 to 20 years we must transform our energy, agriculture, urban and industrial systems, engage non-state actors, and integrate climate action into the broader public policy framework that also addresses jobs, security, and technology."*

There they go again talking about transforming the world due to an external threat that nobody can see or measure except for them. When attempting to show their proof for having to make these decisions the best they can seem to do is show at least a 40% margin of error, but everyone needs to trust that they are telling the truth?

How does the United Nations plan to get these emissions down to zero? Carbon taxes, of course. They want to put a price on carbon, create a global marketplace for that carbon, then control that market. Al Gore and Ken Lay from Enron worked on this back in 1997, of course, Ken Lay was sent to prison for fraud where he died, and Al Gore, who works for the United Nations, is widely known as being a con artist that has used the idea of global warming to make himself over a billion dollars.

One thing everyone can agree on is that the world is going to end because of climate change in 1980. Or maybe in 2000.

"Earth will be doomed by 1980." - Paul Ehrlich, author, 1973.

"Earth will be doomed by 2000." - Noel Brown, senior environmental official, United Nations Environment Program, 1989. He also said that entire nations could be wiped off the face of the earth and create eco-refugees that would cause political chaos.

"No plan B." - Former European Union Climate Chief, 2009. This was said while calling to establish a $100 billion per year fund for climate adaptation, otherwise, the costs of failing to tackle the issue would be greater than the impact of both world wars and the Great Depression combined, he declared, with no proof for his claims.

"Without coherent financial incentives and disincentives, we have just 96 months to avert irretrievable climate and ecosystem collapse, and all that goes with it. We face the dual challenges of a worldview and an economic system that seem to have enormous shortcomings, together with an environmental crisis, including that of climate change, which threatens to engulf us all." - Prince Charles, July 2009.

"We have 12 years to limit climate change." - The Guardian, 2018.

"The world has just only a decade to get climate change under control." - Washington Post from the United Nations, 2018.

"World has three years to stop dangerous climate change." - Christiana Figueres, former executive secretary of the UN Framework Convention of Climate Change, The Guardian, 2017.

They do not have any idea what the hell they are talking about, and the public should have high confidence about that, but the intentional misleading of the public is not something invented by or limited to, climate change policy. Any functional lie is wrapped in mostly truth but dipped in a hard coating of lies to send the general public down the wrong path.

A path that, most likely, is disintegrating because of poor building standards and non-existent maintenance.

Crumbling Infrastructure

The 2017 Infrastructure Report Card by the American Society of Civil Engineers should be a wake-up call to the country because the grades were terrible and the problems are not getting any better. They took a look at a variety of industries and assigned an A through F grade to the different aspects of the infrastructure of America.

The results were horrifying but not surprising as almost all of these areas are top-down, centrally planned, communist-style

Aviation: D

Airports in the United States handle two million passengers daily, with growing congestion expected to continue. Even though the technology is high and the aircraft are economically efficient, the airport infrastructure and air traffic control systems are a mess, with an estimated $42 billion gap in the amount of funding required to keep up with the needed investment.

Bridges: C+

About 40% of American bridges, 56,000 in total, are 50+ years old, with 9% deemed "structurally deficient". Of these deficient bridges, there are 188 million trips made across them each day. The average age of the 614,000 bridges in America is increasing, and the amount needed to fix or replace these defective bridges is now well over $120 billion.

Rail: B

The rail system is split into public and private areas, with the privately-owned rails being financed by corporations and thus is better serviced and maintained. Private rail companies spent $27 billion just in 2015 to maintain their infrastructure and keep their business up and running efficiently, but the public rail system has taken a beating over the past 150 years and requires significant funding, especially for the passenger rails. The expansion has stopped, overhauling the existing rail service has slowed considerably, and the overall quality has plunged.

Dams: D

The dams in the United States are springing leaks, sometimes literally, and the solution calls for $45 billion in federal spending just to fix the existing problems. When the average age of a dam in the United States is over half a century old, it is not surprising that the over 2,100 dams that had been classified as "high-hazard" just a few years ago have ballooned to almost 16,000 today. With 75,000 more dams in the United States, the prices for repair will continue to rise, but like most infrastructure projects in America, the general public will just turn their heads and pretend that the problem does not really exist.

Drinking Water: D

The future of America is as cloudy as the water itself. Estimates by the Water Works Association run into the trillions of dollars needed to fix the broken system of pipes which estimates almost 700 broken water mains every single day that waste two trillion gallons of drinking water. With hundred-year-old pipes running underground, filled with lead and other contaminants, the prospect of replacing them all is an unfathomable undertaking, but it must be done because America's water supply has sprung so many leaks that total replacement has become the only option.

Oh, and most of it is filled, on purpose, with rat poison called fluoride.

Energy: D+

Everywhere Americans look there are power lines running from wooden poles throughout every city in every state. Winter snows and high winds cause downed power lines that cut power to the people at the very moment that they can least afford it, yet 70 years in on a system with a life expectancy of 50 years, and nothing has really changed. The 650,000 miles of high-voltage power lines that run throughout the country are already maxed out, and without replacement of the aging equipment, a move to renewable systems, or both, the power grid will continue to brown out and eventually grind to a halt, that is if an electromagnetic pulse does not knock the whole system offline sooner.

Hazardous Waste: D+

Almost 200 million Americans live within three miles from one of the over 18,000 hazardous waste sites around the nation. Recycling has made a huge dent in the problem, but there are still 22 million acres that are currently dedicated to housing and storing the nation's toxic waste. This is not to be confused with trash or typical landfills, but specifically hazardous waste materials and the infrastructure built to manage, store, and dispose of it.

Inland Waterways: D

America's 25,000 miles of inland waterways are in horrible shape, and the upgrades required to keep them afloat will take 30 years to complete. The dams and 239 locks are outdated and crumbling, the investment needed to make the changes and fixes is astronomical, and the money to do so is not there. This system of transportation moves 600 million tons of cargo yearly, and that accounts for almost 15% of all domestic freight, but the delays affect about half of all ships.

Levees: D

In typical American political fashion, Congress passed the Water Resources Reform and Development Act back in 2014, which expanded the levee safety program nationwide, but the program has not yet received any funding. $80 billion is needed in order to improve and maintain the 30,000-mile levee system in the United States, in large part due to the development and expansion into the floodplains. These levees are responsible for protecting infrastructure, communities, and property estimated to be worth over a trillion dollars, as well as hundreds of colleges and 30 professional sports stadiums.

Ports: C+

About $4.6 trillion of economic activity flows through United States ports each year, about 26% of all economic activity. There are almost 1,000 ports that handle 99% of all overseas trade, but they are dreadfully outdated, dilapidated, and too shallow to allow large ships to dock with them in most cases. The United States has been investing in upgrading these facilities, but not nearly at the rate required to bring them up to a level that would put them in a category to rival Singapore or Hong Kong, and considering how much trade finds its way to American shores, it is baffling to understand why these ports have been so ignored for so long.

Public Parks: D+

Americans go on seven billion recreational outings to public parks each year and depend on the work provided by the National Park Service, U.S. Forest Service, and U.S. Army Corps of Engineers to make the park experience safe and enjoyable, with the states providing the bulk of the maintenance and operations for these facilities. Every President tries to sell off portions of these parks to connected developers, and some quietly are able to accomplish the task. They do generate some revenue, but for the most part, are considered to be money-losing operations for the government, and thus do not receive the financial help that they desperately require to maintain them.

<u>Roads:</u> D

The most obvious fail of American infrastructure are the crumbling and potholed roads that keep expanding, yet always seem to be filled beyond capacity with cars and trucks, starting and stopping for miles and miles. Self-driving cars boast that they will remove inefficiencies associated with human driving and decision making, but that still does not address the problem of too many cars occupying too few spaces. Each year Americans waste $160 billion in fuel and time by sitting in traffic, and 20% of all roads in the country are considered to be in poor condition and require replacement. There is a lack of funding for the roads, even though everyone uses them, and they are becoming more dangerous as a result. Over 35,000 people died on American roads just from 2014-2015, so those flying cars had better hurry up and get here soon.

<u>Schools:</u> D+

American government schools were designed by the likes of the Rockefellers and Carnegie to simulate factory working conditions, thus the desks in straight lines and the Pavlovian ringing bell to inform the children that the next class is ready to begin or that the workday was over, so it is no surprise that the schools are in as bad of shape as the factories themselves. There are 100,000 government (public) school buildings that sit upon two million acres of land, and 50 million K-12 students that attend them each day, not including the additional six million adults. Just because these facilities are important does not mean that they will be treated as such and funded in order to maintain their proper functionality. In fact, each year there is a $38 billion gap in the necessary funding to run these facilities, and as a result, a quarter of the buildings, about 25,0000 of them, qualify as being in poor condition. It is difficult to teach children or help them to learn when they report to poor quality buildings every single day.

<u>Solid Waste:</u> C+

The management of what is known as municipal solid waste (MSW) is in alright condition, in large part because it is managed by private companies instead of government agencies. Trash collection and disposal is run by local or national companies that turn a profit if they run their businesses efficiently, so this industry has been operating well even though Americans contribute more than half of their trash to landfills. Part of what allows these companies to profit is their commitment to recycling 35% of the 258 million tons of MSW and turning another 13% into energy.

Transit: D-

Approximately $90 billion is needed to rehab the nation's transit system due to underfunding and aging systems. Many Americans do not even have access to public transit, a crime against those dependent on this government service for getting to their jobs that are getting harder and harder to come by. New buses are not making their way into the city streets very quickly, and old buses are not being fixed in a timely manner due to budget shortfalls.

Wastewater: D+

At the current rate of growth in America, nearly $300 billion will be required over the next 20 years to connect those 56 million people to centralized treatment systems and sewers. The 15,000 existing wastewater treatment plants are currently overburdened and underfunded to do the job of protecting the health of the people that pay for their services, as well as the environment as a whole. New technologies are coming about, but not nearly quick enough to handle the current and projected demands on the system.

It is clear that America is falling apart, not just as a concept or a society, but literally. The money needed to maintain just the infrastructure of what has been built does not flow to these areas because politicians do not think of them as being very sexy or worthy of bragging about during their next elections, so they get forgotten until it is too late. Much like a car that gets washed but never an oil change, the insides of the machine are breaking down and need to be replaced, and the shame of it all is that it could have been prevented with just some basic maintenance work and a little bit of forethought.

Regulating Government Stupidity

Americans are in violation of countless laws every single day. Some of them are reasonable, but most of them are not. With 4,500 to 5,000 federal criminal statutes and as many as 400,000 regulations that carry some form of criminal penalty, it is clear that one of the many problems in America is not a lack of laws, but a failure to enforce the ones that already exist.

What is crazy is that something that is perfectly legal in one state may carry a jail sentence in a neighboring one. The only real difference is the invisible imaginary line that separates one jurisdiction from another, and the appetite for enforcement by the state and local governments, law enforcement, and the legal system.

• In Oregon, a man was sentenced to a month in jail for simply collecting rainwater in a pond on his own property and refusing to purchase a special permit.[72]

• A California girl had her lemonade stand shut down for a failure to acquire the $3,500 restaurant permit required.[73]

• Vermont can put their residents in jail for denying the existence in God and requires restaurants use colored margarine instead of butter.[74]

• Tulsa's code enforcement department in Oklahoma used a tractor to remove an unemployed woman's well-maintained garden due to a complaint, the same garden she grew in order to feed herself before the judge would even see her in court.[75]

• Idaho has a very active current ban on cannibalism.

• New York City intended to prevent the purchase of more than 16 ounces of soft drinks, officially known as the Sugary Drinks Portion Cap Rule, and it took the New York Court of Appeals to repeal the regulation in 2014.

• It is illegal to dump raw sewage in the ocean without a permit.

• Some human resources documentation must be held onto forever, literally forever. Or at least until the Earth is pelted by another comet.

• In some areas, a person cannot buy raw milk that is not yet pasteurized. Seriously.

• It is a federal crime for a person to make an unreasonable noise at the Pentagon.[76]

• One cannot attempt to change the weather without telling the Secretary of

---

[72] Kendra Alleyne, CNS News, "Oregon Man Sentenced To 30 Days In Jail - For Collecting Rainwater On His Own Property".
[73] Fox News, "California Girl, 5, Cited For Operating Lemonade Stand Without a License".
[74] Criminal Justice Degree Schools, "Criminal Justice Resources: The Top 50 Strangest Laws".
[75] Lori Fullbright, News On 6, "Support Blooms For Tulsa Woman Who Said the City Cut Down Her Edible Garden".
[76] Jason Pye, FreedomWorks, "19 Ridiculous Federal Criminal Laws and Regulations".

Commerce first or risk breaking federal law.

The list of silly laws could fill a book, or maybe two, but the point is that just because something has become a law, does not mean the law makes any sense or actually works to protect the people, which should be the point of the laws in the first place. Sometimes the laws have just become outdated and should be removed, which they never are, and sometimes the origins of the laws stem from corporate involvement trying to legislate protections into their business model to help them defend against competitors or to just tilt the playing field in their favor.

One of the major problems with law enforcement is the selective enforcement of particular laws. When a police officer is sworn into office, they do not ask them to enforce all of the laws that they agree with, they require them to enforce ALL of the laws, even the ones that outlawed dwarf-tossing competitions in Florida.

It is impossible to know all of the federal laws, not to mention the different laws from state to state, which opens up the possibility that if someone in a position of authority wants to have someone that they do not like arrested for something, it can be done. Don't believe this, just go to the inner-cities and ask anyone between the ages of 16-35 if they have ever been pulled over for something trivial, or had their pockets and waistbands searched for drugs just because the officer thought they looked like they matched the description of a suspect in a crime reported in the area?

The Only Law That Matters

The truth is there should only be one law: DO NOT STEAL.

Do not steal people's money.

Do not steal people's ownership of their body... forced vaccination, police brutality, assault, and rape.

Do not steal people's lives... murder.

Do not steal people's freedom...to movement, to trade, to expression.

Do not steal people's dignity...their ability to buy food and shelter.

This one law should never be left in the hands of the most immoral, criminal organization in the world, called government.

Ground Zero Demolition Strategy

Existing structures must be removed to make space for new developments. That is one of the reasons behind the demolition. The other, of course, is to get rid of something that is no longer useful to the people.

Out with the old, in with the new.

Like a tower whose best days are behind it, the Controllers have rigged the American Empire for a controlled demolition that will clear the way for them to build their New World Order on the ashes of one of the best experiments in political history. And it will end the way all empires end: crushed under the weight of its recklessness, strangled by debt, strained by its massive military expansion, weighted down by social entitlement programs, and stung by its own hubris.

America is built on a rotten foundation that has been lying almost from the beginning about having a fair and equal legal system, stable free-market economy, safe monetary policies, and a free and democratic government that protects the inherent rights of its citizens. Because of this weak foundation, the concrete and steel support columns that are supposed to give the building its strength and hold up the country have become increasingly frail and unstable, specifically:

- Critical thinking.

- Education.

- Individual rights.

- The belief in American exceptionalism.

- Peace through the military-information-terror complex.

- Good health and a safe environment.

- Perception of stability and being in control.

Taking down a building requires that the demolition crew follow a specific chain of events so that the building is brought down correctly and without too much collateral damage. Attention to the details of how to remove support from the building will make the difference between a successful implosion and a half-standing structure that will need to be dismantled manually and at a greater cost.

Blow up its support pillars and you are left with ground zero. But in order to do that successfully, you have to first pre-weaken other areas that are providing additional minor support for the structure. This is followed by rigging the main support columns with detonators. These detonators are the tools that the Controllers will use to destroy the support columns in order to bring down the country. Just like the demolition of an actual building, the removal of all major support columns must happen at the same time in order to fully bring down the country in the way they envision.

Then, after sounding the alarm to warn those close to them about the impending destruction, the Controllers will trigger the blast to take down the American Empire and start the great reset.

How To Destroy A Building – Technically

In the old days, before fancy explosives, when a building became functionally obsolete, a crew of serious-looking men in overalls with sledgehammers went to work on it from the top-down, piece by piece.

Later, the crane and wrecking ball was introduced and the process got a whole lot faster.

And dirtier.

A 10,000-pound swinging ball of steel certainly takes the destruction to another level, but progress never stops, and soon the wrecking ball is replaced with a more civilized form of destruction.

When blowing up a building, one size does not fit all. There is a very real science to it, and this science has been evolving for decades. Like anything that involves explosions and massive forms of destruction, the United States military has been fundamental in the development of these methods and materials, but like most things they do, a layer of secrecy is always baked into the recipe.

Whatever the military does, there is always the acknowledged and unacknowledged way of doing it. The general public will never be told about some new technology until decades after the fact, if ever at all. The public has to settle for the traditional way of doing things until a newer version has been invented to replace the secret version that the people never even knew existed.

Basically, Americans get hand-me-down technology once Big Brother outgrows it.

Blowing up buildings is no different, so what they are working with in the commercial building implosion industry is old technology being used until the military dumps their newest products on the market. This hidden technology most certainly includes Thermate, Thermite, and Nano Thermite, but those substances are not currently cleared for sale and use in the United States by registered blasting companies. Instead, they make do with what they have.

For steel structures, blasters typically use the specialized explosive material cyclotrimethylenetrinitramine, otherwise known as RDX. RDX-based explosive compounds expand at 27,000 feet per second, and instead of disintegrating the entire column, it slices through the steel like a hot knife through Spandex.

Dynamite is then used on one side of the column to push it over in a particular direction.

To ignite both RDX and dynamite, one must apply a severe shock.

In building demolition, blasters use what is called a blasting cap. This is a small amount of explosive material connected to a fuse. The traditional fuse design is a long cord with explosive material inside. When a person ignites one end of the cord, the explosive material inside it burns at a steady pace that allows one to get away in plenty of time before the explosion goes off. When it reaches this point, it kicks off the primary charge.

Before a crew blows a building to smithereens, they want to make sure that everyone is out of the way. A blaster will sound the alarm to make sure those involved with the destruction are not standing there when the building comes down. Anyone too deaf or stupid to hear the alarm should consider themselves to have been properly warned and deservingly pulverized.

Blasters using an electric detonator will have two buttons: Charge & Fire.

When the countdown is almost to zero, the person controlling the detonator will hold down the "charge" button, much like an old-school camera flash that is generating enough electricity to illuminate a photo, until the machine is fully charged. Once the blaster's countdown reaches zero, and while still holding down the Charge button, the blaster pushes the Fire button which sends the electric charge to the wires, then down to set off the blasting caps.

A fraction of a second later, there is the beginning of a controlled demolition of a building. A few seconds after that, they have got an enormous pile of rubble and what is left of that building.

The path of destruction in a controlled demolition is called the "demolition wave". It is a visible wave of explosions that moves down the columns of a building a fraction of a second ahead of the speed of gravity. These synchronized explosions are timed to blow out the support columns on the floors beneath the collapse wave in order to allow the building to drop at free-fall speed. A person watching a controlled demolition can actually see the lateral ejection of projectiles and the explosive squibs detonating in sequence in order to take the building down symmetrically.

The benefit of imploding a building is that it essentially takes months of construction work, dust, noise, and inconvenience and condenses it into a few minutes, rather than endless days of guys swinging sledge hammers and wrecking balls. The construction equivalent of ripping the bandage off instead of gently peeling it slowly.

Before the rubble is cleared away, the blasters must be certain that all of the detonators have exploded, and that there is nothing dangerous remaining. They cannot have some construction workers move a beam and set off a secondary explosion two weeks after the building is brought down. That would be a bad look for the demo company, so they have their post-blast crews clear anything that housed a charge or might pose a potential problem during removal and transport. Once that has been completed, a company can safely transport the debris to a local landfill.

Or ship it all to China before investigators have a chance to inspect any of it like on 9/11.

PRE-WEAKENING OF THE BUILDING

Playing a Rigged Game

Whether someone is rigging a building with detonators or rigging a financial market to be compromised, it requires the person to be on the inside and to have enough time to do the job the right way. Having access to the structure is essential, as well as an understanding of how things are supposed to work under normal day-to-day operations so that the infiltration does not raise suspicion.

When one boils things down to their most fundamental elements, a real marketplace should not need too much management. It either works or it doesn't. Someone offers their chickens for sale, another person comes to the market to buy a few chickens, they agree on a price and the deal is done.

The real problems surface when one of the parties is trying to manipulate or rig the market in their favor, which inevitably happens due to human nature.
The current financial system is a rigged game.

From the fiat currency that is printed out of thin air, to front-running market order trades, to arbitrarily setting market rates, employing a "plunge protection team" to prop up the stock market when it dips below a predetermined level, to flooding the market with paper ETC contracts to drive down the physical price of gold, to insider trading before the release of important news. If there is a way to rig a marketplace, those smart bastards on Wall Street will figure it out, then quietly steal as much money as they can get their greedy little hands on.

Perception management is important when trying to make a crime not look like a crime, so very technical and important names are used to give the looting an air of credibility.

When the central banks crank up the printing press and generate billions of dollars that they give to their criminal friends running the big banks, they refer to that as "quantitative easing" and not counterfeiting. Central banks manipulate interest rates, something that would be illegal for anyone else to do so that people cannot calculate the real cost of money.

Any arrests for this? Of course not, because the banks run the world, not the governments.

The people of America no longer even hold out any hope of justice being served because, after years and years of watching these criminal banks steal with impunity, with nobody going to prison for these crimes, the public has essentially gone numb. Not only has nobody gone to prison, nobody has even been put in handcuffs, no perp walks, and not a single executive has even been taken down to the police station for questioning.

It is as if the American public is collectively sitting at a poker table trying to figure out who the sucker is, never considering that it is probably them.

Safe From Prosecution

With unlimited money-printing ability over the past century, the Federal Reserve has bought themselves ample influence and protection from prosecution for their various crimes. No doubt they have blackmail photos of key decision-makers that can be used to dissuade any sort of investigation. They probably helped to finance the political campaigns of nearly everyone in a high political office, so future funding could be in jeopardy if someone decides to try and blow the whistle. The Fed could also threaten the rest of the politicians with pulling their funding as well unless they get their rogue colleague under control. It is no longer much of a secret that the Central Intelligence Agency has been working on behalf of the big banks for half a century, so they are almost a private intelligence and military arm of the banks. In fact, the Dulles brothers set up the CIA to be just that.

The biggest reason for the federal government to not take on the Federal Reserve is that any conflict between the two of them would shake the confidence of the financial markets, and with them being built on a foundation of fraud, greed, and corruption, it would not take much turbulence to create the conditions to destroy the whole financial system. A shift away from the Fed would create contagion in the financial markets that the government and the banks could not manage and control, which would have catastrophic consequences for the American Empire.

This system will be coming down eventually, but the people in charge have other plans for how and when they will crash the markets, and that plan involves them remaining in power after the event and not blaming the problem on their crooked banking structure, which is clearly the root cause of most of the suffering on the planet. It is certainly no coincidence that after every economic implosion the wealth gap between the top .01% and the rest of humanity widens exponentially.

Just the way they like it.

The banking industry has not just screwed up the national debt of the United States, it has screwed up the government and segments of the public trust. If the banks smell money, they will orchestrate a way to put themselves in a position to profit from the privatization of public segments of the government.

LIBOR Whore

LIBOR is an acronym for London Inter-Bank Offer Rate, and it is the interest rate banks charge to loan money to other banks. A manipulated price-setting system, plus the weakness in the regulatory framework, set the stage for rampant fraud and corruption by those in charge.

For the casual investor, LIBOR may not ring a bell because it does not get talked about on the nightly news, but it is the benchmark rate that is underlying many financial instruments. LIBOR is one of the most important interest rates that most people have never heard of, but it is a factor in their lives whether they know it or not.

To put its importance in perspective, LIBOR's rate is a factor in $379 trillion of financial instruments.

As an example, the interest rate quoted to a borrower looking to buy a house might be calculated by the mortgage company as LIBOR + 3%, meaning that if the rate the banks loan money to each other is 2.5%, then the interest a mortgage company charges to the home buyer would be 2.5% + 3%, or 5.5%.

The major banks decided that if they put their heads together, they could rig this market and move the interest rates in the direction they desired, so they set about to discreetly corrupt the system. Their manipulation of the interest rates majorly impacted the interest rate swaps that corporations and governments use to manage their debt. The fraud that these banks were engaged in went on for many years and made them untold billions of dollars at the expense of governments around the world, corporations, and of course, the people of the world.

When their criminal enterprise was finally discovered, the big banks do what they always do when they get caught red-handed committing felonies: they paid a small fine and nobody was prosecuted.

• HSBC agreed to pay $100 million to end private U.S. litigation accusing it of conspiring to manipulate the Libor benchmark interest rate.[77]

• Settlements with the OTC investors totaled $590 million for Citigroup.[78]

• Barclays paid a $120 million settlement due to their involvement in the LIBOR-rigging case.[79]

• Citigroup paid a mere $130 million settlement for their role in the fraud.[80]

• Deutsche Bank settled for $240 million for manipulating global interest rates.[81]

• JPMorgan Chase agreed to a settlement of $13 billion for a variety of offenses.[82]

These banks probably have a budget specifically for paying the fines they incur each year through their illegal activities.

The FOREX Mess

Not satisfied with only rigging a 1/3 of a quadrillion dollar marketplace, the banks set about to game the system in the FOREX market as well.

For over a decade, the currency traders at the big banks manipulated the $5.3 trillion-a-day foreign exchange market by colluding with counterparts and pushing through trades before and during the 60-second windows when the benchmark rates are set.

The traders had been front-running client orders and rigging the foreign exchange benchmark rate for so long that they eventually got sloppy and got

---

[77] Jonathan Stempel, Reuters, "HSBC To Pay $100 Million To End LIBOR Rigging Lawsuit".

[78] Jonathan Stempel, Reuters, "Citigroup Settles Shareholder CDO Lawsuit For $590 Million".

[79] Jonathan Stempel, Reuters, "Barclays To Pay $120 Million In U.S. LIBOR Litigation: Lawyers".

[80] Jonathan Stempel, Reuters, "Citigroup To Pay $130 Million To End LIBOR Rigging Lawsuit in U.S.".

[81] Jonathan Stempel, Reuters, "Deutsche Bank To Pay $240 Million To End LIBOR Rigging Lawsuit in U.S.".

[82] Karen Freifeld, Reuters, "JP Morgan Agrees $13 Billion Settlement With U.S. Over Bad Mortgages".

caught in 2013. Regulators in the United States, U.K., Asia, and Switzerland, either asleep at the wheel or bought off, finally investigated the systemic fraud and market manipulation that had been going on right under their noses for over 10 years, but only after Bloomberg News did a story about it first.

The total amount of money that these criminal banking institutions stole through their FOREX scam is said to be unknown, but for the U.K. pension holders alone it was calculated to be at least $115 billion over the life of the scam.

The U.K.'s Financial Conduct Authority fined the banks for their role in these crimes an embarrassing thin $1.7 billion due to their lack of oversight and failure to control their business practices.[83]

- RBS paid $344 million to settle their involvement.

- Citibank was fined $358 million.

- JPMorgan paid a $352 million fine.

- UBS led the pack with a $371 million fine for their role in these crimes.

- HSBC settled for $343 million due to their participation in these frauds.

These marketplaces are as rigged as "three-card monte", the only difference is that because the fraud is being conducted by people in three-piece suits instead of sweatsuits, it is made to look more legitimate.

Even the credit card companies were getting in on the collusion action until they were brought up on antitrust charges and eventually settled for $6.1 billion for inflating the merchant fees that they charge the retail stores using Visa and Mastercard. Of course, that is a drop in the bucket considering these fees generate $90 billion in revenue each year, but they just cannot help themselves because they are spawn from an industry built on fraud and graft.

The American people have had just about enough of the hypocrisy of the authorities throwing the book at a single Mom caught shoplifting baby formula for her kid, while the criminals on Wall Street loot the American public with impunity.

What the citizens of the United States are now being told about missing money

---

[83] CNBC, November 12, 2014, "Watch Dogs Impose $3.4 Billion Fines In Bank FOREX Probe".

that their government has stolen points to a crime so massive that it is difficult for people to wrap their heads around. This fraud is very real and just might explain where much of the tax dollars have disappeared over the past two decades.

Financial Frauds

A Michigan State University economics professor, piggybacking on the work of former Assistant Secretary of Housing, Catherine Austin Fitts, has uncovered $21 trillion unaccounted for in the federal budget starting in 1998 through the end of the fiscal year 2015. Professor Mark Skidmore, along with his graduate students, went to work examining government documents from the Department of Defense (DOD) and Housing and Urban Development (HUD) to discover an astounding amount of fraudulent spending.

Catherine Austin Fitts, the founder of The Solari Report, had been investigating the missing money since 2000 before Skidmore came across her work and set out to prove her figures wrong. What he ended up finding was that her numbers were wrong.

They were too low.

Fitts had been advising her financial investor clients to be wary of the mortgage fraud at the US Department of Housing and Urban Development (HUD), as well as the manufactured housing bubble that eventually led to trillions of dollars in bailouts, and even more money missing from the US government beginning in 1998.

The Ph.D. Skidmore, who specializes in government spending accounting and economics, usually expects to find transaction discrepancies less than 1% of the total budget, but instead what he found when examining the Army's annual budget for FY 2015, which was $122 billion, was a wildly inflated number. His expectation of finding $1.2 billion in discrepancies was shattered when instead he found $6.5 trillion in inadequate transactions.[84] This amount works out to 54 times more than their entire budget for the year was gone and unaccounted for.

After going back through 13 years of paperwork, Dr. Skidmore was able to determine that $11.5 trillion of the unauthorized adjustments were specifically

---

[84] Michigan State University, "MSU Scholars Find $21 Trillion In Unauthorized Spending; Defense Department To Conduct First-Ever Audit".

run through the Army, and the accounting documents were shady and mysterious. Once the Housing and Urban Development accounts were examined the total figure added up to $21 trillion, but neither Fitts nor Skidmore was certain that all of the fraudulent transactions had been found.

To put the figure in perspective, it works out to $65,000 per American that has been stolen and stashed away somewhere.

All federal agencies are supposed to be audited annually, but the Pentagon has never been audited. Since 1996, $8.5 trillion of taxpayer money has gone completely unaccounted for and nobody is telling the people where it is. The Special Inspector General for Iraq Reconstruction disclosed that the United States DOD is unable to account for $8.7 billion of the $9 billion that they were given.

It is not just money that is missing either. A GAO report found the inventory system for the Defense Department lost 56 airplanes, 32 tanks, and 36 Javelin missile command launch-units.

After Skidmore started asking about the report, the Office of the Inspector General's webpage was taken down. A few months later every figure in the report was redacted under the grounds of the catchall phrase "national security".

The original documents were wisely downloaded, copied, distributed, and saved, so trying to hide the numbers was pointless, but the OIG will try to keep the lie under wraps for as long as they can, even in the face of indisputable evidence of their crimes.

It is important to remember that this is just two of many government agencies, and these particular agencies are not being very cooperative in this investigation. The $21 trillion does not even take into account all of the spy agencies, NASA, Department of Homeland Security, Centers for Disease Control, Food and Drug Administration, Department of Justice, United States Department of Agriculture, Environmental Protection Agency, State Department, Health and Human Services, Department of Energy, Department of Veteran's Affairs, Department of Commerce, Department of Treasury, Department of Transportation, Department of the Interior, Department of Labor, Federal Bureau of Investigation, Social Security Administration, Department of Education, Internal Revenue Service, Securities and Exchange Commission, Federal Communications Commission, Federal Emergency Management Administration, and the United States Post Office.

If these other agencies are also looting the nation, there is no telling how much money is actually missing. It could very easily be well into the tens of trillions of dollars that have been stolen over the years. In fact, every penny the IRS has taken in its history is all theft. Taxation is theft.

The people must also remember the stunning admission that universally loathed former Defense Secretary Donald Rumsfeld made on the day before September 11th, 2001, when he announced in a press conference that his department could not account for $2.3 trillion dollars that had disappeared from the books.[85]

Certainly, this would have been a much bigger story had it not been swallowed up in the news the next day by the events that his administration conspired to orchestrate to take the country into a war where that $2.3 trillion would certainly be needed. He also later speculated that the Afghanistan War would cost no more than $50 billion.

More like $7 trillion and counting, not $50 billion. And ongoing for nearly 20 years now.

The crime wave that is sweeping western governments is the rigging of financial markets, and it has been happening in most global marketplaces for years. It has only been recently that those involved in the fraud have been investigated, but it always ends with nobody doing any prison time and the company getting off with a small fine and no admission of any wrong-doing.

The big banks run Wall Street, and Wall Street has a tremendous amount of influence in Washington. They have set up a feedback loop of bankers that go to Washington, and bureaucrats from Washington that rotate through lower Manhattan.

Nowhere was this more evident than when former Attorney General Eric Holder decided that he did not want to actually do anything to hold those that crashed the economy in 2008 accountable for their mountain of blatant crimes.

Holder even said that he was concerned that the size of some of these banking institutions had become so large that it would be difficult for him to prosecute them because it would have a negative impact on the national economy, and perhaps even the world economy. He called this "collateral consequences" and it allowed him to give the impression that he was doing something about the

---

[85] Daily KOS, "Why Doesn't Anyone Ask Donald Rumsfeld Where The $2.3 Trillion Went?".

criminality on Wall Street when that was all just for show.[86]

This was the era of "too big to fail", and it goes against everything capitalism stands for. In fact, it is a form of fascism, pure and simple, when the state is blended with big business and the two work in concert with one another. It was the reason for the economic crash of 2008, and nothing systemically has changed to prevent it from happening again.

Eric Holder never won a single conviction in court for any crimes related to the financial crisis, and he probably did not try very hard. There was at least $20 billion of fraud right in front of him but he chose to look the other way and not bring a single felony case against anyone. However, should someone get popped with a $20 bag of marijuana in their pocket, he will be prosecuting them to the fullest extent of the law. The reason for this approach is that drug dealers do not offer Eric Holder $10 million a year jobs, but Wall Street banks and big law firms do.

And did. He works for Covington as a reward for looking the other way during the crime spree the banks were involved in orchestrating.[87]

The 10 largest banks in America and the 10 largest banks in Europe have been fined around $300 billion for their roles in market rigging, collusion, fraud, and other violations of the law, but nobody has gone to prison.

The New "C-Word"

When trying to accurately define what the American style of government really is, it is not correct to describe it as solely being fascism, although many important aspects of it certainly are. It is clearly not the republic that it once was, and it certainly never was a democracy, although most people would incorrectly describe it as such.

More than anything else, America is best described as being aligned with the philosophy of corporatism, a term coined by Benito Mussolini. This is a government where a few extremely wealthy people rule over the rest of the population, an oligarchic elite plus corporate interests. The main difference is that in this form of government, none of the rulers were elected to do such, they simply bought their power and influence (example: Bill Gates).

[86] William Cohan, The Atlantic, "How Wall Street's Bankers Stayed Out Of Jail".
[87] David Dayen, Salon, "Why Eric Holder's New Job Is An Insult To The American Public".

This is a very dangerous form of government because too much power is concentrated at the top and the paranoia that the public will finally catch on to what is actually going on leads to authoritarian responses in almost every country that has become infected with this form of control. Corporatism leads to a police state, the rounding up of dissenters, detention facilities, book burnings, and self-censorship. It may sound extreme, but history shows that this is where society ends up.

A report produced by Northwestern University and Princeton University concluded that the American government does not represent most citizens, but rather they are ruled by the rich and powerful "economic elite", and that policies enacted by the United States governmental elite almost always favor lobbying organizations and special interests groups.

In order for corporatism to actually work, the people with the money cannot let the rest of the public know that they are actually running the show, so they select people that they can control through their vast sums of money and put them into a high elected office so that it looks like they are in control. This would best be described as the American political class that runs for President, Congress, statehouses, and those appointed to cabinet positions. Every single person in the American government with a moderate degree of power is in that position by design, and if they decide to break their programming and try to go rogue, there is never enough additional support for them to mount any real sort of uprising.

The political elite is selected for election by the ruling families. This is how a country ends up continuing to have a choice for president that includes either a Bush, a Clinton, or both.

These billionaire ruling families do not include the Clintons or the Bush family, although it is not for a lack of effort on their part. After their political careers ended they certainly behaved much like the ruling families, although they are more psychotic and ruthless, their public perception prevents them from ruling from the shadows like the other families.

The corporatist controllers with the money and political aspirations that are running the United States are families and people like Rockefeller, Carnegie, Koch, Bezos, Gates, Buffet, Du Pont, Vanderbilt, Mellon, Ford, Walton, Soros, Kissinger, Adelson, Sergey Brin & Larry Page, Eric Schmidt, Mark Zuckerberg, Pierre Omidyar, Elon Musk, and others. Families such as these have either been running the country for decades or are a new breed of wealthy technocrats that are stepping up to replace the older ruling families. Their money funds programs pushing to relax restrictions on things like oil drilling, the deregulation of industries they seek to expand into, the regulation of industries that they wish to lock others out of, and the ability to keep their operations as secret as possible.

The corporate leaders talk about free markets, but the last thing they want is actually free and balanced markets. They want rigged marketplaces that favor them, but they want the markets to give the appearance of being free and fair so that the general public thinks that they have a chance to participate and that the playing field is level.

Globalization And The Amazon Economy

Karl Marx gets a bad rap, rightfully so, in Western countries, in part because his ideas ran counter to the guiding philosophy of free markets and capitalism, but his observations about the way economics functions within society were pretty accurate. He was concerned that small, local businesses found in small towns eventually get put out of business by much larger, multinational businesses that are able to undercut their prices through economies of scale. He warned of an invasion, not from the armies of other countries, but from their corporations in what he described as "Imperial Capitalism".

In doing so, not only does the small business go away, but also the connection between the residents of the small town to that business dissolve as well. When enough of these small family-owned businesses go under, part of the town's identity is lost as well.

It is not hard to understand that walking into a Wal Mart is a much different experience than walking into Smith's General Store, where Bob Smith is there to ring a customer up at the cash register. There is a detachment and a loss of culture when big businesses come to town and small businesses are forced to close because they do not have the ability to compete.

From the owner of the small store's perspective, all the years of relationship building, their integration into the community, the history with their customers can all be thrown away just in order to save a couple of dollars?
No loyalty, no friendships, no banked goodwill, no nothing.

Everything that they have built within their community over the decades can all go away the minute a big-box store opens in the next town with lower prices. It looks like all they really ever had with their customers was theoretical loyalty because when that bond was actually tested, it revealed that it was really only about the money.

Marx thought that part of the loss of identity would happen when it became impossible to tell the difference between whether a shopper was standing in a store in Moscow or Mexico City due to the corporate homogenization of the store design and layout.

Is this corporate Darwinism? Are these small businesses being destroyed because they are unable or unwilling to adapt to the new way of conducting business?

Probably, but it is still sad, nonetheless, because they represent a version of the way things used to be, perhaps a simpler time, and it reminds people that the world can be a cruel place for those that do not recognize where things are headed.

A Virtual Global Coup

If an executive worked for a venture capital fund and some young entrepreneur came in and pitched an idea for an online store using Amazon's business plan, the executive would be pressing the little button under their desk that opens the trap door beneath their feet and drops them into a pit of alligators.

It is reckless, wasteful, vindictive, and expensive. And the executive would have been a fool for pressing that button.

One of the major focuses of Amazon was the virtual land grab. Much like the 1800s when the Midwest was sparse and virtually unpopulated by the White Man, the race was to sprint as fast as one could, stake their claim to the biggest or best piece of land, then defend that which they claimed. If they were a one-man operation, staking claims would be hard and defending those claims even harder. If they had a group of people working together, with a viable plan, a map of where they were going, an understanding of what they needed to do as soon as they stake their claim, and the ammunition to defend their spot, as well as the ruthlessness to push others off of their claim, they had a chance to establish themselves and their group as a force to be reckoned with.

When Amazon first burst on the internet scene in 1994, they focused on selling books. As their operations began to grow, their market share of the online bookselling market grew as well. Because they were essentially creating a brand new industry, meaning the selling of books through the internet, it was a mad dash to grab as much market share as possible, then a defense of what they had, while also taking the share away from other companies.

What ended up happening was that they successfully grabbed and defended their share of the online book market, but they had a few advantages that also allowed them to take over the brick and mortar bookstores as well.

First, they did not have the operational overhead costs associated with managing an actual bookstore, or a chain of bookstores. They also did not have to charge sales tax, which might not sound like a huge deal, but it was worth anywhere from 4%-8%, depending on the state.

Secondly, and probably most importantly, Amazon was very clear with their investors from the beginning that they were going to take a very long-term approach for growing this business. They were going to prioritize market share over profits, growth over profits, and international expansion over profits.

Basically, if they had to actually worry about being profitable, it was going to be at the expense of everything else.

Of course, this flies in the face of everything a person learns in business school, or even from running a hot dog cart. If someone cannot make a profit selling their hot dogs, then they are going to be out of the hot dog business pretty quickly. However, Amazon saw the much bigger picture and understood that they were entering a whole new industry and that establishing their dominance, even if that came with a high cost, would be worth it in the long term because if they were the dominant force, then they could make the rules.

Expand as quickly as possible, slaughter all of your competitors by dropping your prices below profitability for you and your competitor until you bankrupt them, then worry about profits after all your competitors are long gone.

Amazon's strategy was so well executed that not only did they crush all of the other online bookstores, they put most of the traditional bookstores out of business as well.

Free shipping costs Amazon over $7 billion a year, but are any of their investors really going to stand up in a shareholder's meeting and tell Jeff Bezos he is doing it wrong?[88] Customers will have to pay for shipping at some point, once all other competitors are out of business, but by then everyone will be so accustomed to shopping on Amazon that shopping any other way will be unusual.

After almost a quarter of a century in business, Amazon has only shown very small profits, but would anyone question their retail dominance? They were able to play this long game because although they did not turn large profits, they had another form of currency that was actually more in demand, and that was their stock. Where profits were missing, the stock filled the gaps, and then some.

Amazon prioritized their share price over their profits because they knew they could use it as another form of currency to finance their operations, which of course they have, and it was used to compensate investors that bought into the plan early on, and those that were always there with fresh money to finance their money-losing operations

The Good

Amazon is an example of globalization in a practical sense. It is easy to see it as a global marketplace, connecting people from all over the planet through its platform and storefront. An even better example of globalization is eBay, where sellers and buyers come together to conduct sales transactions with people that would probably never find each other pre-internet.

This is one of the positive aspects of globalized trade because it allows people separated geographically to meet in one particular spot, on eBay's cyber storefront, and find what they are looking to buy or sell something that is just taking up space in their garage. Having access to this global market has tremendous value, and for hundreds of years, the only real way to make these introductions were through shipping lanes and trading outposts.

It also allows a smaller company to play on the global stage, or masquerade as a much larger company and conduct global trade provided that they have an internet connection. It is not so much that it levels the playing field, but it allows everyone the option of at least getting on the field. Market forces will determine how level the field will get, but a small company can at least take part in the game.

Globalization has been a tremendous benefit for companies looking to outsource

---

[88] Todd Bishop, Geekwire, "The Cost Of Convenience: Amazon's Shipping Losses Top $7 Billion For The First Time".

work to regions where the costs of labor are much lower than through traditional local workers. Most people have a vision of workers sewing buttons on jeans inside massive warehouses in Bangladesh, but it also takes the form of graphic design work in third world countries that get outsourced or medical transcription services that are staffed in the Philippines. The ability to outsource a virtual staff through a variety of different countries puts downward pressure on prices, benefitting the company seeking these discounted services.

Because of endless authoritarian restrictions, regulations, taxes, insurance requirements, tariffs, and product liability in their own country, many companies are forced to have their products made somewhere else like, say, China.

Rise of the Eastern Empire

The growth of China both in terms of population and economy has been nothing short of astounding. When one considers the mess they were in after Mao's cultural revolution, their progress is almost unbelievable.

When Nixon and Kissinger made China a priority for American economic development, in conjunction with Chase Bank and David Rockefeller, it took a very old country that was best known for silk, opium, and an enormous wall, and transformed it into the largest factory on the planet, all in half a century.

Part of that transformation was the realization that in order to make these drastic changes, an exodus would need to take place in which the rural population would migrate to the big cities and industrial hubs. Some people moved willingly, others did not. The authoritarian roots of the country still remained, so some were forcibly relocated to fill the needs and the demographic shift away from an agrarian society and into manufacturing.

• Chinese cities will grow by 350 million people in the next decade due to a shift from rural to urban living.[89]

• By 2025, China will build five million additional buildings, including 50,000 highrises.[90]

• China has 64 million empty homes, as well as entire cities that are vacant.[91]

---

[89] McKinsey Global Institute, "Preparing For China's Urban Billion".
[90] Forbes, "China's Urbanization Is Driving Johnson Controls'; HVAC Growth".
[91] AsiaNews, "Crisis In China: 64 Million Empty Apartments".

- China consumes 53% of the world's cement, as well as half of the world's iron ore and coal.[92]

This process of relocation is still happening, with trends showing even more movement towards cities and away from farms. It is a sort of forced march for the peasants in rural China, spurred by their government, in an attempt to keep up with world demand for the products that their country has come to be known for.

The "Thucydides Trap" is the theory that as one superpower fades and another rises, the chance of war between the two powers is a very likely outcome, and perhaps inevitable. The Greek historian Thucydides first understood this idea framed in the context of the demise of Sparta just as Athens was beginning its ascension to the top of the power structure.

"It was the rise of Athens and the fear that this instilled in Sparta that made war inevitable."

As the most populous country the world has ever known begins to surpass the wealthiest country, will the fear of loss trigger the war of wars between two nations capable of ending life on this planet, or can sanity be injected into the situation? Much like a humiliated drunk, America is a danger to itself and those close to it because it is liable to just start throwing punches at those pointing and laughing.

In the past 500 years there have been 16 cases in which a rising power threatened to displace a ruling one, and 75% of the time it ended in war.[93] As China challenges America's predominance, misunderstandings about intentions, differences in monetary systems, or a desire to ditch the Petrodollar, may lead them into a deadly conflict.

The encirclement of China by the United States' string of military bases already shows a potentially hostile intent on the part of America, as America hypocritically complains about China building islands in their own waters to counter that threat.

China has been making major moves to partner with Africa rather than colonize it, the "American Way" is proving to be less about loving thy neighbor, and more

---

92 Gus Lubin, Business Insider, "18 Facts About China That Will Blow Your Mind".
93 Graham Allison, The Atlantic, "The Thucydides Trap: Are The U.S. And China Heading For War?"

about subjugating him.

The British exploited the dark continent for diamonds, land, natural resources, raw materials, and even people. South Africa, under British rule, designed a cultural system of racism through Apartheid. Belgium and France pilfered their resources and slaughtered the people, with King Leopold II of Belgium responsible for the murder of 10 million Congolese. The United States has blown up countries like Libya and Somalia and built military bases in others like Djibouti.

China builds hospitals for sick Africans, instead of graveyards for dead ones.

- In 2016, America invested $3.6 billion in Africa, while China invested $36.1 billion, more than all of the other countries in the world combined.[94]

- China is the second-largest provider and the top receiver of foreign direct investment.

- China's population is equal to North America, South America, Western Europe, Australia, and New Zealand combined.

- China spends more on education and training as a percentage of GDP than any other country in the world, right around 4%, and its education system is the largest in the world.[95]

- There are more Chinese university students than in both the United States and Western Europe combined.

The "One Belt. One Road" plan to connect Europe and Asia, in conjunction with the rise in cryptocurrencies, is setting the stage for major global disruption and a paradigm shift away from taxes, tariffs, and threats, and into open markets, sound money, and cooperative trade through multiple continents.

The United States should be feeling threatened by these new developments, not because they actually fear China, but because China is making them look bad by comparison.

This is not to say that China is without their problems or a checkered past. They are only six decades removed from their leader rounding up and executing 73,000,000 of his own people for having the audacity to be educated, and they

---

[94] Macau Hub, "China Responsible For One-Third Of Foreign Investment And Jobs Created In Africa In 2016".
[95] Li Yan, People's Daily Online, "China Works Hard To Achieve Its Goal Of Spending 4 Percent GDP On Education".

are certainly headed down an Orwellian rabbit hole with their new social media ranking service that issues points for towing the party line, and removes points for speaking out about the government.[96]

They have some rather large domestic social issues that need to be ironed out, but their openness to business and trade, combined with their plans for developing global marketplaces throughout Eurasia, Africa, and South America make them a horse to bet on for the long term.

The Media's Role in Demonizing China

The American corporate media has begun the push to sell the population that the new threat to freedom and democracy is China, as the United States government simultaneously sells them trillions of dollars of sovereign debt to finance the Ponzi scheme the Federal Reserve has been running for over a hundred years.

China has always been there. This is not a new threat. They did not come down from Zeta Reticuli and start a civilization a decade ago, they have been right where they are for the past 36 centuries. They never pushed into Europe, they never tried to colonize India, and they did not ship all of their prisoners to Australia.

Great Britain did.

The Christian roots of the United States and Britain make them countries seeking to convert other people, or countries, to their way of thinking.

In comparison, the Chinese built the Great Wall 2,000 years ago to keep the invaders out, so it is not in their culture to seek to expand and conquer the way some Western nations do.

If a country's economy depends on military spending, then that country must always have an enemy to justify the expenditures on weapons, intelligence gathering, and military bases.

But if your country is the United States of America, and your economy is as bloated and wasteful as it has been for the past half-century, then the Military-Information-Terror complex must have multiple enemies spread throughout the

---

[96] WikiZero, "Mass Killings Under Communist Regimes".

world to justify 800 military bases in 70 countries and their $1,000,000,000,000 defense budget.

Is China a Threat to the United States?

The Obama administration certainly seemed to think so with his announcement of a "pivot to Asia", and the relocation of two-thirds of the American naval fleet to positions in close proximity to China as a response to their construction of airstrips in the South China Sea on the disputed Spratly Island chain.[97]

Why the Obama administration thought they were in any position to tell China what they can do in the South China Sea, not the South America Sea, is just another example of the arrogance of American foreign policy. If China was building airstrips on Catalina Island, 26 miles off the coast of Los Angeles, then a response would be warranted and expected.

Whether China is actually a military threat is less important because they will be portrayed as a military threat simply because of the way that the American media and weapons industries are interconnected. The weapons makers need an enemy, the media needs life-threatening events to prop up their dismal ratings, and the mega-conglomerates, such as General Electric, own the largest players in both of these industries. A company like G.E. may see a situation like this as a 2-for-1 opportunity to make huge profits.

The more realistic threat from China comes from an economic weapon, not necessarily a military one. They hold trillions of dollars' worth of American debt, and they are the biggest manufacturer and exporter of the cheap goods that the United States depends on.

The way this relationship has been operating is that America spends its dollars to buy cheap Chinese products and have them shipped to the United States. China then takes those dollars that were used to buy their cheap goods and they buy America's debt in the form of Treasury Notes that pay interest to the holder. It creates a cycle that turns sheets of paper into United States dollars that are used to buy products, then those dollars are used to buy an investment in American debt.

This scam allows the United States to generate money out of thin air and then turn it into tangible products. American consumers get cheap Chinese products

---

[97] John Ford, The Diplomat, "The Pivot To Asia Was Obama's Biggest Mistake".

and incoming investment capital. The average American benefits from foreigners providing cheap services and only demanding pieces of paper in return.

Because of China's seemingly endless appetite for American debt, their demand helps to keep interest rates lower, which in turn means that the amount of interest that America must pay to China is both reasonable and affordable.

However, if China decided to slow or even stop its program of purchasing American debt, that would send a signal to markets that one of the biggest buyers of Treasuries, China, is not interested in participating in that program like they always have. Between the loss of a potential buyer of their debt and the message that sends to all other possible buyers of American debt, the interest rates that the United States must pay on their Treasury Notes would instantly spike and throw the bond market into chaos.

Should China decide they wanted to put the United States into a financial recession, it would be a done deal within the span of a week. All they would have to do is stop buying American debt and the world would see that the largest economy in the history of the world is really a house of cards, held together by only an implied trust in its fiat currency, backed by nothing of substance except a dangerous military, and built on quicksand.

The reason why this is not a situation worth worrying about is that China would be committing investment suicide if they destroyed the reputation of the U.S. The Chinese need the United States to continue to function so that all of the American Treasuries that they currently own, estimated to be $1.168 trillion in 2018, retain their value, and also so that America is able to continue to make their interest payments on said Treasuries.[98]

It is in China's best interest to keep America in the game because if their economy tanks, they will be dragging a sizable chunk of Chinese assets down with them. It would be fair to characterize the relationship that the United States and China have a host-parasite relationship because if one goes down, they both go down. China's lack of aggression is less about weakness and more about self-preservation. America's debt levels do not just impact America, but they play a role in China's foreign policy too.

Though China has a nasty reputation for the way they treat their citizens, at least they have resisted the urge to create a private, for-profit, prison system.

---

[98] Investopedia, "China Owns U.S. Debt, But How Much?".

140

The United States, on the other hand...

Profiting From the Big House

The private prison industry should be called the "for-profit prison" industry, but that has such a negative sound to it. Anytime a government monetizes freedom they are creating massive and very serious conflicts of interest.

If one wants to increase the drama, raise the stakes to a level where they are dealing with someone's life and every decision becomes magnified. When a dollar value is attached to a human being's freedom, decisions are made based on money that ruins a person forever.

There are six million people incarcerated in American prisons right now, a figure that exceeds the number that wasted away in the Gulags of Stalin's Russia, and of black American slaves in the mid-1800s.

Time has shown that the State is horrible at running businesses because the greed and corruption always finds a way to infect the operation, but there are some aspects of civil society that are better off not being run by professional business people.

- For every 100,000 Americans, there are 716 people in prison.[99]

- 60% of US prisoners are non-violent.[100]

- 13 million Americans are arrested each year.

- 40% of ex-cons return to prison within three years of their release.[101]

- 1 in 3 black men will serve time in prison in their lifetimes.[102]

- 1 in 6 Latino men will serve time in prison in their lifetimes.[103]

- Since 1980, the number of women incarcerated in American prisons has

---

[99] The Washington Post, "Yes, U.S. Locks People Up At A Higher Rate Than Any Other Country".
[100] Kathleen Miles, The Huffington Post, "Just How Much The War On Drugs Impacts Our Overcrowded Prisons, In One Chart".
[101] CBS, "Study: 40% Of Ex-Cons Soon Land Back In Jail".
[102] Saki Knafo, The Huffington Post, "1 In 3 Black Males Will Go To Prison In Their Lifetime, Report Warns".
[103] Constitutional Rights Foundation, "The Color Of Justice".

increased over 700%.[104]

An executive at a hotel chain will look to reduce labor costs, increase occupancy rates, maximize their advertising dollars, streamline the check-in process, and basically try to do more with less. The more appealing the hotel looks, in comparison to the price being charged, the better the chances of attracting customers.

When these business skills are transferred to the for-profit prison industry, it ends up incentivizing these prisons to increase their occupancy rate by not allowing their current "hotel guests" to leave. A trick that Marriott would love to figure out how to do, to be sure, except that it might qualify as kidnapping.

When a hotel is not running at full capacity, they may beef up their advertising campaign in order to drum up more business. Should the prison industry find itself with too many vacancies, they might have to start enforcing some of the more unusual laws on their books to make sure all of those very uncomfortable beds are filled.

You can hit a prisoner with additional charges that are specific to the prison, but not actual crimes. Failure to clean their cells, being disrespectful to guards, and not following the set of rules that have been established by the Warden may add additional time to the person's sentence.

A traditional public prison is trying to clear inmates out of their facility as soon as they can, but a private prison is trying to invent new ways to keep them locked up. The reason for this is very simple: they are paid by the State for each inmate they keep incarcerated.

• From 1990 – 2009 the number of inmates in for-profit prisons increased 1,664%.[105]

• The private prison industry is estimated to be worth $70 billion.[106]

• Correction Corporation of America housed 90,000 inmates in their 62 facilities.

• In 2011, CCA generated revenues of $1.7 billion.

---

[104] The Sentencing Project, "Incarcerated Women And Children".
[105] Lisa Wade, Mic, "The Number Of People In Private Prisons Has Grown By 1,664% In The Last 19 Years".
[106] John Whitehead, The Huffington Post, "Jailing Americans For Profit: The Rise Of The Prison Industrial Complex".

- 41 of the 62 private prison contracts have minimum occupancy clauses (80%-100%).

- Arizona, Louisiana, Virginia, and Oklahoma have occupancy quotas of 95%-100%.

- Three Arizona private prisons have occupancy quotas of 100%.[107]

- For-profit prisons hold 19% of the federal, and 7% of the state prison population.[108]

- More than 50% of all immigrants detained are held in private prisons.[109]

- Detained immigrants account for $5.1 billion in revenue for the industry.[110]

Their business is locking people up, and business is booming.

The New Slavery

The private prison industry is running a business, not a charity, so they do not have any interest in anything that takes away from their bottom line. There is no incentive to make the place attractive, comfortable, safe, fair, or clean. The inmates do not have a say in where they are going to serve their time, so their opinion of the facility is irrelevant.

In fact, the money that the private prisons receive from the State is not enough for them so they have decided to expand their services from simply being a warehouse of people, into a full-fledged slave labor camp.

A total of 80% of all states have gotten on the private prison slave labor bandwagon, but this is a figure that is guaranteed to rise. There is simply too much profit to ignore.

Private prisons benefit from having inmate labor in a number of ways:

---

[107] American University Business Law Review, "Private Prison Contracts And Minimum Occupancy Clauses".
[108] The Sentencing Project, August 2, 2018, "Private Prisons In The United States".
[109] Equal Justice Initiative, August 8, 2018, "Private Prison Population Skyrockets".
[110] NOLA, August 2, 2012, "Immigrants Are Big Business For Prison Companies".

- They pay their workers practically nothing, in some cases only $.16/hour.[111]

- They have a captive audience that cannot unionize.

- There is almost an infinite supply of potential workers.

- The prisons sell items that are made by their slaves.

- Products produced include military gear, police uniforms (ironically), Victoria's Secret lingerie, furniture, dentures, Microsoft software packaging, Walmart products, and McDonald's uniforms.

- Yearly sales revenue of $500,000,000 worth of prison manufactured items.[112]

- The prisons also market inmate services like call centers, dog training, data entry, and were also used to clean up after the BP oil spill.

Heinrich Himmler would be impressed with the United States' network of forced labor camps. The only thing missing is the Typhus.

This business model of using inmate labor in private prisons, is amazingly beneficial to the companies like CCA and The Geo Group, the largest private operators of for-profit prisons in the United States, and, not surprisingly, incredibly unfair to the prisoners. These companies are publicly traded, so the stockholders also have an incentive to keep the beds filled, the costs low, and the slave labor operational.

Not only is it the management that is betting against the prisoners, but now it is all of Wall Street and thousands of shareholders.

- GEO Group operates 106 facilities in the U.S., with $1.5 billion in revenues in 2011.

- The GEO Group CEO, George Zoley, made $5.7 million in 2011.

- In 2012, the GEO Group and CCA combined to generate $3.3 billion in revenue.[113]

---

[111] David Moritz-Rabson, Newsweek, "'Prison Slavery': Inmates Are Paid Cents While Manufacturing Products Sold To Government".
[112] The Economist, "Prison Labour Is A Billion-Dollar Industry, With Uncertain Returns For Inmates".
[113] Prison Legal News, "Corporations, Colleges, And Cities Dump Private Prison Stock".

- GEO Group & CCA spent $25 million on lobbying and $10 million in political donations.[114]

- From the years 2008-2012, the CEO of the GEO Group made $22,000,000.

- CCA has more than 16,000 dedicated professionals.

- $21,000/year is the cost of an average minimum-security inmate in federal prison.[115]

- $33,000/year is the cost of an average maximum-security inmate in federal prison.

- Some private prisons are paid $100,000/year per prisoner.

Even though slavery was abolished in 1865 with the 13th Amendment, a technicality has allowed it to continue as "punishment for crimes" up until the current day. There are actually more black people performing mandatory, basically unpaid, hard labor in America today than there were in 1830.

Even if an inmate does not participate in the slave labor camp, their mere existence in the private prison system is worth $40,000. A guy out on the street with no job is worthless to corporate America, but if the State can find a way to incarcerate him, he now has value in the system.

Many of these prison administrators are lobbying corporations to pull their manufacturing from Asia, move those businesses back to the United States, and give them access to their slave labor at prices that are even better than the deals they were getting in Asia.

These companies use prison labor:

Abbott Laboratories	Avis	Caterpillar
Allstate Insurance	Bank of America	Chevron
American Airlines	Bayer	Chrysler
American Express	Berkshire Hathaway	Costco
AT&T	BP	ConAgra Foods
Autozone	Cargill	Dell Computers

---

[114] The Washington Post, "How For-Profit Prisons Have Become The Biggest Lobby No One Is Talking About".
[115] The Washington Post, "Wonkbook: 11 Facts About America's Prison Population".

Eli Lilly and Company	Koch Industries	Shell
Exxon Mobil	Limited Brands	Sprint
Fruit of the Loom	Mary Kay Cosmetics	Starbucks
Geico Insurance	McDonald's	State Farm Insurance
GlaxoSmithKline	Merck	Target
Hillshire Brands	Microsoft	Unilever
HP	Motorola	United Airlines
Honda Motor	Nintendo	UPS
Honeywell	Pfizer	Verizon
IBM	Procter & Gamble	WalMart
International Paper	Pepsi	Wendy's
John Deere	Revlon Group	Whole Foods
Johnson and Johnson	Sara Lee	
K-Mart	Sears	

Slavery was not abolished; it was modernized, corporatized, and made mandatory to all colors of people.

For those inmates that finally do get out of these private prisons, they are not out of the woods quite yet. The parole mechanism works to keep them coming back to the prison because of the level of restrictions placed on the inmate as a condition of their release. Early release is the bait that they use to entice a prisoner to bite on accepting parole, but once they do, it is almost impossible for a person to comply with all of the additional rules, restrictions, terms, and conditions. Parole is the feeder mechanism that keeps people coming back to prison over and over.

One can take the total number of felons currently warehoused in American prisons and safely assume that 60% of them will be coming right back almost immediately after release, that is if they are ever actually released.

Those that have served time for a felony realize that once a person is in the American judicial system, it is almost impossible to get out. They are required, by law, to disclose on a job application whether or not they have ever been convicted of a felony. This alone just removed the majority of the possible jobs that a felon could have applied for, just for checking the "Yes" box.

The concept of parole is not a bad idea, but those that have had to change their entire world just to make sure they do not break any of the additional rules of their parole will tell you that the system of parole is designed to make sure that the offender comes back to prison.

So why would the government have any reason to install a revolving door at the entrance to the American prison system?

The people that are in control of the American political and financial systems do not want competition, and as long as a person is incarcerated, they do not pose a threat to their hegemony. The six million incarcerated people is actually a force multiplier because not only are those people wasting away in prison, but their absence from the home puts additional pressure on their families.

A single mother forced to raise her four kids by herself because her husband is doing eight years for owning plants (called drugs) is simply trying to survive, and is therefore not a threat to really succeed.

This then infects the entire community, the neighborhoods, and entire cities, that get trapped in the quicksand of the prison system. The more they struggle, the deeper they sink. The priorities change from trying to get ahead in life, to just trying to make it until the next government check arrives. They will not be trying to figure out how to break out of the system, but rather trying to figure out how to game the system instead, because that is the height of their aspirations.

The threat to the system is neutralized. This softens up the inner city for demolition by removing the family structure that once provided support, both materially and emotionally.

Drug Sentencing Laws

The "Prison Industrial Complex", which is the combination of the public and private prison systems, costs the American taxpayer around $75 billion a year, and it has the highest incarceration rate in the world. According to the Sentencing Project, the prison incarceration rate has increased by 500% over the last forty years, with the prison population exploding by over 800%. The United States has less than 5% of the world's population, but 25% of the world's prison population. With hundreds of stupid new laws being created each year, it is amazing that everyone is not in prison right now for walking a dog on a Thursday while wearing shorts.

There are estimates that the number of federal regulations carrying criminal penalties may be as high as 300,000, but the truth is that nobody is sure how many laws there actually are. This is the height of insanity.

A company that is in the private prison business is really no different than the local gym, as far as the numbers behind the business are concerned. These industries love certainly with the number of members that they can count on each month because this allows them to plan for expenses and get an idea of how profitable they will be when their fiscal year ends.

The gym might lose a few members each year when a person gets honest with themselves and admits that they probably will not actually be going anytime soon, and gain a new group of members after New Year's resolutions kick in. All in all, they might have a consistent group of 10,000 people that they can count on each year, so they make their projections and plan their advertising around those figures.

A private prison is no different in that they would like to know what they can expect this coming year in terms of "members" for their facilities. A prisoner serving 20 years for rape is far more attractive to them than one serving six years for assault with an option for parole after four years. Since these organizations were developed solely to turn a profit, the guarantee of a customer for 20 years is more desirable than a customer that might only fill one of their beds for 20% of that amount. There is a cash-flow figure associated with each prisoner, and Wall Street loves statistics showing guaranteed money flowing in for years to come. These figures then are used to justify higher stock prices for these companies in the private prison industry.

If Gold's Gym could guarantee Wall Street that a huge chunk of their members would stay members for the next two decades, their stock price would spike too.

The rise of "Mandatory Minimums" in sentencing happened at the same time that private prisons were coming online.

That is not accidental.

The people developing private prisons got together with their high power law firm partners that helped them to develop their business in the first place, and actively lobbied their political friends to create a way to guarantee a huge batch of new customers, not just for their current facilities, but for future facilities that have not even been built yet.

Making long prison sentences mandatory removes discretion from the judge's hands and forces them to impose unusually harsh incarceration terms on convicts that might have had a chance of receiving less time. It removes a great deal of uncertainty as to how many beds might be filled in the future, and it shows potential investors why they should invest in them so that they can build even more prisons. Mandatory minimums can make their stock price jump without even adding additional capacity, just because of the reduction of uncertainty.

An increase in stock value also allows the private prison company to have even more money to use to game the system further by expanding out and influencing politicians in other states as well. They can set about to grab as many government contracts as they can get their hands on, and use Wall Street's endless flow of cash to finance the building of more facilities or to help them purchase other private prison companies.

Behind the Numbers

The United States has an obvious double standard when it comes to crime and skin color, and the sentencing laws associated with each issue. Certain drugs are considered to be more "serious" than others, some crimes are investigated in one part of the city but ignored in another, some drivers with a particular skin color are pulled over more often if they are seen driving nice cars than others, and the judicial system that processes these crimes is stretched to capacity.

A statistic that one might hear when visiting Costa Rica is that even though they have only .01% of the Earth's total landmass, they contain 5% of the land animals on the planet.

Pretty cool.

A statistic that a person might hear when visiting the United States is that even though they have only 5% of the people on Earth, they make up 25% of all the prisoners on the planet.[116]

Pretty disturbing.

The U.S. has the largest incarceration system in the world. It has one-fourth of the world's prisoner population despite having only 5% of its entire population.

- According to the Prison Policy Initiative, the number of Americans that are currently in prisons and jails is larger than the population of Houston, Texas, or a

---

[116] Adam Liptak, New York Times, "U.S. Prison Population Dwarfs That Of Other Nations".

little bit under two and a half million people.

• Adding the number of those on probation and parole to the number above would create a population larger than all of Los Angeles, California, roughly 7,000,000 people.

• In 17 states, prisons are filled beyond capacity, according to the *Huffington Post*. The overflow of prisoners end up in private prisons in neighboring states, or into converted prison gymnasiums that house triple-stacked bunk beds. In California alone, it is estimated that one prisoner per week dies due to a lack of medical care from a system that is extended far beyond its capacity.

• A study conducted in 2014 shows that 68% of inmates who leave prison will return over the next three years, and that number bumps up to 77% after five years. About 35% of released prisoners do not even make it six months in the free world before they end up back in prison, according to the Bureau of Justice Statistics.

• The percentage of black American men incarcerated is also higher than one of the most notoriously racist countries in the world, South Africa, during its decade's long system of apartheid, according to the book *New Jim Crow*.

• From the ACLU, 3,281 prisoners are serving life sentences in prison without the possibility of parole for nonviolent crimes. The American Civil Liberties Union added that most of the people on this list had severe mental illness issues and that two out of three of them were black men.

• It is 500% more expensive to keep someone in prison than it is to keep them in school in California and Washington. Most other states have similar rates showing costs exceeding 200% - 300%.

• The reduction in the crime rate surprisingly did not cause a reduction in the pace of incarceration. The incarceration rate actually kept going up even though the amount of crime was going down.

• The total number of inmates in the American prison system has quintupled since the combination of crack cocaine, the War on Drugs, and tougher sentencing laws were introduced to the inner cities.

• In California, 30% of all inmates are incarcerated for drug-related charges.[117]

---

[117] Bureau Of Justice Statistics, "Drugs and Crime Stats".

- In the past two decades, the number of inmates with sentences of "Life Without the Possibility of Parole" has grown by 400%. This kind of sentence was almost unheard of before the War on Drugs policy was instituted.[118]

The intentional hollowing out of the American inner-city began in the 1960s when Nixon, fearful of not getting reelected, instituted a major crackdown on heroin to clear black voters out of the voting booths for good by making them convicted felons. The targeted assault was kicked into high gear through Reagan's insulting "War on Drugs" that placed the Government's large thumb on the scale of democracy. It was taken to new and horrifying levels under Clinton and the Mandatory Minimum laws that disproportionately targeted the inner cities and then pushed into something from a Philip K. Dick novel as Trump enforced Obama's illegal immigrant laws by rounding up, then splitting up families and warehousing them like they were jars of tomato sauce into Walmarts that have been recently converted into private concentration camps in anticipation of these events unfolding.

Another factor that has changed the landscape of American prisons is the shift away from trial and towards a plea agreement. Pushes by the court-appointed counsel to accept plea deals instead of going to trial is partially due to increased workloads on court-appointed defenders. In some situations, a defense attorney averages seven minutes of time to review their client's case before their first hearing.[119]

Seven minutes.

What happened to America?

- Pretrial detention plays a large part in the decision to offer and accept pleas.

- Suspects in custody are far more likely to accept a plea.

- Suspects in custody are less likely to have their charges dropped.

- Between 90% - 95% of cases result in plea bargaining.[120]

- The discretion of the prosecution causes wide discrepancies in sentencing

[118] Christopher Purser, Wiley Online Library, "Incarceration Rates".
[119] Eli Saslow, The Washington Post, "In A Crowded Immigration Court, Seven Minutes To Decide A Family's Future".
[120] Jed Rakoff, The New York Review Of Books, "Why Innocent People Plead Guilty".

outcomes in plea bargaining.

- Suspects who decline a plea and go to trial are more likely to receive harsher sentences.[121]

- Blacks are less likely than whites to receive reduced pleas.

Statistics and numbers can be manipulated to tell quite different stories, but when it comes to the numbers behind the prison industrial complex, it is hard to massage them into anything other than the blueprints for a coming disaster.

There is another aspect to this lack of fairness in the current law enforcement system and that is that rich and powerful people usually do not go to prison unless they have really horrible lawyers. It is not to say that they do not ever get convicted, but when they do it happens in a much different way than with other people.

When Bill & Hillary Clinton's friend Jeffrey Epstein was convicted of soliciting an underage girl for prostitution and was sentenced to 18 months in prison in a plea deal, of which he served 13, the billionaire was able to spend his days out of prison and at his mansion in West Palm Beach as long as he returned to the prison each night to sleep there.[122]

Who knew something like that was even an option? It certainly would not have been if his name was Jeffrey Jenkins from Camden, New Jersey.

This set of double-standards works to undermine the credibility of the entire legal system. The legal system in America had the ability to actually be fair for everyone, but it has become so compromised that it no longer functions properly.

The American legal system must have consistency if it is going to work for the people, but when the world watched bankers steal billions of dollars from the American taxpayers and walk around as if they are gods, it creates a feeling of hopelessness in the public that there might just be two sets of laws: one for them, and another set for everyone else.

Deliberate Urban Decay

---

[121] Human Rights Watch, "An Offer You Can't Refuse".
[122] Julie Brown, Miami Herald, "Cops Worked To Put Serial Sex Abuser In Prison. Prosecutors Worked To Cut Him A Break".

Is there urban decay in the United States? Have a tall glass of water in Flint, Michigan, walk down the street at night in Trenton, New Jersey, or go buy a house in Detroit for $1, then it will be obvious that the destruction of the inner cities began long ago. It was a pre-planned event designed to fill the cities with heroin, crack cocaine, and guns, while removing all disposable income, working-age fathers, and what little hope was left. The plan to break up the families by putting the majority of men in prisons on disproportionately long prison sentences, to destroy civic cohesion by turning neighborhoods against one another through gang violence, and leaving single mothers to carry both burdens of financially and emotionally supporting their families by themselves has put so much strain on them that they come to question their purpose of even being on this planet.

Hard work has been replaced by hope, though they seem to forget that hope is always in the future and never in the present. Their big plan to get out of the inner-city ghetto is to become a rapper, a basketball player, or to win the lottery.

Not exactly a serious plan for success.

Bill Clinton won the Presidential election, in part, because he played saxophone while wearing sunglasses on The Arsenio Hall Show. The black community thought he was the coolest white guy they had ever seen, so they voted for him in droves.

Clinton went on to do more damage to the black community than both of the Bush presidents combined. He doubled the prison population during his eight years in office through tougher federal sentencing laws, with the addition of more laws that targeted urban areas, and his Omnibus Crime Bill that was passed into law in 1994. He allowed for a massive overreach through the civil asset forfeiture laws through laws that he changed, and he poured over $10 billion into the financing of more prisons that would soon be filled to capacity.

Clinton knew he was going to need more prisons because of the other part of his crime bill, the mandatory minimum sentencing guidelines. He tied the hands of judges across the country, and non-violent drug offenders were getting hit with insane sentences that did not reflect the crime that they were found guilty of.

The Omnibus Crime Bill put people in prison on 25-year sentences for selling $20 worth of crack, and it is no exaggeration to say that those people are just now getting released from prison a quarter of a century later.

Bill Clinton used the black community to get him elected, then he went out of his way to put as many of them in prison as he could to show his appreciation.

What a guy.

About 3 out of every 100 adults in the United States was under some form of correctional supervision in 2014.[123] Sadly, 41% of juveniles in the inner city have been arrested by the time they turn 23, setting the expectation that being incarcerated is pretty normal.[124]

It should not be.

Whoever said that justice was blind obviously never lived in the inner cities of America where justice is not at all blind but is racist and vindictive.

When the CIA, otherwise known as the Cocaine Importation Agency, flooded poor neighborhoods with cocaine in the early 1980s, they did so deliberately to suck what little money they had out of their communities and replace it with a hellish new slave master that turned human beings into zombies.

Once the drugs subjugated the poor into a permanent lower class, the State then took their freedom through drug sentencing laws that disproportionately target the poor.

So when is cocaine not actually cocaine?

When it becomes crack.

The actual difference is that crack is cocaine mixed with baking soda and heated to form a solid paste that can be broken into smaller pieces that are smoked instead of snorted. Not a huge physical change, but this type of cocaine was pushed heavily into the black neighborhoods because it was marketed as a more affordable version of traditional powder cocaine that was all the rage at Studio 54 and with the white community in the late 1970s and early 80s.

Once crack exploded on the scene in the mid-80s, the sentencing laws were changed to target crack users and dealers because it now took 100 times more powder cocaine as crack cocaine to receive the same five-, 10-, or 20-year

[123] NAACP, "Criminal Justice Fact Sheet".
[124] The Sentencing Project, "Racial Disparities In Youth Commitments And Arrests".

mandatory minimum prison term.

Crack cocaine was created for, and marketed to, the black community.

That is a fact.

The emergence of crack cocaine coincides with the rise of private prisons, and that is no accident either. The laws had been changed to put young black men in prison for generations, while white men holding the same drug were out on probation.

And the White community wonders why the Black community is so dysfunctional?

How can they not be after what can only be described as a targeted hit job by the law enforcement community in conjunction with the Department of Justice?

The combination of crack cocaine and draconian drug sentencing laws managed to hollow out the Black community of the United States in less than one generation, and this has had a devastating effect on not just the Black community, but the entire nation because it normalized drug use in the lower socioeconomic regions of the entire country.

The "War on Drugs" has been an abject failure for stopping the flow and use of drugs in the United States, but that is based on the assumption that stopping drug use was the mission. Americans must understand that the real reason for this make-believe war was to demolish the inner-cities and put minorities in prison for long stretches, while simultaneously diminishing their ability to ever get a decent job once they get out.

It looks like they "won" the war.

The New Crack

The current opioid epidemic in the Appalachian region of the United States is predominantly a white issue, but the use of drugs in poor areas of the country was established as the norm because of the crack epidemic decades earlier.

Is the opioid crisis an accident, or could it be the new crack cocaine push to target the poor white communities? It should be obvious by now that nothing like this happens accidentally, and that the intentional push of these drugs, in association with rampant over-prescribing by medical professionals, is by design.

If law enforcement wanted to stop this, they would shut down the "pill mills" that exist in most states in the southeast United States and the Rust Belt, but so far that idea has not really been taken seriously.

It is the most confusing of drugs because it is legal for some people, and totally illegal for others. You can have the drug prescribed for a host of legitimate physical ailments, by real doctors, but there is a monster in there. The actual pain may have subsided at some point, but the need for the opioid medicine remains and turns patients into junkies.

What is worse is that opioid medication is a controlled substance and can be difficult to find, so people look for substitutes. The closest substitute for opioid pain medications is opioid drugs like heroin. A patient goes into the doctor's office for a torn ACL and they end up shooting heroin by the end of the year.

Think it cannot happen? It is happening all over the country and the numbers are staggering. The pricing structure makes heroin a very attractive option because where a Vicodin costs a person $80, a bag of heroin might only cost $20 and last twice as long.

Back in 2000, heroin was hard to find and expensive, but thanks to the invasion of Afghanistan and the removal of the Taliban from the poppy fields, the CIA once again controls the flow of drugs into the country. This time they are importing heroin instead of cocaine, but the plan is similar. The profits are used to fund their "black programs", and the drugs are used to hollow out another segment of the American population.

The amount of opium-poppy fields that were cultivated in 2001 in Afghanistan was 8,000 hectares under Taliban rule. Now, under the United States military and CIA control, the number of hectares cultivated per year is over 225,000, so what is America really doing in Afghanistan?[125] It becomes quite obvious that the CIA and U.S. military are not leaving this country anytime soon, or maybe ever.

So the American government is back to the same strategy of importing drugs, collecting the money to finance international terror (otherwise known as American foreign policy), destroying American communities, and demonizing Boogiemen from the Middle East in order to justify massive spending on the

---

[125] Christopher Woody, Business Insider, "Despite 15 Years Of Occupation, Afghanistan's Opium Production Has Only Gone Up".

Military-Information-Terror complex.

Rules for Radicals

"There is no evolution without revolution, and there are no revolutions without conflict, and this is the line that separates Liberals from Radicals." - Saul Alinsky.

Almost half a century ago, a Hard Left community organizer named Saul Alinsky, wrote the playbook of subversive tactics called *Rules for Radicals* to energize a new generation of social warriors seeking change. A few notable followers to the Alinsky method are Bill Ayers, Hillary Clinton, Frank Marshall Davis, and President Barack Obama, among others.

Sarah Palin did get one thing correct when she was campaigning with John McCain, and that was that Barack Obama was "palling around with terrorists". It was not with the Hollywood version of a terrorist wearing a headscarf and holding a sword, but with an actual terrorist named Bill Ayers, a Saul Alinsky disciple, that had been tied to multiple bombings over the past couple of decades. The reason why Obama called himself a "Community Organizer" was because that was how Alinsky thought of himself.

Alinsky had a Machiavellian approach towards changing the prevailing winds of society, and an "ends justify the means" philosophy when making it happen. No tactic was off-limits, and if people had to get hurt in the process then that was the price that had to be paid. He detailed his ideas in a list of rules that he thought his people should live by, and to call his book the "terrorist handbook" is not an overstatement.

He proposes that Mankind has been divided into three parts: the Haves, the Have-Nots, and the Have-a-Little, Want Mores. The Haves ask "when do we sleep", while the Have-Nots ask "when do we eat?". However, the Have-a-Little, Want Mores, the American middle-class, are torn between wanting to change the world so that they can get more, and wanting to keep things the same in order to defend what they already have. They are essentially politically, socially, and economically schizophrenic, as they desire two different outcomes at the same time.

The role of the community organizer is to manage these expectations and help the public to navigate these mood swings between wanting to stay put and the urge to rise up. The 13 rules for radicals help to educate and instigate the middle class to get off their asses and do something to improve their position in life, and if someone should decide to stand in their way, these rules offer advice on how to either go around them or, if they have to, go right over them.

These are the 13 rules for radicals plus additional commentary from Alinsky.

1. *"Power is not only what you have, but what the enemy thinks you have."*

2. *"Never go outside the expertise of your people."* - When an action or tactic is outside the experience of the people, the result is confusion, fear, and retreat. It also means a collapse of communication.

3. *"Whenever possible, go outside the expertise of the enemy."* - Here you want to cause confusion, fear, and retreat.

4. *"Make the enemy live up to its own book of rules."* - You can kill them with this, for they can no more obey their own rules than the Christian church can live up to Christianity.

5. *"Ridicule is man's most potent weapon."* - It is almost impossible to counterattack ridicule. Also, it infuriates the opposition, who then react to your advantage.

6. *"A good tactic is one your people enjoy."* - If your people are not having a ball doing it, there is something very wrong with the tactic.

7. *"A tactic that drags on too long becomes a drag."* - Man can sustain militant interest in any issue for only a limited time, after which it becomes a ritualistic commitment, like going to church on Sunday mornings.

8. *"Keep the pressure on."* - With different tactics and actions, and utilize all events of the period for your purpose.

9. *"The threat is usually more terrifying than the thing itself."*

10. *"The major premise for tactics is the development of operations that will maintain a constant pressure upon the opposition."* - It is this unceasing pressure that results in the reactions from the opposition that are essential for the success of the campaign. It should be remembered not only that the action is in the reaction but that action is itself the consequence of reaction and of reaction to the reaction, ad infinitum. The pressure produces the reaction, and constant

pressure sustains action.

11. *"If you push a negative hard enough, it will push through and become a positive."* - This is based on the principle that every positive has its negative. We have already seen the conversion of the negative into the positive, in Mahatma Gandhi's development of the tactic of passive resistance.

12. *"The price of a successful attack is a constructive alternative."* - You cannot risk being trapped by the enemy in his sudden agreement with your demand and saying "You're right—we don't know what to do about this issue. Now you tell us."

13. *"Pick the target, freeze it, personalize it, and polarize it."*

Once someone knows the rules, the next step is to adjust one's thoughts on ethics. Alinsky has thoughts on modifications to a person's views on how they conduct themselves in order to make them less concerned about what they actually do, as long as the outcome suits their goals.

The Rules of Ethics, according to Saul Alinsky:

• One's concern with the ethics of means and ends varies inversely with one's personal interest in the issue.

• The judgment of the ethics of means is dependent upon the political position of those sitting in judgment.

• In war, the ends justify almost any means.

• Judgment must be made in the context of the times in which the action occurred and not from any other chronological vantage point.

• A concern with ethics increases with the number of means available and vice versa.

• The less important the end be desired, the more one can afford to engage in ethical evaluations of means.

• Generally, success or failure is a mighty determinant of ethics.

• The morality of a means depends upon whether the means is being employed at a time of imminent defeat or imminent victory.

- Any effective means is automatically judged by the opposition as being unethical.

- You do what you can with what you have and clothe it with moral garments.

- Goals must be phrased in general terms like "Liberty, Equality, Fraternity", "Of the Common Welfare", "Pursuit of Happiness", or "Bread and Peace".

His tactics are well known and can be seen at work daily in American politics and in the corporate media. Once a person actually reads the rules for radicals, they practically jump out of the television every night on the nightly news because they become so obvious, and these exact tactics have been completely adopted by the Democratic Party and their supporters.

A practical example of a tactic that the gangster government uses is when they direct the IRS to target the groups they do not like with audits and fake charges in order to tie them up legally, financially, and emotionally. They learned how to do this from guys like Saul Alinsky, who learned how to do this by watching the Chicago Mafia.

For the record, at the beginning of Saul Alinsky's book, he dedicates it to Lucifer, so that might help to make sense of things and understand where he is coming from. At the very least, he is inspired to create chaos and destruction as a way of bringing his version of society to the forefront, which is the core of the New World Order's motto, ORDO AB CHAO, or Order Out of Chaos.

This phenomenon has many names, but let's use Hegelian Dialectic or creating (manufacturing) Order Out of Chaos. They create a problem. They make you panic and react to it. Then they solve it with a pre-made solution. Voila! Total control.

It is all part of the government's campaign – whichever one they are running at any point in time.

How can anyone look at America today and not see the chaos pouring out of every hole in the structure? The pre-weakening of the building has set the structure up for the next phase of the plan.

IDENTIFYING THE SUPPORT COLUMNS

Destroying Critical Thinking

In the sound bite world of modern, Western society, sometimes reading the headline is the extent of the digging into the story. It is as if people allow the story only eight seconds to hook them or else they move on the next one, then the next. If the news cannot tell the whole story in 60 seconds, then the viewer does not want to hear about it.

This clearly presents a problem for topics or concepts that require some unpacking and a bit of a backstory. Most of the serious and important concepts need time to explain, more time to process, and even more time after that for them to really sink in.

Perhaps this is the Twitterization of information where it must be condensed into 140 characters or risk being ignored? This is not to say that getting to the point is a bad thing, but there needs to be room to expand on a point or tell a full story.

This change is more than just annoying or strange, it actually impacts the quality of information. A person can read a headline quickly, but skip the story, then incorrectly extrapolate what the story should be about based on the headline that they read. How many times has a headline been intentionally tweaked specifically to be outrageous, and once the entire story is read it sounds nothing like the headline that grabbed the reader's attention?

For someone that only read the headline and skipped the actual story, they go on about their day with a much different picture in their head about what that story was about. Whether this is fake news, clickbait, or just a misleading headline, the result is the same. People's inability to identify the source of the information, in conjunction with their diminished attention span, plus the media's bias or slant, makes it difficult to know if what they are learning about a particular event is even remotely true.

Get Them While They're Young

These days, just because a kid learned something in school, does not make it true. All one needs to do to understand this concept is to open a history textbook and the lies just pour out of it because history is written by the victors.

There was a time when the ability for critical thinking was a given, assumed to be hard-wired into the brains of all human beings. Those days are gone, and that wiring has either become dormant or rewired in a way that bypasses the normal means of processing information. Part of this change is due to the behavior of the person that has been manipulated by information distribution through television and formal schooling that demands obedience to their version of reality, and punishes any contrary points of view, especially in the education systems.

After a decade of formal education in the United States, the teachers basically beat the critical thinking out of kids and force them to conform to their version of the world. The role of standardized testing is key to this removal of critical thinking because it forces the student to only have one correct answer in order to comply with the results desired from the test. Kids that decide to be contrarian in their answers do so at their own risk because the results of these tests are used as the baseline criteria for admission into college, so there is a limited amount of fighting against this system that a student can engage in before becoming ineligible to move on from high school into more formal education.

Praise Be the Groupthink!

The loss of critical thinking is certainly not limited to students or children. Programming of people takes on multiple forms, but nowhere is critical thinking less welcome than inside religious organizations. This is the epicenter of "groupthink" and critical thinking is most definitely not welcome or appreciated inside the doors of a church, mosque, temple, or anywhere else where organized religion seeks to turn individuals into a group.

This is not to say that there are no beneficial lessons to be learned through religion, but thinking for oneself is not one of them.

The people that find themselves heavily invested in their religious organizations usually find it difficult to question the dictates of the leaders because to do so is seen as being disrespectful, but this lack of oversight by the flock creates the type of blind allegiance that leads to things like looking the other way when a culture of pedophilia infects the Catholic church. When the leaders are above questioning then things have the ability to become corrupted by those seeking power and control.

Nowhere in the history of mankind has more control been consolidated than into the hands of the major organized religions, and these organizations are responsible for the slaughter and destruction of millions and millions of human beings over the centuries in the name of their "God". People that take thousand-year-old manuscripts that have been translated from languages that no longer exist into modern English, with stories that have been passed around from generation to generation, from one region of the world to another, as literal words from God, with no critical thought as to the origins of these words, are the same type of people that listen to Fox News or CNN and believe every word they hear. People must be responsible for their own critical thinking for everything they take into their minds, and no topic is exempt from this, especially religion.

Hollywood D.C.

The destruction of critical thinking and manipulation of minds comes in a variety of methods, most of which fly under the radar due to their classification as being something else entirely.

One of these methods is called predictive programming, and it is when governments or other higher-ups use far-fetched concepts in movies or TV (or events) as a mass mind control tool to make the population more accepting of planned future events.

Result? If and when these changes are put through, the public will already be familiarized with them and will accept them as natural progressions, lessening possible public resistance.

So what would the motive be behind predictive programming?

Easy. It is the government creating a problem so the population will look to the government for a solution. However, because the government planned for the crisis the government will offer a solution that has been planned long before the crisis ever happened.

Think of the Coronavirus crisis. Then think of every dystopian story made popular. *Outbreak, Quarantine, Hunger Games, The Handmaid's Tale* – the list goes on and on. Because the public has been brainwashed ahead of time, they understand how viruses work and how they can destroy the whole world if they do not listen to their masters by staying locked up in their houses.

State-sanctioned propaganda is everywhere, and people line up to buy tickets to see it.

Hollywood has been a favorite vehicle for dispensing patriotism for decades, but few know that there is actually a connection between the Department of Defense and the movie and television studios. If a movie studio wants to use the Pentagon's gadgets and airplanes, they have to agree to let the DOD have final approval on the script.

No script approval by the Entertainment Liaison Office, no aircraft carriers, or tanks.

It is not much of a stretch to think that Tom Clancy novels had some sort of government ties in order to get the storylines right, but why did *Ernest Saves Christmas* need to be run through the DOD for approval first? Was he potentially giving away State secrets, or were they just checking to see how dumbed down they needed to get the programming to appeal to the masses?

Here is a partial list of a few of the movies, without even venturing into the thousands of hours of television programming each year:

Air Force One	*A Few Good Men*	*Jurassic Park*
American Sniper	*GoldenEye*	*License to Kill*
Apollo 13	*Godzilla*	*Manchurian Candidate*
Argo	*Goldfinger*	*Midway*
Armageddon	*Hamburger Hill*	*Navy Seals*
Battleship	*Heartbreak Ridge*	*Patriot Games*
Behind Enemy Lines	*Hurt Locker*	*Patton*
Blackhawk Down	*The Hunt for Red*	*Pearl Harbor*
Captain Phillips	*October*	*Prisoner of War*
Clear & Present Danger	*In the Line of Fire*	*Red Dawn*
Contact	*Indiana Jones*	*The Right Stuff*
Day After Tomorrow	*Iron Man 1 & 2*	*Rules of Engagement*
The Day The Earth	*The Jackal*	*The Silence of the*
Stood Still	*Karate Kid 2*	*Lambs*
Deep Impact	*The Next Karate Kid*	*Star Trek 4*
Executive Decision	*The Killing Fields*	*Sum of All Fears*
Ernest Saves Christmas	*King Kong*	*Taps*

Top Gun	*Transformers*	*United 93*
Tomorrow Never Dies	*True Lies*	*We Were Soldiers*

Godzilla, large dinosaurs, *King Kong*, and all the *Transformers* movies...is there something that the government is not telling the public that perhaps they need to? It looks like they really want the people to fear 100-foot monsters getting loose from islands and wreaking havoc all over the west coast of the United States, while the real villains are 6-foot tall bureaucrats on the east coast at the Pentagon wreaking havoc all over the world.

It is not limited to television and movies that work to influence a generation of young Americans, as certain books fit the bill as well. *On The Road* by Jack Kerouac influenced a generation of young people searching for meaning and adventure in their lives. Other books with a more political slant encouraged young people to get involved in the political machine, but *Rules For Radicals* laid the groundwork for a political revolution decades in the making.

We Don't Need No Education

Let's get honest about the education system in the United States, starting with the "3 R's" that every kid is taught in school: Reading, Writing, and Arithmetic.

Notice anything unusual about the "3 R's"?

If a student was in a school that teaches the Common Core curriculum and they correctly pointed out that two of the words do not actually begin with the letter "R", they would only get credit if they were able to show all 117 steps that it took to reach that answer.

It is a pretty simple concept to understand: the more educated a group of people are, the more options and opportunities they will have in the future. The ability to comprehend and perform difficult tasks sets a person apart from those unable to do so. The fewer the number of people that are that qualified, the more valuable a qualified person becomes.

Raising Sheeple

The Nazis considered educated people to be a threat and potential future enemy. Hitler remarked that if he could control the textbooks then he could control the

State.

What did Pol Pot do as soon as he came to power in Cambodia? He rounded up all the teachers, engineers, lawyers, doctors, and scientists and murdered them as fast as he could.[126]

Education is threatening to those in power. An educated person might be able to figure out the scams that the government is running on them and do something to put an end to them. They may be able to read between the lines to see if the actions are matching up with the rhetoric, or if the government is simply telling the people one thing and actually doing something else.

If a person is running a corrupt government then it would be in their best interest to keep the people as stupid as possible. They do not want to be exposed for their wrongdoing, and they certainly do not want someone to muscle in on their action while they loot the place.

Education is about control. Keep the sheep stupid and fat so they will be too slow to run away, and too dumb to figure out where to run to when the government comes to shear them. This strategy is so obvious and pervasive that it is difficult to put up much of a fight against its existence.

However, if a person is running a government that is on the up and up, then they want more smart people to help them with their plan, in part because they are not actually lying to them. They would view the students as an investment and a partner, not an obstacle that has to be overcome.

The "Specialized Class" of 1922

A little over 100 years ago, Walter Lippman's book *Public Opinions* talked about the "manufacture of consent" as a technique of control that was necessary because the common interest eluded the general public due to the fact that they were not smart enough to figure it out. These important social and political decisions needed to be the responsibility of a new segment of the population that he called the "specialized class", and they were the ones tasked with doing all of the cerebral heavy-lifting. They would be the ones that would dig into the issues, think about the pros and cons of a particular set of laws, then tell the rest of the population the way that they should be thinking and feeling about these pressing topics.

---

[126] Valerio Pellizzari, The Independent, "They All Had To Go".

There is nothing democratic about this method of thinking, but this is the very situation that America finds itself in today. The problem is that in some regards Lippman was correct that the people are not very smart, as well as the very obvious fact that the vast majority of the population has outsourced their critical thinking to the corporate media so that they can be told how they are supposed to feel about things, without having to do any work on their own. This leaves the person susceptible to the biases and slants of the corporate media, with massive swaths of the population reduced to parrots that mimic what they heard the night before on Fox News, CNN, or MSNBC.

The rich know people that they consider to be qualified enough to handle the task of manufacturing consent; the poor do not.

People might go to Walmart to find the best deal on paper towels, but is it really the right place to look for the Director of the Treasury? The chances are high that anyone with the ability to rise above the crime, poverty, drugs, and other traps found in the American ghettos has already left, therefore those in the lower 25% of the socio-economic chart simply do not know anyone from their community that is both qualified, and that they really trust to take up the fight on their behalf.

Of course, the inverse problem exists when one finds a person that is so smart that they are able to easily see the schemes and frauds that can be perpetrated upon the people, or have grown up accustomed to the role of fraud within the system and feel that it is their role to perpetuate this crime because they feel entitled to continue in the family tradition of corruption and graft, like the Bush family. They grew up surrounded by those that manufacture consent, so they know how to operate in those circles. Those just trying to educate themselves to give their families a better life do not have the time, money, or qualifications to attempt to create a new narrative, then organize the massive coordinated effort to push it onto the masses in the United States.

This is one reason why real change is so difficult to come by. It costs a lot of money to rewire the entire system.

Workers, not Thinkers

President Woodrow Wilson admitted that he wanted a portion of the American public to forego the privilege of an education in order to fit themselves to perform specific, manual tasks.[127] This was the height of the Industrial Revolution and industries were springing up left, right, and center, and there were not enough workers to go around. His statement was a bit insulting, but practical, given the economic landscape. Also, it is obvious that not everyone is going to be able to be a doctor or lawyer, so there will be educational layering whether Wilson calls for it or not.

However, as the 21st century begins, there are a few industries that appear to be heading into breakout territory, while others have come to the end of their life cycles.

Computer programming and artificial intelligence will be driving technology throughout the century, both figuratively and literally. In 30 years, having a job as a taxi driver will be as worthless as owning a horse and buggy.

With a realistic understanding of what the landscape might look like for the next generation, shouldn't the education system be recast to prepare kids for the next 100 years, instead of being stuck in the system that Carnegie and Rockefeller funded and built in order to create a nation of "workers, not thinkers"?

Schools are not teaching anything of substance these days, and they certainly are not interested in teaching the children to think critically. They do not bother to teach children how to think because they are so caught up in trying to teach them what to think. The schools have been converted into indoctrination programming centers, and the teachers have been turned into the programmers.

Well, until the robots take their place.

John Taylor Gatto, a lifelong educator, and speaker on the subject of government schooling breaks the school system down into four steps, with each step providing an important function in figuring out where this child should end up as an adult.

The first function of schooling is adjustive. Schools are to establish fixed habits of reaction to authority. Notice that this precludes critical judgment completely. Second is the diagnostic function.

Next, comes the sorting function. School sorts children by training individuals only so far as their likely destination in the social machine.

---

[127] Wisdom of the Hands, "The Meaning Of A Liberal Education".

The fourth function is conformity. As much as possible, kids are to be made alike.

The education system in the United States is badly broken, and this is not even slightly debatable. The only real question is whether the system was broken intentionally or not? Did they break the system so that it will stop producing kids smart enough to see what is really going on? Did the system break under the enormous weight of expectations placed upon it by the rest of the world? Did the American school system break because it was no longer a priority?

The National Assessment of Education Progress shows figures that reflect the reality of this public education fiasco that America is currently facing, and refutes claims that the education system is one of the best in the world.

- 36% of all 8th Graders are considered to be proficient in reading.

- 24% of those 8th Graders in New Mexico qualify as "reading proficient".

- 35% of all 8th Graders are considered to be proficient in math.

- 17% of those 8th Graders in Louisiana qualify as "math proficient".

Even Arne Duncan, the former Education Secretary under Obama has stated that as a nation the United States is not in the Top 10 in anything and that only about a third of all 8th Graders are even proficient in either reading or math. And this is coming from the guy that ran this whole program, so he is not doing himself any favors by admitting to these low numbers but that is what the reality of the situation is in the American education system.

China spends 4% of GDP on education and training. They are taking this problem seriously, while the United States wants to have a conversation about whether teachers should be armed with guns?

Sure, the politicians talk about wanting a better education system, but they run and hide behind budgetary excuses when it comes to actually deliver on their campaign promise. How many of these leaders have their kids in public schools anyhow? The number is probably as close to zero as one can get, and the reason for that is because education is critical, and a great education is only available to those with the financial ability to purchase it through private schooling. Private schools feature smaller class sizes, better teachers, more resources, less propaganda and politics, and more accountability by the administration to the parents.

Something is very wrong here, but luckily the Secretary of Education, Betsy DeVos, is here to fix all of the problems that she witnessed first-hand during her four decades of experience working in the public school system.

Oh wait, she does not actually have experience working in education.

Well, she at least knows a little bit about public schools from when her own kids attended, right?

Nope, only private school for them.

A huge push towards the privatization of schools has increased the number of privately operated, taxpayer-funded, charter schools by 50%, while simultaneously putting 4,000 public schools out of business.

There was considerable push-back from both sides of the aisle when President Trump nominated Betsy DeVos for the position as the Secretary of Education, in part because she is utterly and totally unqualified to hold the position.

This is not to say that Betsy DeVos is a religious zealot or a billionaire simply because her family members are, but it has to make it more difficult to really understand the plight of American families that are struggling to make ends meet and desperately depend on the government to provide adequate schooling for their children.

When Senator Bernie Sanders asked her about working to provide free college tuition to all Americans during her confirmation hearing, she described it as a nice idea, but she was unsure how that cost would be paid for.

When Senator Sanders proposed that reducing the tax breaks currently granted to millionaires and billionaires would easily cover the tuition costs, she simply tried to change the subject.

This is exactly what people were worried about.

What is a Charter School?

A charter school is a school that receives government funding but operates independently of the established state school system in which it is located.

Charter schools receive public money, have an open admission policy to the public, and they provide free education. Charter schools are classified as public schools, according to the U.S. Department of Education.

About two-thirds of charter schools are stand-alone schools created and operated by management organizations that can be nonprofit or for-profit. Enrollment has grown by an average of 12-13 percent annually over the past 10 years. There are currently 6,440 charter schools, with 2.9 million students enrolled, according to the National Alliance for Public Charter Schools, with roughly 500 new schools open each year.

A school's charter typically exempts the school from select state and district rules and regulations. Charter school students, on average, scored slightly less than public school students in both reading and math, according to Stanford.

Public vs. Private Schools

• According to the National Center for Education Statistics, there are 98,817 public schools in the United States. The costs to fund these public elementary and secondary schools each year costs the taxpayers $634 billion, or $12,509 per public school student.

• The average public school class size is 25 kids, compared to around 20 for charter schools, and 19 in private schools, according to the National Center for Education Statistics (NCES).

• There are 34,576 private schools in the United States, serving 5.7 million PK-12 students, and staffed by 442,000 full-time equivalent (FTE) teachers.

• Private schools account for 10% of all PK-12 students, with yearly revenues of approximately $53.7 billion. Of those private schools, 78% are religiously-affiliated.

• Tuition averages for private elementary schools are $7,800, with secondary schools running $13,000 per year, according to the NCES.

If a parent sends their kids to a "free" public school, how much complaining can they really do? They are getting what they paid for.

The government likes to pretend that they are providing free educational services to the children out of the goodness of their own hearts, but the reality of the situation is that they are receiving something very valuable in return. They take advantage of the opportunity to have an entire generation of people for eight hours a day, five days a week, free from parental supervision so that they can indoctrinate and shape their minds in a way that makes them compliant when they become adults, and be assured that they will not be a threat to disrupt the system. They will never seek to think outside of the box, in fact, they will bring their own box with them to school and will willingly get inside it where they feel safe.

Think that kids are not being brainwashed in school? Sometimes it happens in a more subtle and less obvious way, but it is always happening and it is not by accident.

Why do kids know that when the bell sounds, the class is over? Like Pavlov's Dog, they are conditioned to react when that bell goes off to do what they are trained to do. The bell lets them know that it is time to move to leave their current station and proceed to the next station, or classroom.

Why are all of the desks set up in straight rows? Because they are being trained at an early age to conform to a certain pattern that mimics that of an assembly line or a factory. When Carnegie, Rockefeller, and Henry Ford set about to create an education system, they did so in order to create a feeder system that would supply them with an endless stream of employees that were already accustomed to being in a factory-like environment for most of the day. If all these kids ever know are desks in straight rows, standing in a line to get water at the water fountain, and the ringing of bells to let them know when to stand up and walk out of the room or sit down and shut up, working at a factory will appear to be nothing more than an extension of what they are already accustomed to doing, and thus not the sad and depressing place that it surely is.

Who can argue against the truth that childish and childlike people are much easier to manage than critically trained, self-reliant, ones?

Education by the State is necessary for thought control. It creates a foundation on which the State can build upon, and it does so by pulverizing the natural soil and compacting it down into a flat, boring, level, symmetrical square of dirt.

Much like the military, they start by tearing a kid down, shaving their head to strip them of any identity, to make them the same as everyone else, so that they can build them back up the way they need them to be.

Dropping off the Global Stage

Do not think of these so-called education centers as "public schools" because that has a very benign sound to it. They should more accurately be described for what they really are: government schools.

What industries get better when the government gets involved? Not many, and certainly not the education system.

China is spending such a large chunk of their GDP investing in their people because they have become a manufacturing society and they recognize that you need to invest in research and development, be it a machine that makes better wire coat hangers, a cheaper version of concrete, or the education of a person.

The United States' money printing machine always seems to print as much money is needed for stirring up problems in other countries or for building bombs to drop on the Middle East. Is America taking advantage of this unique Petrodollar system that it has had for decades by investing in research and development that does not include weapons of war or bogus medicine?

Clearly not enough.

For many decades the United States has been losing ground in the education area, but it was difficult to quantify exactly how bad things had gotten. As of 2003, a total of 14% of American adults are classified as "illiterate", meaning they have below basic literacy skills. That works out to 34,000,000 American adults that cannot read this horrifying statistic.[128]

McDonald's has large pictures of their food and a numerical ordering system (#3 Meal, etc.) so that the illiterate can still order their food.

This is unacceptable.

If the whole system is a mess, then comparing one school to another might not accurately reflect how far things have slipped because, in comparison to each other, they still might look alright.

In order to get a more accurate gauge of where things actually stand it is

---

[128] The Huffington Post, "The U.S. Illiteracy Rate Hasn't Changed In 10 Years".

important to compare entire systems to one another, not just a few particular schools. One seeking the truth about education results and teaching styles must expand beyond the borders of the United States in order to see how things are being done in other countries.

The Programme for International Student Assessment (PISA) test is used to compare students from various countries against one another. The results of their tests have blown the cover off of the fallacy of superior American education, and has, in fact, exposed the system as one of the worst, and most expensive, in the world.

- American students ranked 26th out of 34 countries in the PISA Math section.

- American students ranked 21st in Science and 15th in Literacy.

- 55% of students in Shanghai were considered top performers.

- 9% of students in American students were top performers.

- The U.S. ranks fifth in spending per student @ $115,000.

- The Slovak Republic scores similarly to the U.S. but spends $53,000 per student.

- Only Austria, Luxembourg, Norway, and Switzerland spend more per student.

- In 1988, America was the world leader in the number of high school graduates and the quality of a high school diploma.

- As of 2018, America is now ranked 36th in both categories.

- Today in the United States, 14% of new teachers resign by the end of their first year.

- One-third of all new teachers in the United States resign within three years.

- Half of all new teachers in America have left the industry within five years.

- A student living in poverty is 13 times more likely to drop out of school.

- High school dropouts are eight times more likely to go to prison.

- Dropouts are more likely to be on welfare and are ineligible for 90% of available jobs.

- A dropout is 50% less likely to vote and earns 50% less than graduates.

There is one bright spot for the United States on the education front, and that is that 380,000 people are enrolled to complete college in their pajamas through the University of Phoenix, an online college.[129]

It is a start.

<u>The Cost of College</u>

It is a widely known fact that college in America is getting more and more expensive each year, and producing results that do not exactly correlate with the extra costs associated with it. There are 44 million students that are either currently enrolled in college or recently graduated, which is carrying some form of student loan debt. The estimates peg this number at just a shade under $1.5 trillion, a figure that has tripled in just 11 years.[130]

It is no secret that Americans have an unhealthy relationship with credit card debt, but the total outstanding credit card debt is nowhere near the levels of student loan debt. The $880 billion of credit card debt that is hanging over the heads of most Americans is only 60% of the outstanding student loan debt, a debt that cannot be wiped clean through the process of bankruptcy, thanks to legislation pushed through years ago by the largest student loan lenders. Every year one million Americans default on their student loans, and it is estimated that by 2023 about 40% of all student loan borrowers will default.[131] Of course, it should come as no surprise since over the last decade the costs of textbooks had almost doubled, student housing had spiked by 50%, and the cost of tuition was up by 63% even though there was no real increase in the quality of the education to correlate with the increase in costs.[132]

Of the students that graduate from a four-year college or university, 71% of them carry student loan debt. Students that graduated from public schools averaged a debt load of $25,500, with private school debt just a hair below

---

[129] Reuters, "U.S. For-Profit Colleges Spend Big On Marketing While Slashing Other Costs".
[130] Abigail Hess, CNBC, "Here's How Much The Average Student Loan Borrower Owes When They Graduate".
[131] Annie Nova, CNBC, "More Than 1 Million People Default On Their Student Loans Each Year".
[132] Bureau of Labor and Statistics, "College Tuition And Fees Increase 63% Since January 2006".

$40,000.[133] The clock starts ticking on this debt bomb six months after they finish college, meaning that decisions made about accepting their first job out of college if there are any jobs available to them, must factor in the student loan debt anchor that is firmly attached to their ankle.

Starting off in the world is a daunting task in and of itself, but doing so already in the hole tens of thousands of dollars makes everything exponentially more difficult and frustrating.

Standardized Tests Gets You Standardized Kids

Standardized testing is not the best way to measure a person's intelligence, but neither are IQ tests. These tests can be culturally biased, for one, and they really only show a person's proficiency in a couple of areas of knowledge.

A child that is more artistically or musically inclined might not be as strong in math, but does that make them less intelligent? IQ tests can measure how fast a person can solve a math problem, but can it measure how they would solve a real problem in their life?

People like to boil things down to a number, then compare their numbers to other people's numbers. There is nothing wrong with this, but it must be understood that not everything can be accurately measured like someone's height or weight. There are far too many variables to take into account when measuring how smart a person is.

For the past 100 years, the method that has been used in compulsory schooling to measure how smart a kid was is to have a teacher discuss a particular topic, provide information to back up what the teacher discussed earlier, and then ask the child to take a test in which they are expected to regurgitate the information back to the teacher. The children that were able to memorize and repeat this information the best would get a higher grade. The higher the grades over the course of the child's decade of schooling, the better the chances of the child getting into a good college. The better the reputation of the college, the better the chances are for this child to find a great job.

This type of schooling rewards memorization over problem-solving. Students are taught what to think, but not how to think.

---

[133] Christine DiGangi, USA Today, "The Average Student Loan Debt In Every State".

This system of education is obsolete and needs to be brought down, provided that there is a better way of doing things. The new education system is slowly being rolled out across the country, but the problem is that most people know very little about what is slated to take its place.

What is coming their way is terrifying. It is the development of the most confusing, least informative, and most expensive piece of educational garbage the planet has ever seen, Common Core.

Common Core

Something unusual happens once a person has bought everything in the store that has a price tag on it: they start looking to buy things that are not actually for sale.

In the late 1800s, Rockefeller and Carnegie had made more than they could ever spend in several lifetimes, so they set out to change society in a way that they thought would be most beneficial to them. They both very much subscribed to the "Golden Rule philosophy", and since they had all the gold, they set about to change the rules.

One area that was ripe for molding was the schooling system that was starting to become compulsory in certain areas of the country. The foundations that Rockefeller and Carnegie started went to work to create incubators for churning out future factory workers.

Today's version of Rockefeller is Bill Gates, the mild-mannered, unassuming tech nerd founder of Microsoft, and he is picking up where the other powerful industrialists left off with regard to shaping education for the next 100 years. His education program is called Common Core, and it has the potential to set the United States back 50 years in the educational arms race against China and Europe.

If education is the key to the future, then the future of the United States is bleak.

The largest sponsor of the Common Core initiative was the Bill and Melinda Gates Foundation, with over $250 million spent to develop and push the national standards.

The Gates Foundations is also involved in purchasing education organizations for the purpose of advancing his Common Core agenda. The following organizations have been funded by, and therefore compromised by, The Gates Foundation:

- American Enterprise Institute: $1,068,788.

- American Federation of Teachers: $5,400,000.

- Association for Supervision and Curriculum Development: $3,269,428.

- Council of Great City Schools: $5,010,988.

- Education Trust: $2,039,526.

- National Congress of Parents and Teachers: $499,962.

- National Education Association: $3,982,597.

- Thomas B. Fordham Institute: $1,961,116.

Bill Gates has spent a fortune on Common Core, a set of national standards for English and Math. There is no local control, the control is ceded to the federal government only, the local and state governments no longer have any say in the curriculum. The reason why the federal government is solely in charge of this pile of garbage is that they always do such a great job when they have no checks and balances.

The Bill & Melinda Gates Organization has invested their money directly into the development of Common Core material and promoting the initiative at the state level, and an estimated $80 billion in total funding related to the Common Core standards will be invested by the federal government.[134]

The tricky part about this program was that under Obama, the states were incentivized to sign on to the Common Core program by tying funding to the United States Department of Education's $4.35 billion "Race to the Top" fund.[135]

This pool of money was a competitive grant created to spur and reward innovation and reforms in state and local district K-12 education. Common Core was a part of this program, so in order to be eligible for this free money that the

---

[134] Joy Pullmann, The Federalist, "Estimate: Common Core To Cost California $10 Billion, Nation $80 Billion".
[135] Peg Luksik, Crisis Magazine, "The Federal Hand Behind Common Core".

Department of Education was handing out, the state had to agree to use the Common Core standards.

Here is the problem with this whole idea of tying money to agreeing to use Common Core: nobody knew what Common Core was actually going to be at the time they agreed to sign on to it. The curriculum was not complete, the standards were not set, and the states were forced to blindly agree to it without knowing what they were in for. If they wanted federal money, and let's face it, all schools need more money, they had no choice but to take on the mysterious Common Core and hope it was not a disaster on wheels.

It is, without question, a full-fledged disaster on wheels. There are currently 43 states and the District of Columbia that have adopted the Common Core standards.

The development of the program was created by the "Common Core Validation Committee", but from the beginning, there were problems with establishing and validating the program. This resulted in five of the 29 members of the Common Core Validation Committee refusing to sign a report attesting that the standards are research-based, rigorous, and internationally benchmarked. The validation report was released with 24 signatures and included no mention that five committee members refused to sign it.

Two former members, Dr. Sandra Stotsky & Dr. James Milgram, refused to endorse the final program and now travel the country giving lectures warning parents and teachers about the Common Core program.[136]

So what caused the only member of the Validation Committee with a doctorate in mathematics, Dr. Milgram from Stanford, to walk away? The fact that there were math questions that had multiple correct answers, and partial credit for incorrect answers, provided that the person showed their work for reaching the incorrect answer.

This is not a joke.

Not only were there incorrect answers that could be partially correct, but the correct answer would be marked wrong if the student did not show their work at reaching the correct answer.

If the question was "3 x 4 = ?" and the student answered "12" because they had

---

[136] Dr. Sandra Stotsky & Dr. James Milgram, "Why I Refused To Sign Off On Common Core Standards".

memorized their multiplication tables and did not need to work out the answer on paper, their answer was marked as incorrect.

Oh, but it gets much, much worse.

If the student was able to show their work at multiplying 3 x 4 but actually came up with 13 as the answer, they would receive partial credit even though the answer was clearly wrong.

Welcome to the future of America, where incorrect math answers hurt people's feelings so everybody gets a participation medal unless you memorized the correct answer, in which case you get nothing and like it.

This is an actual question from a 4th grade Common Core math assignment. Please read the question carefully and then answer it.

"Juanita wants to give bags of stickers to her friends. She wants to give the same number of stickers to each friend. She's not sure if she needs four bags or six bags of stickers. How many stickers could she buy so there are no stickers left over?"

Here is the answer: There is no correct answer to this question!

Common Core is such a mess that one has to wonder how so many smart people could come together to create a curriculum that is so horrible? It is almost as if they tried to make this program confusing on purpose.

Well, what if that really is the answer? What if Common Core was created to actually dumb down and demoralize the next generation of American children? With all the money Bill Gates spent on this disaster, he better hope he kept his receipt so he can get his money back.

The truth of the matter is that Bill Gates also owns the companies that create and sell the textbooks for Common Core, so he has covered himself in this questionable investment by monopolizing the "software" of this educational program that everyone is forced to buy if they want to use his educational system.

Where did he learn how to do that? Oh yes, Microsoft.

The Death of American Exceptionalism

There was a time when America was thought to be exceptional, but sadly, those days are gone.

Too many wars have been waged under false pretenses, too many lies have been told by those holding high office in the government, too many black men have been shot in the back while running away from the police, and too many tax dollars have been spent to build bombs that are later dropped on innocent civilians.

Like most fairy tales, the story of America is pure fantasy and requires the reader to suspend their disbelief in order to just go with it. When Disney released the movie *Fantasia*, it told the story of a Sorcerer's apprentice, played by Mickey Mouse, who borrowed his master's wizard hat and used his book of spells to help him complete his chores faster. His lack of experience came back to haunt him as the army of brooms, mops, and buckets quickly spiraled out of his control and almost destroyed the castle.

The point of the story is not to be a documentary on magic, a study about brooms, or about an overgrown mouse. The story is about what can happen when a person unlocks the power that they cannot control. It is an allegory that is meant to be studied to find the hidden meaning.

The story of American exceptionalism is an allegory as well. It is an idea or a concept, but it is not a real thing. It is a utopian society that Americans strive to live in and be a part of, but it is only as real as a cartoon army of marching brooms and buckets.

It was not one specific event that destroyed this illusion, but rather a lifetime of lies that have been told about America, and to Americans. The United States has always been portrayed as the good guy, and the citizens of that great land are the type of people that look out for those other countries that cannot look out for themselves. They are the defender of freedom, and they believe that everyone is entitled to the truth, justice, and the American way. America never wants war, but they always end up getting dragged into them in order to protect the innocent.

All of this is total bullshit, of course, and none of it is true.

Nowhere has the hypocrisy of American exceptionalism been more obvious than in the wars that it wages around the world against evil regimes and dangerous extremism.

America has been involved in at least one war for 96% of its existence, so the country is hardly getting dragged into these conflicts against their will. They wage wars against innocent people then base their reason for doing so on blatant lies in order to justify their illegal actions. Every war that the United States has been involved with are always sold to the public as a lie. Every single one of them.

The United States public and the world for that matter was told that the Japanese surprised the American naval forces at Pearl Harbor and caught the Navy totally off guard. That is not true, in fact, Roosevelt was aware of the impending attack and had the aircraft carriers moved behind the island instead of being sitting ducks in Honolulu. The boats that were destroyed were older and less valuable to the fleet, but Roosevelt knew that an attack would give him the justification he was looking for to jump into the war in the Pacific, which it did.

The American people were whipped into a frenzy to get involved in Europe to battle the Nazis. The nation entered the war to defend its allies like Britain and France, but the truth is that those countries had been begging America to enter that war for years with no success. America only entered for the last year of that six-year war, after the continent was softened up and the war was almost over.

The history books also failed to mention to the public that a condition for entering the war was that Britain had to give America all of their blueprints for their airplanes, tanks, trucks, bomb technology, and their code-breaking techniques before the United States would agree to come to their defense, but that is not ever mentioned as a reason for entry into the battle because that does not fit with the narrative of American Exceptionalism. America is supposed to come to the aid of its allies because it is the right thing to do, not because they get paid off.

Did America enter the Vietnam War to protect the South Vietnamese from being overrun by the Communists? No, they entered the war after being attacked in the Gulf of Tonkin, except it turned out through declassified documents that there never was an attack on an American ship.[137] It was a completely made-up event. It never happened, yet it was used as the justification to stick the American nose into someone else's business under false pretenses. From that point on, America was involved in a war that resulted in the death of over 50,000

---

[137] Jeff Cohen, Fair.org, "30-Year Anniversary: Tonkin Gulf Lie Launched Vietnam War".

American troops and two million dead Vietnamese and Laotian men, women, and children.

The first Gulf War was fought after Iraq rolled into Kuwait and took babies out of the incubator and left them to die on the cold hospital floor, except that it was discovered that Nayirah, the 15-year-old girl that was a witness to the event, turned out to be the daughter of the Kuwaiti Ambassador to the United States and was coached by Hill & Knowlton to lie to the Congressional Human Rights Caucus as justification for America to go to war.[138]

It was a lie. Just another lie to justify another war.

But there would be far more lies coming to justify future wars in the region, like when the blame for 9/11 was pinned on Afghanistan, even though the hijackers were allegedly Saudis. The story of 9/11 that was told to the American people was a lie from beginning to end, who did it, what happened, and why it happened. One big, fat, lie told to the world to justify the desire of those in the Bush Administration and members of the Project for a New American Century (PNAC) for imperial conquest.

Segments of the public, but certainly not the general public, learned of the list of seven countries that were slated for regime change over the next five years when General Wesley Clark, who was the Supreme Allied Commander of Europe of NATO from 1997-2000, exposed the existence of the letter that was sitting on the Secretary of Defense's desk during an interview with *Democracy Now*. He explained that the belief was that the United States had a "good military" that can "take down governments", so he described how the U.S. had "plans to take out seven countries in five years, starting with Iraq, and then Syria, Lebanon, Libya, Somalia, Sudan, and finishing off, Iran."

So much for not wanting war.

The people watched as the Bush administration, in conjunction with their accomplices in the media, laid a flimsy foundation that would be used to justify the invasion of Iraq, again. America pretended to have their arm twisted to get involved in yet another hornet's nest in the Middle East in order to save the lives of helpless Iraqis from their murderous dictator, by dropping bombs on them.

So what did the media do when concerned citizens spoke out against these illegal wars of aggression? Did they give those people a platform to express their

---

[138] The New York Times, January 15, 1992, "Deception On Capitol Hill".

concerns? Did they push for Congress to actually authorize the war, as they are required to do? Did they hold the Administration to provide proof of their claims of weapons of mass destruction?

No, the media did none of that. What they did was they got their torches and pitchforks and encouraged the American people to destroy anyone speaking out against the war, like Bill Maher, the Dixie Chicks, and Phil Donahue.

American exceptionalism? What is exceptional about any of this?

It has been said that people are now living in a "post-fact world", but really it has been that way for a very long time. The only difference between now and then is that these days people are starting to figure out the lies that they are being fed by the governments of the world, the media, and those in positions of power. It has always been a "post-fact world", it is just that no one ever noticed it.

"And if all others accepted the lie which the Party imposed, if all records told the same tale, then the lie passed into history and became truth.

'Who controls the past' ran the Party slogan, 'controls the future: who controls the present controls the past'." — George Orwell, 1984.

The lie that the Party has imposed is that they are exceptional, and by association, that makes their fellow citizens exceptional as well. It might be easy to criticize the government and remove the belief that they are exceptional, but by doing so, the people must also remove their own label as well. That is not something that most people want to admit, but if they are to get honest with their complicity in this crime, they must acknowledge their role in perpetuating this myth of greatness.

America has not been great in a very long time. In fact, these days, even America's Dad, television star Bill Cosby, turned out to be a serial rapist, so America cannot even get their fake families fixed.

The United States government and their partners in the corporate media, work hard to keep the people thinking that everything is fine, that nothing has changed, that they are still free and they live in a country built on doing the right thing even when it is difficult, that their country is the policeman of the world because nobody cares more about the vulnerable than America, and that the people of the world aspire to be just like them.

This is complete and utter nonsense.

The Flawed Myth of American Presidential Nobility

Several decades ago, when a President spoke to the Nation during the State of the Union address, every television channel would be showing the event. People would stop what they were doing and listen to the President address the people, to hear his words, to read his body language, and to feel a bit inspired.

Something has changed, and it is tough to pinpoint exactly when it happened, but people no longer stop their lives to listen to their Commander in Chief address them.

Maybe it was all of the ridiculous standing ovations and obvious ass-kissing that turned the people off?

Perhaps it was all the years of hypocrisy where the President lectured foreign leaders about their reckless behavior while simultaneously participating in the exact behavior that he was critical of? The whole "do as I say, not as I do" philosophy is a bit tired and ineffective when the American people have witnessed one President after another engage in questionable decision making and outright criminal activity. They have really become the last people in a position to lecture anyone else about bad behavior.

In 2016, President Obama had the audacity to criticize Russia's Vladimir Putin because he invades smaller countries, jails political opponents, controls his country's media, and has driven Russia's economy into recession.[139]

Of course, nobody would suggest that these are positive traits or in any way try to minimize a person's culpability if they engage in these activities, but a little bit of self-awareness is necessary before calling someone else out for this.

Especially if one happens to be guilty of the same exact behavior.

During Obama's eight years in office, he bombed Afghanistan and Iraq, just like the previous President, then added Somalia, Pakistan, Libya, Yemen, and Syria...all smaller countries.

---

[139] Pamela Engel, Business Insider, "Obama Spends Final Press Conference Of 2016 Warning Putin And Russia: 'We Can Do Stuff To You'".

So much for that Nobel Peace Prize that he presumably wore around his neck while ordering drone strikes on civilians, water treatment plants, and hospitals.

It is also pretty ridiculous to accuse Putin of jailing political opponents when Obama put more whistleblowers in prison during his term in office that all of the previous Presidents combined.[140]

This is called "projection", and it is when a person takes all of their faults and issues that they have, and they pretend that the person they are fighting has them instead. If they are cheating on their wife and drinking way too much, they confront their wife and accuse her of cheating on them and drinking too much.

This sort of tactic is infuriating to most people, but in political campaigns, one sees this strategy constantly because it is a favorite trick of sociopaths.

Wondering what to get former President Obama for his next birthday, how about a mirror?

America is still "exceptional" at some things, but most of them are not exactly the types of things one would want to put on their resume.

• Americans consume more prescription drugs than any other country, by a landslide.

• America is home to the fattest people in the world, just go to Walmart and it will become obvious.

• There are 65,000,000 Americans with criminal records.[141]

• America, for all of its preaching about family values and it is looking down on "shithole countries", has the most crime of any country in the world.

• The crime in the United States is not limited to just ordinary citizens because America has more people killed by the police than Venezuela, Somalia, or South Africa.

• The violence towards others is also not limited to adults as America has the highest rate of child abuse deaths than any other country, not to mention the highest pregnancy rate.

---

[140] Spencer Ackerman, The Guardian, "Obama's War On Whistleblowers Leaves Administration Insiders Unscathed".
[141] Law.com, "Employees With Criminal Record Deserve A Second Chance".

- Americans watch the most television, around 28 hours per week, which is not helping the fat problem mentioned earlier.

- Everybody knows that the United States has the most governmental debt of any country, but the people also have the most personal debt.

- American students have the highest student loan debt of any country, roughly $1.5 trillion, and thanks to lobbying by the lenders to the Congress, that debt cannot be forgiven through bankruptcy, and private student loan debt even passes to family members after death.

- America is only ranked 18th according to the World Happiness Report.

- The United States spends more money on defense than China, Russia, India, Saudi Arabia, France, the U.K., and Japan combined.

- America spends more money on airport security, over $110 billion on the Transportation Security Administration (TSA), even though they have a 95% failure rate and have never caught a terrorist.[142]

- Only 35% of Americans even have a valid passport, and on a yearly basis, 96.5% of the population never leaves the country.

- A survey conducted by the University of Pennsylvania's Annenberg Public Policy Center showed that 37% could not name any of the five rights protected by the First Amendment, and only 48% could name freedom of speech.

- According to the same survey, 18% said Muslims do not have all the same rights as other U.S. citizens, and 15% said atheists did not either.

- Four out of ten Americans did not know who the Vice-Presidential candidates were in the lead up to the 2016 debates, and a third were unable to name even one of the three branches of the U.S. government: legislative, executive, and judicial.

The United States Empire always held itself out as some shining beacon of freedom, democracy, and fairness, but it is none of those things. The sad truth is that America has been living on its reputation for a very long time, and the government has been using the corporate media to hide as many of their

---

[142] NBC News, "TSA Chief Out After Agents Fail 95% Of Airport Breach Tests".

transgressions as possible over the decades.

The population has been dumbed down through GMO foods, their education system, by Big Pharma, through fluoride, and from lead paint.

They have been ignored by their parents, their teachers, and their government.

And they have been stripped of all their rights, but it does not seem as if they have noticed...or care.

Rights, Not Privileges

The rights of individuals have been slowly removed by the government, and what that does is make the country a little bit less exceptional every time it happens. Over the years, the image and perception of America have taken a hit because the things that once made the country great have gone away once bills like the Patriot Act and the NDAA were passed under the lies of stopping terrorism and protecting the citizens. The world sees the problems, but Americans are still sadly stuck in the past and clinging to the myth that they are the freest country in the world and the defenders of liberty.

"The most profoundly revolutionary achievement of the United States of America was the subordination of society to moral law. The principle of man's individual rights represented the extension of morality into the social system — as a limitation on the power of the state, as man's protection against the brute force of the collective, as the subordination of might to right. The United States was the first moral society in history. All previous systems had regarded man as a sacrificial means to the ends of others, and society as an end in itself. The United States regarded man as an end in himself, and society as a means to the peaceful, orderly, voluntary co-existence of individuals. All previous systems had held that man's life belongs to society, that society can dispose of him in any way it pleases, and that any freedom he enjoys is his only by favor, by the permission of society, which may be revoked at any time. The United States held that man's life is his by right (which means: by moral principle and by his nature), that a right is the property of an individual, that society as such has no rights, and that the only moral purpose of a government is the protection of individual rights." - Ayn Rand, author.

The Bill of Rights was the first ten amendments to the United States Constitution, and it worked to add specific rights and guarantees of freedoms. It focused on the rights of citizens and imposed limitations on the government's authority through explicit declarations that all powers not specifically delegated to Congress by the Constitution were reserved for the people or the states.

Though the Constitution of the United States provided a balanced system of government and clearly defined the government's role and operation, it did not assert the individual rights of the citizens. The Bill of Rights, inspired by Thomas Jefferson and drafted by James Madison, did provide for these rights.

There are currently 27 Amendments to the Constitution.

- The 1st amendment covers the freedom of religion, press, and expression and specifically prohibits Congress from making any rulings to the contrary.

- The 2nd amendment preserves the right of the citizens to have weapons and form a militia.

- The 3rd amendment prohibits the government from forcing citizens to house soldiers in their homes.

- The 4th amendment protects citizens from unreasonable searches or seizures of their property.

- The 5th amendment ensures that the government cannot take property from citizens without compensation and establishes some of the conditions for a fair trial.

- The 6th ensures that citizens receive a trial before a jury.

- The 7th amendment ensures a speedy trial.

- The 8th amendment outlaws cruel and unusual punishment.

- The 9th amendment asserts that the Bill of Rights, itself, should not be interpreted as the only rights that U.S. citizens should enjoy.

- The 10th amendment gives any power that is not specifically attributed to the United States government in the Constitution to the individual states or to the citizens.

- The 11th amendment makes states immune from suits from out-of-state citizens and foreigners not living within the state borders; lays the foundation for sovereign immunity.

- The 12th amendment revises presidential election procedures by having the President and Vice President elected together as opposed to the Vice President being the runner-up.

- The 13th amendment abolishes slavery, and involuntary servitude, except as a punishment for a crime.

- The 14th amendment defines citizenship, contains the Privileges or Immunities Clause, the Due Process Clause, the Equal Protection Clause, and deals with post–Civil War issues.

- The 15th amendment prohibits the denial of the right to vote based on race, color or previous condition of servitude.

- The 16th amendment permits Congress to levy an income tax without apportioning it among the states or basing it on the United States Census.

- The 17th amendment establishes the direct election of United States Senators by popular vote.

- The 18th amendment prohibited the manufacturing or sale of alcohol within the United States. (*Repealed December 5, 1933, via 21st Amendment.*)

- The 19th amendment prohibits the denial of the right to vote based on sex.

- The 20th amendment changes the date on which the terms of the President and Vice President (January 20) and Senators and Representatives (January 3) end and begin.

- The 21st amendment repeals the 18th Amendment and makes it a federal offense to transport or import intoxicating liquors into US states and territories where such transport or importation is prohibited by the laws of those states and territories.

- The 22nd amendment limits the number of times that a person can be elected president: a person cannot be elected president more than twice, and a person who has served more than two years of a term to which someone else was elected cannot be elected more than once.

- The 23rd amendment grants the District of Columbia electors (the number of electors being equal to the least populous state) in the Electoral College.

- The 24th amendment prohibits the revocation of voting rights due to the non-payment of a poll tax or any other tax.

- The 25th amendment addresses succession to the Presidency and establishes procedures both for filling a vacancy in the office of the Vice President, as well as responding to Presidential disabilities.

- The 26th amendment prohibits the denial of the right of US citizens, eighteen years of age or older, to vote on account of age.

- The 27th amendment delays laws affecting Congressional salary from taking effect until after the next election of representatives.

How many of these laws have been broken by the government in the name of "spreading democracy" throughout the world, or because of their desire to keep its citizens safe from terrorists at home?

Since 1975, a total of 3,438 Americans have been killed by all terrorists, and that includes 9/11 in which over 3,000 of those people died.

Between the years of 2008-2015, the Cato Institute showed that the chances of dying from getting stung by a bee were 20,000% more likely than getting killed by a foreign-born terrorist, but there was no massive push to exterminate all bees, except by Monsanto.

Half a million Americans will die from the broken medical system over the next two years, so where is the massive overreach by the government to force doctors out of their hospitals, to confiscate medical equipment from the hospitals that continue to allow their patients to be extorted by the medical insurance agencies, to imprison the Oncologists that are pushing toxic products on their patients?

If the United States government was serious about cracking down on those trying to harm Americans, they would invade the Food & Drug Administration's office and arrest the senior executives for fraud, corruption, and assault.

Instead, they have kept up a fake reign of terror, printing trillions of dollars to feed the collusion of the Military Cabal, Big Pharma and Big Tech, and their ever-faithful propaganda pet, called Mainstream Media.

The Military-Information-Terror Complex

It should be clear to those with an understanding of American foreign policy that the War on Terror is based on a fake premise. Because America always needs an enemy, those in charge of foreign policy decisions made the call to manufacture the Islamic State to fill the role of the amorphous terrorist that is not tied to a particular country, but rather a general region, and has connections to one of the most popular religions on Earth, making this an enemy that could be just about anyone and located almost anywhere.

The funding of these "terrorists" actually comes through the United States, in conjunction with their partner countries in the Middle East, and it forces America to chase its tail in the global busy work of hunting for an enemy that they themselves created in order to justify moving trillions of dollars from one pot managed by the federal government to another pot managed by the Military-Information-Terror complex. Foreign policy decisions are made according to this paradigm, but it is important to understand that this is also the point of the War on Terror, to create a pretext for decision making that allows America to get a foothold in the Middle East in a way that justifies, and in some cases, begs for the involvement of the United States in areas of the world that they should really have no reason to be.

They have created a problem in order to motivate the public to demand something be done, then stepped in to offer their solution. The Hegelian dialectic of foreign policy is shrouded in deceit and operated from Langley, Virginia, and the District of Columbia. The "War on Terror" should be more accurately named the "War of Terror", on the people in many countries, conducted by the American government, and paid for by the U.S. taxpayers.

What these policies have done is replace the industrial economy that fueled America's growth in the 1940s through the 1970s, with a Permanent War economy that is only focused on creating jobs through things like the arms industry, defense contracts, engineering firms that rebuild after America bombs the hell out of foreign countries, the spy agencies, the tech surveillance boom, and affiliated business concerned with the never-ending wars around the world, coming as a result of the empire-building of the United States.

So who or what is the Military-Information-Terror complex?

The "Military" component of the group is composed of multinational offense contractors and other arms manufacturing companies.

Boeing	Halliburton	Rolls-Royce
Lockheed-Martin	Honeywell	Harris
Raytheon	Triple Canopy	Huntington Ingalls Ind.
General Dynamics	Aegis Defence Services	SAIC/Leidos
General Electric	Bechtel	Blackwater/XE/Academi
Northrop Grumman	Exxon	Textron
BAE Systems	Shell	Vinnell Corporation
TRW	Chevron/Texaco	AirScan
United Technologies	BP/Amoco	DynCorp
L-3 Communications	Dow Chemical	G4S
KBR	Airbus Group	SERCO

The "Information" component of the group is comprised of tech companies, corporate media outlets, chip makers, and private security firms.

Facebook/Instagram	CoreLogic	Viacom
Associated Press	Datalogix	CBS
Twitter	Exactis	PBS
Amazon	23 & Me	Reuters
Yahoo	TimeWarner	Black Cube
EMC	Comcast	Newsweek
Intel	News Corp.	Recorded Future
Apple	Sony	National Amusements
In-Q-Tel	CNN	CrisisCast
D-Wave	Disney	Palantir
Acxiom	MSNBC	Cybereason
Experian	Washington Post	Kroll & Associates
Epsilon	New York Times	

The "Terror" component is the governmental agencies tasked with actually stopping terrorism, as well as the private companies, Think Tanks, and NGOs that create the atmosphere and manufacture fake evidence to justify the War on Terror.

NSA	DARPA	Anti-Defamation League
Department of Defense	CFR	Institute Policy Studies
MI-5	Stratfor	Open Society
CIA	Carlyle Group	Stanford Research Inst.
Mossad	IAI	Hoover Institution
MI-6	Brookings Institution	Atlantic Council
FBI	Blackstone Group	World Economic Forum
NATO	Heritage Foundation	Council National Policy
GCHQ	Bohemian Club	Kissinger & Associates
KGB	United Nations	Interpol
Department of State	Cato Institute	Skull & Bones
DHS	Club of Rome	PNAC
TSA	Committee of 300	Amer. Enterprise Instit.
National Recon. Office	Trilateral Commission	U.S. Supreme Court
AIPAC	The Aspen Institute	Bilderberg
Booz Allen Hamilton	Tavistock Institute	Human Rights Watch
RAND Corporation	Department of Justice	ICTS

These are some of the companies that are responsible for terrorism around the world, but it is by no means a complete list. Not for preventing it, but for creating it.

Feeding the American War Machine

The Permanent War economy is not limited to just the United States. The Stockholm International Peace Research Institute reported that $1.68 trillion was spent by all countries on military defense in 2016. These companies have a vested interest in keeping America at war, any war, real or fabricated.

• Lockheed Martin: 2017 $44.4 billion (87% of their total revenue) came from the U.S. government or were contracted to other nations through the U.S. government.

• Boeing: 2017 $28.9 billion from the U.S. government, accounting for 79% of the company's "Defense, Space & Security" revenue.

- Northrop Grumman: $21.8 billion from the U.S. government, or roughly 85% of their revenue.

- Raytheon: 80% of its sales come from the U.S. government.

- General Dynamics: 61% of its revenue comes from the U.S. government.

Cost of the American War Machine

- The estimated interest payments on the debt used to finance these wars will add another $7.9 trillion to the total over the next 35 years.

- The Department of Defense claimed that they spent $1.5 trillion on wars since 2001.

- The actual amount spent on wars since 2001 was $5.6 trillion, an average of $23,000 per American taxpayer, or almost four times more than their earlier estimates.

- George W Bush's budget for the War on Terror was about $1.161 trillion while he was in office.

- Taxpayers spent more than $800 billion on the Iraq War alone.

- Obama's spending on Iraq and Afghanistan totaled another $807 billion.

- The first Trump-era Pentagon budget was $700 billion, and it was easily passed with bipartisan support.

The cost of the War on Terror in Iraq, according to the National Defense Budget Estimates for 2017:

FY 2001 – $31 billion	FY 2007 – $192.5 billion	FY 2013 – $49.6 billion
FY 2002 – $59.1 billion	FY 2008 – $235.6 billion	FY 2014 – $88.0 billion
FY 2003 – $111.9 billion	FY 2009 – $197.1 billion	FY 2015 – $67.0 billion
FY 2004 – $105.0 billion	FY 2010 – $181.0 billion	FY 2016 – $89.5 billion
FY 2005 – $102.3 billion	FY 2011 – $162.4 billion	FY 2017 – $80.3 billion
FY 2006 – $127.0 billion	FY 2012 – $119.6 billion	FY 2018 – $126.8 billion

The Scope of the American War Machine

Terrorism is a very serious thing, except that there is a disproportionate amount of money flowing towards defending against something that is so rare that a person is 17,600 times more likely to die from heart disease than from a terrorist attack, and heart disease is one of the biggest killers of American men.

These days a person is eight times more likely to be killed by the police than by a terrorist and is over a thousand times more likely to die from a car accident.

Considering how much money is spent each year to fund the Transportation Security Administration (TSA) one would think that the chance of getting killed by a terrorist plot involving an airplane was much higher, but it turns out that a person is 11,000 times more likely to die from a normal airplane accident.

The reality of the situation is that the real purpose of the "War on Terror" is not to protect the people from terrorists slitting their throats or blowing up an airplane they are flying on, but to use this fake issue to redraw the map of the Middle East and destroy countries that are geographically strategic for the American Empire and their allies in the region.

If protecting Americans from harm was the real objective then the military would bomb the Federal Reserve, Monsanto, and Congress. Instead, the money has flowed into financing wars that voters do not want, in countries that most Americans do not care about, for reasons that still do not make any sense.

- In 2017, American Special Operations Forces were deployed to 149 countries.

- In the Iraq War, 4,488 U.S. soldiers were killed and another 32,226 were wounded.

- The War in Iraq lasted longer than the Vietnam War.

- The Pentagon has at least 44,000 troops deployed that identify their location as "Unknown", according to a report by the Defense Manpower Data Center under the Office of the Secretary of Defense.

- There are a total of 76 countries involved with America's fake War on Terror.

- In 2017, there were 4,609 contractors in Iraq, with another 23,600 still in

Afghanistan.

Timeline of Afghanistan War Costs

The Afghanistan War is a military conflict that began in 2001 and has cost $1.07 trillion. This baseless war costs the United States $4 million per hour or roughly $96 million per day. Does anyone think that they could have found better things to spend the money on at home? There are homeless people in record numbers, but the politicians understand that the homeless do not vote, so in the immortal words of Judge Smails, "you'll get nothing and like it".

Those costs go towards three different areas:

• There is $773 billion in Overseas Contingency Operations funds directed to the Afghanistan War.

• There is an increase of $243 billion for the Department of Defense.

• An increase of $54.2 billion to the Department of Veteran Affairs budget.

FY 2001 - $37.3 billion	FY 2007 - $57.3 billion	FY 2013 - $53.3 billion
FY 2002 - $65.1 billion	FY 2008 - $87.7 billion	FY 2014 - $80.2 billion
FY 2003 - $56.7 billion	FY 2009 - $100 billion	FY 2015 - $60.9 billion
FY 2004 - $29.6 billion	FY 2010 - $112.7 billion	FY 2016 - $30.8 billion
FY 2005 - $47.4 billion	FY 2011 - $110.4 billion	FY 2017 - $5.7 billion
FY 2006 - $29.9 billion	FY 2012 - $105.1 billion	

Some may propose that spending is spending, and it all sort of flows through the system and works its way around to make up the economy of the United States, but some spending is better than others for spurring economic growth and generating a return on investments. The media has repeated the false claim that wartime spending is a huge driver of economic growth when the truth is that it really only benefits very specific industries while creating a drain on the majority of the economic growth.

Considering that some economists have determined that $1 billion in education spending will add $1.3 billion to the economy while creating 17,687 jobs, this does not sound like the best way to be spending all of that money.

Or, even better, not extorting the people who live in the US in the first place and allowing them to spend their own money on what they wish. What a crazy idea.

"Private Pyle, What is Your Major Malfunction?"

For an American male coming out of high school, sometimes college is not part of their life plan. Maybe that is for economic reasons, or perhaps there was not an emphasis on learning and their grades were not high enough to qualify them for anything other than community college.

Some of these kids are looking for any reason to escape their current situation, so joining the military becomes an attractive option. This is not to say that the only people that join the military are those without any other options or crappy home lives, but as long as one has a high school diploma and are physically capable, the military will take them because they are confident that they can mold them into the soldier they want them to be.

Why would anyone enlist in the American military these days?

Remember the way American soldiers were treated in their own country when they returned home from the Vietnam War? Angry Americans that opposed the war were spitting on them.

How were American troops treated by the United States government when they returned back from wars in Iraq and Afghanistan?

For many of them, their medical benefits were declined. For those veterans that were approved, many were put on a cocktail of psychotropic drugs. These drugs had side effects that included suicide, which might explain the rash of soldier suicides of troops coming home from combat.

With two wars in the Middle East running simultaneously, and a feeling of distrust from the general public towards the politicians that were creating these wars, the United States military was having a hard time filling their ranks with people that wanted to get shot at for some reason. The Pentagon made the decision to offer the highest enlistment bonuses that they had ever offered for soldiers to re-enlist, and then in many cases clawed back that money if the person was unable to be put back into the theaters of war.

Clearly, loyalty is a one-way street in the eyes of the United States military. The United States military has to spend $1 billion every year on advertising in order to convince kids to sign up and join the armed forces.[143] If joining was such a great idea then the budget would be zero and that money could be spent to feed the homeless or fix Flint's water problem.

That ain't happening.

The World's Police Force

Should the U.S., with its enormous military might, act as a global sheriff, policing the world's trouble spots?

Some Americans like to think of their country as the world's police force, and in some ways they are, but one has to be specific about the type of police force they are referring to. Are they talking about the dumpy officer that hangs out at the donut shop and helps stranded motorists fix their flat tires, or are they actually picturing the juiced-up egomaniac cop that was picked on in high school and is looking to settle some perceived score with those that have done him wrong or in any way challenge his authority?

Does it depend on what the goal is? Is this to try and intimidate foreign countries into doing what the United States wants them to do? Are they actually trying to help other countries clean up their problems? Is this just a cover story that allows America to stick its nose in other countries' business?

It does not require all that much introspection to realize that American foreign policy is a bit hypocritical. They build military bases in foreign countries, threaten neighboring countries with harm from these specific bases, then act legitimately surprised when both the host country and the neighboring country have a problem with this.

What if the roles were reversed? Would the United States submit to the laws of other countries on American soil? Of course not, the mere thought of it is preposterous, but the United States expects Iraqis in Iraq to obey the American interpretation of laws enforced by armed U.S. troops.

Over the years, the image of America has transformed from being the helpful public servant looking out for their community, into the cop that pulls someone over for no reason, slowly walks around their car, shining his flashlight inside to see if there is anything worth taking. It has become painfully obvious that the

---

[143] Foundation For Economic Education, "A Billion Dollars For Propaganda And No Oversight".

American government plays the role of the police officer for the rest of the world, but they decided to base their character on Harvey Keitel's role in *Bad Lieutenant* instead of on Andy Griffith from Mayberry.

The Very Thin Blue Line

It is not to say that all police officers are maniacs and psychopaths, but it is fair to mention that just because they have made the decision to devote their professional lives to enforcing the laws, they do not always follow them themselves.

Some laws are illogical, immoral, outdated, overbearing, contradictory, Orwellian, bizarre, un-Constitutional, or just plain stupid. Nobody follows all of the laws, and that isn't necessarily a bad thing.

These are not the laws that concern citizens with regard to the lawbreaking by those in positions to enforce the laws.

The Free Thought Project's 2016 study found that an average 21 police officers are arrested and charged with actual crimes each week, with many of the charges for sex crimes and sexual abuse, including, but not limited to, forcible rape, statutory rape, sodomy, and pedophilia-related crimes against children.[144]

A seven-year study that was reported on by the Washington Post showed that of the police officers charged with sexual crimes, four out of five of the officers that were charged were actually found guilty of their crimes. These crimes included 422 for forcible and statutory rape, 352 cases involving forcible fondling, and 94 sodomy cases.

According to the study, sexual misconduct is the second leading complaint filed against officers, with just under 1,000 police officers losing their jobs for committing sexual assaults like rape, child pornography, Peeping Tom behavior, having sex while on duty, sending texts or emails to underage victims, and the always popular cop fantasy of being forced to perform sex acts in order to avoid being arrested.

When one expands their perception of these crimes to include all of the countless crimes that go unreported due to intimidation, previous criminal background of the victim, the fear of not being believed, and the very real possibility of future

---

[144] Tess Owens, Vice News, "When Cops Commit Crimes".

retaliation, it is easy to understand that these figures do not nearly reflect the actual number of crimes being committed by those in positions of power.

The criminal behavior of those tasked to protect the public acts to erode the confidence of the people and chip away at the pillars of law and order that hold civil society up. People expect a portion of the public to be criminals and defective human beings, but they falsely assume that those that have made the decision to educate, train, and devote themselves to serving and protecting the public will actually hold up their end of the bargain. One dirty cop is far more damaging than 100 convicted criminals because of the psychological effect that it has on the public and the realization that just because a person is wearing a badge, it does not mean that they are the good guy.

The frustration of the citizens is compounded by the fact that their taxes fund these police organizations, and they feel as if their own tax dollars are being used to fund people that are actively working against their own best interests. This contributes to the hollowing out of America because the rule of law has been turned against the people, a sign that always seems to precede the end of an empire.

By the way, the police have no legal requirement to protect the public. They are actually there to protect the political class and its extortion racket called the IRS.

With asset forfeiture laws in the U.S. now, they are actually by far the biggest thieves by a large margin.

The Fear & Death Administration (FDA)

The freedom one has over their own body should never be given up, under any circumstance. If the government takes the right to make decisions about a citizen's body, that is the equivalent of handing their life over to the State. One cannot expect the State to have the same sense of urgency that others would have about maintaining their health.

The State is reckless and operates without much oversight, which is a very dangerous group to hand one's life over to, and history is littered with examples of the government treating their citizens as being essentially disposable.

Although the push for wars is one of the more dangerous aspects of the current news configuration, the mainstream media does not only shill for the Military-

Information-Terror complex, they whore themselves for Big Pharma like their financial lives depend on it, because they do.

Watching a 30-minute episode of the national nightly news is all the research one needs to do in order to fully understand how the media and Big Pharma work together. How many commercials were for prescription medicine manufactured by pharmaceutical companies? The number is usually around 50%.

Americans make an assumption that if they see a drug being advertised on television that it is safe, not just because the company that made the drug had to have it tested and approved by the Food and Drug Administration, but also because it is being advertised on national television, so, therefore, it must be safe or else it would not be marketed to everyone. It is an extremely dangerous assumption and one that is based on the presumption that there is an additional layer of protection created by the mainstream media vetting the products before allowing them to be sold during their commercial breaks.

There is no additional protective layer, and just because they made a commercial for a new medicine that does not mean it is safe. Hell, just listen to the long list of side effects that they have to disclose during the commercial.

Having FDA approval does not mean that the drug is safe or effective; it only means that the FDA has approved taking money from the company that is making this drug. The FDA would probably approve crack cocaine if they could somehow convince the CIA to give them a portion of their profits.

Americans also assume that advertising prescription drugs on television is normal, but only the United States and New Zealand allow these forms of medicine to be hawked to unsuspecting consumers through the hypnotic flicker of television programming.[145] It seems that the unintentional humor associated with the long list of side effects does not even prevent people from lining up to ask their doctor if some new drug that has not even been tested on prisoners is right for them.

The media in America has convinced the people that there is a pill to cure everything, and if it does not exist yet, just wait and it will be available shortly after they fast-track it through testing. There is a blind assumption that if a medicine is to the point of advertising on television, it must have been fully tested and certified as safe and effective, otherwise, the manufacturer would not spend the money to market it to the general public.

---

[145] Piers Fuller, Stuff, "Kiwi Doctors Lobby For Crackdown On Drug Ads".

History is filled with medicines that were later recalled or had class-action lawsuits against them because the product was killing people left, right, and center. These drugs slipped through FDA testing without being flagged as deadly, which makes people wonder what exactly the FDA is doing with all of the taxpayer money they siphon off each year.

Interesting Facts About the FDA

• On average, it takes about 12 years to get a drug from the research phase to the patient.

• In 1988, the FDA formalized its "fast track" designation.

• In 1992, the FDA rolled out the approval process to allow drugs to go ahead if they are intended to treat a serious illness.

• The majority of these drugs were trialed in 1,000 or fewer patients to get FDA approval.

• In 2009 there were 1,742 different drugs that were recalled.

• According to the Journal of the American Medical Association, between 2001-2010, one out of every three drugs that made it to market had a safety-related issue.

• Mental illness-related drugs that were fast-tracked through the approval process had a much higher number of safety events.

• Some drugs that were fast-tracked had a large number of adverse events that required additional warning labels.

• Many of the fast-tracked drugs are not first in class and are less innovative.

• In 2011, 10 million people suffered a serious injury due to medical error in America.[146]

• Out of those 10 million injuries, 2 million-4 million of these were caused by

---

[146] Ray Sipheard, CNBC, "The Third-Leading Cause Of Death In U.S. Most Doctors Don't Want You To Know About".

prescription drug use.[147]

• The Center for Disease Control is not required to disclose the number of deaths caused by the medical industry, but that does not mean that those figures are not available through other channels.

• The 3rd leading cause of death in the United States is the American medical system, with a total of 225,000 deaths per year.

• Every two years, more Americans die from their broken medical system than died in all of World War 2.

• The people that live in America in 2017 are 24.5 times more likely to die from a doctor than from a gun.

• Every year 106,000 Americans die as a result of FDA-approved medical drugs having an adverse effect.[148]

• In 2017, there were 80,000 deaths from infections contracted in American hospitals.

• Another 20,000 people died because of hospital errors, as well as another 7,000 deaths per year due to errors with hospital medication.

• In an average year, 12,000 more deaths were caused as a direct result of unnecessary surgeries.

Marketing Disease to Sell the Cure

GlaxoSmithKline hired the public relations firm Cohn & Wolfe to help them create a market for a drug they had, but no disease for it to cure. Over a two-year period they set about inventing a new phobia that they called "social anxiety disorder", a term was only referenced a total of 50 different times during the two prior years.

By pushing the fake concept of "social anxiety disorder" in every possible direction they could, the PR company ended up creating a billion references in

---

[147] Unity Behavioral Health, "Prescription Drugs Responsible For More Deaths Than Illicit Drugs".
[148] Daniela Perdomo, AlterNet, "100,000 Americans Die Each Year From Prescription Drugs, While Pharma Companies Get Rich".

the press, culminating with the advertising campaign in 1999 called "Imagine being allergic to people".[149]

Madison Avenue has jumped into the disease manufacturing business because there is a ton of money in it for them. For every dollar Big Pharma spends on direct-to-consumer marketing, such as magazine advertisements and television commercials, they collect $4.20 in revenue. This is a massive payoff for the Pharma company. The public relations firms create these products that sell themselves so they take a nice chunk of this money, and the television networks and magazine platforms are still in business in large part because of the advertising dollars they collect from hawking prescription medicine.

The biggest bang for their bucks comes through spending marketing dollars, not research and development dollars. As consumers and users of their products, it would be better for the public if they placed a larger focus on the science behind their medicine instead of the science of public relations, but once the MDs were replaced by the MBAs, the focus shifted away from the well-being of the patient to the bottom line.

Of the top 100 largest Big Pharma companies surveyed, 64 of them spent at least twice as much on marketing and public relations than they spent on research and development, with 27 companies spending ten times as much on the selling of their medicine than they spent on developing it.

The business of sickness is sickening.

If a person wants to control someone, there is no better way than to hold the key to their health in their hands. The desire for self-preservation trumps just about everything else, and when facing impending death, the potential risks are meaningless. One can even justify the side effects associated with a brand new medical treatment if death was the only other alternative.

If the disease or condition was not life-threatening, then the potential side effects play a much more important role in decision making. The calculation includes an understanding that the person will not actually die from the particular disease, so how much permanent discomfort are they willing to take on in exchange for immediate relief from the non-life-threatening situation.

The medical industry in the United States, and Big Pharma, in particular, have gone about marketing their medicine in a very clever, but evil way over the past

---

[149] Karen Schwartz, AdWeek, "Marketing Disease To 'Sell' The Cure".

two decades. Instead of identifying a disease, then figuring out how to cure it through their new medicine, they have been inventing new diseases that do not actually exist and claiming that their medicine cures it.

Whoever heard of "restless legs syndrome" until a couple of years ago? What about "dry eye disease", how many poor people are suffering from that horrible "disease"? However, will humanity survive without the cures for a bouncing leg and a dry eye?

The drug companies then go about selling cures for these diseases with a straight face, not understanding that it is diminishing their credibility with the general public to cure any of the real diseases that their other products are supposed to cure. It is obvious that they are lying about curing Restless Legs syndrome with their medicine, so is it not reasonable to assume that they might be lying about their other medicines curing real diseases such as Hepatitis or High Blood Pressure?

The Polio Myth

At Tulane University, Dr. Alton Ochsner was so convinced that his new polio vaccine was effective that he inoculated his two grandchildren in front of his class of students. From there they pushed forward with the mass inoculation of the children in the general public.

Within a couple of days, children all over the country fell sick from polio, some were crippled, and some even died from his new vaccine. As for Dr. Ochsner's grandkids, well his grandson died from the vaccine, and his granddaughter contracted polio but survived.[150] As you can imagine, an enormous lawsuit was filed.

Most people have never heard about this, but it happened.

Another sneaky thing that Big Pharma is guilty of doing is claiming that a disease has been eradicated because of their vaccine when in actuality, they simply changed the name of the disease to something else, or they changed the diagnosis criteria. This greatly contributed to the decline of documented cases of polio following the introduction of the vaccine, and that has always been the one disease that the big pharmaceutical companies have touted as their greatest accomplishment.

---

[150] The New York Times, May 5, 1955, "Bulbar Polio Kills Doctor's Grandson".

What happened when the definition of polio was changed was that many thousands of cases were no longer counted as polio, which in turn gave the impression that the polio vaccine was working.

It was not.

Once the vaccine was introduced to the population they started to split the cases into either polio or polio-like. They then no longer counted polio-like cases as being polio, which obviously created a drop in polio that was happening at the same time as the vaccine being released, thus giving the impression that the vaccine was responsible for the drop in cases when it was really just a reclassification issue.

The polio-like illnesses were not eradicated, in fact, they are still infecting people at the rate they were before the vaccine was released, except because they go by names like transverse myelitis and Guillain-Barre syndrome, both of which cause polio-like paralysis, and ironically, are known adverse reactions to vaccination.

Recently, Dr. Orenstein, a former Associate Director at the CDC, instructed clinics to remove all of the old trivalent vaccines right away and replace them with a new oral one because they were causing polio in children all over the world. Smallpox was changed to monkeypox, then the rate for smallpox went down. Of course, monkeypox, which did not exist before, skyrocketed to levels only seen by smallpox, because it was smallpox, it was just using a brand new name that no one was looking for.[151]

If you cannot beat 'em, just change the name. This is the level of criminality that one encounters when dealing with the medical industry in the United States.

The Law of Unintended Consequences

America has the cure for cancer...well at least they think they do.

Probably the most feared medical condition a person can come down with is cancer, in large part because of the reputation that it has for killing people of all ages, sometimes rather quickly, but always painfully.

---

[151] Nicholette Zeliadt, Scientific American, "Pox Swap: 30 Years After The End Of Smallpox, Monkeypox Cases Are On The Rise".

There are all sorts of types of cancers, and they come in a variety of forms. Some types grow quickly, some give hints before they are discovered, some come out of seemingly nowhere, some are curable and others kill people 100% of the time.

- 1 in 20 - Chances of getting some form of cancer in the early-1900s.

- 1 in 16 - Chances of getting some form of cancer in the mid-1900s.

- 1 in 10 - Chances of getting some form of cancer in the late-1900s.

- 1 in 3 - Chances of getting some form of cancer in 2019.[152]

If a person is diagnosed with cancer, the first treatment option that comes to mind is usually chemotherapy. Most people really do not know exactly what chemotherapy actually is, but they think that it will kill their cancer, make them feel like hell, and probably cause all of their hair to fall out. A decent trade-off for anyone diagnosed.

Chemotherapy is like dropping an atomic bomb on a hostage situation. Sure, the bad guy is now dead, but so is everyone in the city and now the place is a toxic waste site.

What people do not realize about chemotherapy is how ineffective it actually is, how unbelievably expensive the treatment is, that doctors are massively incentivized to recommend it to their patients, and how it works like fertilizer on cancer. It is hardly the cure for cancer that it is made out to be.

People assume that medicine is good for them and that the reason why one would be taking the specific medicine is that it will help them to heal in their struggle against the disease.

But what if the medicine was the problem?

Would a person's decision to take the medicine change if they knew that the doctors stood to make a ton of money from one type of medicine, and almost nothing from another type of medicine? Should the potential for a conflict of interest concern the patient?

---

[152] Honor Whiteman, Medical News Today, "1 In 2 People Will Develop Cancer In Their Lifetime".

Consider the accounting behind the medicine:

- $10,000 - Wholesale price a doctor pays for chemotherapy drugs (per shot).

- $50,000 - Retail price a doctor sells the chemotherapy drugs to their patients (per shot).

- $40,000 - Estimated profit for the doctor (per shot).

To be clear, nobody is suggesting that doctors that treat cancer should do so for free, or even at a discounted rate. There is a business that is being run in conjunction with treating these cancers, and the better a doctor is at removing cancer from people, the more in demand their services will be. The higher the demand, the higher the price.

The grey area comes when there is more than one possible option for a patient that has cancer, and one of those options makes the doctors a ton of money, while the other option generates almost no revenue for the doctor.

The chemotherapy option costs a small fortune, is almost completely ineffective, and demolishes the immune system of the patient, making infections and other diseases more likely.

The holistic approach to healing and the use of CBD Oil will put almost no money into the pockets of the doctors, but it will allow the patient to retain their immune system in order to fight back against cancer. The traditional medical community frowns on this as a form of pseudo-science since it is not blessed by the medical establishment, the Food & Drug Administration, the Centers for Disease Control, and law enforcement.

Chemo by the Numbers

- 75% - The percentage of American cancer patients that used chemotherapy, but also the percentage of Oncologists who said if they had cancer they would not participate in chemotherapy trials due to its "ineffectiveness and its unacceptable toxicity".[153]

- 16.3 million - Since 2000, the number of cancer patients that have died from chemotherapy.

---

[153] John Robbins, *Reclaiming Our Health: Exploding The Medical Myth And Embracing The Source Of True Healing.*

- 1,665,540 - New cancer cases diagnosed each year.

- 585,720 - Cancer deaths in the United States.

- $125 billion - Projected medical costs of cancer care, according to the National Cancer Institute.

- 39% - Projected medical cost increase by 2020.

- 2.3% & 2.1% - Chemotherapy success rates in Australia and the United States.[154]

- 90% - Percentage of chemotherapy patients that die 10-15 years after treatment, though their deaths are never attributed to the chemotherapy.[155]

- 1,400% - Percentage increase of chemotherapy users to develop Leukemia.

- 68% - Percentage increase in chemotherapy drugs since 2003.

The Centers for Disease Control and the Food and Drug Administration has a long history of turning a blind eye to defective and deadly drugs and letting the drug makers skate off with minor fines and little to no punishment. In some cases, it took 55 years of complaining about a dangerous drug, like Darvon, before the FDA actually stepped in to stop the company from selling a drug that had killed over two thousand people.

One reason for this is the revolving door between high government regulatory positions and positions within pharmaceutical companies, and nowhere was this more obvious than when the former director of the Centers for Disease Control and Prevention, Dr. Julie Gerberding, was named the president of Merck's vaccine division.

Gerberding's main job while running the CDC was the promotion of vaccinations while simultaneously downplaying the adverse reactions. She was in charge of the CDC when whistleblower Dr. William Thompson and a few of his CDC colleagues destroyed their evidence regarding the Merck MMR vaccine and the connection to autism. Gerberding was aware of that evidence and allowed it to be destroyed so as not to tie the Merck vaccines to causing autism, an action

---

[154] Dena Schmidt, Natural Health 365, "5-Year Cancer Survival Rate For Chemotherapy 2.1%".
[155] John Robbins, *Reclaiming Our Health: Exploding The Medical Myth And Embracing The Source Of True Healing*.

that should have led to prison time instead of a multi-million dollar job.

You scratch our back and we will scratch yours.

People can accept a person taking a better job with a competing firm, or making a change that financially benefits them through another line of work, but the conflict of interest that is created when those creating the policies that are put in place to protect people, in general, and children, in particular, are enticed to leave the job guarding the henhouse and go to work for the fox makes people wonder when the offer was actually first made? Was a job offered many years ago as a condition of destroying the evidence by Gerberding, or was Merck simply rewarding her for her loyal support over the years?

Perhaps neither were the case, but it creates the possibility that there could have been a conflict of interest. It goes without saying that Merck certainly was able to pay her substantially more money and stock options than the CDC could, so maybe everyone working at the CDC does not even need to have a conversation with the Human Resources Director at Merck to understand what happens when they play ball.

The people that are put in charge of these regulatory government agencies, like the CDC and the FDA, accept a huge responsibility when they agree to the position. Unlike the jobs that most people hold, these jobs are actually a matter of life and death, so there is no room for even the appearance of a conflict of interest, let alone an actual one.

- 4.45 billion - The number of prescriptions filled in 2016, just in the United States.[156]

- 32 billion - The number of prescriptions filled between 2009 and 2016.

- $25 billion - Big Pharma's revenues from mass inoculations like vaccines and flu shots.[157]

- $329.2 billion - The amount Americans spend on prescription drugs every year.[158]

- $17.5 billion - Johnson & Johnson's yearly sales and marketing budget.

---

[156] Statista, "Total Number Of Medical Prescriptions Dispensed In The United States From 2009-2016".
[157] Bourre Lam, The Atlantic, "Vaccines Are Profitable, So What?".
[158] Mark Koba, CNBC, "Deadly Epidemic: Prescription Drug Overdoses".

- $8.2 billion - Johnson & Johnson's yearly research and development budget.

- $3 billion - The advertising budget for marketing prescription drugs directly to consumers per year.[159]

- $24 billion - The advertising budget for marketing prescription drugs directly to doctors per year.[160]

When a major pharmaceutical embarks on trying to bring a new medicine to market, the costs associated with doing so are enormous, the time frame is long, and they face several regulatory hurdles along the way. When a company has invested so much money into a drug, and they have moved it through the regulatory process to the finish line, the idea of one person at the FDA or CDC torpedoing the deal surely gives the CEO of the drug company night sweats and panic attacks.

From a business standpoint, it would probably be a smart idea to make sure that the person at the regulatory agency with the final decision-making ability has been incentivized to not stop the product from crossing the finish line, regardless of the risks that the product may carry.

It is not so much that these medications are ineffective, but that many of them are actually deadly. History is littered with class-action lawsuits brought by victims against the manufactures of these defective drugs.

Fen-Phen

Fen-Phen was a well-known weight loss drug until it was pulled from stores in 1997 after a 24-year run that impacted 6,500,000 people. Many consumers experienced heart disease, with 50,000 different people filing lawsuits against the maker, Wyeth, making it one of the most expensive product safety recalls of all time, an estimate of $21 billion in settlements and legal fees.[161]

Baycol

---

[159] Ana Swanson, The Washington Post, "Big Pharmaceutical Companies Are Spending Far More On Marketing Than Research".
[160] Ana Swanson, The Washington Post, "Big Pharmaceutical Companies Are Spending Far More On Marketing Than Research".
[161] Justinian Lane, Dangerous Drugs, "$21 Billion Set Aside For Fen-Phen Lawsuit Settlement".

In only four years, Baycol was responsible for 100,000 deaths of patients trying to cure their high cholesterol. Bayer paid out $1.2 billion after it was determined that the drug caused a dangerous disorder called Rhabdomyolysis that destroys kidneys.[162]

Vioxx

Vioxx was the largest drug recall in history after being prescribed to more than 20 million people as a pain reliever for arthritis. The drug was responsible for an increased risk of heart attack and stroke, with as many as 140,000 Americans suffering from heart disease as a result of taking the drug that was manufactured by Merck.

Both Merck and the FDA were slammed for ignoring the evidence of the dangers of Vioxx before they finally recalled the product in 2004, after five years on the market. Merck settled Vioxx litigation in the US for $4.8 billion, with another $1 billion in legal expenses.[163]

Bextra

Bextra was a non-steroidal anti-inflammatory drug, made by Pfizer and prescribed to treat arthritis and pain from other inflammatory disorders. It was taken to market in 2005 but removed within a year for many of the same reasons that Vioxx was removed.

Bextra still resulted in $1.8 billion in legal awards against Pfizer and was one of the largest criminal fines ever imposed in the US. The Pharmacia & Upjohn Company was fined $1.195 billion, after admitting to criminal wrongdoing with "intent to defraud or mislead" in relation to the promotion of the drug.[164]

Accutane

Accutane was finally recalled after 27 years on the market for causing an increased risk of birth defects, miscarriages, and premature births when used by

---

[162] Melody Peterson, The New York Times, "Papers Indicate That Bayer Knew Of Dangers Of Its Cholesterol Drug".
[163] Alex Berenson, The New York Times, "Merck Agrees To Settle Vioxx Suits For $4.85 Billion".
[164] 24/7 Wall Street, "The Ten Worst Drug Recalls In The History Of The FDA".

pregnant women, as well as being linked to both inflammatory bowel disease and suicidal tendencies.

Over 7,000 lawsuits were filed against the manufacturer over the side effects including multimillion-dollar verdicts.[165]

Darvon

It took more than half a century, but eventually, Darvon was pulled from the market, but not before killing 2,110 people from 1981 to 1999. The medicine was eventually recalled due to toxicity to the heart, even though the FDA was petitioned multiple times to remove the drug, which they did not do until 2006.[166]

Dangerous or questionable drugs make it through the regulatory process and onto the market all the time, with some ending badly for both, the patients, and the drug companies. One must consider the possibility that someone at the top of the regulatory agencies decided to look the other way.

It hurts when one discovers that the people that they trusted do not give a damn about them. It really is a difficult pill to swallow, no pun intended. If people hope to evolve as a civil society, they do themselves a disservice to deny the existence and evidence of humanity's evil past. It needs to be acknowledged because people must know how bad things can get when they live their lives in constant denial. They cannot pretend that people like this do not exist because they count on everyone's ignorance to give them cover to put their horrible plans into action.

Do No Harm...To Their Stock Price

At first mention, it might sound outrageous to think that there is an active and ongoing push to destroy the good health of Americans. Sure, there is quite a bit of unhealthy food being sold today, and the people that purchase that food do so at their own risk. Many Americans consume too much alcohol and do not get enough exercise.

That is not what this is about.

There is a covert push of dangerous drugs, chemicals, and other substances in

---

[165] Shari Roan, Los Angeles Times, "New Study May Deal Final Blow To Acne Drug Accutane".
[166] Consumer Reports, "Darvon, Darvocet Pulled From Market Due To Potentially Fatal Heart Problems".

order to intentionally destroy the health of people in America, as well as in other parts of the world.

The reason for the push of toxic substances is that healthy people do not visit the doctor enough, whereas sick people do. Also, the sickness of a person in one aspect of their health can work to break down the areas of their health in which they have always felt fine. If one does not take care of the engine in their car, eventually the belts and fans start to fall apart from being asked to overcompensate for the weaker areas. The body is no different in that it can only overcompensate for a weaker area for so long before it too becomes broken down.

It may sound like a conspiracy theory that the medical industry was actively working against the best interest of their patients, but how then does one account for some incredibly toxic and deadly substances being pushed on patients dressed up as cures for illnesses?

In America, the government loves the people so much that they even add fluoride to the water, for free, so that everyone's teeth will be stronger and whiter. That is so nice of them to add a neurotoxin to the water supply, and Americans do not even have to tell them that they want it.

The public perception of fluoride is that it is added to toothpaste in order to increase the strength of teeth and keep them whiter.

The actual truth about fluoride is that the Nazis added it to the drinking water in their work camps because it is a neurotoxin that makes people more docile and easier to manage.

A report from the world's oldest and most prestigious medical journal, The Lancet, has officially classified fluoride as a neurotoxin and put it in the same category as arsenic, lead, and mercury. The cumulative effects of fluoride can cause ADHD, liver damage, brain damage & sterility, and sodium fluoride is the main ingredient in Sarin nerve gas too.

Some people realize that fluoride is a neurotoxin that lowers IQ, so they buy toothpaste for their family that is fluoride-free, while others still blindly accept the ridiculous lie that the American government adds it to the water supply to help people's teeth.[167] For those that believe that this must be some big misunderstanding, it is important to know that the Food and Drug Administration

---

[167] Naturimedica, "Fluoride: Harvard Study Confirms Fluoride Reduces IQ In Children".

(FDA) requires the companies that make toothpaste with fluoride to put a warning label instructing those that accidentally swallow their product to call the poison control hotline or head to the hospital.

The drinking water in America is not naturally loaded with fluoride, it must be added to the water intentionally. If it is classified as a neurotoxin, then it is added to the water supply, it is hard to explain this as being anything other than an intentional poisoning of the people. Most of the people do not have a clue that it is destroying their health and contributing to lower IQ rates, but someone at the decision-making level certainly does, which should make them an accomplice to the intentional poisoning of the majority of Americans.

To be more accurate, a substance named hydrofluorosilicic acid, which is a waste product from the aluminum industry is added to the water supply and it is extremely harmful. The traditional version known as fluoride is listed in Toxicity Class II, considered to be moderately toxic and required to be labeled "harmful or fatal if inhaled" and "harmful or fatal if swallowed", and it is estimated to be fatal at a dose between 5 - 30 grams.[168]

It does not have to kill a person in order to have a lasting impact. There are 53 studies connecting the dots between the ingestion of fluoride and a reduction in intelligence, as well as a study conducted by Harvard that showed the overall cognitive function of kids was cratering for those with higher exposure to fluoride. Some studies pegged the actual I.Q. drop at seven points, so this is not a trivial amount of cerebral horsepower.

From one natural liquid to the most unnatural liquid, the case for the legitimate creation of diet sodas might be even harder to justify than the addition of fluoride to the water supply.

A different type of poison almost did not make it into the world of artificial sweeteners, but after multiple rejections by the FDA, and the eventual recruitment of everyone's favorite villain, Donald Rumsfeld, to grease the bureaucratic wheels, aspartame finally made it through the approval process, but not before giving 50% of the mice it was tested on cancerous tumors.[169]

Some of the side effects of aspartame are seizures, multiple sclerosis (MS), headaches, dizziness, vision problems, depression, numbness, vertigo, severe

---

[168] Arjun Walia, Collective Evolution, "97 Percent Of Europe Doesn't Put Hydrofluorosilicic Acid In Their Water - Why Do We?".
[169] Dr. Joseph Mercola, "Aspartame: This Artificial Sweetener Produces Cancer In Rats".

PMS, hyperactivity in children, chronic fatigue syndrome, fibromyalgia, birth defects that may include mental retardation, epileptic seizures, insomnia, nausea, painful rashes, and in certain cases even memory loss.

But at least people won't be fat.

Corporate Media: Paid-for Perception

The American corporate media is one of the most dangerous institutions on the planet because they set the narrative for the people of the United States on behalf of the government. In the latter part of the 20th century, the mainstream, corporate media has operated as the public relations arm of the White House and Congress to sell the "plan" to the American people. Because of the powerful role that the United States plays on the global stage, this has worked to push their plan beyond the American borders and into the world as a whole, although not with the all-encompassing effect that it has within the United States.

The way that information is collected now by the media organizations is almost unrecognizable to what it once was in the mid-1900s. The emphasis on accuracy has been jettisoned in favor of speed, and the focus on telling important stories that matter to the people has been shelved in order to suppress uncomfortable stories that paint powerful people in a negative light.

One very noticeable problem is that even though the number of networks and channels has grown, the number of owners of all of these platforms has gone the other direction. The ownership of the media companies has been consolidated into the hands of several multinational conglomerates, which has dire consequences that are being felt, not just in the United States, but throughout the entire world.

Organized Mainstream Control

This control of information works in the form of pushing out a specific message through all media outlets at the same time to give it a sense of importance. After all, if every news channel is talking about the same thing, it must be important, right?

It also works through the systematic suppression of other news stories, just like the coordinated pushing of a story, only in reverse. By ignoring an event, it gives the impression that it must not be that important if none of the news organizations are talking about it. This is the control of information through omission.

The coordinated discussion or silencing of a particular event works extremely well with the older generation that has spent decades looking to the media to tell them what is really happening in the world. If they do not see it on the Nightly News then, to them, it probably did not happen, otherwise, they would have heard about it. For those viewers that have a limited amount of time to get their news, a 30-minute news broadcast is going to be the extent of their digging into current events.

The viewer will pick their favorite news presenter and stay relatively loyal to them, in part because they have learned to rely on their expertise to walk them through the important topics that they need to know about what happened in the world today. Those that sell it well are rewarded with massive paydays, thus making walking away due to a bad case of guilt or conscience almost nonexistent. They can walk away from that multi-million dollar salary if they want to, but there are an endless number of other people willing to sell their soul and read a teleprompter five nights a week.

War is glorified by lobotomized news anchors like NBC's compulsive liar, Brian Williams, who gets a hard-on every time the United States launches a cruise missile strike, while simultaneously comparing the "beauty" of our weaponry to a Leonard Cohen song.

There is nothing beautiful about war, and Brian Williams would know this if his helicopter ever really did get hit by an RPG, and not just the ones he imagines in his big, well-coiffed, empty head.

This is what George Orwell warned the people about, that the meaning of words would become inverted and taken hostage by those that control the media. The words "beautiful" and "weapons" do not belong in the same sentence in a society that is healthy and evolved.

The filter of conscience has been removed from those in control of our corporate media and people are suffering the effects of a society that looks to the nightly news to tell them how to think about the world, then wonders why they feel so empty.

Those in control of the media have been caught lying so many times that they simply cannot be trusted to tell the truth about anything, let alone a serious topic like the reasons for going to war. They are puppets, and the people in control of these media puppets are the same people that financed the campaigns of the political puppets to get them into office or pay them a couple of million dollars a year to read the news off a teleprompter.

Deceptive Mind Control

However, there was another reason why negative stories are on our nightly news, but they will not hear the news anchors talk too much about this. There are a couple of agendas that the government of the United States pushed on the general public, and the nightly news has been a great vehicle to deliver those messages.

The American Empire has the financial and military capacity to take on unpopular tasks around the world without owing the people an explanation about why they are doing what they are doing, but things go much easier if they can get the population on board with their decisions first. This is where the corporate media comes in because they play a fundamental role in explaining the reasons why the United States and their minions must invade a country like Iraq.

Rather than jam a war down the public's throats, the Military-Information-Terror complex uses their seemingly endless pool of money and influence to slowly, but consistently, bang the drum for war through their partners in the media. They do this by stocking the news organizations with retired generals playing the role of "Military Analysts" that just so happen to also sit on the Board of Directors for some of these large weapons manufacturers. They speculate about the different ways of removing a certain dictator from power, clearing a batch of "terrorists" from a particular region, or imposing a "No Fly Zone" on a country that is not doing what the United States has instructed them to do. The media then leverages the implied trust that this former General has with the viewing audience to create a list of potential options that must be considered, then the permanent puppets that man the anchor desks close the doors to the echo chamber and pound away at these very limited options until the insanity starts to wear off and the concept of invading a country that has done nothing to the United States starts to seem like not only a reasonable option but a priority that needs to be put into action immediately.

This is how you manufacture a war for the American people: First, propose a far-fetched military idea, talk about it constantly all day and all night for eight months straight, and then wait for the American people to demand it.

News "Made in China"

This is why the American corporate media is so dangerous. They have the ability to start hot wars through a simple formula of concocting lies, manipulating the way the viewers felt about those lies, followed by constant repetition.
But they call the Alternative Media "fake news"?

The Nightly News is so fake that it says "Made in China" on the label and falls apart the first time someone tries to actually put it on and wear it.

Their hysterical overreaction when President Trump flipped the script and slapped the "fake news" label on CNN showed their insecurity about being exposed as an entertainment channel and not an actual news organization. The reaction of the mainstream media proves that the "fake news" is not actually fake because they are so obviously threatened by it, otherwise, they would simply ignore it.

It struck a nerve because in their hearts they know it is true. The news anchors reading the news know it. The executives at the top know it. A large and growing segment of the viewers know it, and pretty soon the entire world will know it too.

Did NBC run a special broadcast to refute Elvis being spotted at a Chick-Fil-A, or eating Ding Dongs at a Winn Dixie store? No, why not? That is fake news, right? So where is the massive overreaction from the mainstream media?

They had fake news right in front of their faces when President Obama pretended to drink a glass of Flint, Michigan water during a campaign, but they failed to recognize such an obvious stunt, in part because they liked the guy.[170]

The discovery of the actual fake news being pushed by the major news organizations sent some people into a frenzy of retaliation against these big corporations, but they did not turn out as well as some had hoped.

Filmmaker and Author William Brandon Shanley decided to pursue multiple lawsuits against the corporate media seeking a modest settlement of $1 trillion. The media were not big fans, as one can imagine, but it should not be a surprise

---

[170] Brian Manzullo, Detroit Free Press, "Michael Moore Calls Barack Obama Drinking Flint Water 'Disappointing'".

to hear that William Shanley wound up getting arrested on what he called "trumped-up" phony charges to silence him.

Shanley is now out of jail and has picked right up where he left off with his lawsuits. It should go without saying that he is risking his life by doing this, so it will not be a surprise if it is later discovered that William Shanley decided to kill himself by tying a red ribbon around his neck and hanging himself from a doorknob.

Control Alt Delete

The delivery method of mainstream media news stayed relatively constant for about 50 years. Newspapers carried the torch for decades, as people waited until the paperboy delivered yesterday's news today. News magazines like *Time* and *Newsweek* delivered last week's news this week. Because the information actually needed to be printed on paper and physically distributed to each person, the process was inherently time-consuming and created a lag between what was happening, and when the consumer found out about it.

The television news industry gave the public the anchorman, a trusted source of reliable information that would be the viewer's connection to the news of the nation five nights a week. These experienced journalists had been out in the field for years sharpening their skills by digging into important stories and weeding through fluff and lies to get to the truth. When they presented the nightly news, they did so with the confidence that only comes from being a seasoned journalist at the top of their game. The viewers bonded with these anchormen and decided which nightly news broadcast to watch based, in part, on which anchorman they liked the most. There was less loyalty to a specific network as there was loyalty to a particular news presenter, and people came to feel like they actually knew these people, though the vast majority have never even seen them in person, let alone actually knowing them.

Each night viewers would invest 30 minutes of their time to get a handle on the day's most important events so that tomorrow they can go about their day with a basic understanding of what is happening in America. There was so much happening that cutting the most important topics down to only 30 minutes was quite difficult, but the printed newspapers were able to fill in the gaps left by television's tight schedule.

The first disruptor of the media came in 1980 when a little company in Atlanta challenged New York and Washington D.C. as the epicenter of newsgathering. When CNN launched their 24-hour news platform on cable television, they were not limited to only 30 minutes, and they were not restricted to showing their news at only one set time because they had 1,440 minutes to go into more depth about some of the most important topics of the day. They discovered that they had the opposite problem with the traditional nightly news: they had too much time.

As other networks jumped into the cable television news industry, they all found themselves having the same problem of filling the hours each day with interesting and thought-provoking topics for discussion. They were also stepping on each others' toes as they all rushed to cover the same events, in the same manner, using the same tactics of interviewing witnesses to important events, speculating about the events back in the newsroom with multiple journalists on-camera sitting at the large anchor desk, then echoing the same thoughts over and over until the story fell out of the news cycle and was forgotten.

As large companies started to purchase these news organizations, the content became more homogenized, the sets started to resemble each other, the presentation of the news seemed indistinguishable from one another, and eventually, there was almost no differentiation between the "news" on CNN or MSNBC. These channels no longer were listed on television guides as "news channels" because they had been reclassified as "entertainment". It was becoming obvious that they were no longer in the news business. These networks were only really interested in selling advertising space for their shows, whether those shows were professional wrestling, The Kardashians, or the Nightly News with Brian Williams, all scripted entertainment starring semi-real characters for the dumbed-down masses, just in a different package.

Then the internet came along and turned the journalism industry, among others, on its head.

Now the news could bypass the printing and distribution steps and go straight to the reader in real-time. No longer were people tied to the network's schedule of airing the news at only 6 pm, and they did not even have to be in front of a television to watch CNN's 24/7 news broadcasts. People now had instant access to a broad selection of different news organizations, both domestic and international, on their computers, tablets, and smartphones, wherever they went, and at any time during the day.

The online platform reduced the barriers to entry that prevented small news organizations from really competing with the established American news organizations of ABC, CBS, NBC, CNN, Fox News, and MSNBC in a meaningful way before. They now had access to a wide distribution channel, provided that they had a computer server and enough bandwidth, and the costs were almost nothing.

The rise of the alternative media, loosely defined as a media organization that is not controlled, financially or otherwise, by a larger corporation, has been the most serious threat the corporate media has ever faced because they are exposing these established newsgroups as nothing more than the de facto public relations arm of the White House, the Pentagon, and the CIA, to name a few.

These large media conglomerates approach this threat with their typical philosophy of "If the only tool you have is a hammer, every problem has to look like a nail" so they buy the alternative media companies in order to shut them up, or they lie about them in an attempt to discredit their work.

They want to control the alternative media so they can delete it.

Control. Alt. Delete.

Invert & Multiply

One of the hallmarks of corporate media is their staggering hypocrisy. In 2018, Sinclair Broadcast Group sent a memo to all 200 of their local media news organizations requiring an anchor delivered journalistic responsibility message to be recorded and shown that night on the news. Sinclair was concerned about the recent "fake news" that was gumming up the system and messing with their ability to freely lie to the people, so in order to prove to the viewers that they were serious about independent journalism, they recorded 200 messages with 200 different local anchors reading the same exact message off a teleprompter.[171]

Because nothing says journalistic integrity like everyone saying the same words, the same way, at the same time, about the same subject.

One of the funniest parts of the whole debacle was that Sinclair Broadcasting Group did not have a clue that this might be perceived as fake news, and they were shocked at how they were mocked relentlessly by all of the other media organizations for creating a fake journalistic integrity message to complain about

[171] NPR, "Sinclair Broadcast Group Forces Nearly 200 Station Anchors To Read Same Script".

fake journalism and integrity.

The teleprompter reading is not limited to those on the news. In the lead-up and push for the war in Iraq in 2003, soon-to-be Canadian Prime Minister Stephen Harper and Australian Prime Minister John Howard both delivered the exact same speech three days apart, one to an audience in Australia and one to an audience in Canada. The speeches were identical, word for word, and it showed with clarity that even the people we perceive to be at the top of the power pyramid are reading a script given to them by those in power above the offices of Presidents and Prime Ministers.

Because of the sheer number of radio stations and local television channels, it is easy for these conglomerates to invert the news, then use their hundreds of stations as a force multiplier to make it appear that a particular story is hitting a person from many angles. To the average news viewer, hearing a story on the radio, then watching the same story later on the local news works to reinforce the story. If a person hears something from two different sources then it seems more legitimate. The problem with this line of non-scientific evidence vetting is that even though the news appears to be coming from two different sources, it is really the same company just dressed up to look like two different organizations, just the way they want it to appear.

False information is cheap but debunking it is expensive.

The Consolidation Problem

Over the last 30 years, the amount of multinational companies that own the companies that produce the news has shrunk from 50 down to five. When there are 50 companies putting out the news, then there are 50 versions of the news. The viewer can take their pick of which version of the news suits them best.

In theory, there should only be one version of the news, which is the truth, but that is not happening in modern American society, or really any society these days. The assumption is that as the number of versions of the news is consolidated, the better the chances are that the news is getting closer to the truth.

That is not what happens. In fact, the exact opposite happens.

When there are 50 news organizations giving 50 versions of tonight's nightly news, they work to check and balance each other by exposing the idiocy of the other network's version of events. There are also too many different organizations to be coerced by the government to bury a story that paints them in an unflattering light, or for a corporation to push back against when one of their products kills a bunch of people and the media wants to cover the story.

By not being part of a multinational conglomerate, these organizations had to be great, or else they would fail and go out of business. They had to be trusted and reliable or else they would lose viewers to the other 49 news organizations, so they did not have the luxury of leaning on the parent company for money if things went poorly.

When the number of news organizations shrinks, society does not get closer to the truth, they get closer to the lies because the number of people that need to be brought under control shrinks. The consolidation of the number of executives in positions of power for decision making in these mega-media organizations has allowed for the agenda of the corporate media to be shaped over the decades through the Bilderberg Conference. They no longer needed to try and herd cats now that they had the five CEOs all sitting in a room together for three days getting on the same page about how particular newsworthy events will be dealt with for the immediate future.

The corporate news is the lie that convinces the average viewer to willingly work against their own best interest.

Operation Mockingbird

The CIA instituted a program called Operation Mockingbird that was designed to turn newspaper and television newsrooms into mouthpieces of the CIA, thus the symbolic Mockingbird that mimics what it hears. They infiltrated the newsrooms by either compromising existing reporters, or they inserted their agents covertly to keep an eye on things. By the 1950s, the CIA had over 10,000 agents secretly installed in various businesses, media organizations, universities, film studios, radio stations, and think tanks.[172]

Some of the media assets participating in Operation Mockingbird included CBS, ABC, NBC, Time, Newsweek, United Press International, Reuters, Hearst Newspapers, Associated Press, Scripps-Howard, and Copley News Service. Additionally, hundreds of journalists secretly carried out assignments according to

---

[172] Carl Bernstein, "The CIA And The Media".

documents on file at CIA headquarters, from intelligence-gathering to serving as go-betweens.

Although the CIA claims to have shut the program down in the 1970s, it is obvious to anyone with the eyes to see and the ears to hear that the mockingbirds are still chirping away. The "Mockingbird Media" of the 1950s has been replaced by the "News Parrots", a group of good looking repeaters that get paid a whole lot of money to read someone else's words from a teleprompter on the nightly news, regardless of whether the stories are true.

The control of the media was an early focus of the CIA because they understood the importance of mass media broadcasting, and they realized what a perfect partner they would make for misdirecting the public away from topics that they did not want to be investigated or talked about. The CIA could use the media to lie directly to the American people, they could demonize people while deifying others, they could misdirect and send the viewers on wild goose chases, and they could create and maintain the narrative of who the "good guys" are, and who the "bad guys" are that Americans must watch out for.

And the CIA could do all of this without firing a single shot.

Former Director of the CIA, William Casey, was quoted as saying that they [the CIA] would know that their disinformation campaign was a success when everything that the American people believed was wrong. So this begs the question of why MSNBC would hire former CIA Director John Brennan to be a Senior National Security and Intelligence Analyst on their network?

They are obviously trying to compete with CNN and their stable of spooks like former Director of the CIA & former Director of the NSA, Michael Hayden, and former Director of National Intelligence, James Clapper, a man that is on video lying to Congress.

The networks have filled out their rosters with Department of Defense Chief of Staff, Jeremy Bash, former Chief of FBI Counterintelligence, Frank Figliuzzi, former Deputy National Security Advisor, Fran Townsend, former Chief of Staff for FBI Director James Comey, Chuck Rosenberg, former Homeland Security Advisor, Juan Zarate, former National Security Advisor, Tony Blinken, former House Intelligence Committee Chairman, Mike Rogers, former Senior Advisor to the National Security Council, Samantha Vinograd, former CIA officers Philip Mudd and Steven Hall, and former FBI agents James Gagliano and Asha Rangappa.

When a news organization hires the former Director of the Central Intelligence Agency to be an analyst on their network, they are no longer in the news business. This should be painfully obvious to anyone with even the slightest bit of understanding about how the news industry should work. It is a joke. The television news networks fill their ranks with professional liars and spies, then accuse the alternative media of being "fake news". Their hypocrisy knows no bounds.

The lack of trust by the American people towards their television news programs is reflected in the viewership statistics that show major changes in the corporate media's grip on the distribution of relevant information that they have had for decades. The only group of Americans that really get their news from their television are the 65+ community, but for all other categories, it is a mass exodus away from their TV and to the internet to find news that is relevant to them.

• From 2016 to 2017, the move from television to the internet has been massive, with those ages 30-49 dropping 10%.[173]

• The 50-64 age range faded by 8%, while their internet news usage rose by 6%.

• In the 18-29 age category, only 23% get their news on the television.

• The 18-29 and 30-49 groups have 52% of their people going online to consume their news instead.

• The 65+ crowd still clocks in at 82% getting their news from their favorite newsreader, which explains all of the pharmaceutical ads for a whole slew of diseases, but even their viewership numbers are down 3% in just one year.

• The percentage of age 65+ viewers that are now getting their news online jumped by an astounding 10% in just 12 months.[174]

Whether the reason is convenience or reliability, the numbers show that television news is in free fall, and they have no one to blame but themselves.

Their Disinformation Business

---

[173] Pew Research Group, "About 6 In 10 Young Adults In U.S. Primarily Use Online Streaming To Watch TV".
[174] Amy Mitchell, Pew Research Group, "Pathways To News".

The intentional promotion of false stories and lies has always been a cornerstone of the CIA's charter. Their job is to collect good information and keep it secret, and they use disinformation to muddy the waters in order to throw people off of their tracks. Disinformation is horribly damaging to a free society and a very effective tool for those in power to cover up for their criminal deeds.

There is an art form to lying professionally, but once the tactics are exposed and people become aware of them, they become far easier to spot going forward. Football players study hours of game film of the opposing team they are preparing to play so that they will be able to quickly recognize their formations and understand what plays they are running in order to position themselves accordingly.

It is no different when it comes to spotting disinformation, and there is plenty of CIA game film to study. These are a few of the tactics that disinformation agents are taught in order to obfuscate the truth, promote lies, discredit those that are uncovering their crimes, and marginalize truth-tellers.

• They will sometimes question the motives of the people exposing the truth and will imply that they have a financial stake in questioning the official story.

• They will call the truthseekers names like conspiracy theorists, right-wing, left-wing, unhinged, crazy, unstable, racists, terrorists, anti-semitic, homophobic, Christian fascists, zealots, Constitutionalists, anarchists, Communists, Socialists, among other things, even when there is no proof of their association with any group.

• They will attempt to deflect attention from the real meat of the story, their lies, and shift the focus onto the person exposing it instead. It might be spun that the person has an axe to grind with the writer or speaker and that they are dragging their own personal opinions into their analysis of the situation, making them less valid.

• There will always be an attack against the weakest portion of the person's rebuttal of the disinformation, then this will be used to imply that everything else they are saying must be equally as weak.

• The disinformer will never, ever, admit that they are lying, so one should not even bother waiting for it.

• Expect the disinformer to ferociously pushback over the top with a statement like "How dare you accuse me of lying about something as serious as this?". The more enraged, vicious, and vocal; the bigger the lie they are trying to hide. [See Bill Clinton].

• Do not expect a professional disinformer to ever actually debate the real topic and actual heart of the lie, but rather to dismiss everything as being rumors, internet lies, baseless accusations, speculation, personal attacks against their character, or a hit piece by their opponents or rivals.

• They will always attempt to deflect the accusations by accusing the accuser of being guilty of the very thing that they themselves are guilty of. This is known as projection, and it is very widely used by lying scumbag politicians, especially those wearing pantsuits. As an example, if they know they are actually colluding with Russia, then they will often accuse their enemy of colluding with Russia preemptively, even before they are accused of it, and put that burden of defense on them. This works to remove the ability of the truth-teller to accuse them of that crime because it will look ridiculous and childish like they don't have much to work with if their only defense is "No, you're colluding with Russia".

• Once the person that was the target of the projection responds with a verbal denial, usually emotionally, the next step is for the projector to accuse the truth-teller of being overly sensitive to the criticism, usually because it is actually such an obvious lie, that it must be proof that they really are guilty of the projected issue.

• The best way for a disinformer to hide something that they do not want to be known is to ignore it and simply refuse to talk about it. If that does not work, they might just act stupid and pretend that they do not know what the person is talking about. Simple and effective.

• The opposite of playing dumb is to play far too intelligent and dazzle them with big words or baffle them with bullshit. The more technical the rebuttal, the greater the chance that the disinformer is trying to hide the lie behind big words and scientific answers that the average person is ill-equipped to respond to.

• A hybrid version is for the disinformer to describe the whole situation as far too complex for even them to explain, and therefore, too complicated for the truthseeker to figure out as well. They hope everyone will lose interest in the topic due to a lack of understanding and stop talking about it.

- When participating in a debate, be that a television political debate or one featuring the talking heads on the corporate news, disinformers love to announce that all of the claims against them are old news and have been discredited long ago.

- Disinformers will demand proof from those challenging their version of events, then if proof is presented, they will claim that the evidence is incorrect, irrelevant, or invalid.

- It is not unheard of for disinformers to simply manufacture new lies to try and validate their old lies. Then create even more lies to back up the others.

- Multiple streams of the same disinformation talking points will be activated and pushed into the corporate media at the same time to give the impression that where there is smoke, there must be fire.

- Any good disinformation is 80% truth mixed with 20% lies. Just enough truth to check out factually to the casual observer, but not enough truth to actually be correct.

- Disinformers will often try to act annoyed that they are even being questioned about a particular event as if the case has already been closed and the science settled while trying desperately to change the topic completely.

- Politicians have been known to employ a tactic called a "limited hangout" which is a partial admission to a lesser offense in advance, in order to give the impression that they are voluntarily disclosing all of the information when, in fact, they are keeping the juiciest details hidden.

- Another version of the fake confession is when people admit to vague indiscretions or crimes as "mistakes that were made", while never placing the blame on anyone in particular.

- Disinformers love to blame their accusers of wanting to dwell on the past, while they want to put everything behind them and focus on the future. They seek to distance themselves from their lies by trying to run from their past and into the future.

When everything else fails, the disinformer might just crawl back into the hole from whence they came and disappear. Or in the case of some of the political families that run Washington, the truthseekers disappear. They are not above employing criminal law enforcement officers and judges that are either corrupt or have been compromised to do their bidding, and even the nightly news cannot deny the existence of both types of criminals as they show a countless number of stories about corruption inside the halls of justice in America.

The Legalization of Lies

When most Western people look at North Korea, one of the first things that jump out at them is the unbelievable layers of control that have been put in place to prevent their citizens from knowing the truth about the outside world. As an outsider, it is obvious that they are being fed information that paints a very different picture of reality than what it actually is.

What does not get discussed is that Americans are also being controlled to see the world in a particular way, and the people's arrogance that something like this would never be possible to pull on them makes them even more susceptible to it. Propaganda is a distortion of the truth that governments use to create a uniform belief in a certain way of thinking, feeling, or viewing some aspects of their lives. It is the control of the flow of information by the State, and it is the essence of tyranny.

For several decades, a law prevented the U.S. from pushing government-created programming to Americans, but on July 2nd, 2013, they decided that they no longer cared if that programming was directed towards Americans. The Smith-Mundt Modernization Act of 2012 lifted the ban on government created programming, and it effectively nullified the old Smith-Mundt Act of 1948, which explicitly forbade information and psychological operations aimed at influencing U.S. public opinion.

What does a corrupt government do when they want to pass a law that they know will be wildly unpopular with the citizens? They hide it inside a bigger bill that they think people will like. In the case of the Smith-Mundt Modernization Act of 2012, they crammed it in to the National Defense Authorization Act of 2013 (NDAA) and passed with all of the other stupid ideas masquerading as some form of terrorism prevention.

The result of this law was that it allowed thousands of hours per month of government-funded programs to be created and distributed via television, radio, and internet. If people want to talk about "fake news", but they are not mentioning the Smith-Mundt Modernization Act of 2012, then they really are not getting to the root of the problem.

Their slogan in the corporate media should be "your new home for government-funded propaganda".

The people have always wanted to know the truth about what was really going on inside the government, and there was a time when the media wanted to know too. The Old Media was a check on power, but the New Media only cares about checking their falling ratings.

The Old Media might have wanted to know what really happened with SEAL Team Six and why they went against protocol and put all of them in a 30-year old helicopter to fly through an area of Afghanistan that is known to be a shooting gallery? Why did the military lie about it to the press, and why was the New Media so willing to blindly accept their explanation with no interest in digging into the story to confirm any of it? What about the parents that pushed back against the flimsy story sold to them by the Obama administration, and where is the New Media to hold them accountable?

There was a time when the media wanted to know the facts behind scandals such as the Iran Contra Affair back in the 1980s when Oliver North lied to Congress, and they even destroyed him and tried to take down the President over it.

What happened to the New Media with regard to the scandal known as Fast & Furious, where were they? They caught the Obama administration and Eric Holder red-handed running guns through the Mexican drug cartels and nothing ever came of it because the media just pretended there was nothing to it, then they waited out the news cycle and they changed the subject.[175]

They were complicit in the suppression of the real story of the Obama administration rigging the FISA court and weaponizing the CIA, NSA, and the FBI, and they acted as if it did not happen. Brennan used the CIA to settle old scores, James Clapper lied to Congress about "not wittingly" spying on the American people and the media turned their heads in unison like the rest of the world was crazy for expecting them to actually do something about it.[176]

The truth about the situation was that the media had no balls and they were

---

[175] Paul Speery, New York Post, "The Scandal In Washington No One Is Talking About".
[176] Steven Nelson, Washington Examiner, "Lawmakers Want James Clapper Prosecuted For Surveillance Testimony Before Statute Of Limitations Runs Out".

scared to death of Dick Cheney. They were afraid to question the Bush administration because they were concerned that they will appear soft on terrorism and unpatriotic, and they feared being perceived as being possibly racist if they questioned the Obama administration.

They do not have that fear about questioning the Trump administration because they do not believe that any of those people are still going to be around a year from now, and rightfully so, but now the media has decided to act tough and show everyone that they are not afraid to question the White House. Oh but they certainly were terrified during the two previous administrations, and they are still scared of Darth Vader in a pastel pantsuit who somehow always gets a pass on her criminal deeds being brought to light in the media.

The Clinton News Network

So where are the actual journalists that work for these media companies, and what are they doing with their days? It clearly is not journalistic work because if they were in the business of being an actual journalist they would have questioned why Loretta Lynch was able to have a meeting on the tarmac with former President Bill Clinton, and they would never have allowed themselves to be dismissed as a band or morons that actually believe that they were simply discussing grandchildren.

Where was the media when the Benghazi event went down and the Clinton State Department pushed the embarrassing story that an internet video sparked the violent demonstration that led to the death of Christopher Stevens?

Why did the media not ask whether or not the FBI took possession of Hillary Clinton's email server and examined it? They never did, for the record, and the media never asked about it because they did not want to know the truth. A real news organization would want to know the answers to questions like these, especially when the head of the FBI announces that he has been lied to on multiple occasions by Hillary Clinton, but they just went silent.

Where was the trusted mainstream media when it came time to investigate the Uranium One transaction in which the Clinton Foundation brokered the deal to sell 20% of America's uranium to the Russians?[177] Has Charles Ortel's work on the massive fraud that is the Clinton Foundation been featured on MSNBC anytime since 2016? It would make for an interesting story for a news organization that

---

[177] Peter Grier, The Christian Science Monitor, "What's The Real Story Behind Hillary Clinton, Russia, And Uranium?".

was actually interested in real conspiracies that involve Russia and powerful American political operatives unless of course, they are only interested in stories that portray the Clintons like the heroes and not as the operators of one of the largest criminal enterprises on the planet.

The Clinton Foundation and the recently defunct Clinton Global Initiative, an enterprise that was shut down the day after the 2016 election when it became clear to the world that the influence-peddling was no longer an option for the second-place finisher in the American election, have been described by Ortel as the largest criminal enterprise on the planet, and that is really saying something considering the drug cartels, mafia, and the CIA are in competition.[178]

Did the media question the flimsy story of the death of Seth Rich, a DNC staffer that was allegedly murdered during a robbery, even though his wallet, his phone, his watch, and his gold necklace were all left by the thief? It does not take a seasoned FBI investigator to realize that the story simply did not add up, especially once one factors in the reality that he was the leaker that provided Kim Dotcom with information from the DNC that proved that Bernie Sanders' nomination was suppressed by Hillary Clinton and others in the Democratic National Convention.[179] This information was sent to Wikileaks and Julian Assange, and leads to another story that lacked in substance, but was universally portrayed to be of a legitimate origin: the narrative that Russia hacked the 2016 election.

The mainstream media has been polishing that turd for so long that it says more about their lack of actual pull within the establishment political apparatus that despite 24/7 coverage and a unified front by the Democrats and their partners at CNN and MSNBC, they still have not been able to convince the public that Russia actually had any role in Trump's election victory because it is so plainly obvious to anyone that Hillary Clinton was the reason why Hillary Clinton lost the election.

It was not because of the Russians, not due to voter fraud, not as a result of "fake news", not due to James Comey talking about her plethora of lies, but rather because she was such an unlikeable candidate that she made Donald Trump seem like a reasonable alternative. A candidate with zero political experience, the type of guy that was on record telling men to "grab 'em by the pussy", a notorious liar, a golf cheat, a serial exaggerator, a womanizer, and spray tan addict beat Hillary Clinton, and that is the truth of the matter. It was not because of Russia, it was because she was a horrible Presidential candidate. All

---

[178] Michael Sainato, Observer, "The Clinton Foundation Shuts Down Clinton Global Initiative".
[179] Rachel Alexander, The Stream, "Evidence Piling Up That Seth Rich Leaked DNC Emails To Wikileaks".

she had to do was be a normal human being and she would have destroyed him in the election, but she simply could not do that.

Perhaps Hillary Clinton lost the election because she had a campaign manager in John Podesta that is suspected of being a pedophile, who had a brother that was a banned lobbyist and collector of pedophilic-related art, she had accepted money and at least six trips on the private jet of a convicted pedophile named Jeffrey Epstein, as had Trump, a trip her husband had also made on 26 different occasions, her right-hand-woman was married to a convicted pedophile in Anthony Weiner, and claimed her favorite pizza place in Washington D.C. is Comet Pizza, a well-known pedophile establishment. Maybe there were too many pedophiles in decision-making roles within her circle of influence for America to feel comfortable with that? Photos of her and good friend Harvey Weinstein did not help either, especially when it came out that they have been very good friends for well over 20 years. People are judged on the company that they keep and in the case of the Clintons, it is a bunch of sex offenders, Kevin Spacey, Harvey Weinstein, and billionaires running Brownstone Operations to entrap political and business rivals.

American politics is as dirty as it comes. The corporate media is so corrupt that nothing they say can be taken at face value. The American military has been used as a tool for regime change by the wealthy families that run the country. The American education system has been completely subverted and compromised.

As bad as all this is, the reality of the situation is that these are only annoyances in comparison to what is being used to rig the detonators to the American Empire.

RIGGING THE DETONATORS

The American Printing Press in Action _Before_ Coronavirus (BC)

Long before the panic plandemic reared its ugly head in 2020, the Federal Reserve Bank had been crazily spinning in its wheel, printing more and more money.

That is because the United States government spends money like Nicolas Cage on a coke bender. Of course, a Gulfstream jet, two yachts, 18 motorcycles, 50 vintage and new cars, including some Ferraris, a couple of Mercedes, a Rolls Royce, a few Bentleys, a bunch of Aston Martins, and the Shah of Iran's Lamborghini Miura SVJ, are prudent investments.

And much like the American government, he also had a bit of an impulsive side and a strange taste for weird stuff like a $270,000 dinosaur skull, several shrunken heads (of people, of course), two albino King Cobras, a million-dollar Superman comic book, and meteorites (plural).

Money well spent.

The United States throws trillions of dollars down the Military-Information-Terror complex rathole every single year, with nothing to show for it except for a dozen illegal wars, a fleet of F-35 that cannot fly on back-to-back days or any place with sand, and warehouses filled with "smart" bombs that always seem to fall wildly off course.

At least Nick Cage has some cool snakes to show for all of his reckless spendings.

There are two main reasons why the United States has the ability to conjure up money out of thin air like they have a printing press.

The first is that they actually have a printing press that they call the Federal Reserve Bank, and the second reason is the Petrodollar.

The Federal Reserve Bank will always print more money for the American government, even though it is not a governmental organization. It is a private bank, owned by a consortium of other central banks, and managed by the monetary mothership in Basel, Switzerland, the Bank for International Settlements (BIS).[180]

If the American people made only one decision in an effort to improve the country, the most important and far-reaching choice they could make would be the abolition of their private central bank, the Federal Reserve Bank.

It would improve the lives of millions of people overnight and would remove the cancerous tumor that has been responsible for the financial illness we call inflation that has whittled the value of a dollar by 96.1% in just over one century.[181]

The reason why someone's Grandfather could buy a loaf of bread for a nickel is that back then there was far less money in circulation, and the money that was in circulation was actually backed by something tangible.

It is important to note that America had central banks before the Federal Reserve was established, but they were smashed into pieces on a couple of occasions because they were destroying the country.

Nowhere is the corruption and contamination of the American Empire more obvious than the relationship between the Fed and the United States government where every governmental whim is financed without a thought to the consequences. And why not, after all, it theoretically costs nothing to crank up the printing press and churn out a huge stack of money to buy a new batch of tanks or build military bases in 140 countries.

The Federal Reserve Bank creates and regulates the money supply of the United States, but it is a private bank that does not answer to any government agency. The Fed is run by a director that is appointed but not voted on. The decisions that the Fed makes are not subject to any oversight by the Federal Government, though they greatly impact everyone in the country.

Understanding what the Federal Reserve actually is is fundamental to figuring out why the American monetary system behaves the way it does. The public is led to believe that this bank is a part of the United States government.

It is not.

---

[180] Ellen Brown, Global Research, "Who Owns The Federal Reserve?".
[181] John Williams, Shadow Stats, "Hyperinflation 2012".

Former Fed Chief Alan Greenspan admitted that the Federal Reserve is an independent agency and that no other agency of government can overrule the actions they take.[182]

The Fed sets interest rates and loans the money that they create from literally nothing out to the other banks. Those banks, in turn, lend that money out to people and businesses at a higher interest rate than they borrowed it for, thus making a profit.

But there is a catch.

The concept of creating money out of thin air, then attaching an amount of interest that must be paid back along with the money at a specified time, makes this equation collapse on itself.

Wall Street's Secret Bailout

When Hank Paulson held a gun to the collective heads of the American taxpayer in 2008 and threatened to blow their financial brains out unless he received $700 billion to stop the bleeding of his friends on Wall Street, known to the world as TARP (Troubled Asset Relief Program), no one ever thought to look around the corner to see what the Fed was doing.

The Federal Reserve was giving out turkeys like Nino Brown on Thanksgiving, trying to bribe the neighborhood so that they can keep their scam running for a little bit longer. In the banking game, poultry just will not cut it, so the Fed put the word out that they were open for business, but not for the common person. They only deal with other banks, so after TARP was done looting the American government for money to help the poor bankers, those same bankers walked down the street to the Fed and that was where things got serious with the bailout that nobody ever heard about.

These are the banks that were invited to the "secret" bailout:

Citigroup – $2.513 trillion	Barclays PLC – $868 billion
Morgan Stanley – $2.041 trillion	Bear Stearns – $853 billion
Merrill Lynch – $1.949 trillion	Goldman Sachs – $814 billion
Bank of America – $1.344 trillion	Royal Bank Scotland – $541 billion

[182] RT, "The Great Bank Robbery: How The Federal Reserve Is Destroying America".

JP Morgan Chase – $391 billion

Deutsche Bank – $354 billion

UBS – $287 billion

Credit Suisse – $262 billion

Lehman Brothers – $183 billion

Bank of Scotland – $181 billion

BNP Paribas – $175 billion

Wells Fargo – $159 billion

Dexia – $159 billion

Wachovia – $142 billion

Dresdner Bank – $135 billion

Societe Generale – $124 billion

All Other Borrowers – $2.639 trillion

The final amount of money that was essentially printed out of thin air: $16.1 trillion dollars.[183]

That's trillion with a "T".

Exchange Stabilization Fund

The Exchange Stabilization Fund was created by the US Treasury in 1934 with the proceeds from the gold confiscation scam that the United States government pulled on its citizens. The Federal government ordered all Americans to turn in their gold in exchange for $20 per ounce. Anyone who did not exchange their gold for dollars would be arrested.

The Treasury then revalued all the gold that they confiscated to a value of $35 per ounce, essentially robbing the people of a 75% increase in the value of the gold that they once owned, and successfully completing the biggest robbery in recorded history without shooting anybody.[184]

And the government wonders why the citizens do not trust them?

The Exchange Stabilization Fund was created to defend the "integrity" of the dollar, and it is above any oversight from Congress, and the authority of the ESF is literally above the law. The operations of the ESF are classified as an area of "National Security", and therefore they do not have to release any of their financial documents to the public.

The ESF essentially operates as a slush fund to finance covert operations without the interference of Congressional oversight. Because the money is off the books and free from scrutiny, it is impossible to know for sure how much money is

---

[183] Campaign For Liberty, "The Fed Dished Out $16 Trillion In Emergency Lending".

[184] J.D. Seagreaves, Silver Monthly, "Government Confiscation Of Gold: It Happened Before - Could It Happen Again?".

stashed there, but a fair guess would be multiple trillions of dollars. You can throw a whole lot of parties with multiple trillions of dollars.

The Federal Reserve takes the majority of the heat for the monetary policy in the United States, but the Exchange Stabilization Fund is every bit as evil and dangerous to the well-being of the citizens.

Terrorists in Nice Suits

When the banks introduce free credit into the market for their corporate buddies, a couple of things are bound to happen. The corporations use this money to speculate on things like mergers & acquisitions, real estate, buybacks of their own stocks, dividend increases, and the purchase of other stocks. It fuels bubbles in the stock and real estate markets because free money makes everything seem cheap, and as long as more free money is available, the new money into these markets will continue to push up the values.

When the Fed flooded the banks and corporations with $16 trillion for "financial assistance" after the markets tanked in 2008, that money was first used to shore up their balance sheets, then used as the fuel that created the stock market boom that was about to come. Since early 2009, the S&P 500 stock index ballooned by 300%, which is exactly what one would expect since the money was never contingent on capital investment, the hiring of new employees, home loans, auto loans, or any other conditions. The S&P 500 grew 80% higher than its peak during the 2007 boom.

These bubbles never end well for the common participants, but the wealthiest always seem to be able to exit the scene just in time to benefit from the drop in values of assets when they step back in years later to purchase them again for pennies on the dollar.

Of course, this is nothing new.

During the Great Depression's trigger event, the stock market crash of 1929, most of the average investors were cleaned out while those that manufactured the event were sitting on the sideline poised to profit from buying back assets at depressed prices.

This is a classic "pump & dump" scheme that has been at the core of all market manipulation throughout the last century.

The tide of fear connected to the stock market receded from 2011 to 2018 and drew everyone from the beach down into the ankle-deep water to pick up all of the treasures that the receding water exposed.

But the people have forgotten what happens to all of that water.

It does not just vanish, it simply moves offshore and gathers into a tsunami that catches everyone off guard and destroys everything that did not have the sense to understand what was coming.

J.P. Morgan believes that a gargantuan financial crisis is right around the corner, and when it hits, the solution that the controllers propose will seem like nothing short of a rigged and criminally orchestrated fraud, as the Federal Reserve, for the first time ever, enters the market to purchase stocks.

So who owns the majority of the stocks in the United States?

The 1% does.

And what type of stocks make up a chunk of their portfolios?

Banking stocks, of course.[185]

When the stock market collapses due to being built on a foundation of fraud, disinformation, collusion, and the stock buyback programs fueled by free money from the Fed, the banks will be pulling the ripcords on their golden parachutes while the Federal Reserve cranks up their magic printing press again to create more fiat dollars and silently inflate the money supply in order to buy the stock of Goldman Sachs and Citigroup so that they are assured of not becoming worthless.

Heads, the bankers win. Tails, the people lose.

The Visible Hand of Crony Capitalism

Crony capitalism is defined as an economy in which businesses thrive, not as a result of risks they take, but rather as a return on money amassed through a nexus between a business class and the political class.

---

[185] Rob Wile, Money Magazine, "Richest 10% Of Americans Now Own 84% Of All Stocks".

This has been the mission statement of the United States for at least the last 30 years, and probably longer.

The original economist, Adam Smith, described the "invisible hand" as enlightened self-interest, and a market force that helps the demand and supply of goods in a free market to reach equilibrium automatically.

If a person makes a product and charges too much for it, nobody will buy it. This is both Common Sense 101 & Economics 101. Their competitor may sell a similar product and charge much less, so they would need to either lower their price to a point where they are competitive, or else they will never sell anything and the market will punish them.

The government does not need to interfere with this process because the process itself sorts everything out. This is known as "price discovery". The Sellers and Buyers will come to an agreement that they consider to be fair. If the price offered for a product is too low, the Seller simply will not sell. If the Buyer is unable to find any Sellers willing to take his offer, maybe his offer is just too low and will need to be raised in order to entice someone to sell.

This is why they call it an invisible hand because it does not need anyone messing with it to make the market fair for the people.

Crony capitalism gives the invisible middle finger to the people.

When one manipulates either side of the equation, be it the demand or supply side, they end up with numbers that are invalid and warped. If the local butcher kept his thumb on the scale every time people bought meat from him, they would get fed up and go somewhere else. Of course, he realizes this, so he either does not do that to his customers, or he tries to hide it.

When the government puts its big thumb on the scale, it does not care if the people know it or not because they are the only governmental game in town, so to speak, so they do not have an incentive to make people the very best offer possible. In fact, sometimes their offer is downright horrible, such is the case with many aspects of the American government.

Historically, printing money that does not exist has led to depression, which led to hyperinflation. In the past, the dollar recovered. But what if it doesn't this time? Or the next time? The question one has to ask is whether the death of the dollar when it comes, will be from natural causes, or premeditated murder?

Bank Holiday

When opening a traditional bank account in the United States, it is very important to read the fine print. One cannot count on asking the bank manager about the little technicality that they slipped into the contract because the chances are that he will have no idea what they are even talking about. They will not hear the tellers talking about it, their friends will not inform them about it, and they sure as hell will not hear it mentioned in the television advertisements, but it is important nonetheless.

When a person deposits their money into a bank account, it becomes the property of the bank.

This is worth repeating because it is so important: their money becomes the bank's money the minute they put it in their bank account. This is called a "Bank Sweep Program" and it is the automatic transfer (sweep) of cash in the brokerage account into a deposit account at a bank that may or may not be affiliated with the broker-dealer.

The bank account holder is no longer in the first position as far as the ownership of that money is concerned. It is now the bank's money and the account holder becomes an unsecured creditor.

This is not a good position to be in, but it gets worse.

People must understand that the banks WILL take the money from the accounts when something bad happens. The money will be taken. After all, it is, technically the bank's money. They have the right to take it, it is legal for them to take it, and the account holder cannot do a damn thing about it.

And the bank knows that.

That money can now be used by the bank to pay their obligations and debts, without the consent of the account holder. After all, it is their money now.

If a person thinks this cannot happen in the modern banking world, all they have to do is see what happened in Cyprus in the Mediterranean in 2013. The citizens of the island awoke to find that their entire banking system was frozen, and they were shut out completely. No ATM withdrawals allowed, no cash available from the local bank around the corner, no access to savings accounts, and no online bill payment services.

No nothing. Think about how scary that would be.

The first move after discovering this is to check and see how much food one has in their fridge and pantry and to make the calculations about how much time that actually buys them before they have to explore some illegal options just to survive another day.

The precedent has now been set for outright bank account confiscations, with Cyprus acting as the test case. Of course, they do not call it a bank account seizure or confiscation, instead, the banks, media, and government do what they always do, and that is to give the criminal act a sweet and disarming name, like a "bank holiday".

Isn't that a warm sounding name for the theft of a person's life savings? They made it sound like their money went on a vacation, which technically it did, only it forgot to invite them to join it.

The "holiday" part is because the bank closed down and the employees were told to go home, and like a normal holiday, it was probably planned well in advance. This bank holiday in Cyprus was a dress rehearsal for what is coming for the rest of the world very soon. Adjustments are being made and calculations are being factored so that the mistakes that were made with Cyprus do not happen when they roll out this plan on the big world stage in the very near future.

People thought they hated the government's problems that they created, just wait until everyone sees their solutions.

What Americans experienced in 2008 was the "Bailouts" of Wall Street and the banks, but what they have to look forward to during the next economic collapse are "Bail Ins". This is where instead of asking the government to fund insolvent banks with taxpayer money, the banks just steal the customer's money, thus bailing in, instead of out.

People will go to bed on Friday and everything will be alright, then wake up on Saturday and be told that the banks are closed for the weekend and probably Monday as well, just until they sort out the mess. Yes, this will be billed as an inconvenience, but not anything to panic about.

There is everything to panic about.

This is how it will be presented if the banks decide to tell the people the truth.

There are no guarantees that they will opt for the honest approach because, after all, they are banks, and banks are inherently dishonest.

The more likely scenario is that the people will go to sleep on a Friday night then awake to "Breaking News" that the Russians have infected the United States banking software with a virus to cripple the system. The system is being fixed by bank professionals that hope to have everything back online Monday, maybe Tuesday at the latest.

This, of course, will be a gigantic lie. It will be used as a distraction while they loot the banks from the inside and move the digital money out of everyone's accounts before the people have a chance to pull their money out.

It is important to note that the Federal Deposit Insurance Corporation (FDIC) only has $.02 for every dollar on deposit with a bank, and those accounts are capped at up to $250,000. Everything over a quarter of a million dollars is not insured, and everything under only has 2% of actual cash in reserves to cover the losses. If a local bank goes under because the manager decided to loot the vault and move to Guatemala, the FDIC will step in making sure those with accounts below the threshold are made whole.

If the whole system goes down, because of a bail-in, there will not be any money left in the bank because the bank is stealing it, and there will only be 2% at the FDIC because they are no real help. However, depositors will not be left totally empty handed. They will receive something that should make everything alright. Their money will be converted into equity in the failing bank that just stole all of their life's savings. They will receive ownership stock shares of the bank in exchange for their money. A forced liquidity investment in a company that is so broke that they just stole all of their client's money in order to not go under this week.

See, everything is fixed (sarcasm font).

How to Avoid Going on a Forced Holiday?

If hiding their money in their mattress makes people uncomfortable, they can take some of their money and buy gold and silver because that is an option that retains value and cannot be printed into infinity by the central bankers. When buying gold and silver, it is important to understand that actual gold and silver is different from ETFs or "paper gold". People need to own actual gold coins or bullion because the gold funds have been oversold and there is not enough actual gold or silver backing them up. It is important to know that there is a difference between tangible gold coins and paper contracts giving the holder the right to buy gold at a certain price. One has value, and the other may not, especially when the system goes down.

After all, who created ETFs? Wall Street did, so people know it is a scam.

Economic Darwinism

Most people think that Darwinism means that only the strong survive. That is not the underlying premise of the concept. It actually does not have anything to do with strength.

Darwinism is that only those able to adapt will survive. If the environment changes suddenly, those that recognize it quickly, figure out what to do about it, then put their plan in place, will be moving on to the next round on Planet Earth. If the Dodo bird is unable or unwilling to accept its new paradigm, it might find itself in an evolutionary dead end.

Darwinism is not limited to the animal kingdom, as humans have witnessed over the past century. There are areas of their lives that change quickly, and if they are asleep at the wheel, they can easily be left behind.

There are examples of "Economic Darwinism" throughout the business landscape, and just because a person, family, or company dominated a segment of business for a generation, does not assure them continued success in the future.

When was the last time someone bought a roll of Kodak film? How is the biggest pager company doing these days? When was the last time kids were excited to go home and play Atari after school?

If the Invisible Hand balances things out, then Economic Darwinism is like a fat kid on one side of the See Saw. The other kids can try as hard as they like to push their side down, but their skinny ass might want to think about swinging on the monkey bars instead.

When the government gets involved with marketplaces in order to prop up an aspect of the economy that they feel is important to stimulate, it delays the natural transition to something better. If the current situation was working, usually a stimulation would not be necessary.

The reason for going the stimulus route might be that an election is coming up and it is believed that by injecting an artificial flow of money into a situation, the voters may reward the incumbent by reelecting them. It could be that a politician has a donor that already helped to finance their previous campaign and expects legislation to benefit him in some way. Maybe the politician sees himself in the future taking a cushy job or being hired to "give speeches" in a particular industry that he has assisted with massive amounts of government money.

Theoretically, what about starting a couple of unjust wars that destroyed large portions of two countries, then giving billions of no-bid contracts to a multinational engineering firm that an unnamed person used to be the CEO of to rebuild it all, wouldn't that count?

Yes, Dick, it would count.

There are far too many reasons to list as to why a politician may want to direct money to one area instead of another, but the underlying point is that by doing so it disrupts the natural balance created by invisible marketplaces. In a crony capitalist system, terrible companies with great connections can rise to the top, while well-run companies with no political juice dry up and blow away.

The United States has been creating this paradigm over the past 40 years, and nowhere has it been more prevalent than in the warfare economy, otherwise known as the Military-Industrial complex.

Smedley Butler talked about it. Eisenhower warned about it.

Clearly, America was not listening.

There is a very well thought out trick that the multinational conglomerates have been pulling off for a long time now, and it is fairly simple.

As an example, take a large conglomerate that is interested in making a ton of money so they diversify into many different industries through acquisition. They buy media companies, they invest in aerospace groups, they acquire a controlling interest in missile manufacturers, and they finance new construction and development projects. They then use their media arm to sell the need for a war in some foreign country to the American people, while simultaneously making a fortune from advertisers looking to capitalize on the important stories in the run-up to war. They offer their aerospace service to the military in case they need some more planes to launch the missiles that they just so happen to manufacture while promising to rebuild the destroyed country with their real estate development company and engineering firm when the whole war is over.

They make money on every angle, and the general public never notices that all of these companies have the same ownership. Surely pushing for a war through media channels they own while simultaneously selling them the bombs to carry out the war would be of some interest one would think.

Not in America. Americans do not want to get bogged down in the details, just tell them who to hate and they will take it from there.

The Slowest Camper

The late author Michael Ruppert once pointed out that if a person is in a camp with a bunch of other campers and a bear attacks, they do not really need to be faster than the bear, they just need to be faster than the slowest camper.

Crony capitalism is the government handing their favorite camper a large stick to bash another camper in the leg first before turning and running away from the bear. Sure, they will survive, but all of the other campers will instantly hate and distrust them, and with good reason.

A politician that is in charge of a massive budget to build 100 detention camps to warehouse illegal immigrants, as an example, is going to give some company a fortune to do the job. It is fair to say that the politician probably would love to take a tiny little piece of that large budget, but to do so might be too obvious, so what happens is that the money flows to his buddy's commercial real estate development company for them to build the facilities, then once he retires from public office he becomes the Senior Advisor to the CEO of that same development company and is paid $3 million a year to "advise" the company while playing golf with clients.

One need only take a look at Eric Holder's cushy gig with Covington & Burling to understand "no show" jobs are real, and they are the reward for services rendered previously, not necessarily for future services yet unperformed.

The reason why President Obama was paid $400,000 to speak at Cantor Fitzgerald was a reward for the favorable decisions he made in the bond industry over the course of his presidency.[186]

Ex-president Bill Clinton was paid $750,000 to give a speech in Hong Kong to a Swedish telecom company called Ericsson that ended up on a watch list because of their dealings with Iran.[187] After Bill collected his bribe, er, speaking fee, his wife Hillary Clinton, who just so happened to be the Secretary of State, excluded Ericsson from sanctions.

Probably a coincidence.

George W. Bush still receives $175,000 to give speeches to companies and organizations, even though he is barely capable of putting a sentence together. Unless part of that fee allows the audience to pelt him with rotten eggs, that is a colossal waste of money just to hear that guy speak.

But, of course, it is not about the speech.

This is how bribery is done in the United States. In other countries, they fill duffle bags with cash and hand it to the President. In America, they hire the ex-President for an imaginary job that he does not have to show up to, pay them 100 times more than the going rate, then write off the cost as a business expense.

Do not think for a second that bribing politicians is limited to Banana Republics and failed states, or that those people Americans have voted for have enough integrity to exclude themselves from this kind of behavior.

They do not.

Atlas Chugged

---

[186] Ben McLannahan, CNBC, "Obama To Be Paid $400,000 For Cantor-Fitzgerald Speech".
[187] John Solomon, Washington Times, "Bill Clinton's Foundation Cashed In As Sweden Lobbied Hillary On Iran-Related Sanctions".

Ayn Rand felt that true capitalism was the only morally valid socio-political system because it allows people to act in their own self-interest, if they chose to, and reap the rewards. If someone wanted it bad enough, then they would go and make it happen. If they did not, then they should get the hell out of the way or risk getting run over by someone more motivated.

She was not the warmest woman in the world.

If one had to boil down her philosophy to a sentence it would be "Man's own self-interest and their individual rights are the most important tools for developing a great country". These things are enough of an incentive to push the country forward, and if a person does not care enough to look out for themselves, then why should society?

Respect is earned.

Wealth is created.

But what if a person was too fat, stupid, or lazy to even act in their own self-interest because the government gave them everything they needed, then what happens?

What happens is a collapse of the modern world, according to Rand.

What happens is that society gets the "projects" of a large, hollowed-out, city in America. A bunch of people standing around, not doing anything, waiting for their government check to arrive. There is no incentive to get an actual job, not that they would even be a viable candidate for it because by doing so they run the risk of no longer qualifying for the free money that they are currently receiving for doing absolutely nothing. They would have to decide if they would rather do nothing and get paid a little bit for it, or do something, lose out on the free money, and get paid even less than before?

When people are incentivized to do nothing, they will do nothing to the best of their ability.

The altruistic approach is giving a man a fish, whereas the capitalistic approach is teaching a man to fish.

The American way is to make the fisherman get a license from the State before he can go fishing, then the State takes one fish for themselves, they give one of his fish to the guy taking a nap under a tree, and they leave one fish for the guy that actually caught it.

The Crony America way is to bribe the guy from the State to make fishing in the lake illegal to everyone else except his friends, then sell the fish to the other people for triple the original value.

It is time to go fishing somewhere else, this is getting ridiculous.

Tapeworm Economics

In her case study titled "Dillon Read & Co. Inc. & the Aristocracy of Prison Profits", Catherine Austin Fitts describes what she calls "tapeworm economics" and how the tapeworm game is played.

Private investors arrange for new laws to be created, with a little help from their politician buddies whose campaigns they finance, that benefit the industry in which they wish to invest. These new laws usually do not have society's best interests at heart, just their own financial goals. The investors partner up with powerful law firms that have a kind of revolving door that moves people between high government positions and their own boardroom. The powerful politicians arrange for large government contracts to be granted to the companies that have hired their old law firm to assist with the creation of a particular investment vehicle. Once these investments pay off, the companies use a portion of the profits to finance the campaigns of the politicians seeking reelection, and the "tapeworm" is fed.

The blending of private companies with powerful government agents is the definition of Fascism, and over time it bleeds the economy to death because it destroys actual productivity in favor of the manipulation of numbers, inefficient production, and fake marketplaces. The best bid does not get the contract in this model, only the most connected and powerful bid actually wins the business.

This creates a system where there is massive incompetence through crony capitalism, and where negative behavior is positively reinforced.

Nowhere is this feedback loop of corruption more obvious and prevalent than on Wall Street, where there is a well-worn path from Lower Manhattan to Washington D.C. This problem is not limited to one political party or investment bank, it is fully-encompassing and it captures all of the powerful players in both finance and government. Nobody working in high finance or politics can ignore this parasitic relationship because there is an insane amount of money involved, and this money is the blood that flows through the system and keeps the beast alive.

This philosophy cannot simply be voted out of office because it is more than a few bad apples ruining it for the rest of those upstanding politicians. This is a systemic problem that requires a new way of thinking and a complete overhaul of the current political system because as long as politicians need money to finance their campaigns, there will always be someone willing to hand them a check in exchange for favors.

The Bar From Star Wars

Corporate Cronies have been inserted into high-ranking positions of power inside the federal government administration, showing yet another signal of an empire in decline. The selling off of regulatory positions to people with a ton of money, but no obvious experience, is another box that is ticked on the checklist of collapse. This is in no way limited to President Trump, as all presidents are guilty of it to some degree, but he has made no attempt to hide his nepotism or favoritism for those that kissed his ass during the election.

Hell, he even hired fellow former reality show participant, and current maniac, Omarosa Manigault, as his Director of Communications for the Office of Public Liaison in the White House, a woman he later described as a "lowlife" when she wrote a book implying that he likes to drop "N-Bombs" during meetings, even though she could not prove it and admits she never heard it in person.

Amway's Betsy DeVos, with a net worth of $1 billion, was tapped to run the Department of Education. The lady who was picked to run the public school system because she had no experience in education, government, or public schools, making her the natural fit for this cabinet position. Her brother is Blackwater founder, Eric Prince, a man that made over a billion dollars through the privatization of the wars in Afghanistan and Iraq.

Steve Mnuchin was appointed to head the Treasury, which was a good thing because he certainly does love money. He had a net worth of $385 million after a spotless career in some of the shadiest industries in the world: film producer, hedge fund manager, and as the Chief Information Officer at Goldman Sachs. His job was to steal money for Goldman Sachs through his computer programs that would front-run the market, making losing money an impossibility.

Commerce Secretary, Wilbur Ross, founder of WL Ross & Co., had a net worth of $2.5 billion and was implicated in the theft of $120 million of other people's money while running his firm, a firm that has been fined by the Securities and Exchange Commission for millions of dollars.[188] He also ran the bankruptcy-restructuring advisory practice for the Rothschilds for many years while at N M Rothschild & Sons, where he met Donald Trump while advising him on one of his many bankruptcies.

Former Secretary of State, Rex Tillerson was the CEO of Exxon Mobile and had about $300 million stashed away when he agreed to be insulted by Donald Trump for a year or so. Considering the Secretary of State is a position focused on regime change in foreign countries, and countries with oil are always a prime target, it makes sense that Trump went with a guy that knows the importance of the American Petrodollar, and how to use the threat of embargos to subjugate other countries and force them to bend to their demands.

Elaine Chao, the wife of slack-jawed Mitch McConnell, had an estimated net worth of $22 million and is the obvious choice to become the Secretary of Transportation because nothing says "I love public transportation" like having enough money to buy your own train.

Ben Carson, a former doctor and Trump's pick for Secretary of Housing and Urban Development, probably had very little experience in the urban areas of the country, especially considering his $22 million net worth. However, he did confess to trying to stab his friend with a knife when he was 14, which did give him some street cred.[189]

David Shulkin was worth $17 million, which makes him very relatable to all of the military veterans as the Secretary of Veterans Affairs. Those same veterans loved it when the Secretary took his wife with him to Wimbledon and made the taxpayers foot the bill, then acted like a jerk when the press called him on it. Shulkin finally admitted he should not have done it and repaid the money.[190]

Tom Price was the Secretary of Health and Human Services, and he had serviced himself to a net worth of $10 million. He also helped himself to two dozen

---

[188] Dan Alexander, Forbes, "New Details About Wilbur Ross' Business Point To Pattern Of Grifting".

[189] Fusion, "Ben Carson Tells Jorge Ramos About The Moment He Almost Killed Someone At Age 14".

[190] Dan Mangan, CNBC, "Veterans Affairs Boss David Shulkin Improperly Accepted Wimbledon Tickets, Allowed Wife To Fly To Europe On Taxpayers' Dime, Scathing Report Says".

charter jet flights instead of flying commercial, like he was required to, and thus lost his job within a couple of months.

Even a lifetime politician like Rick Perry had managed to accumulate $2 million after giving lots of "speeches", which was funny considering how crappy he was at both talking and thinking. If the criteria for consideration was "irony", the obvious choice to head the Energy Department was Rick Perry, the very same Energy Department that he could not remember during the debate that cost him a chance at becoming America's Next Top President. Of course, there were no conflicts of interest when considering him for the Energy Department gig, just the three different energy company boards that he sits on, one of which was developing the extremely controversial Dakota Access Pipeline.[191]

Environmental Protection Agency chief Scott Pruitt might not have been as wealthy as the rest of this cast of characters, but he made up for it by taking shadiness to a higher level. He traveled in first-class from Washington to New York and then again to Cincinnati and Rome, with his aides flying coach, which was par for the course with this group. But he also hitched a ride on military planes at a cost of over $36,000 for a single trip from Cincinnati to New York, which was not money well spent. He also was confirmed to have been out of the office for 43 out of 92 days in 2017, and he stuck the taxpayers with the bill for his numerous flights back to Oklahoma where he lived, a theme that runs deep through the Trump administration. He was eventually fired, just like many of the others.

Shotgun Capitalism

The current political system is all about control. It might be controlled through access to money, or controlled through the limitation of money. It could be controlled through access to information or control through the limitation of information.

But it can also be about control through access to dirt.

There are two kinds of captured politicians: those that want to work with powerful business interests, and those that have to.

One does not rise to positions of power within the United States government

---

[191] Associated Press, December 14, 2016, "Rick Perry Is A Board Member Of The Company Behind The Dakota Access Pipeline".

without being controllable in some way. If they do not willingly get onboard with the program, they will be forced to get on board through blackmail.

Former Representative Dr. Dave Janda explained that the best advice that he ever received when he first entered politics at the national level was to stay away from the parties if he could and leave early if he actually did go. When the first party ends, they lock the doors and pull the blinds down before the real show begins. This is where powerful people are recorded without their knowledge while they engage in illegal behavior from drug use to pedophilia, and in some cases ritual sacrifices.

Seriously.

This is not some far fetched plot from a Tom Clancy novel, this happens all the time in Washington D.C. This is as serious as a heart attack, it is 100% real, and it is effective in order to control a person, not just until the end of their political career, but forever.

Former Speaker of the House, Dennis Hastert was extorted for millions of dollars over the course of 40 years for raping kids while he was their wrestling coach, not to mention how many other things he was forced to do while in political office in order to keep the secret safe.[192]

The British people could not figure out why British Prime Minister Edward Heath gave away almost all of Britain's fishing rights to Europe in order to join the European Economic Community, later to be renamed the European Union (EU). He was a notorious pedophile that was extorted for years by other governments across the world, including parts of his own government. To protect his secret he had no choice but to do what those with the goods on him wanted him to do.

General Petraeus, Elliott Spitzer, Senator Larry Craig...the list goes on and on of people in positions of power being brought down through sexual scandals for not doing what they were instructed to do.

It should be becoming clear that this is a tool that is used all the time and must cause people to start thinking about these public scandals in a new way.

A company making a play for a lucrative contract with the government might secretly arrange for money to find its way to the politician making the decision in their favor. Or, they might also purchase some incriminating video featuring that

---

[192] Rod Dreher, The American Conservative, "The Annals Of Dirtbaggery".

same politician from a person running a "Brownstone Operation", like the one that convicted pedophile Jeffrey Epstein was operating from his private jet called "The Lolita Express", and his island in the U.S. Virgin Islands called Little Saint James, aka "Orgy Island".[193]

Not every high-ranking politician is a pedophile, but everyone is controlled to some degree. People simply do not get to the highest levels without being compromised. Since a "crony" is defined as a close friend or companion, this is not Crony Capitalism in the traditional sense, but instead a hybrid version of it where one person is forced into this relationship. A better name might be "Shotgun Capitalism".

It does not have to be this way.

People can get involved with changing the world, but their understanding of this political marriage to big business is fundamental because it is obvious that money is the root of the problem, so people can make decisions with their money to remove it from this form of business.

Leaving big banks in favor of local credit unions is a great start. Refusing to purchase products and services from companies that are involved with shady dealings on Wall Street, harsh product testing on animals, or polluting the environment is something everyone can do with very little effort. Getting their news from other sources than the corporate media is vital because being educated about the world is a great thing, provided that the education that they are getting is accurate and unbiased.

Humanity has the option to withhold their attention, influence, money, and energy from those people or things that simply have not earned it. Maybe one individual's boycott will not make a dent in the quarterly earnings of one of these companies, but a large enough collection of individuals will be noticed, and since money is all they really care about, the removal of money from their business will surely get their attention at some point.

The Athlete's Foot of Washington D.C.

Lobbyists are the Athlete's Foot of politics, found in disgusting bathrooms and infecting unsuspecting people that don't know any better than to stay away from them.

---

[193] Maureen Callahan, New York Post, "The 'Sex Slave' Scandal That Exposed Pedophile Billionaire Jeffrey Epstein".

The idea of lobbying was developed as a way to help a politician become more knowledgeable about a particular topic. There was just a limited amount of time that a Congressman had, so lobbyists would help to educate them about their particular area of specialization, be that healthcare, agriculture, military, or some aspect of the business industry. This way of condensing and streamlining information into smaller portions, allowed elected officials to give off the perception that they knew quite a lot about a variety of industries.

What happened over time was that these lobbyists found they had far more influence than the general public, or maybe even the politicians themselves believed. The elected officials leaned on them for information and advice, and once that started to happen, the lobbying industry really took off.

If a company could not get to the politician directly to pitch their service, perhaps they could get to the trusted lobbyist and have that person present their idea, product, or service. That influence does come at a cost, and thus the industry of lobbying was created.

Grifters and scumbags like Paul Manafort and the Podesta brothers that found themselves with tremendous influence with people like the Clintons and the Trumps sold access to these powerful Washington insiders to the highest bidders and put a literal fortune into their bank accounts in the process.

What becomes crystal clear when looking at the lobbying industry is that if an industry has a lot of money to spend, and they do not mind working with some unsavory characters, almost anything is for sale. That influence can come in the form of favorable legislation, a reduction of regulations, the suppression of information, and even the criminalization of free speech.

Energy Transfer Partners is the hated company behind the very controversial Dakota Access Pipeline, and they have been accused of using their money to fund lobbying to change the laws surrounding protesting because so many people have protested against their project. Rather than adjust their project, talk with the protestors, or bribe officials to push their proposal through, they instead hired the American Legislative Exchange Council (ALEC) to lobby for measures to increase the length of prison sentences for protests related to "critical infrastructure".

They have made a decision that if they cannot win an argument with the people that disagree with their pipeline, they will just try to criminalize free speech and make sure that the laws put those people that are protesting them in prison for long stretches of time.

That is not all that they have done to silence dissent. Energy Transfer Partners has also hired an unlicensed private security firm, TigerSwan, to surveil, infiltrate the groups that are protesting their project, and even attack them during protests. They also filed multiple lawsuits and used the threat of additional lawsuits to try to silence their critics. They sued Greenpeace for almost a billion dollars claiming that they were guilty of a RICO crime of racketeering, and they presumably did so with a straight face knowing that they are the ones guilty of the organized crime.

This is what America has become.

There are 14,000 lobbyists working in Washington D.C. where roughly $2.5 billion is spent each year by a variety of companies, industries, organizations, charities, and rich people. Money flows into the campaigns of politicians, but a lot of it sloshes into lobbying organizations that use their connections to influence policy. Some of the largest and most influential companies invest vast fortunes into lobbying efforts because the return on their investment is so massive.

These are just some of the publicly traded companies that have spent the most money on direct lobbying over the last decade:

General Electric: $201.5 million   Exxon Mobil: $155.8 million
Verizon: $143.2 million   Boeing Co: $173.3 million
Blue Cross/Blue Shield: $225.5 million   AT&T: $165.2 million
Pfizer: $123.8 million   Raytheon: $65.7 million

Newcomers from the tech industry have come to understand the benefits of greasing the wheels of power, and these are some figures showing their spending in 2017:

Facebook: $11.5 million   Apple: $7 million
Amazon: $12.8 million   Google/Alphabet: $18.1 million
Microsoft: $8.5 million   Comcast: $15.3 million

So how effective were their lobbying efforts? Really effective, and a detailed list can be found at OpenSecrets.org.

When Northrop Grumman's sales increased from $5.2 billion to $11.1 billion on their $148,000,000 lobbying investment, it resulted in a profit 40 times larger than the year before. The increase was even more staggering for Lockheed Martin who saw their $144,000,000 in lobbying investments generate $7.2 billion, or 50 times more profit than the year before.

It is hard to find anything with a 5,000%+ return like the legalized bribery of lobbying, and it is a destabilizing factor because it allows money to directly purchase influence and shape public policy. Decisions are not being made based on what is the right thing to do, the smartest thing to do, or the best use of taxpayer funds. Decisions are being bought and sold by people that are compromised and unethical, and the American public pays the price, both figuratively and literally.

However, when outright bribery does not get the job done of influencing the public to settle the way in which they desire, sometimes they need to bring in the big boys to influence public opinion in a very different, and more serious way.

False Flags For Change

A "false flag" is a horrific, staged event, that is blamed on a political enemy and used as a pretext to start a war or enact draconian laws in the name of "national security".

A false version of an event is given to the general public by the government and their accomplices in the corporate media with the intent of manipulating the emotions of the people, while simultaneously manufacturing an outburst of patriotic support that the government can then use as their justification to introduce laws that would normally be unpopular.

It is psychological warfare using mass trauma.

So far, the Coronavirus plandemic has been the biggest one, but there have been many others.

Sometimes these events are staged and totally fake, like the Boston Bombing, and sometimes the events are real but the people responsible are masked, like 9/11. The common denominator is that the government and the media know that these events are not what they claim them to be, but they must sell the lie to the public in order to fulfill their agenda. The agendas change, but the stories are always lies, and they want the public to be fearful, angry, vengeful, and outraged enough to "do something" about the problem that the government created.

There is ample evidence of governments dressing up as the enemy and terrorizing their own citizens in order to justify some foreign war or domestic operation they wish to kick off. When a country wants to go to war against another country, but they do not have an honest justification for doing so, sometimes they pretend to be the other side and invade themselves.

The Reichstag fire that enraged the Germans when it was discovered that the Poles had been responsible, was a perfect example of a false flag by the Germans against themselves in order to justify the slaughter of well over a million Poles, and the reduction of Warsaw, the most heavily bombed city during World War 2, to literal rubble.[194]

False flags have been a tool of psychopathic governments for so long because they are very effective as a tool against their citizens. The average person is at an enormous disadvantage when trying to comprehend the idea of attacking one's self in order to blame it on a political rival to generate the pretext for going to war.

Governments may run the operation from start to finish like 9/11 and the 7/7 London Bombing, outsource the job to contractors as they did to Craft International for the Boston Bombing, coordinate an Integrated Capstone Event between FEMA and the Department of Homeland Security like the Sandy Hook drill, or simply order law enforcement to stand down and allow the event to happen, as they did for both the Shoe & Underwear Bombers.

Almost all wars are started by false flag events. That is how it is done.

In order to pull these events off in a way that is believable, the governments must use their assets in the corporate media to push the narrative that they have crafted and sell the hell out of the story in a coordinated manner. The vast majority of Americans do not believe that the media would intentionally lie about a larger terrorist event, but they would be mistaken. Operation Mockingbird was a CIA operation that was put in place 50 years ago in order to corrupt the media and infiltrate their operations. That program is still operational, the framework is still in place, and the nightly news is still the intellectual property of the Central Intelligence Agency.

---

[194] Tony Patterson, The Telegraph, "Historians Find Proof That Nazis Burnt Reichstag".

Although they have been manufacturing these bloody stories and selling them through the corporate media for decades, they are surprisingly bad at it, and the alternative media has been able to analyze these events and zero in on the lies. The truth of the matter is that it really is not very hard to find the glitches in their stories, especially when one knows what to look for.

This is how the corporate media television news reports a staged or false flag event:

• The corporate media announces who carried out the attack within a matter of minutes.

• There is no logical motive for the mass attack, but the media creates one that seems disjointed and clunky.

• The corporate media starts demonizing the "terrorist", even though an investigation has not actually begun.

• The corporate media channels all report the same major components of the story in unison, with no diversion from their identical talking points, and even their tone of voice, speech pattern, and vocal tempo are choreographed, and practically identical regardless of the television channel.

• The "Breaking News" trigger phrase will be pushed immediately by the corporate media as an indicator that this story is important.

• Intentional disinformation deliberately inserted to marginalize those seeking an alternative narrative.

• The flow of information from the scene is assigned and controlled by only one authority figure.

• A victim body count will be pushed in order to traumatize viewers, as well as graphic descriptions of the horrifying event, with no regard for younger viewers.

• The corporate media almost immediately calls for gun control, even if a gun was not used in the event.

• In the days following the event, televised charity events featuring celebrities are exploited to create funding campaigns and call for new legislation to "do something" to fix the situation that is alleged to have caused or allowed the event to happen.

Where things tend to get away from the corporate media is when the alternative media jumps on board and starts to sort through the information without the obvious bias that comes with working for a controlled television news network or channel. These are the things that the alternative media notices and reports on that are vastly different from the story, and important aspects of the event that the corporate media either ignore or are oblivious to.

• Independent investigative journalists later discovered that some people had prior knowledge of the event, but the corporate media covers up that information.

• There happens to be a training exercise being held at the same time that simulates an attack that is very similar to the actual attack.[195]

• The alleged "terrorist" has no real military or weapons training, yet he carries multiple guns. He usually leaves a manifesto in their car or at their home because they get killed or "suicided" at the end of the attack so that they can never speak about the incident.[196]

• The physical evidence from the crime scene gets lost, contaminated, or even intentionally destroyed, and the surveillance cameras either malfunction or the footage is confiscated and labeled "Classified" by the FBI.[197]

• Most eyewitness video evidence is either grainy, out of focus, or non-existent, and the good quality footage either gets confiscated by the FBI, or the person's cell phone memory gets wiped on "national security" grounds.

• Independent eyewitnesses gave conflicting accounts about what actually happened at the event, but those eyewitnesses that were interviewed on the corporate news give unrealistic and overly-detailed descriptions of what they claim to have witnessed.

• Alleged victims are discovered to be crisis actors that appear in multiple events, promoting faked or staged cell phone footage to further push the

---

[195] Jon Rappoport, Global Research, "Training Exercises Dovetail With Mass Shootings. What Are The Odds?".
[196] Mike Romero, Physics 911, "Mohammed Atta: Terrorist, Patsy, Or Scapegoat?".
[197] Michael Stratford, Classroom, "Why Were The 9/11 Pentagon Tapes Seized By The FBI?".

intended account of events or to authenticate the story.[198]

•   Families of victims show odd behavior, no emotion, fake crying, or even laughter during interviews. This is known as "duping delight" and it is a clear and obvious indicator of deception.[199]

•   The families of the victims either have acting backgrounds or ties to government agencies, and the "victims" receive millions in federal payoffs or charity proceeds.

•   There are wild fluctuations and changes in the critical details from the first accounts of the story, especially from real eyewitnesses that are not involved in the marketing of this event.

•   Several of previous false flag events or drills have similar patterns and inconsistencies that have been cataloged by the alternative media over the years.

•   The retroactive construction of the final story often takes weeks, but the plot is unrealistically figured out by the media, in conjunction with law enforcement, in a matter of minutes which is inconsistent with logic, especially when sorting out complex events like 9/11.

Opinions on false flags may be different if the population knew how many "terrorist events" had drills running at the same location that was simulating the identical situation, but that information is never discussed on the nightly news. There were dozens of drills running on 9/11 simulating terrorist events.

The 7/7 bombings were running a drill simulating an explosion in the exact tube stations, at the exact same time, according to Peter Power, the person that was running the drill who went on television to admit to it.[200]

The Boston Bombing was announced in advance through the Boston Globe's Twitter account that there was going to be a drill simulating a bombing in front of the library where the marathon ended.[201]

---

[198] Who What Why, "Boston Marathon Bombing: A Primer".
[199] Kyle Hunt, Renegade Tribute, "More Duping Delight After Yet Another Hoax Shooting".
[200] Michel Chossudovsky, Global Research, "The London 7/7 Mock Terror Drill: What Relationship To The Real Time Terror Attacks?".
[201] Boston Globe's Twitter Account, April 15, 2013, 12:53 pm, *Officials: There Will Be A Controlled Explosion Opposite The Library Within One Minute As Part Of Bomb Squad Activities.*

Twice.[202]

What are the chances?

Then there's the Big One.

The Johns Hopkins Center for Health Security released the following statement about nCoV and their pandemic exercise:

In October 2019, the Johns Hopkins Center for Health Security hosted a pandemic tabletop exercise called Event 201 with partners, the World Economic Forum and the Bill & Melinda Gates Foundation. Recently, the Center for Health Security has received questions about whether that pandemic exercise predicted the current novel coronavirus outbreak in China. To be clear, the Center for Health Security and partners did not make a prediction during our tabletop exercise. For the scenario, we modeled a fictional coronavirus pandemic, but we explicitly stated that it was not a prediction. Instead, the exercise served to highlight preparedness and response challenges that would likely arise in a very severe pandemic. We are not now predicting that the nCoV-2019 outbreak will kill 65 million people. Although our tabletop exercise included a mock novel coronavirus, the inputs we used for modeling the potential impact of that fictional virus are not similar to nCoV-2019.

• "Event 201" was the fourth major pandemic exercise that the Center for Health Security has run – a mere three months before the official outbreak of...guess what...a coronavirus pandemic.

• The first, called "Dark Winter", was held in 2001 and simulated a smallpox attack on Oklahoma. The timing was just a few months before 9/11.

• This was followed by "Atlantic Storm", to see how world leaders would manage the catastrophe of a fast-moving global epidemic of a deadly disease.

• Finally, there was "Clade X" – a daylong pandemic simulation held by the Johns Hopkins Center for Health Security, in May 2018 – also funded by the Gates Foundation.

But wait, there is more proof that all world "leaders" were reading off the same Covid-19 script.

---

[202] Boston Globe's Twitter Account, April 15, 2013, 12:53 pm, *BREAKING NEWS: Police Will Have Controlled On 600 Block On Boylston Street.*

- The Global Preparedness Monitoring Board's 2019 Annual report confirms that the United Nations (including the WHO) conducted at least two systemwide training and simulation exercises, including one covering the deliberate release of a lethal respiratory pathogen.

What it really boils down to is that once a government uses false flag events to terrorize their population in order to get what they want from them in terms of a reaction, they can never stop. They will always have to keep the lies and the propaganda going, and the United States has been either authorizing, or actually conducting false flag terrorist events against their citizens since at least the Oklahoma City bombing, and more than likely before that.

A society that is built on a foundation of lies and self-directed terrorist attacks by their own government is a society that will eventually crumble once a critical mass of the population awakens to the reality of their situation.

The United States is at that point.

Neverending Wars

"He picked up a piece of paper. And he said, 'I just got this down from upstairs', meaning the Secretary of Defense's office, 'today'. And he said, 'This is a memo that describes how we're going to take out seven countries in five years, starting with Iraq, and then Syria, Lebanon, Libya, Somalia, Sudan and, finishing off, Iran". – Wesley Clark, General of the United States Army (R), March 2007, talking about a conversation he had inside the Pentagon back in 2001.

When Wesley Clark made this jaw-dropping admission on the television show *Democracy Now!* in 2007, it gave the public a glimpse into the workings of a psychopathic government mentality that puts world domination and resource control above humanity and suffering. What General Clark exposed is premeditated murder, by the Bush regime and all of his blood-thirsty buddies both in government and in big business, against millions of people in the Middle East all because of money and power.

If people are trying to make sense of the world they live in, but they just cannot seem to make the pieces fit, they should try looking at it from a new perspective and attempt to come to terms with an unpleasant fact. The banks have the real power, and those banks make lots of money during wars, therefore as long as there are powerful banking institutions and a layer of management that values profits before all else, there will be wars. It is really just as simple as that.

The American Empire plans its wars of aggression well in advance, and though they give the impression that they are always retaliatory in nature, they are carefully orchestrated years in advance. Evidence for this can be found in the war plan for the invasion of Afghanistan that was crafted before the events of 9/11 even took place.

They follow a pattern of demonizing another nation, then using their alleged actions as the pretext for initiating economic sanctions first, in order to soften up the target financially from the inside, followed by direct military action always framed as just and limited to military targets.

Sanctions as a Tool for Regime Change

Sanctions are used as a tool to cut off funding and punish countries that are not falling in line with the diabolical agenda of what author Peter Dale Scott named the "Deep State". As an example, they may fear that Iran is selling a portion of their oil for yuan or rubles, a direct violation of the Petrodollar scam, so they slap sanctions on Iran through their compromised politicians in Washington in order to prop up their crooked banking and oil company buddies. A couple of things are a result when something like this happens, and it happens all the time, (cough cough) Venezuela.

First, the money from around the world that normally flows into a particular country that has crossed the United States, in this example, Iran, gets choked off quickly because they can no longer sell their oil through the traditional channels that are controlled by OPEC and the United States. This forces sales to go underground or around the sanctions if they can. Sales still happen because there is usually so much money at stake, but it certainly works to complicate the process and at the very least slow things down.

The United States uses the SWIFT (Society for Worldwide Interbank Financial Telecommunication) system that enables banking institutions to send and receive financial transaction information securely for everything dollar-related. They have been known to switch off permission for countries that annoy America, making it virtually impossible for them to conduct international banking using the dollar.[203]

---

[203] Henry Farrell, The Washington Post, February 28, 2015, *Russia Is Hinting at a New Cold War Over SWIFT. So What Is SWIFT?*.

Second, this destabilizes the country, financially at first, then politically if the situation does not get fixed. As more of the citizens are affected financially, they start to lean on their political structure to demand that something is done about the current situation. Sometimes that means caving in on whatever the issue was that got sanctions slapped on them in the first place, but also the CIA funds the political opponents of the current regime and has them push for a removal of the people in power.

Third, the exportation capability of the country grinds to a halt which creates a supply shortage around the world for the items that the country is accustomed to exporting, like oil, which in turn drives up the prices for the particular items. Less supply, same demand, higher prices.

Fourth, the corporations that pushed their partners in government to put sanctions on a country find that they are now able to sell their products for a much higher price now that their competition has been effectively locked up and put out of business for a while.

Fifth, part of these profits find their way back into the American political system in the form of campaign contributions that can now be unlimited thanks to the Citizens United decision. The money that flowed into the American political system works to keep the policies the same since the people benefitting are the ones throwing their money behind these politicians. This leads to more sanctions being forced on other countries that do not cooperate, and the loop continues.

During an interview on "60 Minutes" on May 12th, 1996, Reporter Lesley Stahl asked Secretary of State Madeleine Albright a question about the sanctions the United States imposed on Iraq after the 1st Gulf War.

Lesley Stahl: *"We have heard that a half million children have died. I mean, that's more children than died in Hiroshima. And, you know, is the price worth it?"*

Secretary of State Madeleine Albright: *"I think this is a very hard choice, but the price – we think the price is worth it."*

Her response was what one would expect from a Globalist hellbent on redrawing the Middle East while thinning the herd and trying to justify their imperialist ambitions. A reprehensible statement that underscores the mentality of empire builders that operate under the philosophy that the ends always justify the means.

Placing sanctions on countries and imposing "No-Fly Zones" is a passive-aggressive way of declaring war without actually doing so, and neither of those things makes Americans safer. Just stop and ask how placing sanctions on Syria makes the United States safer?

It does not, and the suggestion that somehow it does is ludicrous.

America has been involved in some kind of war during 225 out of the nation's total 242 years of existence. Another way of looking at it is that during the entire span of American history, 93% of the time America is involved in at least one war. The United States has also never gone a full decade without being involved in a war of some kind, and they still operate 800+ military bases in 80 different countries.[204]

The lies about the role of the military changed after World War 2 when the Department of War was rebranded as the Department of Defense. There was never anything defensive about the foreign policy of America even back then. The military does not have all that much defense to play, especially when one considers that two really large oceans do a pretty good job of creating a natural line of defense across half of the country's borders, a third line is guarded by an ally, and the fourth line is getting a wall if a particular orange-skinned man has anything to say about it.

Perhaps he does not realize that Mexico has ladders?

The American military has been described as the defenders of freedom and the spreaders of democracy, neither of which are even remotely accurate and are outright lies. Despite what the television ads might say, there is no way to "be all that you can be in the Army" because the Army is not what most people think it is.

If one imagines America's foreign policy as a "carrot or stick" philosophy, with the American dollar as the carrot, then the United States military is the stick. For countries that play ball, and that might encompass a variety of positions on the field that a country can play, economic riches and military protection are in their future. For countries that refuse to bow down to the Empire, the American stick of exceptionalism will begin to poke at them, slowly at first, then more consistently until it becomes a full-blown bludgeoning under the guise of

---

[204] Darius Shahtahmasebi, Antimedia, "The U.S. Empire Has Up To 1,000 Baes In 80 Countries".

spreading democracy and removing dictators.

American foreign policy and the strength of the United States dollar are defended and enforced at the barrel of a gun, and where gold and righteousness once backed these two concepts, now only the strength of the military stands in their place.

So if America's foreign policy is forced on other nations under the threat of violence, what exactly is America's foreign policy agenda?

The answer is as sickening as it is shocking, but America's foreign policy is set by the multinational corporations that fund the politicians' political campaigns and put them into high office. That is the tradeoff that happened every election cycle undercover, of course, until Citizens United was passed and legalized bribery by the world's corporate masters.

Smedly Butler talked about this in his book *War Is A Racket* when he explained that the United States military was involved in the Banana Wars on behalf of U.S. Fruit Company, and how J.P. Morgan financed coups to try and overthrow dictators to secure the profitability of his company.

This is nothing new, but the understanding of how things really operate has begun to come to light over the past decade as more and more people wake up to the fraud that has been perpetrated by big businesses against the interests of the citizens of the world, their own customers, in many cases.

Part of the reason why the United States has engaged in many massive wars and countless coups in the Middle East is due to oil, and no amount of lies coming from the mouths of George W. Bush, Dick Cheney, and Donald Rumsfeld can convince the public otherwise. This is so obvious that it requires little defense, but Afghanistan is a different story.

The story that was told to the American people about why the United States was compelled to commit hundreds of thousands of troops and trillions of dollars toward invading this stone-age country was because Osama bin Laden had directed his minions from his cave fortress in Tora Bora to attack the United States on 9/11, a story that is so flimsy and laughable that everyone that retold that version of events with a straight face should be ashamed of themselves.

The real reason for invading Afghanistan had zero to do with the Taliban, or Al-Qaeda, or ISIS, or bin Laden. It was about finally being able to run and secure an oil pipeline on behalf of the oil interests that practically run the United States, it was for the trillions of dollars in unmined minerals that are locked underground and in the mountains, it was to establish a base for opium production in one of the few regions in the world suitable for growing the basic ingredient of heroin, and it was to create a war that would destroy the country and require a resupply of arms from the Military-Information-Terror complex, as well as the rebuilding of the country through the massive engineering firms like the one whose CEO left to become the Vice President of the United States and the controller of America's military ambitions.

If it had actually been about terrorism then the United States would have been gone after three years of mopping up a bunch of guys on horses that cannot shoot their AK-47s straight, but instead, it does not appear that they plan to ever leave.

Smedly Butler was correct, war is a racket. It always has been, and it always will be. Given a long enough timeline, it actually destroys both sides, as the empirical ambitions and spreading the military too thin always come back to haunt the aggressor in the end. Think this cannot work to end the American Empire, just look at the United Soviet Socialist Republic.

The United States of Socialist America

In order for the Controllers' plan for a New World Order to actually work, there cannot be any "superpowers" strong enough to push back against their agenda for world domination.

The United Soviet Socialist Republic was dismantled in the 1990s and was cleared out of the way, and here is how it was done.

The United Soviet Socialist Republic (USSR) is by definition an oxymoron since one cannot be socialist and a republic at the same time and many of the countries were "united" at the barrel of a gun. This was the Russian Empire, for lack of a better term, that formed after the second world war and lasted until 1991 when all hell broke loose and the entire government collapsed in what seemed like a matter of weeks.

The reality of the situation was that the columns of the empire had been rotting away for years, out of sight from the average Russian citizen, until one day the whole thing just collapsed. For those that had an understanding of what was really happening behind the Red Curtain, the end was inevitable. For many outsiders in America, they were not surprised that the empire imploded, but they were stunned at how fast everything went down. There were warning signs everywhere for those with the eyes to see them, but the myopia was so severe that those with a front-row seat were unable to see what was happening right in front of their eyes.

What happened to the Russian Empire will happen to the United States Empire, and for those unable or unwilling to heed the warning signs, the price they pay for ignoring the obvious will be steep.

- The Russian invasion of Afghanistan had a big impact on the attitude of the developing countries and the third world against Russia. And for years the Soviets were preaching that they were supporting the developing countries to maintain their freedom. However, when the USSR invaded Afghanistan, people found that Russia was not a reliable ally. The same way Soviets invaded Afghanistan they could invade any country as well. The occupation of Afghanistan caused irreversible internal conflicts between the Soviet republics and the Soviet government. By the time Mikhail Gorbachev took the position of general secretary in the Community Party and ordered the Red Army to withdraw from Afghanistan, the economic and military resources for the invasion were drained.

- Oil cratered from $66 per barrel in 1980 down to $20 by 1986, no doubt due to external forces that had a vested interest in bankrupting the USSR's oil industry. This was not the reason why the USSR broke up, but it was part of chipping away at its economy and internal funding mechanisms.

- And, in 2020, under the guise of a supposed "pandemic", oil was taken down from $60 to as low as -$35. Yes, negative $35 in April 2020 for the exact same reasons as before: to take down the USA's empire based on the Petrodollar. The USA might be more accurately described as the USSA.

- People living in western countries remember the images of Russian bread lines and old Babushka ladies freezing while waiting to shop in grocery stores with empty shelves, but that is simply how the corporate media framed the situation to paint the picture that they wanted of a country in decline economically.

- The military parades were pumped nightly through the television sets and into American homes in order to scare the populace into not complaining about the arms buildup that was sucking trillions of dollars out of the United States government and into the pockets of defense contractors that continued to push the Red Curtain scare in order to keep their businesses booming. The Military-Industrial complex framed their situation to paint the picture that they wanted of a threatening country on the incline militarily.

What did not make it onto the nightly news in America was the real situation that was actually happening in the USSR and that was that their empire was coming unraveled socially. The integrity of the country was disintegrating, and even Gorbachev's prime minister Nikolai Ryzhkov acknowledged this when he laid the blame on their culture and that those of them in positions of authority all, without exception, stole from themselves, took bribes, lied in the papers and from podiums, hung medals on each other, and wallowed in their lies.[205] It was a cultural gutting in conjunction with the graft that caused many of the most educated and intellectual Soviets to flee the country out of a lack of respect by the government towards them. They felt unappreciated and ignored, as well as oppressed both politically and spiritually.

This is the way the United States currently behaves, and it is like looking into a crystal ball to see the future of the United States. America, in its current form, cannot be allowed to continue. It is time for the American Empire to be destroyed so that it does not pose a threat to their plan. The balkanization of the empire will seek to weaken it by breaking off chunks from the main core, much like what happened to Russia and its satellite countries, and to Yugoslavia around the same time. Debasing the currency will almost always take down a society, but there are many reasons why a government feels that they have to resort to using this tactic. The murdering of its own citizens by governments is typically frowned upon by the remaining living citizens, so that starts a chain reaction that eventually leads to the overthrow of the government. The exact sequence of events might not align, but the outcome is usually the same.

There was an obvious economic component to the demise of the USSR, as well as political and social ones. Central planning is a form of government that simply does not work no matter how many times it is tried, and it always leads to lies and corruption inside the government, and economic hardship for the masses as the size of the population grows. The arms race against the United States slowly bled the country dry, plus they loosened up their grip on the Eastern Bloc countries giving the impression that they were losing control of their satellite territories, but the reason that both Ryzhkov and Gorbachev gave for the collapse of the Soviet Union was actually due to the decimation of morality.

---

[205] Leon Aron, *The "Mystery" of the Soviet Collapse.*

Gorbachev's restructuring of the USSR, known to the world as "Perestroika", was a political movement started years earlier that was designed to reform the Communist Party of the Soviet Union through a policy of openness, otherwise known as "glasnost", which would work to begin the process of the decentralization of power.

Clearly, this was a monumental task, and one that brought a ton of heat on Gorbachev, but he felt that moving away from the arms race and using that cash to reform the government and improve the lives of ordinary Soviets was the right thing to do. This is part of the reason why Oliver Stone, through his amazing 10-part docuseries *The Untold History of the United States*, describes Mikhail Gorbachev as one of the most important men of the 20th century.

The decentralization of power meant that the empire could no longer retain their colonies like Lithuania, Latvia, and Estonia, so they were spun off like a company going through bankruptcy that splits their divisions into separate entities and sells them off for pennies on the ruble. These countries eventually fell into the hands of NATO, and the breakup of the USSR started to look remarkably similar to the collapse of the British Empire after both world wars when they had expanded beyond their social desire and economic ability to carry those costs and had to divest itself of some of its assets around the globe, like India and Singapore.

The decentralization of the USSR into smaller republic states also took on the appearance of the United States in some ways with independent states' rights plus a smaller central federal power, whereas the previous governmental model had all power retained by the central government.

The irony is that as the USSR began to take on the characteristics of the United States, the United States started to take on the characteristics of the USSR by consolidating power into the hands of the few in the federal government, and by attempting to dictate foreign policy to other countries through the threat of force.

There is an old saying that "history repeats itself", but a more accurate metaphor would probably be that history does not repeat itself, but it does rhyme. The same exact situations, caused by the same exact things usually do not happen, but there are similarities in events that cause similar outcomes.

The Off-Balance Sheet Wars

What is referred to as the "Black Budget" is really just a covert slush fund financed by the Department of Defense with money that is never detailed in the reports by the department? In 2013, the Department of Defense received around $2.6 trillion, with an estimated $50 billion being diverted to the Black Budget. This is chump change compared to what is really being diverted into the underworld economy.

This unacknowledged money is used for financing some aspects of the spy agencies, secret military technologies, and a whole bunch of other covert projects. The money gaps get filled in by the illegal sale of drugs and the trafficking of kids that a branch of the CIA runs, as well as the sale of Treasury bonds by HUD and the DOD out the front door, while the money goes missing out the back door, a figure that Professor Mark Skidmore and Catherine Austin Fitts calculated as being at least $21 trillion.[206]

One might assume that with all this money at the disposal of the intelligence agencies, terrorism would be a thing of the past. This would be a classic miscalculation as the intelligence agencies create the terrorists that they claim to be saving the world from. They devised these organizations like Al-Qaeda as a group of mercenaries on a list that they can pull from in order to kick off violence in countries that are not going along with their plan.

In fact, the translation of the words Al-Qaeda into English is "The Base", as in, the database.[207] The database of names of the mercenary army that they used to defeat the Russians in Afghanistan in the 1980s.

Like their buddies running the pharmaceutical companies, they invent the disease in order to sell the world the cure, only in this case the disease is terrorism and the cure is more money for the military and the destruction of the Middle East.

The American Empire does not want a safe and stable world because as long as there is an external threat to the security of the nation, those in power can remain in power under the guise of protecting the people. Wars are not fought between good and evil. When it gets to the point of a war between two countries it is a war between evil and evil, with both sides financed by the global banking syndicate that is just as bad, if not worse, than the two countries fighting each other.

---

[206] Laurence Kotlikoff, Forbes, "Has Our Government Spent $21 Trillion Of Our Money Without Telling Us?".
[207] Collins Dictionary.

The people do not feel protected by those government agents that are currently in power because their foreign policy has actually made America a much bigger target than it has ever been. Even though 9/11 was a false flag operation, Americans feel like the country squandered the goodwill that it had throughout the world by starting indiscriminate wars, illegally detaining people without trials, bombing villages, bringing in private military contractors that murdered civilians without just cause, torturing suspected terrorists in offshore penal colonies, using depleted uranium and white phosphorus, and acting like maniacs all over the Middle East.

One thing that is becoming clear to many people after almost two straight decades of war in the region is that the United States and its allies are not there to spread democracy and liberate the Middle East from terrorists. They did not invade these countries to bring peace, they brought war, and it is becoming more obvious by the day that the American military has no intention of ever leaving.

According to Wikileaks on September 21st, 2018, the US Senate voted 93-7 for a $674 billion military spending bill, again choosing to spend more than half of the federal discretionary budget on the military and spies. Every single Senate Democrat supported the bill, so it seems pretty clear that the myth of Democrats being anti-war should be finally put to rest.

Every day there are 22 American soldiers, or roughly 8,000 each year, that would rather kill themselves than to continue to suffer, after participating in these wars of aggression.[208] People think that the only country that is destroyed by war is the one being invaded and defeated, but the American Empire is showing that they too are losing these wars, although in a much different way. Maybe the bridges, roads, and power plants inside the United States are not being bombed by a foreign adversary, but the infrastructure of America is being worn down, the people themselves. There is almost no support for the war in Afghanistan inside the United States, and nobody really has a good explanation for why the military is still even there, except for some leftover Pentagon and White House talking points about "freedom and democracy", or something like that.

The truth about war is that it destroys both sides but in different ways. The bleeding of money, soldiers, and support that the Afghanistan War caused the USSR and destroyed their empire, will be the undoing of the American Empire as well.

---

[208] Carl Andrew Castro, University of Southern California, "Suicides In The Military: The Post-Modern Combat Veteran And The Hemingway Effect".

Just as the people running this planet planned.

Division of the Public

If the goal was to divide the people into smaller and smaller groups so that they can be more easily controlled, what would be the best way to make that happen?

Obviously, a division by race and the color of one's skin is the most obvious, both from a visual standpoint and from a cultural one as well.

Beyond race, there is political division through the red team vs. blue team of American politics, as well as gender division through the "Me Too" movement where all men were lumped in with Harvey Weinstein and vilified whether they were guilty of deviant behavior or not.

There was the creation of multiple gender pronouns and the division that came through that, gun lovers vs. gun haters, border wall enthusiasts against ladder lovers, and all the way down to people divided over whether a dress was really black and blue, or was actually white and gold.

There is an endless number of ways to divide people into smaller groups, so what is the point, who is doing it, what are their methods, and what are their motives?

The controllers of America want the people to be outraged and overreact, but not to actually engage with one another, less the plebs discover that they have way more in common with one another than they realized. In order for the controllers' plans to work best, they need the masses to be fearful, panicked, and self-destructive, not calm and rational.

The Cloward-Piven Strategy

The idea of dividing the people into smaller groups is not a new strategy, not even for the United States. The many have been controlling the few for at least half a century in American politics, but most people do not know that there is actually a name for the strategy that these political controllers implemented years ago.

The Cloward–Piven strategy is a political strategy developed by Democratic-leaning Richard Cloward and Frances Fox Piven, American political activists, and sociologists, in 1966. They theorized that in order to get rid of the welfare system that they thought was dysfunctional and clunky, they could break the system by inviting everyone to join the system all at once, thus causing the system to overload, the welfare offices to be overwhelmed, and the states to go practically bankrupt. Once the United States public welfare system was destroyed, they wanted to replace it with a guaranteed annual income that they theorized would end poverty while reforming the system along lines more politically feasible.

They noticed that many people were eligible for welfare but were not receiving it either because they were unaware or unwilling to apply for it. Their plan called for a massive push to inform those eligible for welfare and encourage them to immediately apply, thus crashing the system. Once they pushed as many of the poor people as quickly as they could into the welfare system, they then incited class warfare between the middle and upper class against the lower class. This included racial division, ethnic tension, political clashes, immigration battles, and stigmatizing welfare recipients.

Cloward and Piven felt that this would force the government to scrap the current system and bring in a new system that would take the burden off of the local and state governments and place that financial cost upon the federal government instead. They hilariously believed that this would actually help the Democratic party by unifying them and showing them as the caring and compassionate people that they proclaim to be because they had heroically stepped in to solve the problem that they had just created. They were going to create a national solution to poverty that would help the poor, help local agencies, and help state budgets, all while transferring the financial and bureaucratic obligation on to the federal government.

The people receiving this free money in the form of a welfare check would be indebted and loyal to the Democrats and vote for them as long as the checks kept arriving. This would instantly create a huge new batch of Democratic voters that would support local, state, and national candidates all while being financed by the federal government.

The Clower-Piven model is still a fundamental strategy used by American Democratic politicians to garner votes from those on the lowest rung of the socioeconomic ladder. The open border policy under the Obama administration allowed the flow of undocumented people to funnel into the country while the administration worked to either provide them with a path to citizenship or amnesty, thus allowing them the ability to vote, hopefully for Democrats.

The Republicans were no better, they just did not want the immigrants in the country at all.

A massive flow of illegal immigrants also works to destabilize the country on the receiving end because it puts heavy burdens on infrastructure, schools, welfare, low-level jobs, the legal system, prisons, and so on.

America has been turned against itself, just like Clower & Piven theorized that it would, but the amplification of the division by the corporate media was probably something that they could only dream of.

And nowhere has it been more evident than in the convenient changing-of-the-narrative than *circa* May 2020; George Floyd's death by Covid-19 and the start of The Great 21st Century Race War – turning family against family, friends against friends, and black & white against white & black.

Division By All Means

The clearest division of the public is through skin color and ethnicity, though these days the country is appearing more and more homogenized. Beyond the obvious color of people's skin, the division continues through things like religious beliefs, political leanings, socioeconomic standing, and education levels.

People are different, that is not a problem. In fact, that is part of what made America work back when it actually worked. The problem is when these differences are looked at as being divisions, and these characteristics are not viewed as diversifying the gene pool, but contaminating it. When one group of people feel like their blood is more valuable than someone else's because they have more money, things start to get serious and people get defensive and offended.

Religion, long proclaimed to be a unifying force, has done more to divide people into smaller groups than all the governments in the world combined. The Crusades, the Spanish Inquisition, the Mayans ripping people's hearts out on the top of a pyramid...all of these brutal murder campaigns were conducted under the cover of their religion but actually used to kill people that have differing beliefs.

Though mass sacrifices are not a big problem in the United States, the division of the public on religious grounds is very much alive and unwell. The persecution of Muslims that started in the hours after 9/11 has not slowed down, as brain-dead, racists Americans attacked Hindus wearing turbans because they did not know the difference between the two religions. The hardcore Christian right preaches about being good to one another while demonizing Muslims. Christian fascist Joel Ostein preaches about compassion for our fellow man, then refuses to open his massive church with a capacity for 19,000 people, once the home of the Houston Rockets NBA basketball team, to those people displaced by Hurricane Harvey in Houston until the media pressure to do so became so overwhelming that he had to. Lunatic preacher and founder of the 700 Club, Pat Robertson, is constantly calling for everyone that is not white to be removed from his world, especially those in Haiti that got what they deserved from the earthquake because they signed a deal with the Devil a couple of hundred years ago.

Nationalism is another tool used for division, where people associate their identity with a flag from their nation, then set about to attack anyone from another country simply because they were born in a different place on the planet. Hollywood is the biggest pusher of this division, as every other movie released is in some way connected through the Department of Defense's public relations arm, and where glorifying war while promoting the American Empire agenda are the goals.

In reality, there is nothing sophisticated about scaring people in order to control them. This is a tactic that has been used in conjunction with the always popular divide & conquer strategy. These methods have been around forever and are still being used today because they are easy to pull off, and they work really well. They are simple and effective as a tool for reducing a person's access to information, but what if the problem is not a lack of information, but too much information? The results can be just as devastating.

Information Overload

Information has always been useful and now exists the technology to process this information in a way that was never possible before. Just about everything is digital these days, and if a person asked a college kid what "microfiche" is, they would probably tell them it was the name of a punk band.

Times change and the way people source information has changed as well. There is a downside to all of this information that people now have almost instant access to, and that is that they are drowning in statistics, and it is harder and harder to determine the accuracy and the value of this information.

Fans saw professional baseball plug along for 100 years with pretty much three different offensive categories: Batting Average, Runs Batted In (RBI), and home runs. With the emergence of Sabermetrics, they now have stats for OPS (On-base Percentage plus Slugging Average) and WAR (Wins Above Replacement), but fans can also dig deeper to see how well a guy hits left-handed pitching on Thursday day games at home before heading out on the road for a week.

Sometimes there is just too much information, and it waters down the value of the entire batch.

If too much information has the ability to water down the results like a really weak Margarita, then bad information is like adding antifreeze to the blender: it kind of looks the same, but it will end the party real quick.

As an emerging society, people are drawn to these statistical categories as a way of quantifying everything. The trend has the very real possibility of evolving (or devolving, depending on one's opinion) to a point where a computer program running the latest version of Microsoft Decision 8 can sift through all of the available information and render a decision.

Is that what people really want? What about the so-called "gut feeling" that humans get about a person or situation? Can real people ever account for that when building decision-making platforms for computers? People do not even know how that works inside their own minds, let alone how to account for it in a program model.

The less connected people get as a society from having to make decisions, the less human they become. People are starting to have the conversation about how Artificial Intelligence (AI) will impact their society moving forward, and what sort of changes are to be expected. What current industries will be replaced by AI robots, and what sort of new industries will emerge?

The arrival of the automobile destroyed the horse and buggy industry and put all of those workers in the unemployment line, but it created a massive new industry for things like the rubber used for making tires, asphalt for the roads, and oil and gasoline for engines.

The guys that made leather saddles switched to making leather seats for cars instead. The companies that made metal frames for the buggies had the opportunity to evolve and design the steel chassis for the automobile.

Some clung to the horse and buggy industry and suffered the consequences of a failure to recognize a paradigm shift. Others, like the Rockefellers, used this new industry to vastly expand their empires and create multigenerational wealth.

The emergence of Artificial Intelligence is another one of those pivotal moments in human history where new technology has the capacity to raise humanity to the next level, or possibly end it once and for all.

Online Usage, Cell Phone Addiction & Email Statistics

Groups that gather information for their reports, such as Pew Research Center, MediaKix, eMarketer, SmartInsights, Nielsen, and comScore, paint the picture of a gradual creeping in of technology into just about every aspect of our lives.

These figures show the direction our society is heading, for better or for worse.

- Americans spend 23.6 hours/week online.

- Worldwide there are 269 billion emails sent and received each day.

- This number grows by 8 billion each year.

- The number of worldwide email users is now 2.9 billion.

- Americans spend an average of 5.3% of their time emailing, and 13.4% of their time texting.

- 72% of parents have slept with their phone, compared to 62% of non-parents.

- Cell phones are now toted by more than four in five American adults (82%).

- Mobile now accounts for about 65% of total digital media consumption.

- The average American adult spends 2 hours, 51 minutes on their smartphone every day.

- College-age adults (18–24) spend significantly more time on mobile phones than older demographics, at 4 hours, 5 minutes per day.

- In 2018, Americans spend an average of 1 hour, 56 minutes on the top 5 social media platforms alone, ranked as YouTube, Facebook, Snapchat, Instagram, and Twitter.

- 77% of the population in the United States has a social networking profile.

- Facebook has some 1.86 billion accounts.

- YouTube and Whatsapp add 2.2 billion more social media accounts.

- Adults typically send and receive an average of 10 texts a day.

- Teens, on average, send and receive 50 texts per day.

- Only 5% of all adult texters send more than 200 text messages a day.

- About 15% of teens send more than 200 messages a day.

- There are 2.34 billion social media users worldwide.

- The users are expected to increase to 2.95 billion by 2020.

- Four out of five Americans, or roughly 196 million, have a social media profile.

The shift into the Digital Age has been an ongoing process that really started once mobile phones became cheap enough for the typical person to own one. These days, all one needs to do is look around to see the impact that they have made on our society. People walking into fountains at the mall because they are too busy looking at their phone, antisocial kids glued to a tablet computer, or the anxiety of getting on an airplane without your personal electronic device, are all things that did not even exist just a decade ago but are pervasive in today's society.

Between central banks, Wall Street, crony capitalism, the lobbying industry, false flag attacks, endless wars, the division of the public into smaller and smaller factions, and information overload, it is clear to anyone awake to what is happening that the detonators have been rigged to take the American Empire down.

The real questions are who is responsible, and how much time is left?

WHO WIRED THE BUILDING?

Who Is the New World Order?

"We have in this past year made great progress in ending the long era of conflict and the cold war. We have before us the opportunity to forge for ourselves and for future generations a New World Order—a world where the rule of law, not the law of the jungle, governs the conduct of nations. When we are successful—and we will be—we have a real chance at this New World Order, an order in which a credible United Nations can use its peacekeeping role to fulfill the promise and vision of the U.N.'s founders." – George H.W. Bush, Address to the Nation Announcing Allied Military Action in the Persian Gulf, January 16, 1991.

During the 20th century, many statesmen, such as Woodrow Wilson and Winston Churchill, used the term "New World Order" to refer to a new period of history evidencing a dramatic change in world political thought and the balance of power starting after World War I, but more noticeably during and after World War II.

They all saw these periods as opportunities to implement idealistic proposals for global governance only in the sense of new collective efforts to identify, understand, or address worldwide problems that go beyond the capacity of individual nation-states to solve.

These proposals led to the creation of international organizations, such as the United Nations (UN) and the North Atlantic Treaty Organization (NATO), and international regimes, such as the Bretton Woods system and the General Agreement on Tariffs and Trade (GATT), which were calculated both to maintain a balance of power as well as regularize cooperation between nations, in order to achieve a peaceful phase of capitalism.

The grouping together of nations into treaties like NATO creates the middle point between the sovereign and individual nations that made up the past couple hundred years, and the planned one-world government that is coming in the 21st century. It is meant to be an incremental move towards a world government so that the people of the world can ease into it, and also so that the change is not so overwhelming and obvious.

David Icke refers to this as the "Totalitarian Tiptoe" where freedoms and liberties can be taken away a little bit at a time without drawing too much attention or protest, whereas trying to take everything away all at once would elicit major pushback from the population.

The New World Order has a clear goal, and that is the destruction of individual national sovereignty and the integration of all countries into a one-world government. That is their plan in a nutshell, but they have been navigating through the political landscape long enough to understand that they cannot come right out and announce their intentions and expect everyone to be on board. In order to get the public to back this plan to ditch the sovereignty of the nation-state and join together as one mega-government, they have to make it seem like it was the peoples' idea, not theirs.

One tried and tested method is the Hegelian Dialectic, otherwise known as "Problem-Reaction-Solution", where a problem is manufactured in order to get the reaction from the people to do something to make the problem go away. Of course the government steps in to solve the problem with a solution that just happened to be the solution that they wanted to impose all along but did not have the support until this new problem came about, the one they invented for that purpose.

In order to fully comprehend their methodology, one must really reduce their mental capacity and force themselves to think like low-level criminal hoods, then the plans make more sense. They do not require complex planning, for the most part, but one has to think like a criminal or a sociopath and adhere to the philosophy that the ends always justify the means. There can be no hesitation to pin the blame on an associate because loyalty counts until it doesn't.

In order for a small group of megalomaniacs to take control over billions of people, they have to understand how the world functions, where the choke points are, how to use the information to convince the people to enslave themselves, how to spoof their identities in order to pin the blame on others, and know when the timing is right to put their evil plan in place. They can take the world to its knees with a baseball bat to the legs, or by a pressure point in someone's neck, it depends on how they want the situation to look.

The first thing that is needed is a coalition of the willing. These are people that stand to benefit greatly through consolidation of power, be that financially, politically, or both. These families and organizations that have been held together through the centuries because of their dedication to making money, their secret religion, a desire to retain and expand their power, and their deeply-held beliefs that they are preordained to rule over the rest of humanity because of their bloodlines, are more easily described as "globalists", or the description that David Rockefeller gave himself in his autobiography, "internationalists".

In his book "Memoirs" Rockefeller admits he is part of a secret cabal working to destroy the United States and create a new world order. Here is the direct quote from his book, pg 405:

"Some even believe we [Rockefeller family] are part of a secret cabal working against the best interests of the United States, characterizing my family and me as 'internationalists' and of conspiring with others around the world to build a more integrated global political and economic structure - One World, if you will.

If that's the charge, I stand guilty, and I am proud of it."

And...

"We are grateful to The Washington Post, The New York Times, Time Magazine and other great publications whose directors have attended our meetings and respected their promises of discretion for almost forty years. It would have been impossible for us to develop our plan for the world if we had been subject to the bright lights of publicity during those years. But, the work is now much more sophisticated and prepared to march towards a World Government. The supranational sovereignty of an intellectual elite and world bankers is surely preferable to the national auto-determination practiced in past centuries." - David Rockefeller to Trilateral Commission in 1991.

And...

"The end goal is to get everybody chipped, to control the whole society, to have the bankers and the elite people control the world." - Nick Rockefeller (Aaron Russo interview).

This secretive group of internationalists is said to have funded, and in some cases, caused most of the major wars of the last 200 years. Their favorite method of shaping public opinion is, primarily, through carrying out false flag attacks to manipulate populations into supporting them. Their control of the banking system has allowed them to tighten their grip on the world economy, deliberately causing inflation and depressions at will. The people behind the New World Order are thought to be international bankers, in particular, the owners of the private banks in the Federal Reserve System, Bank of England, and other central banks, and members of the Council on Foreign Relations, Trilateral Commission, and Bilderberg Group.

Calling For a New World Order

David Icke said: *"It may be bliss not to know a tornado is coming because you have no need to worry or take action. But while your head is in the sand your bum is in the air, the tornado is still coming."*

That is exactly what is happening here because pretending it does not exist will not make it go away.

A discussion about the plan for world domination by a group of powerful elites will get one funny looks at the dinner table, to be sure, but when they take it to the next level by identifying them as the "New World Order", they will get eye rolls as well. The reaction is usually reflexive and not actually based on any real knowledge about the subject, but more like an assumption that anything as crazy as a plan by a select few to run the world must be fictional because it sounds more like a bad movie than a dose of reality.

It is hard to blame someone for initially thinking that it all sounds a bit nuts, but the New World Order is very real and extremely dangerous. It is no longer a secret plan, it is *the* plan. They have long since given up on trying to keep the whole thing under wraps, now that they have the pieces in place to kick off their plan to take America down and fold it into the much larger New World Order, or to be more specific, New World Reorder, since they intend to reshuffle the deck in terms of where the power will lie after America is dismantled.

The history of warfare and political succession shows that when power is removed it will create a vacuum that will be filled by the most organized group with power-grabbing aspirations. It does them no good to simply remove the current control structure unless they have the solution already packaged and ready to be sold to the people.

The current control structure is the Nation-State, where countries are defined by their borders, culture, language, flag, and in some cases a specific currency.

The New World Order's control structure will be a top-down authoritative system, controlled internally by a police state, and externally by the United Nations and their World Army. Borders will be removed, the currency will be centralized through a digital system that they control with biometrics, a social media ranking system, much like the one China has recently rolled out, will analyze and monitor the behavior of the people and assign a citizenship score to all people to measure their compliance.[209] The internet will only be accessed through an Internet ID card that is issued specifically to each person, where their history and activities will be monitored and restricted.

It is going to be horrible.

It is important for people to understand that the desire for a select few to control the entire planet has always been the plan of megalomaniac dictators over the centuries, so this is not some new idea that they just came up with. Where it is different from before is that now the technology exists to actually do it, to really put their plan in place and have it work. This is a very real outcome, and although it might sound alarmist, people must understand that everything that they need to make this hellish future reality has already been invented and quietly deployed. All they are waiting for is the right time to switch it on.

If this all sounds a bit far fetched, just listen to the New World Order priests tell the people what they are planning on doing. According to their warped sense of karma and justice, as long as they let the public know what horrible things they have in store for everyone and the people do nothing to stop them, they are covered from a karma standpoint. A strange set of values, for sure, but they honor their code of conduct and take it seriously.

"The New World Order cannot happen without U.S. participation, as we are the single most significant component. Yes, there will be a New World Order, and it will force the United States to change its perceptions." – Dr. Henry Kissinger, World Action Council, April 19, 1994.

"Each of us has the hope to build a New World Order." – Richard Nixon, former President, United States of America.

"Now, we can see a new world coming into view. A world in which there is the very real prospect of a New World Order. In the words of Winston Churchill, a 'world order' in which 'the principles of justice and fair play protect the weak against the strong'. A world where the United Nations, freed from cold war stalemate, is poised to fulfill the historic vision of its founders. A world in which freedom and respect for human rights find a home among all nations." – George

---

[209] Alexandra Ma, Business Insider, "China Has Started Ranking Citizens With A Creepy 'Social Credit' System - Here's What You Can Do Wrong, And the Embarrassing, Demeaning Ways They Can Punish You".

H.W. Bush, 1991.

"The 'affirmative task' before us is to create a New World Order." – Joe Biden, former Vice President, United States of America.

"We are moving toward a New World Order, the world of communism. We shall never turn off that road." — Mikhail Gorbachev, former President, USSR, 1987.

"We are on the verge of a global transformation. All we need is the right major crisis and the nations will accept the New World Order." – David Rockefeller, Founder, Club of Rome & Chase Bank.

"A New World Order is required to deal with the Climate Change crisis." – Gordon Brown, former British Prime Minister.

"After 1989, President Bush said a phrase that I often used myself, that we needed a New World Order". – Bill Clinton, Former President, United States of America.

"We've got to invest in countries that have no educational infrastructure, have no means for young people to get ahead. We've got to give them a stake in creating the kind of World Order that I think all of us would like to see." - Barack Obama, 2014.

"The President, George Bush, has talked time and time again about the New World Order, and this is the best chance to begin to establish the New World Order, and that's why the stakes are so high. It's not just Kuwait. It's not just Iraq. It is a question far more fundamental than that. It is a question if, in fact, an allied coalition of 28 nations deploying forces to the Persian Gulf can, in fact, establish order there in a very volatile region, and if we establish order and establish peace and security, which I think we will, it will have a tremendous impact on future tyrants and dictators that will think about going in and gobbling up a weaker country." – Dan Quayle, former Vice President.

"The Trans-Atlantic Partnership was never just the foundation of our security, it was the foundation of our way of life. It was forged in experience of the most bitter and anguished kind. Out of it came a new Europe, a New World Order, a new consensus as to how life should, and could, be lived." – Tony Blair, former British Prime Minister.

They certainly do not seem to be trying to hide their intention to bring about a

New World Order, the only real question is what is the New World Order? Is it an actual government organization, is it a frame of mind, or is it just the idea of a centrally controlled power structure?

It is a little bit of all three.

There certainly is a united front being shown through the Presidency of the United States, as well as the ruling parties in the United Kingdom. This comes to be because of the way the organizational chart is constructed, and how people seeking high political office must work their way through the systems in order to ascend higher in the pyramid structure.

The criteria for moving up a level has less to do with actual qualifications and more to do with being properly compromised to a point that is adequate to assure that they can never go off the reservation, so to speak.

They must implicate themselves in these crimes so that they all have a vested interest in remaining silent about the illegal things that they have been a part of, just like in a street gang.

Blood in, blood out.

Of course, they will never be brought to justice, in large part because they have cross-pollinated with other radicals within the political administration, and become so entrenched that simply pulling the weeds will not solve the problem.

Shining the light of truth on government corruption only forces those rats to run for cover in the private sector. Once the light turns off, the rats will rotate back into the public sector, maybe under a new administration, definitely with new connections and associations, and the whole process starts up again.

They do not publish a list of everyone that is a part of the New World Order, but a quick look at the people involved with the Project for a New American Century is a good place to start. Those in positions of influence within the American, British, and Israeli governments that always seem to be pushing for another new war, while trying to control the narrative on the last war, are members, without exception.

Those who want to send Americans to war, but have not been to war themselves, are illegitimate. The criminals that share responsibility for 9/11 are not Arab hijackers armed with box cutters and pocket-sized Quorans, but rather a faction of the American Military-Information-Terror complex, the members of the Project for a New American Century (PNAC), a handful of cooperating foreign governments, and a slew of double agents operating within the White House.

The members of the Project for a New American Century should be tried for their crimes, including treason, and if found guilty, executed. That is what happens when spies get caught.

The "Permanent State"

As Ron Paul once said, *"In an empire of lies, the truth is treason"*.

The people that talk about the "Deep State" as being the figment of an overactive imagination of conspiracy theorists either do not know how to define what or who the group really is or they simply don't know what they are talking about. The names used to categorize these people are varied, but the group is real.

It is not a conspiracy, it is a measurable observation.

The Deep State is a parallel un-elected government, secret until recently, organized by a faction of the intelligence agencies, operated by a branch of the Military-Information-Terror complex, and financed through illegal activities such as securities & bank fraud, the drug trade, human trafficking, weapons sales, extortion & blackmail operations, counterfeiting, black budget projects, or outright theft. The organization is international and not aligned to any particular country, though the bulk of the participants are located in the United States.

It is true that this organization is deeply entrenched into the controlling hierarchy of the governments, but they are so deeply entrenched that they have actually become a permanent part of the structure. Administrations come and go, but the Permanent State remains.

The Permanent State is an All-star team of powerful and vicious people that work with one another to accomplish their goal of consolidating power into a one-world government. They are ruthless in the pursuit of their objective, cruel towards those that stand in their way, evil in their methods of exerting their control, patient in their planning, and sociopathic in their approach.

Make no mistake about it; people are murdered every single day to ensure that they never talk about "something" ever again. The people in charge will not be leaving witnesses to their crimes.

Members of the Permanent State would be people like Henry Kissinger, Bill Gates, Sheldon Adelson, George Soros, The Bush & Clinton families, John Brennan, James Comey, Rupert Murdoch, Dick Cheney, Donald Rumsfeld, Barack Obama, Richard Perle, Bill Kristol, Paul Wolfowitz, Eric Schmidt, Mark Zuckerberg, and many more names that most people would never recognize.

A new generation of Permanent State swamp monsters is stealing the headlines these days as they work to take control of industries, like Jeff Bezos, who owns the bulk of Amazon. His ownership stake in Amazon is worth well over $100 billion, part of which he used to purchase the Washington Post. He has a $600 million dollar contract with the CIA to provide cloud services for them through Amazon, plus he sits on the Board of Advisors for the Pentagon.[210] It does not get more Permanent State than being one of the wealthiest people on the planet and owning a massive media organization while simultaneously doing almost a billion dollars' worth of business with the CIA and the Pentagon.

It is not to say that every one that is wealthy is in on it, or that everyone within the CIA is involved because they are not. The Permanent State will find and compromise important people within specific companies and quietly draw them into the organization by giving them whatever it is that gets them off. For some people it is money, for others, it is pure power. Some guys like hot women, while others quietly want young boys. Whatever they want, the Permanent State has it, but they will not get it for free. The strings that are attached are thick, and much like joining a gang, once a person is in, it is very difficult to get out.

How hard is it to understand that people should always be distrustful of those in a position of power? It is obvious that anyone who tries to exchange their rights for security from the State will end up with neither, and that those tasked with guarding the henhouse are usually the foxes themselves. In the case of the Permanent State, most of these people have never subjected themselves to the public scrutiny of running for an elected office either, so not only do they want to control the public, but they want to do so without giving too much information about who they really are and without asking for permission.

Once someone knows what to look for, it becomes much easier to identify the groups and individuals working to push their agenda onto the oblivious public in order to shape society in the way that they see fit. The signs are everywhere, but

[210] Max Weinberger, Business Insider, "Amazon Is Launching A 'Secret' Cloud Service For The CIA".

the best place to look is the well-known organizations that boast of their involvement with shaping world political policy.

Council on Foreign Relations

Hillary Clinton, while acting as Secretary of State and in a surprisingly honest moment, admitted that the CFR tells her what to do and how to think about the future and that she finds that delightful.

Their mission is to create an unlevel playing field for its members through foreign policy planning, and they have become blended with the government because many of their members go back and forth between the Council and powerful positions within the U.S. government. Entire presidential administrations are pieced together from members of the Council, and it has been this way for at least the last 30 years. The George W. Bush administration was all CFR members, including Dick Cheney, Colin Powell, Donald Rumsfeld, Condoleezza Rice, Scooter Libby, Tim Geitner, Paul Wolfowitz, Richard Armitage, and Richard Perle.

The Council on Foreign Relations is like the Mafia of politics that control politicians through money and influence. Although the perception is that voters make the decisions about how they want things to be in America, politics is actually run by the big multinational banks and organizations like the Council on Foreign Relations, with methods such as blackmail, veiled threats, murder, and war.

The CFR is committed to the dissolution of all national boundaries, including that of the United States, resulting in the creation of a one-world government. They promote the disarmament and submergence of U.S. sovereignty and national independence. They draw their financing from tax-exempt foundations like those founded by David Rockefeller, and their influence is unmatched in the areas of Wall Street, the corporate media, big business, tech, and the military industry.

The Council on Foreign Relations is a part of the New World Order, and their goals are to destroy the United States from within and establish a one-world government that they control.

This is not just speculation or conjecture, it was stated by James Warburg, son of CFR founder Paul Warburg, to the Senate Foreign Relations Committee on February 17, 1950, when he said that *"We shall have world government, whether or not we like it. The question is only whether world government will be achieved*

293

by consent or by conquest."

The Council on Foreign Relations is the talent pool from which some of the most important positions in government are filled by the players that are currently controlling the United States of America. The Council on Foreign Relations has produced 23 Defense Secretaries, 21 Treasury Secretaries, 19 Secretaries of State, and 16 CIA Directors in the past. Obama's cabinet was stuffed to capacity with members such as John Kerry, the Secretary of State, Jeh Johnson, the Director of Homeland Security, Ashton Carter the Secretary of Defense, and Jacob Lew, the Treasury Secretary.

The Bilderberg Group

Sometimes people get a glimpse into how the world really works if they take the time to seriously listen to those that are actually running the show. David Rockefeller had a habit of telling the truth about his actual intentions for these think tanks and organizations that he founded during his century on planet earth. In his autobiography titled Memoirs, David Rockefeller wrote:

"If the Council on Foreign Relations raises the hackles of the conspiracy theorists, the Bilderberg meetings must induce apocalyptic visions of omnipotent international bankers plotting with unscrupulous government officials to impose cunning schemes on an ignorant and unsuspecting world."

They do.

The Rockefeller family was not content just running some of the world's biggest corporations. Their true intention still is to run the world, and their vehicles for doing so are the Trilateral Commission, the Bilderberg Group, and the Council on Foreign Relations.

The Bilderberg Group is a collection of influential leaders in the world of business, politics, and media. Founded in 1954 by David Rockefeller and the royal family of the Netherlands, The Bilderberg Group sets the agenda for the developed world for both the short-term and long-term. Held yearly, the Bilderberg conference is designed to spark dialogue between 150 business, finance, academic and political leaders in Europe and North America.

The conference is a forum for informal discussions about major world issues where no minutes are taken, no reports are written, no policy statements are issued, no resolutions are proposed, and no votes are taken. Everything is off the record and only certain trusted members of their media inner circle are invited. Recent topics for discussion included:

Globalization	NATO
Cyber Security	Middle East
Terrorism	European Strategy
Current Economic Issues	Russia
Artificial Intelligence	Iran
Chemical Weapons Threats	United Kingdom
Greece	USA

Topics of discussion at the meetings include the world economy, country-specific economics, global affairs, current and future wars, new technology to be rolled out, scientific breakthroughs to be announced, and decisions on when and how to collapse the dollar.

After the coming financial collapse in America, as well as the takedown of the American Empire, the Bilderberg meetings will, no doubt, have played a pivotal role in starting the dominoes falling in the order designated to take the system down in a coordinated manner. This will have been where the world currency was proposed, debated, and decided on. These are the most important meetings in the world, and the general public has no idea that anything is even happening, let alone that their fate is being decided by a bunch of unelected psychopaths that honestly want them all dead.

The Trilateral Commission

Formed in the early 1970s the Trilateral Commission is made up of prominent leaders from North America, Europe, and Japan. It was founded by David Rockefeller and Zbigniew Brzezinski. Brzezinski was a professor at Columbia University, a pusher of one-world idealism, and the author of several books that have become the policy guidelines for the Trilateral Commission.

If one goes by the description of the organization that is found on their website, they do not sound like that bad of a group of concerned citizens, but anytime David Rockefeller is involved things tend to take a dark turn.

"The Commission was originally created in 1973 to bring together experienced leaders within the private sector to discuss issues of global concern at a time

when communication and cooperation between Europe, North America, and Asia were lacking.

The Commission has grown since its early days to include members from more countries in these regions, and it continues to find that study and dialogue about the pressing problems facing our planet remain as important today as in 1973. Problems and threats have changed, but their importance has only increased due to the more interconnected and interdependent world in which we now live."

They like to discuss global concerns, one assumes, because they want to help out and fix some of the problems.

In his book, former Senator Barry Goldwater described the Trilateral Commission as the vehicle for multinational consolidation of the commercial and banking interests by seizing control of the political government of the United States. He thought they actually planned to consolidate the four centers of power, being the political, monetary, intellectual, and ecclesiastical, in order to create a worldwide economic power superior to the political governments of the nation-states in order to run the world.

That does not sound very promising for the future of the planet, in general, and the United States, in particular.

The coordination of these different industries is necessary when turning the world in a new direction towards a one-world government. When the world shifts into a new paradigm, the politicians are told how to vote, the businesses are told what to sell, the media is told what to say, and the organizations that are controlling everything are the Council on Foreign Relations, the Bilderberg Group, and the Trilateral Commission.

The truth is that there are two types of people in politics: those who control people and those who are controlled.

The Rockefellers had one more organization that they funded in order to shape society in their favor, and most people actually have heard of it, although they have done a fantastic job of disguising it to look like a charity determined to save humanity and rid the planet of suffering: the United Nations.

The land that the United Nations sits on in New York City was a gift from the Rockefeller family, and they are very much involved with the organization. Once people dig into the truth behind this evil organization it is obvious that their public mission statement and their actual mission are two very different agendas.

United Nations' Agenda 2030: The Plan to Destroy America

Nothing exemplifies the globalists' desire to control society like the playbook written by the United Nations called "Transforming Our World: the 2030 Agenda for Sustainable Development". This document is an assault on mankind from every direction, and the repercussions of this plan have the ability to end humanity in a very real way.

The controllers at the United Nations have put together a plan to save humanity called Agenda 2030, and these are their 17 stated goals for sustainable development, most of which are designed to do the exact opposite. What they are actually seeking is the permanent establishment of a New World Order dressed up by the United Nations to advocate for global peace and prosperity through sustainable living.

1. End poverty in all its forms everywhere.

2. End hunger, achieve food security and promote sustainable agriculture.

3. Ensure healthy lives and promote well-being for everyone.

4. Ensure quality education.

5. Achieve gender equality for all women.

6. Ensure sustainable management of water for all.

7. Ensure access for all to affordable and sustainable energy.

8. Promote sustainable economic growth and productive employment.

9. Invest in upgrading infrastructure and sustainable industrialization.

10. Reduce inequality.

11. Make cities safe, resilient, and sustainable.

12. Ensure sustainable consumption.

13. Take urgent action to combat climate change.

14. Conserve and sustainably use the oceans.

15. Promote sustainable use of terrestrial ecosystems.

16. Promote peaceful and inclusive societies for sustainable development.

17. Revitalize the global partnership for sustainable development.

The actual plan of Agenda 2030, not just the 17 talking points but their goal, is to create two different groups of humans like the feudal society of serfs and kings.

The lower class of "useless eaters" gets fed the nutritionally deficient GMO food and they can chase it down with fluoride-laden polluted water, the same water that will be strictly rationed due to water shortages. They will be forced to live in 300 square foot micro-apartments inside high-density cities in order to combat global warming, and their carbon footprint will be monitored and taxed through the smart grid while imposing forced austerity on the masses. Due to the tight living quarters, vaccination will be mandatory for "herd immunity", and all children will need to be fully immunized with all 100+ shots before they are allowed to attend the government schools teaching Common Core.

The upgrades to the infrastructure will be due to the privatization of current public roads, bridges, and waterways, and public safety features will include the removal of all guns from the citizens. In an effort to thwart terrorism, all cash will be outlawed and instead, everything will be moved into digital currency in the form of a microchip that everyone will have implanted under their skin to conduct all financial transactions, courtesy of the World Bank.

In order to protect the ocean from additional pollution, the mega-cities will be constructed inland and the oceans will be rezoned as protected areas with no access for the masses. The same goes for National Parks as the federal government will move to reclaim the majority of the land in the United States, including all of the minerals and oil, while the citizens are forced to migrate into large cities. The Chinese did the same thing starting in 1979 when they began moving the first of the 340 million people from rural areas into the cities, just as Kissinger, Rockefeller, and Mao had discussed in order to build up their manufacturing labor base.

This is the New World Order that George H.W. Bush always talked about where humanity has *"a real chance at this New World Order, an order in which a credible United Nations can use its peacekeeping role to fulfill the promise and vision of the U.N.'s founders"*.

The vision that their founders, David Rockefeller, and his family, had for the world was this dystopian nightmare city.

They have suicide nets installed at Foxconn, the iPhone manufacturing company in China so that their employees have to find different ways to kill themselves.

Welcome to the future of the world under Agenda 2030...suicide nets so that the useless eaters do not kill themselves from hating their jobs so much.[211]

It is important to note that the United Nations specializes in keeping the world in poverty through their policies, and their mission is to remove national sovereignty worldwide.

Implementing Agenda 2030 requires that the concept of the nation-state is abolished, and that America, in its current form, will need to be destroyed for their plan to work. The last of the superpowers in world politics must be dismantled to remove any possible resistance, so the United Nations has a vested interest in seeing the American Empire fall. The strong will need to be made weak, the educated will need to be re-educated, and the wealthy will need to be bankrupted for the United Nation's future society to be implemented.

There is a precedent for this ambitious plan to end the dominance of a superpower and that is what happened to the Soviet Union and the Balkanization of the fraying edges of the empire. It started in Afghanistan when the Soviets were drawn into a 10-year war that depleted their war chest, destroyed their morale, and bankrupted the country. America was talked into that very same trap, but in their case, the duration of the occupation has been almost double, and the costs are easily tens of times more expensive than what the USSR invested in trying to control what Bryzenski called Eurasia, the most strategic location in the Middle East and possibly the world.

The plan to Balkanize the American Empire is well underway, one only needs to open their eyes to see the similarities. It might end the way it did for the USSR where anything not named Russia ended up falling off, leaving just the torso of

---

[211] Reuters, "Foxconn Hit By 10th Jumping Death; Nets Installed".

the empire to carry on, albeit with much less influence.

The British lost their control of India, the Dutch lost their grip on Indonesia, and the Portuguese let go of Brazil. The American Empire will probably lose the territories they control like Guam and the U.S. Virgin Islands, the hundreds of military bases across the world, their political influence in foreign countries, their financial control over foreign governments, and maybe even places like Hawaii and Alaska. A deep enough blow to the parent country will force it to retreat in order to preserve the homeland, and by doing so it will mean releasing their grip on policies concerning luxury countries that are not vital from a strategic standpoint.

The Wolf in Sheep's Clothing

Better make sure that Russia did not interfere with the elections. It would be a crime if a foreign country had somehow infiltrated the American political establishment in order to set political policy towards a particular country unbeknownst to the vast majority of the American people. Catching Boris & Natasha, dual American and Russian citizens, working away deep inside the United States political system would certainly be the lead story on the nightly news for the next 2,000 nights in a row.

Unless they were not actually working for Russia but for Israel. If that was the case the public would never hear anything about it.

How can people be so sure about that? Because it is currently happening and nobody talks about it at all for fear of being labeled an "anti-Semite" or a "Russian apologist".

The United States government has a huge problem that nobody is ever willing to mention.

Some of the most important and powerful people working inside the American political machine are dual American and Israeli citizens, but the public will never hear that on the nightly news due to the suppression of information by AIPAC, the American Israel Public Affairs Committee, an organization that has been practically running Washington D.C. for almost 70 years.[212]

There is an unbelievable number of people with dual citizenship at the highest

---

[212] Foreign Policy Journal, "The Best Congress AIPAC Can Buy".

levels of both the state and the federal government. Having dual citizenship is not an issue for the vast majority of people in America, but holding two different citizenships does create the potential for a conflict of interest.

Those holding high-ranking positions within the government that demand a person put "America First" should have to choose citizenship from one country, otherwise, it creates a problem. These dual citizens have the ability to vote in a way that benefits their other country of citizenship, at the expense of America. It does not mean that they will, but it does mean that they could.

The common thread shared by these dual citizens is that they are all from Israel, and not just a couple, but hundreds.

Part of the reason for America's confusing policy towards the Middle East is because a sizable chunk of the politicians pushing this policy is Israeli citizens working at high levels inside the United States government. Is this America's foreign policy or Israel's?

To be clear, this is not about their religion, but it is a factual statement about their citizenship of two different nations at the same time while serving in a governmental capacity and making policies for the United States. It is not unreasonable to question the possibility of a conflict of interest existing, in fact, it is crazy not to.

Under President Obama, these were just some of the dual U.S./Israeli citizens that occupied high-ranking positions, meaning that in addition to being citizens of the United States they are also citizens of Israel.

Names one might recognize from the previous administration include Rahm Emanuel, David Axelrod, Tim Geithner, Peter Orszag, Gary Gensler, Richard Holbrooke, Elena Kagan, Larry Summers, Cass Sunstein, Kenneth Feinberg, Ben Bernanke, Paul Volker, Neil Barofsky, Robert Reich, Michael Mukasey, David Frum, Jack Lew, Janet Yellen, and Stanley Fischer.

No Russians on this list so far.

Congress was and still is filled with dual citizens, not from Iran or Turkey, but from Israel. Certainly, many of these names should ring a bell, like Gabrielle Giffords, Eric Cantor, Barney Frank, Shelley Berkley, Adam Schiff, Henry Waxman, Alan Grayson, Chuck Schumer, Dianne Feinstein, Carl Levin, Al Franken, Barbara Boxer, Richard Blumenthal, Ron Wyden, convicted pedophile Anthony Weiner, and soon-to-be convicted criminal Debbie Wasserman-Schultz.

Anyone with an understanding of 9/11 and the role of the Project for a New American Century will recognize many of these dual-citizens like Michael Chertoff, Richard Perle, Paul Wolfowitz, Douglas Feith, Elliott Abrams, Richard Haass, "Scooter" Libby, Robert Zoellick, John Bolton, David Wurmser, Eliot Cohen, Ari Fleischer, and Henry Kissinger.

But the problem is Russian interference with the American election?

Ok, sure.

What about Israeli interference with the American election? What about the Israeli interference with every aspect of the American political system? What about the blatant hypocrisy of being called a racist for having the audacity to point out this obvious conflict of interest?

Remember when Vladimir Putin gave that awesome speech before Congress and he got 30 standing ovations? Oh wait, that was Netanyahu that received standing ovations from his fans in the United States Congress. Anyone that stood up to give Putin a standing ovation would find their political support had vanished before they had a chance to sit back down, and they would be labeled as traitors and fast-tracked to the gallows.

The only thing the American media can talk about seems to be Russia's alleged influence in the 2016 elections, meanwhile, Israel sends their guy over to give a speech to Congress and the media is totally fine with it. This is a joke, and it works to expose the outright hypocrisy of the mainstream media in conjunction with the purchased governmental officials holding positions of high office inside the United States.

One country overtly interferes with American politics and things are fine, but another country is alleged to have tried to influence the election and there must be nonstop investigations into that country even though there has been little proof, if any, of the crimes being alleged. How come the world cannot see how obvious this is?

The United States has agreed to give Israel $38 billion over the next 10 years, even though that money could be used to pay for the American education system, used to fix bridges, cover the costs of student financial aid programs, fix potholes, or be distributed back to the citizens of the United States for them to buy beer with.[213] Anything is better than handing that money to a foreign country with no strings attached for them to do who knows what with.

This is what happens when criminals are running a government and playing with other people's money, they give it away to their friends because they know the citizens will never do anything about it. It is also one of the signs of a dying political system.

AIPAC's Role in Destabilizing the American Empire

The biggest and most powerful lobbying group on the planet, let alone the United States, is the American Israel Public Affairs Committee (AIPAC). Their stated purpose is to lobby the Congress of the United States on issues and legislation related to Israel, so they meet with members of Congress and hold events where it can share its views, but they do not consider themselves to be a political action committee. Everyone else does, but they do not.

Those with influence, like AIPAC, always have the potential to be dangerous if their influence is recklessly used in a way to benefit some people, it might have a side effect that is harming others.

AIPAC has very defined goals, and they use their influence to swing laws and policies to benefit them. This creates problems because their interests are hidden and the general public is not made aware of what these goals actually are. This is especially true because the organization with the power is a foreign country, and the interests of this foreign country are not aligned with those of the United States, even though they pretend to be America's ally.

They are not.

They are only looking out for themselves and they have been using the American Empire to do their dirty work for them for decades. AIPAC uses their influence to fuel a cycle of violence in the Middle East in order to destabilize the region so that no other country is able to rise up and challenge their authority, and they have done so by using their political connections to draw the American Empire into wars that do not seem to benefit anyone other than Israel.

They always push policies that benefit Israel and harm Palestine.

---

[213] Reuters, "Key U.S. Lawmakers Want To Boost Israel's $38 Billion Defense Aid Package".

The push for war with both Syria and Iran is directly a result of the influence of AIPAC's lobbying efforts, in conjunction with the Military-Information-Terror complex.

They force American politicians to subscribe to the policy of full one-sided support of Israel, or they turn off the money, and they reportedly must sign a loyalty pledge to AIPAC, which is prohibited for American politicians because of an obvious conflict of interests.

It is not anti-Semitic to talk about Israel's influence on the American political machine, but it might be anti-American to support it.

Non-Governmental Oppression

The way in which these globalists and technocrats structure their influence operations are through foundations that they create to function as stand-alone Non-Governmental Organizations (NGOs) that work as tax shields and also provide a couple of extra layers of legal security, not that they are ever concerned with prosecution for their crimes.

According to NGO.org, a non-governmental organization (NGO) is any non-profit, voluntary citizens' group that is organized on a local, national or international level. Task-oriented and driven by people with a common interest, NGOs perform a variety of service and humanitarian functions, bring citizen concerns to Governments, advocate and monitor policies, and encourage political participation through the provision of information. Some are organized around specific issues, such as human rights, environment, or health. They provide analysis and expertise, serve as early warning mechanisms, and help monitor and implement international agreements. Their relationship with offices and agencies of the United Nations system differs depending on their goals, their venue, and the mandate of a particular institution.

It used to be that the best tool for destabilizing a foreign country was the NGO, but it turns out that they are really great at destabilizing their own country as well.

A hundred years ago there were only 21 NGOs, but now there are over 10 million of them operating around the world, with 1.5 million located inside the United

States.[214] Many times these are tax shelters dressed up to look like a charity in order to disguise the true intentions of the organization.

NGOs get political cover as well as the goodwill that comes with looking like a charity organization, and since people do not like to accuse charities of being shady without rock-solid evidence, these organizations usually skate through without much scrutiny by the corporate media, not that they in the media are in the business of actually digging deep into organizations being run by their own corporate overlords.

At first glance, a crooked NGO will look like an organization devoted to the benefit of humanity, but once the layers are peeled away the true mission of the organization is discovered. This is a favorite method of the New World Order because they have discovered that they can use NGOs to infiltrate a country, manipulate opinions, and change the laws to benefit their goals without starting a hot revolution.

This is a list of the number of NGOs controlled by recognizable political operatives:

George Shultz: 76	Bill & Hillary Clinton: 35
David & Jay Rockefeller: 73	Colin Powell: 35
Zbigniew Brzeziński: 62	Paul Wolfowitz: 35
Thomas Pickering: 57	James Baker: 34
George H.W. Bush: 54	Donald Rumsfeld: 34
Madeleine Albright: 54	John McCain: 33
Rothschild family: 54	Condoleezza Rice: 32
George Soros: 49	Dick Cheney: 30

These organizations might hand out turkeys to the poor on Thanksgiving, but this is just for window dressing and it certainly is not their main objective. This is really just a way for well-known politicians to retain power after leaving office without drawing too much negative attention.

Soros has been a major player over the last decade with his Open Society Foundations, which is a hilariously ironic name considering his vision of the future is anything but open. In 2017, Soros transferred $18 billion of his fortune into his Open Society to fund his dystopian fantasies, and through his foundation, $11 billion has already been spent to shape global society in a way that he sees

---

[214] ACCA Global, "Vetting Of Local Staff And Suppliers Is A Further Complication. Vetting Is Required By Donors, Particularly Government Bodies Such As USAID".

fit, like financing uprisings like the Arab Spring, and the mobilization of hundreds of thousands of displaced Libyans into Europe.[215] In the United States, Soros was the financial backer for Black Lives Matter and other social movements meant to appear organic in nature but clearly had his fingerprints all over them.

Part of the problem that these foundations create is that they are desperate to make the social uprisings appear to be authentic and real, when they usually are not, then use the organizations to change society in a way that suits them. They try to implant their ideas into the heads of average Americans in order to make it seem like it was their idea all along which, given the current state of the average submissive American, is not very difficult.

Once the people ponder this implanted idea of social change, it is critical for them to act on it in order for the idea to become a reality. This is where the financial element to the NGOs come into play as the buses show up to deliver protestors to Ferguson, Missouri and the migrant invasion of asylum seekers that all suddenly and miraculously got the idea to walk on the same path at the same exact time, are fed and housed during their staged, thousand-mile walk to the southern border of the United States.

This is not social unrest, it is political theater financed by private organizations that want society changed so that they can benefit at the expense of all the suckers that helped them put their plan in place. The key is to make the people demand the change that the controllers wish to implement.

Over the last twenty years, a new type of fungus has sprouted up from the NGO roots but it features a component that is very different from its predecessor. Where the NGO took money from the rich like George Soros to fund their operations, the new breed hopes to steal from the average American citizen and give to the people running the foundation, like Robin Hood in reverse.

A Foundation of Lies

If the Clinton Foundation is an actual charity organization that does important work in places like Haiti and Africa, then why did they shut down the Clinton Global Initiative a couple of weeks after Hillary Clinton lost the 2016 Presidential election?

---

[215] Juliet Chung, The Wall Street Journal, "George Soros Transfers $18 Billion To His Foundation, Creating An Instant Giant".

Did they fix all of the world's problems then shut the doors because there was nothing left to do? Did they put all of the donor money that flooded into Haiti to good use by building homes and roads for the people after the devastating earthquake? Did they use all that money to drill water wells in Sub-Saharan Africa?

The answer, of course, is obviously, "no". They do realize that they are not allowed to just keep all of that money, right?

The Clinton Foundation's real mission is not saving the poor, but selling influence to the highest bidder. The foundation is not a charity, and a series of misfilings pointed out by Charles Ortel and investigative journalist Jason Goodman should trigger an actual investigation. The Clinton Foundation also has major problems with their taxes, and huge discrepancies between the number of money donors claim to have given to the Foundation, and the amount of money declared on their taxes. In fact, Ortel and Goodman calculated that the fraudulent charity organization may be as large as $100 billion when measured from 1997 when it was founded, and described the Clinton Foundation as one of the largest criminal enterprises on the planet.[216] That money was raised from people all over the world, but a surprising number of them happen to be convicted felons, adding to the shadiness of the whole operation.

IRS documents show that of the $500 million the foundation raised over a four-year period starting in 2009, only 15% was actually spent on "programmatic grants."[217]

So what did they spend the remaining $425 million on?

According to their filings, they spent $32 million on travel expenses, and $110 million on salaries. Did they hire the New York Yankees to run the Clinton Foundation? An additional $290 million was classified as "other expenses" which could mean anything, except probably clean water, food, and housing for Haiti.

The 1.5 million people that were affected by the earthquake were still homeless years after the money had been donated, with little done to improve their country even though donations were in the tens of billions of dollars.

Organizations that made large donations to the Clinton Foundation would end up

---

[216] Tyler Durden, Zero Hedge, "Clinton Foundation Is Charity Fraud Of Epic Proportions, Analyst Charges In Stunning Takedown".
[217] Aaron Bandler, The Daily Wire, "7 Things You Need To Know About The Clinton Foundation".

receiving the contracts to help Haitians on the ground, though most of the money would go missing and flow anywhere else but where it was needed. The contracts went to companies that had less to do with actually rebuilding, and more to do with financial connections to the CGI.

There is one silver lining in all of this, literally, and that is that the Clinton Foundation was able to, thanks to the support of their generous donors, give Chelsea Clinton a wedding dress that was fit for a princess, while children in Haiti picked through the garbage looking for food.[218]

National Deceit Against Americans

The National Defense Authorization Act (NDAA) is another in a long line of ironically named laws that masquerade as freedom defending legislation while simultaneously stripping citizens of actual freedoms. And like other unpopular bits of legislation, it was signed into law on New Year's Eve of 2011 by President Obama, while the rest of the country was partying and not paying attention to the fact that their rights were being stripped from them.

Sections 1021 and 1022 of the NDAA authorizes the indefinite military detention, without charge or trial, of any person, even American citizens, and applies the "Law of War", to United States soil, making America a battlefield, legally.

There is much to dislike about this bill, but the part on Counterterrorism is the most alarming because of the arbitrary process of determining what can get an American citizen detained indefinitely without trial. Should someone determine that a person committed a "belligerent act", that is enough to keep a person in prison without charges until the end of the conflict? The "War on Terror" is a vague and nonsensical war against an idea.

Subtitle D — Counterterrorism

SEC. 1021. AFFIRMATION OF AUTHORITY OF THE ARMED FORCES OF THE UNITED STATES TO DETAIN COVERED PERSONS PURSUANT TO THE AUTHORIZATION FOR USE OF MILITARY FORCE.

(a) IN GENERAL. — Congress affirms that the authority of the President to use all necessary and appropriate force pursuant to the Authorization for Use of Military

---

[218] Samuel Osborne, Independent, "Chelsea Clinton 'Used Clinton Foundation Funds To Help Pay For Wedding', Hacked Wikileak Emails Claim".

Force (Public Law 107–40; 50 U.S.C. 1541 note) includes the authority for the Armed Forces of the United States to detain covered persons (as defined in subsection (b)) pending disposition under the law of war.

(b) COVERED PERSONS. — A covered person under this section is any person as follows:

A person who planned, authorized, committed, or aided the terrorist attacks that occurred on September 11, 2001, or harbored those responsible for those attacks.

A person who was a part of or substantially supported al-Qaeda, the Taliban, or associated forces that are engaged in hostilities against the United States or its coalition partners, including any person who has committed a belligerent act or has directly supported such hostilities in aid of such enemy forces.

(c) DISPOSITION UNDER LAW OF WAR. — The disposition of a person under the law of war as described in subsection (a) may include the following:

Detention under the law of war without trial until the end of the hostilities authorized by the Authorization for Use of Military Force.

The above section is not just "sort of" unconstitutional, it is so unconstitutional that it violates numerous amendments, including the Fourth Amendment, the Fifth Amendment, and also the Sixth Amendment.

Quick civics lesson:

• The Fourth Amendment makes it illegal to conduct seizures of property or people without a warrant.

• The Fifth Amendment prevents the government from depriving an American citizen of their life, liberty, or property without due process of the law of the land.

• The Sixth Amendment ensures a public trial by an impartial jury.

The Founding Fathers of the United States would easily qualify as "terrorists" under this definition because of their "belligerent acts" towards the British and would have been subject to indefinite detention. There would not even be an America if it was not for their belligerent acts, and there will not continue to be an America if legislation like the National Defense Authorization Act is used as the rule book for what will and will not be tolerated in the country instead of the Constitution.

Whatever happened to the Declaration of Independence?

"We hold these truths to be self-evident, that all men are created equal, that they are endowed by their Creator with certain unalienable Rights, that among these are Life, Liberty and the pursuit of Happiness. — That to secure these rights, Governments are instituted among Men, deriving their just powers from the consent of the governed, — That whenever any Form of Government becomes destructive of these ends, it is the Right of the People to alter or to abolish it, and to institute new Government, laying its foundation on such principles and organizing its powers in such form, as to them shall seem most likely to affect their Safety and Happiness."

If an American is not protected from being illegally searched, having their property taken, having their life ended, and being unable to have a fair trial, then what the hell is the point of having any laws?

Maybe that is the point? Maybe that is the reason for this evil provision of the NDAA? Maybe the goal is to remove these protections from the citizens and repeal these rights so that it is not America any longer, and so that those that are planning to take down the American Empire may do so with impunity?

One thing is for sure, the NDAA was not created to protect the American public.

It was created to terrorize them.

Executive Orders

Sometimes Executive Orders trample the Constitution, and when that happens, the President usually does not get bogged down in pesky little details like whether or not their actions are actually illegal, but rather, they focus on doing the bidding of those that put them in office. When one actually sees some of the Executive Orders that blatantly violate the Constitution, it is no wonder why people have been screaming that the rule of law is dead.

• Executive Order 9066 - In 1942, as America's involvement in World War II had just kicked off three months earlier, President Roosevelt signed an Executive Order that rounded up 120,000 Japanese or Japanese/Americans living on the

West Coast in the United States and put them in concentration camps for fear that they might launch a surprise attack.

- Executive Order 4311 - Gerald Ford submarined his chances to remain the President of the United States for another term by issuing a pardon of Richard Nixon in September of 1974 in order to spare the country of the stress and anxiety of having a former President on trial for the list of crimes he committed, all of which, by the way, has now been made legal over time. Though technically legal, the Executive Order was unbelievably controversial, and no doubt was never forgotten by the future Presidents that always felt they had it in their back pockets to absolve themselves or other Presidents of their crimes against the people.

- Executive Order 6102 - This was signed by Roosevelt in 1933 and it expressly forbids the private ownership of gold. This was in response to the Great Depression, which of course was engineered by the Federal Reserve, so the government did not want the people to hold anything of real value so that they, in conjunction with the Fed, could manipulate the money supply. Once they held all of the gold or as much as they could threaten the people to exchange under the Trading with the Enemy Act, they immediately revalued it from $20 to $35 per ounce, banking an instant 75% profit for themselves while screwing the American people in the process.

- Executive Order 13524 - Through this Order, INTERPOL now has jurisdiction inside the United States beyond the other law enforcement agencies, even over the Federal Bureau of Investigations.

- Executive Order 13606 - Basically, the government can confiscate whatever they want from the people, and they can conscript Americans into working for the government without compensation. They can seize property, persons, or resources at any time, in "peacetime and times of national emergency" without having to pay for it. This was one of Obama's gifts to the psychopaths that controlled him.

During the eight years of President Obama, drone strikes against American citizens, 23 Executive Orders pertaining to gun control, and the PRISM spying program were all enacted in complete violation of the United States Constitution. No voting by the Congress, no debating by the people, and no honest discussion about this on the corporate nightly news.

Obama accepted the Chairmanship of the UN Security Council, a violation of

Section 9, he signed the UN Firearms Treaty, a violation of the 2nd Amendment, while also falsely claiming the United Nations may legally usurp Congressional war powers.

When did the United Nations move into the first position with regard to the laws of the United States, and who was Obama actually working on behalf of?

Clearly the United Nations.

Obama exposed the method of operations of a Navy SEALs team, a crime, and started another war, this time in Libya, without the approval of Congress, another crime worthy of impeachment under the War Powers Act.[219]

Where were the outrage and the protesting in the streets of the United States? These things were quietly and illegally made a part of American life. It is hard to imagine how anything such as this can be looked at as a good thing for the American people, and the reason for that is because they are clearly not a benefit to the people, but a benefit to the government.

The American government does not pass laws to sit on them and not use them, they pass them because they are thinking a couple of steps ahead. They pass these laws because there is a plan that requires them to make these crimes legal in advance so that their actions will not land them in Leavenworth for the rest of their lives.

Unless they get a pardon, which they know will happen.

No-Fly List

A hallmark of the freedom-stripping Patriot Act and a by-product of the fake "War on Terror" is the FBI's No-Fly List. Like being banned from a local dry cleaner for writing bad checks, the No-Fly List is a database of suspected terrorists that might possibly blow up a commercial airliner, even though, unlike the check writer, these people have not committed a crime. At least the guy trying to pass off rubber checks can see his face plastered next to the cash register as a warning, but these people on the FBI's list usually have no idea they are even on the list until they first decide to try and get on a plane.

So what are the stringent criteria for landing oneself on the dreaded list that

---

[219] Jeffrey Kuhner, The Washington Post, "The Betrayal Of The Navy's SEAL Team 6".

began back in 2003? Someone at the FBI just needs to think that a person might be a terrorist. Or looks like a terrorist. Or maybe acts like a terrorist. If they smelled like a terrorist that would be enough. Also, if they dressed like a terrorist it would certainly get them on the list, or if they listed "terrorist" as their current title on a job application.

In September 2015, Yahoo Travel compiled a list of eight things a person might have done that could lead to their name being added to the FBI's No-Fly List:

- Having a similar name to someone on the No-Fly List.

- Outstanding warrants from law enforcement not related to aviation activity.

- Being suspected of direct terrorist activity.

- A clerical error by the FBI.

- Making comments that are not politically correct.

- Turning down an offer to become an FBI Informant.

- Traveling to the wrong country.

- Controversial social media posts.

Luckily for everyone, if those things ever do happen, nobody at the TSA is actually going to put two and two together and figure it out. Now if a person has toenail clippers, that is a different story.

The New World Order is a real thing, and its members are actively working to destroy the United States from within. The Permanent State has been put in place to make the transition possible. The Council on Foreign Relations, the Bilderberg Group, and the Trilateral Commission are greasing the political and banking wheels to wire the American Empire for demolition, and the NGOs are providing the political cover to keep the public from noticing that the locks are being changed because their government has been sold and the new owners want everyone out.

But there will still be many people that never understand what is happening, even when the warning signs are right in front of their faces. For those people in the dark, there is still time to sound the alarm and explain to them what to be looking for right before the American Empire is brought down.

RINGING THE ALARM BELLS

Wealth Inequality

When a person sits down to watch a movie, there is a lot of information and activity that is easy to miss unless one is specifically looking for it. There is a funny video showing a bunch of young people dribbling basketballs and passing them back and forth between each other, but when the video stops and the voice-over reader asks the viewers if they noticed the breakdancing guy in a bear outfit that walked right behind the whole basketball scene, most people have to rewatch the video and then it appears clear as day, right where it was the whole time, only seemingly invisible to most viewers.

The breakdancing bear is sounding the alarm on the controlled demolition of the American Empire, but most people do not notice him walking in the background and waving his sign about the impending doom. Once they stop to examine the video and specifically look for the bear, it is impossible not to see it because it is right there in front of everyone's face, but most people just happen to be looking at all of the other things and never notice the obvious until someone points it out to them.

There are signs of what is coming, just like there are always signs before something terrible happens, but if one is not in tune or open to examining the information, it seems to appear invisible until after the fact when looking back on the event when, once again, the information becomes clear, obvious, and a bit embarrassing that it was not spotted sooner.

These are the signs of impending doom, as we sound the alarm to wake people up to the reality of the situation.

Wealth inequality creates major fissures in a society, and not just in the form of jealousy of the poor, complaining from the working class, and outright hatred from the unemployed. It usually comes due to shifts in the balance of power and governmental regulations favoring the rich, or the removal of regulations through the lobbying paid for by those in a position to afford it and benefit the most.

When Amazon and Walmart pay their workers below a living wage, while the stockholders make more money in a minute than most of their employees will make in an entire year, it becomes clear that there are two different economies operating within the same marketplace. A push by the company for its employees to attain food stamps from the government to subsidize their low wages is an unsustainable business model and a public relations disaster waiting to happen.

However, the problem is that those executives running the companies do not care if there is a public backlash against them for treating their employees like slaves, and they also do not mind if the public thinks they make too much money, in fact, they would be proud of it, that is, if they ever stopped working long enough to read the gossip magazines or the comments left on videos.

The Dislocated States of America

The economic disparity between the "Haves" and "Have Nots" had widened so much that by the late 1990s, the Top 10% of the nation held 76% of the wealth. To take that even further, the 1% accounted for half of that 76% figure, so the concentration of wealth was extreme even two decades ago, but things have only gotten worse.

During the two decades from 1980-2000, the wealth of the lower 60% actually declined, so the gap widened financially, while also putting even more distance between the sides from a social standpoint as well.

• In America, the top 1% retain about 35.5% of the wealth, with the top 20% of the population accounting for 87%.[220]

• The lower half of the American population combined to hold only 1.1% of the wealth of the country.[221]

• As of 2018, the average net worth for the 1% household is $14 million.[222]

• A new billionaire is created every other day in the United States, while the median lower-income family has a net worth of just under $11,000, according to Pew Research.

• Jeff Bezos, Bill Gates, and Warren Buffett have a combined net worth of

---

[220] Robert Frank, CNBC, "The Top 1% Of Americans Now Control 38% Of The Wealth".
[221] World Centric, "Social & Economic Injustice".
[222] Suzie Khimm, The Washington Post, "Who Are The One Percent?".

about $400 billion, or about the same as the lower 60% of the American population.

• The gap between upper-income families and median low-income families jumped from 40 times larger in 2007, to 75 times larger in just nine years due to stock market gains and real estate appreciation.

There are massive differences between the American experience for white people and those in the black and Hispanic communities. The only thing similar is the flag, everything else might as well be happening thousands of miles away.

• The average white family had 68 times more wealth than a Hispanic family and an astounding 86 times more wealth than a black family.[223]

• About 25% of black households have a negative net worth compared to only 10% of white families.[224]

• For the few black families that succeed financially and join the 1%, their children are just as likely to end up in prison as white kids growing up in a household that only earns $36,000.[225]

• For every $100 in family wealth for white families, the black families hold a mere $5, according to the New York Times.

• In the 30 years from 1983-2013, the median household income of a Hispanic family was cut in half, while the income of a black family was reduced by 75%.

• The poorest 50% of Americans saw their net worth shrink from $11,000 to $8,000 since the recession of 2008 up to 2017.[226]

• Over the same period of time, the median household income for a white family increased by 14% from $102,000 to $116,800, according to The Institute for Policy Studies.

The gap in income is not limited to the United States, nor is the damage that it causes. The income problems that plague other countries spread and infect the United States as well, and these figures include the American wealth statistics in

[223] Brian Thompson, Forbes, "The Racial Wealth Gap: Addressing America's Most Pressing Epidemic".
[224] Quentin Fottrell, MarketWatch, "One In Five American Households Have 'Zero Or Negative' Worth".
[225] Emily Badger, The New York Times, "Extensive Data Shows Punishing Reach Of Racism For Black Boys".
[226] Linda Qiu, Politifact, "Sanders: African-Americans Lost Half Their Wealth Because Of Wall Street Collapse".

their calculations.

- Just 1% of the world's population control more wealth than the rest of the other 99% combined.[227]

- Reducing that figure even further, the richest 42 people in the world had more wealth than the poorest 3.7 billion put together.[228]

- 2017 was a great year for the 2,043 billionaires around the world because their wealth increased by three-quarter of a trillion dollars.

- The bottom 90% saw their wealth fall from 33% to 22% in less than three decades, while the top 1% increased their share from 30% to 39%.[229]

- At the rate of appreciation since the Great Recession, the 1% will soon hold wealth equating to $305tn – up from $140tn back in 2008.

- Compared to the rest of the world, the United States holds the 40th highest level of inequality out of 150 countries, putting them on par with Cameroon and Jamaica, according to the CIA Factbook.

At the current rate of appreciation, it is only a matter of time before the wealth inequality will become irreversible and will create a feudal system of Kings and Serfs, ushering in a new Dark Ages, unless the public wakes up to what is actually happening in the world, and the media does its job and reports how dire the situation has become.

The slow death of the American middle class was ramped up once NAFTA was put in place and the speculation from Ross Perot about a "giant sucking sound" came true as jobs were sucked out of America by Mexico. This was followed by the mass migration of factories to China and the gutting of the rust belt of America, just like they knew it would.

The Globalists that pushed for NAFTA operate under the philosophy that they don't really care in which country they earn their profits, as long as their profits are greater than the year before. They have no allegiance to America, so if things get too expensive to produce them in their own backyard, then they will simply move their operations somewhere else, thus the concept of Globalism.

---

[227] BBC News, "Oxfam Says Wealth Of Richest 1% Equal To Other 99%".
[228] The Guardian, "Inequality Gap Widens As 42 People Hold Same Wealth As 3.7 Billion Poorest".
[229] Edward Wolff, The American Prospect, "How The Pie Is Sliced: America's Growing Concentration Of Wealth".

When a company that is paying $30/hour to an employee discovers that now they can get away with paying only $3/hour with no benefits of any kind, it becomes less a decision involving the heart and more a decision predicated on the math of the situation. When 50,000 factories all decide to close their doors and move their operations overseas, it creates a hole in the American economy that hits the middle class the hardest by pushing wages down, and it forces both parents to participate in the workforce, if they can, just to get back to where they once were.

There is nothing accidental about this outcome, as it was obvious to anyone with an economics background how things would play out. It was done completely by design to gut America and widen the wealth gap even further because the people that own the companies that moved overseas were the same people that financed the campaigns of the people that put that legislation in place. They wanted to be able to move their factories to a place that costs them 1/10th of what it costs back in America.

What the country gets is a nation of government dependents. Here is a look at the results, by the percentages.

- As of 2019, 50% of American workers make less than $30,500 a year.[230]

- Almost 40% of Americans would not be able to cover an unexpected expense of $400 and would resort to selling something that they own or borrowing money from a friend.[231]

- In the United States, 33% of households have trouble paying their energy bills.[232]

- According to 62% of Americans, their personal financial situations have not improved since Donald Trump was elected President.[233]

- The cost of living is higher than the median income in 84% of U.S. states.

- More than 50% of the country now receives more in government transfer

---

[230] Tyler Durden, Zero Hedge, "Middle Class Destroyed: 50% Of All American Workers Make Less Than $30,533 A Year".
[231] Ylan Mui, The Washington Post, "The Shocking Number Of Americans Who Can't Cover A $400 Expense".
[232] Associated Press, September 19, 2018, "One-Third Of Households Struggle To Pay Energy Bills".
[233] Alyssa Newcomb, NBC News, "Most Americans Say Finances Haven't Improved Since 2016 Election".

payments than they pay in taxes.[234]

• The bankruptcy of those 65 and older has increased by 500% in the past two decades.[235]

• A little over 33% of Americans have no retirement savings at all, and a full 40% of those that consider themselves to be middle class believe they will live in poverty during their retirement years.[236]

• Since the late 1970s, the amount of money spent on healthcare has increased by 2,900%.[237]

The Washington Post, owned by Amazon billionaire owner Jeff Bezos, described the situation in America as being "nearly a perfect economy", giving insight into just how detached from reality they really are, or what perspective they are surveying the damage from.

It is a perfect economy in which to be a billionaire because the rules of the game are tilted in their favor, but the wealth inequality in America is only one of the obvious signs of a society in decline. Another is that anyone that stands up to identify and expose the problem is demonized and labeled as a conspiracy theorist, or worse.

In a society where blowing the whistle on overt corruption is viewed with disdain, it does not take very long before the whole social structure comes down, as it should so that a new foundation can be created based on fairness, truth, and doing the right thing.

The War on Whistleblowers

Whether a person is working in government or in a factory, sometimes people on the inside need to speak out about what they are seeing in order to keep themselves and others around them safe. Going over the head of the boss to speak to the owner might be viewed as a risky venture, but when a person is sounding the alarms about something very serious and nothing is happening, the decision to make some noise might save someone's life.

---

[234] Scott Hodge, Tax Foundation, "60 Percent Of Households Now Receive More In Transfer Income Than They Pay In Taxes".
[235] Michelle Singletary, The Washington Post, "Retired And Broke: Bankruptcy Filings Surging For Seniors".
[236] Emmie Martin, CNBC, "Here's How Much Americans Have Saved For Retirement".
[237] Austin Frakt, The New York Times, "Medical Mystery: Something Happened To U.S. Health Spending After 1980".

Exposing a dangerous culture within an organization can go one of two ways: either they are applauded for coming forward or they are shunned and ostracized. There is usually no middle ground.

Those that are allowing an unethical, or even illegal, culture to flourish are going to view any challenge to their way of doing things as a threat, so whistleblowers must decide how firmly they actually believe that things need to change, because one thing is for certain, something will change, and it might be that the whistleblower is looking for a new line of work.

There are aspects of the American government that are so corrupt that they need to be shut down completely, like a house that is so decrepit that there is really nothing worth salvaging. Just bring the wrecking ball in and start all over. Because of the compartmentalization of divisions of government, and the secrecy surrounding it, the criminals that are running things have the perfect structure for hiding what they are actually doing. They hide behind legal documents like non-disclosures, they hide within secret societies through blood oaths, they hide in plain sight through aliases, they hide behind closed doors through off-the-record conversations, and they hide behind the threat of retaliation towards anyone that talks about things that they should not be talking about.

If a person goes around their boss at work, he might fire them. If they go around their boss at the CIA, they might end up dead and their autopsy will list the cause as a suicide. History is filled with countless examples of people that spoke out and were silenced forever.

To truly understand the culture of corruption within some of these fragmented organizations, it usually requires someone with first-hand and inside knowledge about how it all really works. To encourage whistleblowers to come forward, protection from retaliation must be offered and actually provided, otherwise, nobody will ever feel safe enough to step up and speak out. People who come forward to disclose corruption and wrongdoing put their careers and lives on the line, but they feel compelled to do so because it is the right thing to do. What they demand in return is protection.

When a whistleblower steps up to disclose wrongdoing within a governmental organization, they are afforded certain protections to entice them to come forward with their information. The "Whistleblower Protection Enhancement Act" (WPEA) provides millions of federal workers with the rights they need to report government corruption and wrongdoing safely. It works to shield people that come forward from retaliation from those powerful people that have the ability to wreck them financially, emotionally, and even physically. The WPEA says that the rights of the whistleblower will be protected and appreciated.

Not so fast. They claim to offer those that blow the whistle on corruption a shield, but the problem is that the shield they are offering is made out of cardboard.

Government workers that have signed secrecy agreements, that work with classified documents, or are involved in any covert programs are not covered by the Whistleblower Protection Enhancement Act. Their secrecy agreements supersede the WPEA, so they are not considered whistleblowers when they disclose information, but they will be considered to be breaking the law. They have no protection and are 100% at risk.

The most well known and obvious government agencies that are not covered by the WPEA are the CIA, NSA, DOJ, FBI, DOD, and DOS. There are another 1,271 different government organizations involved in secrecy, with an additional 1,931 private companies that fall under this exemption.

Intelligence agencies operating outside of the United States are not covered, and neither are the 10,000 intelligence locations inside the United States. Almost a million people in the United States have "Top Secret" clearance which carries stiff penalties for disclosing information. Add to that all of the workers inside the Military-Information-Terror complex that are not covered, as well as 4.8 million people living in the United States with security clearances, and what America has, is a whistleblower protection law that does not protect whistleblowers. This does not count any of the people outside of American borders.

The Whistleblower Protection Enhancement Act does not protect whistleblowers because the people covered by the law are not going to be in a position to actually have valuable or classified information that blows the whistle on anything of any great importance. The government will offer a person protection, as long as they do not have access to anything that is dangerous to them.

By using the state secrets privilege, the intelligence community can stop an investigation into dirty issues. It can also shut down any lawsuits that might paint them in a negative light. Whistleblowers are targeted by government agencies and treated as traitors.

For those that like the James Bond movies and have always dreamed of being a secret spy, gathering important information to help save their country from the evil of foreign governments sounds pretty cool. Those people might be interested in an unpaid internship with one of the dirtiest organizations in the United States. The Department of Homeland Security needs help catching terrorists, and all a concerned citizen needs to do is spy on their neighbors for them. DHS has even started a marketing campaign that encourages citizens to rat out their friends, family members, and casual acquaintances.

The campaign featured Janet Napolitano looking straight into the camera and implored the American people that "if you see something, say something".

Seriously.

They have even trained garbage men on what to look for in the trash that might indicate that the quiet lady that keeps to herself over on Maple Drive is actually a sneaky terrorist quietly assembling bombs in her basement.

Empty crates of dynamite and crumpled boxes of fuses might give her plan away, but if someone was an actual terrorist would they really be dragging their bomb-making garbage to the curb twice a week? This is silly, insulting to the intelligence of the American people, and a colossal waste of time and money.

Why doesn't Janet Napolitano explain to the American people why any of them should trust her? Edward Snowden came forward and "said something", how is that working out for him?

Chelsea Manning "saw something" and they gave her 30 years in prison.

Thanks to Wikileaks, the world knows how dirty the war in Iraq was, and how criminal the people running the show actually are. Where are his great thanks from the Department of Homeland Security? Hillary Clinton's only question was "can't we just drone this guy?", which should be considered conspiracy to commit murder if the government decides to actually enforce any of these laws that they have imposed.

Thomas Drake, a former Senior Executive at the NSA, was reduced to working part-time at an Apple store after going public about the Trailblazer program that sucked up all communications within the United States, not to mention billions of dollars in unnecessary costs.

Bill Binney also cost himself his career at the National Security Agency for speaking out about Trailblazer's collection of all information, including every phone call made and received in the United States. What was his reward?

They ruined his life and damn near killed him.

Ray McGovern, a man in his 80s, spoke out against the NSA and the confirmation of CIA torturer Gina Haspel and got dragged out of the hearing and had his shoulder dislocated.

Michael Hastings wrote a scathing article about General Stanley McCrystal that got him fired from running the Iraq War, then his car blew up after hitting a tree at 100 mph on San Vicente Blvd at 4 am in Los Angeles, only hours after he told his friends that he had to get out of town to lay low.

There was the alleged robbery and murder of Seth Rich, the Democratic National Committee analyst that provided proof that the DNC conspired to suppress votes for Bernie Sanders so that Hillary Clinton could be the nominee. He downloaded information to a thumb drive that was given to Kim Dotcom, who in turn made the information available to Wikileaks and Julian Assange. He was murdered in an alleged robbery in a park in Washington D.C., except that the robbers forgot to take his wallet, his watch, his gold necklace, or his cell phone. Sounds like a hit, not a robbery.

It is interesting that John Podesta said "I'm definitely for making an example of a suspected leaker whether or not we have any real basis for it.", and then Seth Rich ends up dead. He does not sound like a guy that is really into whistleblower protection.

But lest one think that silencing the press was only a Republican tactic, remember that more journalists were jailed by Obama and his bulldog, Eric Holder, under the Espionage Act than under all of the previous administrations combined. They described it as a "zero tolerance" policy towards leaks.

Joseph Stalin had a zero-tolerance policy too, as did Hitler.

Obama targeted whistleblowers through his use of the Espionage Act, more times than all other Presidents that came before him combined, and The United States has a history of treating people who "saw something" then later "said something" like criminals and traitors. So what message are they actually trying to send, that they want people to speak out or shut up?

The intent is irrelevant when discussing the Espionage Act. The law makes no distinction between an American citizen disclosing classified information and a foreign government doing the same thing. As far as they are concerned, a foreign spy is no different than an American journalist. Both must be silenced by any means necessary.

A person does not need to actually share the information with the public either, as the act of retaining the documents is enough to get a person put away in prison for a decade or more.

Obama's Department of Justice brought charges against eight people accused of leaking to the media — Thomas Drake, Ed Snowden, Jeffrey Sterling, Shamai Leibowitz, Stephen Kim, Chelsea Manning, Donald Sachtleben, and John Kiriakou. These people either went to prison or will be arrested if they set foot in the United States again. Kiriakou did time in a federal prison where he had to sit at the Aryan Brotherhood's table during meals so that he would not get shanked or worse. This is serious business.

Manning, Snowden, McGovern, Drake, and Binney were not protected by the Whistleblower Protection Enhancement Act, so it is not really "protection", it is all just an "act" This is what is called "security theater", or the perception that there are protections in place. The name says "Whistleblower Protection Act" so it must protect whistleblowers, right?

Does the "Patriot Act" protect patriots? Does the National Defense Authorization Act actually defend the nation? Is the Federal Reserve Bank federal, or does it have any reserves?

Of course not.

These names are chosen to confuse and pacify the public that does not bother to figure out if the laws are actually helping, or are just a smokescreen to give the impression that something is being done to solve the problem.

That is some Whistleblower Protection Program they've got...

But Janet Napolitano wants the American people to get involved and let them know if they see something? Well, what is in it for the people?

Of course, it goes without saying, but the answer is "nothing".

There is another form of whistleblowing that comes with some implied safety precautions and that is the right to a free press. In theory, a journalist would discover a story that had been intentionally hidden from the general public for any of a vast array of reasons, then they would present it to their editors and if proven to be true, the story would be run in the newspapers and the publisher would stand by their reporter and defend them against the pushback from the embarrassed or infuriated government officials. The publication would claim journalistic integrity as their reason for pushing back against the government or the military, and they would remind those critical of the media's decision that they function as the fourth column of government and that their oversight is a form of checking and balancing the State so that they do not run rampant over the rights of the citizens.

People who come forward to expose corruption put their careers on the line and their lives at risk by disclosing this information, and they do so because it is the right thing to do. All they ask for in return is protection from those powerful people that have the ability to destroy them once the news of their corruption is made public.

Those journalists that stood up to the Bush administration's push for war, and there were not many, were destroyed in every way you can destroy a person. Bill Maher lost his television show *Politically Incorrect* on ABC for speaking out, as did Phil Donahue on MSNBC, even though both had some of the highest ratings on the networks.

Remember what the reaction was when one of the Dixie Chicks blasted Boy George Bush? The public grabbed their torches and pitchforks and ended their careers because they had the audacity to actually question the need for a war against Iraq, a country that had no role in 9/11 and posed no threat to the United States.

The American government hates things like this, so they found a way to guilt the media into keeping quiet about important issues like these by suggesting that by speaking out about these topics they would be putting our troops and agents in the information gathering and spying business at risk of being killed.

When Seymour Hersh published his story on the My Lai massacre in Vietnam, there was massive resistance from the military because of the perception that this would turn public support even more against the war, which of course it did.

Did his editor bury the story in order to save the Army from the public relations nightmare that was surely coming their way? No, he pushed the story out and stood behind the journalist because it was the right thing to do, and also because the story was true. Hersh won the Pulitzer Prize for Journalism that year, and the story exposed what unchecked power does to otherwise good soldiers.

It is amazing how far journalism has fallen over the past couple of decades where real news was once protected by those determined to defend it, to where America is now, where fake news is created by those very same people, and the idea of journalistic integrity is a relic of a time long ago.

Weaponization of Words

Words are very powerful, so is it any surprise that those in positions of power seek to control the meaning of certain words for their own selfish reasons? Of course not, and this is not some recent discovery that Donald Trump just figured out. The control of language was sought the day after language was invented, and those in positions of power and influence have used this control to keep some words hidden while promoting others. They have altered the meaning of words to suit their agendas, they have used them in religious texts to tell magical stories that only they can decipher, and they have used words to demonize, marginalize, and victimize the weak, the stupid, the gullible, the trusting, and the willfully ignorant.

Those who control words control the people; those who control people control the world.

There are techniques, some simple and others complex, for distorting the meaning of words to shield a particular group from criticism, or for lumping people together in order to attack them as a whole. Those that understand these techniques for language manipulation are highly sought after in places like Madison Avenue, Hollywood, and Washington D.C. where liars, con artists, psychopaths, and predators constitute a disproportionate percentage of the population.

Understanding the playbook employed by those trying to manipulate words makes one less susceptible to their influences, and it allows for the dismantling of the argument put forth by the would-be controller by calling them out and explaining to those around them that they are being manipulated by the other person's words.

One way to manipulate people is to play on their emotions. People seem to check their logical brains and function purely from their lizard brain when they are emotional. Advertising agencies do this all the time, and the corporate media are masters of this. With a limited amount of time to paint the picture of the situation the corporate news is trying to convey, they use images of sad, scary, or troubling things to draw out a particular emotion from the viewer. Perhaps the image is of a small child shivering and covered in debris from a chemical gas attack that the media wants to pin on Syrian president Assad, so they show this image over and over until the viewer associates that poor child with the brutal dictator that is intent on killing his own people. The proof for the claim is supposed to be the photo itself, but the truth behind the photo is never really known, only assumed.

Another fertile spot to see emotional manipulation in the media is political campaign ads where the candidates attack each other in order to see who can paint the other person in the worst light. They prey on people's emotions like outrage, fear, and disbelief, rarely proving their claims with any level of certainty.

Staying on the political campaign trail, this is where opponents try to insult and discredit each other by "grouping" their opponent's supporters into batches of people, and then labeling the group in a way meant to marginalize them. The 2016 election circus saw this play run as Clinton attempted to tie Trump supporters to "White nationalists", and then called the rest a "basket of deplorables" in an effort to tie the candidate to a group of people on the fringe of society that nobody would want to be associated with their campaign. Grouping is just the plural version of labeling with the intention of discrediting, only in this case many people get labels put on them instead of just one. Why call one person a racist or a homophobe when they can round up a bunch of people and call them all racists and homophobes in one fell swoop?

1984: The Instruction Manual

When George Orwell wrote his frightening fictional vision of the future, *1984*, he did not intend for it to be an instruction manual for enslavement or a documentary from the future. One of the more memorable aspects of the book was the creation of an entire vocabulary of new words and terms to describe the totalitarian control system that Big Brother had implemented to watch over the people. In and of itself it is not that interesting, but when compared to what the world is currently dealing with, and where humanity is headed in the near future, it is amazing to see how accurate these make-believe terms are, even though they were written 70 years ago.

Newspeak - The official language of Oceania was called Newspeak, and it was the politically correct speech in the mold of North Korea. Newspeak was based on traditional English but without traditional political ideas and concepts. They sought to remove the overall number of words in general in order to limit the range of ideas that could be expressed by the people.

Through the political correctness police found on many college campuses, words that were commonplace just a decade ago in America have been deemed off-limits by the social justice warriors that are obsessed with protecting everyone's feelings and handing out last place trophies.

Memory Hole - If a document portrayed the government in a way that was critical, or if a person had somehow crossed the State and was disappeared, the documents would be put into the memory hole where it was whisked through a series of suction tubes down to the furnace where it was destroyed, and thus erased from history forever.

This is what Google has done with information that runs counter to the official government narrative, first by burying results deep in the search results through their algorithm, then by removing them altogether.

Doublethink - The ability to hold two completely contradictory beliefs in one's mind at the same time, and accept both of them without conflict.

Hillary Clinton is pretty good at this, as evidenced by her speech to Goldman Sachs where she explained that she thought it was always important to have one opinion for the general public, and another one for the people listening to her paid speeches.

Crimethink - This is a thought crime against the State, which included thinking anything that conflicted with the principles of IngSoc. They believed that all crimes began with a single thought, so if they could control thoughts then they could control crime.

The de-platforming of social media accounts that run counter to the views of the government by their partners in Silicon Valley is Version 1.0 of the Crimethink concept.

Fake News Words

Some terms that are thrown around by the corporate media are so Orwellian and nonsensical that one really has to laugh at their audacity of using them in their nightly news broadcast with straight faces. The problem is that after being said thousands and thousands of times, the true meaning and the absurdity of the words all kind of fades away, and a new meaning is created through repetition.

For years the corporate media has been talking about how the Federal Reserve has come to the rescue of the American economy over and over again by instituting a policy called "quantitative easing", which sounds really important, official, and technical until one realizes that it is just a fancy name for printing money out of thin air and debasing the value of the currency.

Take, for instance, the War on Terror. The actual meaning of this term does not make any sense because it is not possible to declare a war on an idea, but beyond that, what is lost is that war _is_ terror, so to create a war against terror cannot happen because the act of declaring war is a terrorist action.

After 17+ years of hearing the term, what it has come to mean to most Americans is fighting wars in the Middle East against people that the United States and their allies do not like anymore. If they have done something to irritate America then they are terrorists, especially if they happen to have brown skin, and because they are classified as being involved in the "War on Terror", different rules for engagement and capture apply to them. They become "Enemy Combatants", and therefore, they can be housed in Guantanamo Bay without trial, and thanks to the NDAA and the Patriot Act, the "Enemy Combatants" can also live inside the United States and be American citizens with "extremist" views, snatched in the middle of the night, and legally taken to any number of black sites around the world to suffer "Enhanced Interrogation" including "Waterboarding", otherwise known as torture.[238]

What qualifies as "extremist" views? According to the Department of Homeland Security, an Orwellian Newspeak name, if ever there was one, an "extremist" could be an alternative journalist, a gun's rights activist, a veteran, a member of a patriot group, a person concerned with open borders, a cryptocurrency advocate, someone with a Gadsden flag sticker, or a variety of other descriptions.

If one's view is not in line with that of the government, they run the very real risk of being labeled as an "extremist", or being "radicalized", and suffering the

---

[238] Naomi Wolf, The Guardian, "The NDAA: A Clear And Present Danger To American Liberty".

consequences that come along with that arbitrary designation, including being put on a "Watch List" or a "No-Fly List". The authorities do not even need to have probable cause any longer in order to detain an "extremist" now that they changed the terminology to "reasonable suspicion", which begs the question "what qualifies as unreasonable suspicion"?

When information about corrupt government actions bubble to the surface and embarrass the agencies that were involved, they do not apologize and change their behavior, they simply change the name of what they were doing. When news broke about the NSA's mass surveillance of the American people, they did not actually stop collecting everyone's data, they just steered the public away from the term "mass surveillance" and towards "bulk collection" to give the appearance that it was as if they were just collecting everyone's junk mail, Pottery Barn catalogs, and coupons that come in the mailbox once a week.

Nowhere does the American Empire try to minimize their involvement, whitewash their crimes, and skew reality more than when discussing their illegal wars of aggression throughout the world. It started after World War 2 when the Department of War changed its name to the Department of Defense in a transparent attempt to hide their imperial ambitions.

The way the American Empire engages in regime change is incremental, starting with the funding of terrorists inside the targeted country, only they have always called them "freedom fighters", which has a nice ring to it. These days the terminology of choice is to refer to them as "moderate rebels" because that sounds better than "paid psychopathic mass-murdering rebels" which is what they actually are.

If the Empire's "moderate rebels" do not get the job done of clearing out the entrenched government, then their next plan is to murder the leader through a targeted assassination program that has been sanitized and rebranded as "extrajudicial killing", although it still has "kill" in the name, for now. No doubt it will soon become known as "targeted erasing" or "extrajudicial hugging".

Before the war that they really want gets started, the United States needs to sell it to the citizens as something noble and justified in order to have the support from the people. One way that they do this is by demonizing the current leader by spreading false stories through the CIA-controlled corporate media about the "dictator" killing his own people, then they frame the invasion as a "humanitarian intervention" to make it sound legitimate. They will paint the picture of an out of control maniac about to commit genocide against his own people, so they must launch a preemptive "intervention" to stop the killing before it gets started.

When the bombs start dropping on the civilian population it becomes difficult to make the case that the mission was a humanitarian one, what with all the dead humans and everything. Once the American military moves in, they will actually start committing genocide against the population by "neutralizing" them, but they will dress it up with a more subtle name, "ethnic cleansing" like it is some new brand of happy laundry detergent. "It gets the brown out...of the skin...by killing it!"

With every "humanitarian intervention" there is always "collateral damage", which sounds like when a person accidentally bumps a shopping cart in the parking lot with their car. What "collateral damage" actually means is the murder of civilians from bombs and bullets that miss their intended target from an occupying army that invented the reason to be in the country in the first place.

That is the cost of "spreading democracy" to foreign countries that "hate us for our freedoms" and are in desperate need of "Western values".

It is murder dressed up to sound accidental and semi-respectable, but a person that exposes and calls out these facts is called a "conspiracy theorist", a term created by the CIA back in the 1960s to discredit those that were investigating their involvement in the killing of John F. Kennedy.

The reason for all of these illegal and unnecessary wars around the world is to protect the American Way which really has been grounded in the concept of "globalism", where all countries are free to conduct business with one another internationally without control in the form of tariffs and taxes. The people in modern-day society that pushed for the creation of this were the Rockefellers and Rothschilds who wanted borders opened and restrictions lifted. They did this through their proxies in Washington D.C. that passed trade deals like the Trans-Pacific Partnership and NAFTA.

What they were actually doing was setting the groundwork to begin the process of erasing national sovereignty so that they could centralize power for their New World Order that they dream of. They started the process of grouping countries into larger groups so that they could control them easier, which is why the European Union was formed, and why the North American Union between Canada-United States-Mexico has been on the drawing board for years.

The seemingly harmless term, "globalism", is the trojan horse of the one-world government, and a perfect example of how words can be presented to the public as having one meaning, while they actually mean something far different and more sinister.

A person that finds themselves disagreeing with the globalist philosophy of government is no longer thought of as just a hippy or a protestor, but are now called "anarchists", and are described by the corporate media as dangerous because they want to break windows, light tires on fire, and overthrow the government.

Whoever came up with the advice that "sticks and stone may break my bones, but words will never hurt me" has obviously never been accused of a thought crime, called a conspiracy theorist, and thrown in jail as an anarchist for peacefully protesting a trade deal in a public park. The censorship of these thoughts has migrated from the real world into the cyber world, as internet censorship has been ramped up in recent years because the controlling power structure has noticed that most people are moving online to source their news and information.

It does beg the question, do flat-Earthers believe in globalism?

Internet Censorship

Never before have Americans seen the internet censorship in action as much as during the Coronavirus pandemic. Facebook, YouTube, even the comments sections on news sites have blocked and removed anything that opposes their mainstream paid-for narrative with alarming alacrity.

Censorship is what happens when powerful people get nervous, so the rise in online censorship is both a good thing and a horrible thing.

It is good in the sense that those in positions of power are legitimately nervous about the weakening grip they hold on society. The "alternative media" has been making things more difficult for the controllers over the past half-decade, starting with the revelations from Edward Snowden and Julian Assange, both were rewarded with sequestration and isolation in foreign countries for their troubles.

It is a horrible thing in the sense that the controllers do have the ability to switch off those voices that dare to stand up to their plan for an Orwellian Ministry of Truth by de-platforming them one at a time, or in the case of Alex Jones, colluding to remove him from multiple platforms all at the exact same time.

Not everyone in the alternative media had their channels taken away, but most faced some version of digital censorship that comes in a variety of flavors.

The first salvo in the information war on social media came in the form of demonetization, where the videos or content that were uploaded onto the platform were prevented from showing advertisements, thus removing any financial benefit that might have been associated with a particular video or post.

The videos would still be available, but the commercials would be removed.

The throttling of reach to a content provider's subscriber base is another early method used because it is so difficult to quantify, and it does not send off alarm bells to either the provider or the receiver of the content. A content provider with 100,000 subscribers to their video channel that is used to getting 25,000 views of any given video that they post might be alarmed to realize that those viewership numbers drop to 3,500, with no obvious reason for the decline.

What is happening is that the service provider is not making the content available to all of the subscribers of the channel, so as far as the end-user is concerned, the video does not exist. Many of those that specifically enable notifications of new video content being uploaded had their notifications switched off by the provider, unbeknownst to them.

A more overt version of this is called "shadow banning" and that is where the posts or videos are not seen by anyone, they basically ban the content without officially announcing the ban. Another method is for the platform to simply delete the posts or the videos at a later time, or to go back into the history of the channel and selectively delete videos that they have now deemed to be a violation.

The most common method of deleting video channels and social media accounts is to accuse the content provider of a "Violation of Community Guidelines", a catchall phrase that makes the accusation that the content provider has posted something against their rules and subsequently the entire channel has been terminated from the platform effective immediately.

No discussion, no appeal, no judge, no jury, no rights, and no more channels. What is crazy about these cases, and there are many, is that what sometimes gets a channel de-platformed is a video that had lived on that channel in peace and love for the past three years without any issue but now all of a sudden was so offensive that not only is that video deleted, but every video the person ever created is gone as well.

Facebook might put a content creator in "Facebook Jail" for 30 days where their content cannot be seen or modified, before popping back up after a month. Another "violation" may result in a 90-day suspension, or even the delisting of the account altogether. Twitter is a fan of the suspension method as well, as account holders regularly login only to discover that they have been censored for something they have said, maybe the day before, maybe the year before, and their account has been put on ice for a specified period of time.

Search engine companies could have their algorithms adjusted in a way so that certain types of information, or information coming from particular websites, would be pushed so far down in the results pages that it was essentially hidden from the public. Even entire domain names have just been switched off and deleted.

Lately, a favorite of the establishment media and their partners in the social media industry has been to label anything that conflicts with their worldview as being "fake news", which is hilarious for those that know the truth about how fake the "real" news actually is, and how under the control of the Central Intelligence Agency they have been for a half a century. Sure, a company can protest or challenge the ruling, but by that point, the damage is already done to their image and reputation.

Then there are the ever-watchful guardians of the cyber-realm, those demigods of knowledge – the "Independent Fact Checkers".

Especially in the time of COVID-19 people had to wonder who this army of "independent fact-checkers" are who have been employed by Facebook and YouTube. They must be incredibly smart, wasted as a fact-checker for sure when they are able to divine the truth on highly complex topics where qualified experts in their field have a differing of opinion.

The rise of "fact-checking" companies like Snopes that are anointed as the authority on truth and back up the mainstream media's points on polarizing issues are a bad joke. The media never bother to mention the fact that Snopes has been proven to be a completely compromised husband and wife operation that are suing each other over a variety of issues, including marital infidelity and the husband's penchant for hookers, and have no business being in the investigative journalism industry in any way, shape, or form. They get paid to nod their heads in unison with the mainstream media, that is their job.[239]

Also, the announcement that Facebook plans to hire 20,000 people to sort through the news stories to determine the truth is so Orwellian that at first glance one has to do a double-take to make sure they are not actually reading a satire article from The Onion.[240] The grunts that are sifting through the news stories are going to get to the bottom of fake news by asking their bosses at Facebook what version of the news they want to portray, then stuffing anything into the "memory hole" that does not fit with the narrative.

What could be more "real news" than that?

Facebook also stole a play out of China's playbook by announcing that they plan to rank the trustworthiness of their users in order to tackle fake news. They plan to measure behavioral clues from the users that they monitor in order to see who is a problem and who is to be trusted to post or more accurately critique, the news that Facebook considers to be real.

Everything is fake news except for what comes from the mainstream media and social media giants, which is entirely real, true, correct, honest, impartial, well-researched, unbiased, fair & balanced, thought-provoking, and objective, as far as the brainwashed viewer is concerned.

This content flow restriction is not limited to individuals only. Businesses that are perceived to cater to alternative viewers such as gold and silver resellers, prepping supply distributors, cryptocurrency marketplaces, and alternative news sources have all been under attack.

Website hosting companies like WordPress have started kicking off certain alternative media websites from their hosting platforms. A company might have been operational for many years then wake to find that their entire website has been taken offline, and the owner has been locked out of their website altogether, with no access to their content and information, and no warning so that they could back up their data.

If community guidelines were being broken, how come the content was not removed years ago? Why the coordinated effort to suppress thoughts that run

---

[239] Keith Kelly, New York Post, "Bitter Divorce Fuels Snopes' Slow Demise".
[240] Anita Balakrishnan, CNBC, "Facebook Pledges To Double Its 10,000-Person Safety And Security Staff By End Of 2018".

counter to the mainstream media narrative? Why are platforms and hosting operators censoring their own customers and messing with their ability to run their businesses?

Clearly, it was because of what they were saying, and how they were saying it.

This clampdown on freedom of speech online should not come as much of a surprise, as the idea of reconfiguring the way the internet works has been on the drawing board for quite some time. Because of the anonymous nature of the current version of the internet, called Internet 1.0, it allowed a person in one location to interact on websites in faraway locations without having to disclose their identity. Their computer was identified through an IP Address, but the user was still anonymous.

It is like walking into Nordstrom's to browse through the men's department, before walking out into the mall and heading over to another store.

But what if one had to swipe their driver's license before they could even walk into the store, would that change the shopping experience? Would a person hesitate because of the lack of anonymity? Obviously, Nordstrom's would want to know exactly who was walking through their stores each day so that they could market to them, but would a person decide not to enter a store specifically so that they do not show up the store's mailing list?

If the way to enter a mall had always been to swipe a driver's license in order to enter, it would be normalized and probably accepted as the way things are.

However, if the population remembered that an ID was never required before, there would be push-back, boycotts, and outrage. If a person showed up to the mall today and was required to show their driver's license before being allowed to enter they would probably give the security guard the finger, get in their car and go home, and post to social media how stupid things have gotten.

What if a terrorist walked right through the unguarded, but video surveilled doors of a mall on a Sunday afternoon with a suitcase full of explosives and blew the place to smithereens, killing 3,758 people, including 897 children? Now would the people demand ID readers on the doors of all malls?

Of course, and that is how these things get done.

The Internet 2.0 will be accessed only by those holding an Internet ID Card.

Those without a card either by choice or by decree, will not be allowed to access online services including web browsing, online banking, booking travel, video chatting, social media, email, streaming video services, cloud storage, news, the new platform of television, online radio, navigation and other features for automobiles, rideshare services, and mobile payments.

Good luck functioning in the modern world without an Internet ID Card.

Want to post a video critical of the government on YouTube? Go for it, but their Internet ID Card might be shut off.

Beyond the obvious overt censorship that comes with a system like this, there is also the unquantifiable self-censorship that inevitably accompanies these changes. One need look no further than East Germany to understand what happens when the omnipresent fear that the KGB was listening to all the phone calls chills the population, or the fear of triple-generation deportation to the salt mines of North Korea for any dissenters, in conjunction with the reward system for ratting on those neighbors suspected of committing thought crimes.

It makes a person wonder what sort of "suitcase event" is going to happen on the Internet 1.0 to bring about the demand for the cybersecurity provided by these Internet ID Cards that will soon be making their entrance onto the world's stage?

What is Really Going on Here?

The mainstream media and their lackeys in the social media arena would not be censoring their own customers and suppressing free speech if they did not feel threatened by the alternative media, or if they felt like they had a handle on the truth getting out. They do not, and they realize this which is why the push is so massive and coordinated. The mainstream media is trying to silence the alternative media because they talk about those wacky conspiracy theories, while they are participating in a giant, coordinated conspiracy of their own to silence free speech.

The mainstream media is so reviled and distrusted, and their ratings have tanked so badly that they can no longer compete against the alternative media so they coordinate their efforts, as documented at the Bilderberg Conference, with the social media companies to just ban the alternative media so that CNN, MSNBC, the Washington Post, Politico, and others no longer have to even compete against them for viewers.

"If you can't beat 'em, have your buddies silence 'em".

To really understand the deeper reason why companies like Facebook and Google/YouTube would agree to participate in the suppression of free speech, it is important to understand how many of these companies first came into existence.

Money that was used to finance the seed funding operations of many tech companies came from the CIA's venture capital arm, a company called In-Q-Tel that was founded in 1999 in order to finance data gathering companies in Silicon Valley so that it did not look like the CIA was running them.

In-Q-Tel poured money into a variety of tech start-ups, and they hold powerful positions and a tremendous amount of equity within these companies. They have a say in the operations of the companies, and that is a point worth remembering because when a company takes money from a venture capital firm, they do so with certain strings attached. They also are dependent on regulatory agencies for certain classifications and licenses, so double-crossing or defying the CIA would be done at one's own business, and personal, peril.

In-Q-Tel funded Keyhole, which later became Google Maps, so the CIA is involved in the mapping aspect of Google's business.

If the Central Intelligence Agency wants Facebook and YouTube to flip the switch and turn off Alex Jones, The Anarchast, or Aunt Josie's Cat-tastic Channel, consider the switch flipped.

Does the mainstream media want the alternative media silenced so that they do not have to compete with them?

Yes.

Do the United States government want the alternative media silenced so that they do not show that the DNC documents were not hacked by Russia but leaked by Seth Rich or expose their history of lies?

Yes.

Does the CIA and the Military-Information-Terror complex want the alternative media silenced so that they do not blow the whistle on their plans to frame North Korea, Iran, and Russia in order to kick off a major war that puts trillions of dollars into their pockets?

You are goddamn right they do, and that is what the internet censorship is all about.

The Department of Defense has their own version of the Bilderberg Conference called The Highlands Forum, and it aims to provide the Pentagon with a network of social media and big business connections that can help to further their spying efforts and provide them with a talent pool to draw from. Representatives from a variety of companies are a part of this forum, including private spy agencies like Booz Allen Hamilton, SAIC, and RAND Corporation, as well as tech giants like AT&T, Microsoft, Google, IBM, Cisco, eBay, PayPal, General Electric, British Broadcasting Corporation, and even Disney, to name a few. They form small workshops where they discuss how the companies can integrate their services with the large government spy agencies and the military, for a price, of course.

The line between private tech companies and large governmental departments is blurry these days. When Amazon signs a massive deal to host the CIA's cloud computing needs, it is easy to wonder where Amazon the global marketplace ends and where Amazon the cloud computing platform begins, and how much access the CIA has to all aspects of Amazon's business data?

Media Matters...Until It Doesn't

Media Matters For America is a non-profit organization founded by David Brock and funded, in part, by George Soros. They are a far-left organization that's sole mission appears to be to bring down Donald Trump and silence anyone with a differing opinion to theirs, usually conservatives but not exclusively. Anything to the center and right is fair game for them.

"Media Matters for America is a web-based, not-for-profit, 501(c)(3) progressive research and information center dedicated to comprehensively monitoring, analyzing, and correcting conservative misinformation in the U.S. media.

Launched in May 2004, Media Matters for America put in place, for the first time, the means to systematically monitor a cross-section of print, broadcast, cable, radio, and Internet media outlets for conservative misinformation - news or commentary that is not accurate, reliable, or credible and that forwards the conservative agenda - every day, in real-time.

Using the website mediamatters.org as the principal vehicle for disseminating research and information, Media Matters posts rapid-response items as well as longer research and analytic reports documenting conservative misinformation throughout the media. Additionally, Media Matters works daily to notify activists, journalists, pundits, and the general public about instances of misinformation, providing them with the resources to rebut false claims and to take direct action against offending media institutions."

In 2017 their playbook for the next four years that was given to donors and high-level operatives was leaked and ended up being made public. This manifesto was enlightening because although their mission was becoming clear as day, to actually see it in print was frightening. They use the term "here is what success will look like" to describe what they have up their sleeve.

• *Serial misinformers and right-wing propagandists inhabiting everything from social media to the highest levels of government will be exposed, discredited.*

• *Internet and social media platforms, like Google and Facebook, will no longer uncritically and without consequence host and enrich fake news sites and propagandists.*

• *Toxic alt-right social media-fueled harassment campaigns that silence dissent and poison our national discourse will be punished and halted.*

They mention that they have Facebook and Google (parent company of YouTube) onboard with their operation to silence what they call "propagandists" by de-platforming them, which explains why all of the alternative media sites began getting shut down in unison during 2018.

Media Matters intends to expose and discredit what they describe as "serial-misinformers", a term that is so Orwellian that it is laughable, especially considering that Media Matters pulls a large chunk of their money from George Soros, a Globalist that has been misinforming the world for the past half-century.

The document goes on to admit that they were the ones behind the push to de-platform social media Facebook pages, YouTube channels, and Google search links to sites that they deem to be fake news in a section titled "Collaborating With Social Media Platforms".

"Collaborating With Social Media Platforms"

Outlets that push fake news are completely dependent on Facebook to spread their lies, and ad networks like Google to fund them.

Media Matters has a unique insight to help fix problems in this part of the media landscape.

After Facebook responded to our campaign by acknowledging the problem of fake news and agreeing to do something about it, we began a dialog. It became clear from these conversations that Facebook needed our help in fully understanding the problem and identifying concrete solutions. Further, it also became clear that we had information and insight that they didn't have that was helpful in educating them on the full scope of the problem. For example, Media Matters had a detailed map of the constellation of right-wing Facebook pages that had been the biggest purveyors of fake news - as well as insight into the food chain of fake news and how it was moving through the Facebook ecosystem.

Similarly, after Google revised their terms of service in order to prohibit so-called fake news sites from using their advertising network, it was Media Matters that had the information necessary to identify 40 of the worst fake news sites to which this policy applied."

If forcing the social media platforms to silence those with dissenting voices does not work during the course of their four-year plan, Media Matters has a backup plan that seems crazy, even by their standards.

"We will train hundreds of thousands of individuals on how to identify fake news and alt-right smears in their social media networks and equip them with the tools to fight them on their own."

Good luck, David.

Media Matters pretends that only the Republicans lie to the people as if the Democrats are always telling the truth. The people running Media Matters are not really afraid of the lies that Donald Trump tells about them, or the lies that their political enemies spread about them. Those lies do not bother them.

What Media Matters is really trying to silence is the truth. They do not want the public to know the truth which is why they are so desperate to label it as fake news. If it was so fake, then why worry about it? If it was such an obvious lie, then why the panic and the need to bring down the whole social media establishment.

Shakespeare said it best, and this can be directed at David Brock and his boyfriend, James Alefantis, owner of Comet Ping Pong and the 49th most powerful person in Washington D.C. (for some unusual reason): *"The lady doth protest too much, methinks"*.[241]

It is worth noting that Facebook also brought in a think tank called The Atlantic Council to assist them in determining what was fake news, but what they failed to mention is that The Atlantic Council is funded by NATO and the Military-Information-Terror complex, so any news that was critical of the globalist agenda was clearly going to be labeled as fake news. Facebook also worked with The German Marshall Fund which has similar ties and is funded by the United States government directly, despite its name, so it is not just Media Matters that is trying to shape reality through limiting free speech on social media platforms.

The control over the perception of the world has been the goal of the corporate media since the 1960s, at least, but the social media platforms have really been instrumental in the shaping of society over the past decade. Though the flow of information through the media and social media platforms is made to appear organic, it is clearly not the case. The product that the colleges are turning out these days looks to have been shaped by something very different than just one generation previous. Where college once toughened kids up and turned them into adults that were better equipped to go out into the real world, these days the students are finding themselves softened up to the point where they are ill-prepared to deal with reality, and employers are discovering that most of them are unhirable.

Safe Spaces, Trigger Warnings, and Snowflakes

The "pussification" of America is an actual problem. Every generation tells the tales of how when they were kids they walked five miles to school, every day, in the snow, uphill, both ways. These days, college kids in the United States have gotten so soft that new vocabulary words had to be created to explain things that never existed before, like "safe spaces", "snowflakes", and being "triggered".

---

[241] Reid Cherlin, G.Q., January 18, 2012.

A safe space is a place on a college campus where students can feel comfortable talking about their experiences and hide from those with differences of opinions that make them feel all icky inside. This safe space is where they can find support from others with similar fears and afflictions, like an Alcoholics Anonymous meeting, except without all the cool stories. The safe spaces function like an echo chamber where only similar opinions and philosophies are allowed, and disagreement is met with hysteria. Although the concept is that it creates an environment where people can explore and express their feelings, what actually ends up happening is that they shut out anything that challenges their current belief system and this actually works to retard their emotional development.

If college is supposed to prepare students for the outside world, then safe spaces are doing those kids a tremendous disservice by insulating them from the reality of the world they will soon be forced to deal with. Their boss at their first real job is not going to be as understanding as the liberal Dean at their college that catered to their every whim and gave them a hug and a tall glass of warm milk.

These safe spaces have been the incubator to create "snowflakes", or people who are unable to emotionally deal with being offended by views that conflict with their own. Snowflakes seek safe spaces the minute their college books Milo Yiannopoulos to speak, or when the person that they did not vote for becomes the President of the United States. Every snowflake is perfect and special, but very fragile.

Being "triggered" is a term that describes what a snowflake heard that made them seek out a safe space. It could be something as innocuous as a professor explaining that the course he teaches contains sensitive material of a nature that some students might find uncomfortable and off-putting. It might be that someone like Ben Shapiro comes to their school to debate another political activist and they hear something that makes them sad, or that they disagree when he starts making sense in a way they had never considered before and it makes them want to scream.

There was a time when America did not hand out trophies for last place.

Those days are over.

According to a poll of 1,659 current college students taken by LendEDU, a student loan consolidation and refinancing organization.

- 37% felt safe spaces were "completely out of touch with reality".

- 36% thought safe spaces were "absolutely necessary".

- 25% were indifferent to the whole idea of them.

This coddling of kids has been a result of the noble idea that parents want to make things easier for their kids than they were for them, but the last generation had it pretty damn good, so the current batch of kids are getting treated like kings and queens by their parents since they really did not have all that much strife to overcome themselves. Though the purpose might be well-intentioned, the result looks a whole lot like entitlement on a mega scale.

Safe spaces are stupid. The world is not a safe space, and the sooner the kids figure this out, the better off they will be when learning to function in the real world. Without adversity, lessons are not learned, ingenuity is not fostered, and people are not tested to see what they are made of. These parents are not doing their kids any favors by trying to protect them from the big bad world.

Generation XYY

If an XX chromosome combination is a girl, and XY chromosome combo signals a boy, then America is slipping down the path towards XYY, the generation of multiple sexual identities.

Every day on the online mainstream news websites there is multiple stories about gender identity bravery about how a girl realized she was actually a boy at age nine, and why the child should be celebrated for being so heroic. If there were only one story every now and then, it might be interesting, but instead, it looks more and more like an orchestrated push towards the normalization of multiple gender identities.

To be clear, being unsure of one's gender must be a confusing and lonely experience, on top of the normal struggles of just being a kid, but it is not common. It is being covered by the mainstream news at a disproportionate rate that gives it the appearance of being a normal process that lots of kids have to deal with.

The push through the media about gender identity stories is undeniable if one is paying attention, so it begs the questions "why"? What is the end game here about normalizing the abnormal? Who is behind this push to create 51 different gender identities and criminalize the use of incorrect pronouns?

Like most things the media does, it is probably designed to divide the people into smaller and smaller groups that can then be turned against each other to keep the masses bickering over meaningless and trivial matters so that they will not have the time or desire to dig into the real problems that plague America, and that is not whether or not there needs to be a third bathroom.

To clarify, sex refers mainly to biology and is a function of chromosomes, hormones, and internal and external anatomy, where gender is more about a personal sense of who a person is, like being a man, woman, transgender, or other. Many countries and societies are expanding their use of gender terms, and nowhere is this being noticed more than on the social media platform Facebook where a person can be anything they want to be, even a non-person.

The new list of Facebook gender choices are Agender, Androgyne, Androgynous, Aporagender, Bigender, Body Dysphoria, Cis, Demigender, Dyadic, Female to Male/ FTM, Gender Apathetic, Gender Fluid, Gender Nonconforming, Gender Questioning, Gender Variant, Genderqueer, Greygender, Intersex, Male to Female/MTF, Maverique, Neither, Neutrois, Non-binary, Novigender, Other, Pangender, Polygender, Social Dysphoria, Transgender, Transsexual person, Transmasculine, Transfeminine, and Two-spirit.

Even people that describe themselves as being an alternative gender to the standard two choices have got to admit that this is pretty ridiculous.

Pronoun use is an important issue for those that do not consider themselves to be in the traditional gender roles. Some gender-fluid people choose to use pronouns other than she/her/hers and he/him/his. A few examples of gender-neutral pronouns are they/them/theirs and ze/hir/hirs.

This is not a joke.

A person's gender cannot be assumed from their appearance, so one is advised to ask their preferred gender pronoun before addressing them. A failure to take this seriously may result in being branded as "homophobic", a vague and misleading term that sounds like it was created at the Tavistock Institute to attack those that were exposing the alarming number of closeted homosexual men that were a part of Margaret Thatcher's cabinet.

The media has taken these new gender designations and whipped the public up into a frenzy looking to lynch anyone that is ignorant enough to refer to someone as "she" instead of "ze" while normalizing the insanity of 51 different identities and doing all of this with a straight face.

And they wonder why nobody watches the news anymore.

The media is focused on extending additional and unnecessary freedoms to people that really do not need them, while the government is busy removing freedoms from the people that do.

Constitution Free Zone

A glaring example of the hypocrisy of the American legal system is the discovery that there is a "Constitution-Free Zone" that was put in place by the U.S. Department of Justice way back in 1953. They defined this zone to be 100 miles inland from all of the borders.[242]

Just ponder that concept for a moment.

Mind you, the 100-mile inland border is inside of the United States, but somehow does not conform to the rules of the rest of the country. Upon a casual glance, it might seem that this band of the lawless territory is a rather insignificant area until one discovers that 2/3's of Americans live inside this zone.

The next logical question to consider is "why bother having a Constitution if it does not apply to over 200 million Americans"?

This type of random probing contradicts the 4th Amendment which guarantees that:

"The right of the people to be secure in their persons, houses, papers, and effects, against unreasonable searches and seizures, shall not be violated, and no Warrants shall issue, but upon probable cause, supported by Oath of affirmation, and particularly describing the place to be searched, and the persons or things to be seized."

None of this is stopping the Border Patrol from setting up citizenship checkpoints and arbitrarily searching buses and detaining those that are unwilling or unable

---

[242] Lornet Turnbull, Yes Magazine, "Two-Thirds Of Americans Live In The 'Constitution-Free Zone'".

to answer their questions to their liking. They admit that they sometimes set up these stops just to "see what we can catch", which would be fine if one was fishing, but it is a violation of the Constitution and the assumption of innocence, for those that care about things like that.

Checkpoints cannot be primarily used for drug-search or general law enforcement efforts, but sometimes they are.

The Border Patrol is refusing to allow Americans to travel on these interstates unless they disclose their citizenship status to the officer questioning them. Some of the signs that these agents are looking for include the driver speaking with a foreign accent, looking suspicious, or a failure to answer their questions.

That seems like a pretty vague and unscientific way of dealing with this immigration problem.

Military Occupation

What would a military occupation actually look like in America?

Sadly, one does not have to use their imagination very much because it has been playing out in real life more and more.

In America B.C. (before Corona), it looked like Ferguson, Missouri where riot police with face shields and batons used sound cannons, where the protestors were threatened by the police and even physically beaten, where demonstrators were put in chokeholds and pepper-sprayed, shot with smoke grenades, and arrested in mass.

It looked like the break up of the Occupy Wall Street protest in Manhattan with intimidation through the use of unmarked black helicopters and aggressive riot police, jamming the internet so that protestors could not live stream the event, the restriction of the press, the arresting of the press, cell phone confiscation, the use of Stingray devices to intercept phone calls, and the importation of private military contractors paid for by the banks.

It looked like the aftermath of the Boston non-Bombing event where cops in black military-style gear, black masks, and helmets, rode in Armored Personnel Carriers going door-to-door with search teams and police dogs, confiscating guns from law-abiding citizens while ordering people to stay in their houses or face arrest.

It looked like Baltimore with snipers on the roof, soldiers dressed in battle fatigues carrying machine guns, strip searches, indefinite detentions, and drone surveillance with thermal cameras.

This has been an incremental deterioration of rights to the point where Americans do not even think twice about the obvious fact that the old image of a nice, approachable police officer dressed in his blue uniform has been replaced with a cop in head-to-toe black military gear, with the only difference being the removal of camouflage and the replacement with solid black, who looks at the people with suspicion and contempt. The NDAA allows the military to arrest Americans and detain them without being charged, a blatant violation of the Constitution.

None of this matters, and clearly, nobody seems to care.

FEMA camps and private prisons?

Fine.

"Constitution Free Zones" 100 miles from the border, and "Free Speech Zones" 100 yards from the Democratic National Convention?

Who cares, go for it.

This is what it is like to live in a Police State where a person is considered to be an "enemy combatant" in their own country.

This is how it is when they transform the homeland into a "battlefield" in order to allow themselves to technically comply with the new laws they passed so that they can murder American citizens without a trial or due process, so they can remove Posse Comitatus in order to flood the street with soldiers instead of police officers, and so they can treat Americans like they are the enemy.

Welcome to America, the new home of Martial Law, coming to a city nearby in America. But the real question is "why"?

They do not pass these laws unless they intend to use them, and they have gone out of their way to try and normalize armed military operating within the borders of the United States. None of this is normal if the people in charge believe that things will remain as they are.

Do they know something that the rest of us are not being told?

They do. They realize that the end of the financial system of central banking is near and that martial law will have to be enacted in order to deal with the social unrest that will arise in the aftermath of the collapse of the American Empire. It might look like a drill or some kind of exercise right now, but when looking back after the empire falls it will be so obvious that the reason for the militarization of the police, the creation of American the Battlefield, the Constitution Free Zones, and the FEMA camps built next to railways was to prepare for the collapse of American society and the chaos that would arise because of it.

And at no time has the evidence been more transparent than the tyrannical measures taken by governments around the world during the Coronavirus plandemic. And the intentional ignition of the race war that is spreading over the globe like molten lava – destroying everything in its path.

Gun Control in America

The 2nd Amendment to the Constitution is the right to bear arms in the United States. The government does not like the idea that hundreds of millions of Americans have guns, so they will do whatever it takes to convince the public that they need to confiscate all of their guns for their own protection.

"A well-regulated Militia, being necessary to the security of a free State, the right of the people to keep and bear Arms, shall not be infringed."

As long as the government knows that the people are armed, they will be less likely to try to take advantage of them. This is just a simple assessment of the situation.

• American civilians own an estimated 265 million - 330 million guns, or roughly 40% of the guns in the world, according to the Graduate Institute of International and Development Studies in Geneva.

• America has the highest rate of per capita firearm ownership in the world, with a little less than one gun for every American.

• Only 22% - 31% of American adults own a gun.

- About 40% of Americans say they own a gun or live in a household with one.

- Just 3% of American adults own a collective 133 million firearms, an average of 17 guns each.[243]

- There are 7.7 million Americans that own 40+ guns each.[244]

- Since 2006, Americans have purchased 122 million new guns.

There is a massive push towards gun control by those in political power worldwide, not just in America, but in many other countries as well. The American military, the local police, and the authority-hating criminals will probably not hand over their guns, as they are not the type of people to generally follow the rules.

The slaughtering of citizens by their own government almost always starts with gun confiscation in order to disarm the public. This might sound alarmist or paranoid, but in the last century, the #1 killer of people around the world, estimated to be 144,000,000, came at the hands of their own government.

- 61,911,000 Murdered: The Soviet Gulag State.

- 35,236,000 Murdered: Mao's Communist China.

- 20,946,000 Murdered: The Nazi Third Reich.

- 10,214,000 Murdered: The Depraved Nationalist Regime (China).

- 5,964,000 Murdered: Japan's Savage Military.

- 2,035,000 Murdered: The Khmer Rouge Hell State.

- 1,883,000 Murdered: Turkey's Genocidal Purges.

- 1,670,000 Murdered: The Vietnamese War State.

---

[243] Lois Beckett, The Guardian, "The Gun Numbers: Just 3% Of American Adults Own A Collective 133 Million Firearms".
[244] Lois Beckett, The Guardian, "The Gun Numbers: Just 3% Of American Adults Own A Collective 133 Million Firearms".

- 1,585,000 Murdered: Poland's Ethnic Cleansing.

- 1,503,000 Murdered: The Pakistani Cutthroat State.

- 1,072,000 Murdered: Tito's Slaughterhouse.

- 1,663,000 Murdered: Orwellian North Korea.

- 1,417,000 Murdered: Barbarous Mexico.

- 1,066,000 Murdered: Feudal Russia.

- After China established gun control in 1935, 10,076,000 political dissidents were murdered from 1948 - 1952, plus another 35,000,000 over the next 35 years.

- When Nazi Germany implemented their version of gun confiscation in 1938, 13 million people that were not loyal to Hitler's Third Reich were executed in just six years.

- From 1929 to 1953, about 20 million dissidents were murdered by the Soviet Union, with that number rising to 62,000,000 over the next three decades.

- In just five years, the Khmer Rouge in Cambodia killed 2,000,000 educated people because they considered them to be a threat to their regime. When examined later, Pol Pot and his Khmer Rouge had ended up murdering 30% of their own people.

The American government secretly imports guns for the criminals to use because that creates tension among the people so that they can be more easily divided against each other. It also works to create the impression that because there are mass shootings all of the time (allegedly), there have to be more gun control regulations. The irony of America's stealth push for gun control is that every time there is another fake school shooting, people do not turn in their guns, but rather they go out and buy even more guns.

Every country that is quietly screwing their own people over with crazy restrictions or a divide & conquer philosophy will, at some point, seek to remove guns from the hands of those they feel might stand in their way. Because part of America's culture and image is so intertwined with the idea of having guns, it will be a slow process to change the culture so that guns no longer play a role in what it means to be an "American".

If the United States government decided that guns were going to be made illegal the following day and that all citizens would be required to give up their weapons, it would be met with so much resistance that it would have the exact opposite effect. With this in mind, the controllers set about to make this an incremental process that gradually removed certain types of guns over a much longer period of time so as to avoid the backlash that would come with an outright ban.

There have always been shootings, but the way that the corporate media chooses to cover them has changed drastically. These shootings, whether organic or fake, are seized upon by the media in order to push the narrative that only criminals have guns, and sometimes those guns are used to kill children, so the solution to the problem is to remove the guns. The media does not cover knife attacks, baseball bat attacks, or when some guy loses his mind and smashes up another car with a tire iron. They are only interested in shootings that involve military-style rifles like AK-47s and M-4s, especially those using extended clips and bump stocks. Their plan is to slowly put bans into place that prohibit the selling of these add-on items and take away the hardware piece by piece.

After the Integrated Capstone Event at Sandy Hook, a joint venture between the Department of Homeland Security (DHS) and the Federal Emergency Management Agency (FEMA), that drill was used to push and pass legislation for gun control across the country. Laws were proposed like reinstating the assault weapons ban and restoring a 10-round limit on ammunition magazines, as well as making gun trafficking a federal crime, and implementing universal background checks for gun sales.

In the three years after the Sandy Hook drill, 39 states have passed at least 117 new pieces of legislation to make gun laws stricter, according to the Law Center to Prevent Gun Violence. Lawmakers in New York and Connecticut worked to ban the possession of large-capacity magazines and semi-automatic weapons.

The overriding theme of the Las Vegas shooting at the Mandalay Bay hotel was the number of guns the alleged shooter had in his room. So what was the media pushing together in the days and weeks after the shooting? There have to be more laws to reduce a person's ability to own multiple guns and specifically assault weapons.

After the Parkland High School shooting, another very dubious mass shooting that has all the markings of a COINTELPRO event, 50 new laws were enacted restricting access to guns. The laws ranged from banning bump stocks to allowing authorities to disarm "potentially violent" people, a law so vague that anyone can be deemed to be potentially violent.[245]

The next big shooting event will also focus on a few specific aspects of gun ownership until there is enough momentum to push forward with a new set of laws to remove the item from being sold, be they bump stocks and extended capacity clips, or hollow-point bullets and scopes. Once those items are no longer available then the shooting after that might be carried out by someone armed with a shotgun, until there is a public outcry to ban all shotguns. And then rifles, then handguns, until the people wake up one day and realize that not only have they given away their right to own guns, but they have begged the government to take that right away from them.

Chairman Mao is famously quoted as saying *"You disarm the population before the slaughter"*, so what should make the Chinese version of tyranny look any different than the American style? They both will taste like blood and smell like death, and they will have been enabled by the very people that the government eventually turns against.

Criminals In Blue Costumes

Civil asset forfeiture is a legal process in which law enforcement officers take assets from people suspected of involvement in illegal activity without necessarily charging the owners with wrongdoing. While civil procedure usually involves a dispute between two private citizens, civil asset forfeiture involves a dispute between law enforcement and property such as a briefcase filled with cash, a Ferrari, or a house, if those things happen to be suspected of being involved in a crime. To get their seized property back, owners must prove that the car, the cash, the item, was not involved in criminal activity.

To be clear, they do not have to prove that this property is the result of a crime, they just have to believe that it might be involved or gained through illegal activity. The burden of proof falls on the shoulders of the person that had their property taken. The person does not need to even be charged with a crime. In fact, the person is not even involved with this case because it is the Police against the Property, not the Person. The case will be called something like "The State of Oklahoma vs. One Silver Necklace & Four Gold Coins".

---

[245] Matt Vasilogambros, The Huffington Post, "After Parkland, States Pass 50 New Gun-Control Laws".

It would be hilarious if it were not so scary.

There is another version of this called Criminal Forfeiture which is what happens when the person is being charged with a crime and the police go after their property. The evidence required is "beyond a reasonable doubt", whereas the requirement for civil asset forfeiture is only "a preponderance of evidence", which is about as vague as one can get in a court of law.

The potential for abuse with a system like this is obvious, but what makes it even more dangerous is that federal and local law enforcement agencies have come to depend on this as a revenue stream to finance their operations. There is a very real incentive for the police to classify the property as being involved in a crime, therefore subject to immediate confiscation with no rights for the owner of the merchandise.

The idea behind Civil Asset Forfeiture is that the police department would bust a big drug kingpin, take his huge pile of cash, and use that money to finance their operation to catch the next drug lord. This would work to weaken the drug dealer by reducing his ability to conduct business, while simultaneously helping to fund the operations of law enforcement.

In theory, this could work.

In reality, this is a disaster.

If a person thinks that arrogant cops are a problem when they give out a speeding ticket for going 3 MPH over the speed limit, wait until they write up their police report claiming that they suspect them of being a drug dealer and they take their car, all the money in their wallet, and what was left of their faith in law enforcement.

No judge, no jury, no rights.

This is no exaggeration, and people might be surprised to learn that there are thousands of examples of this very scenario being played out all across the United States. It has gotten to the point that most law enforcement budgets actually factor in the assumption of revenue from seizing people's possessions as a way of financing their operations.

Many cities across the country have been going down a similar path for decades when they decided that they would make the police officers revenue generators to go along with their law enforcement duties. That motorcycle cop that is hiding in the bushes with his radar gun pointed at cars probably has a quota of speeding tickets he is required to meet if he wants to stay on good terms in his precinct.

The city or county is dependent on that ticket revenue to partially fund their operations, so if a decision needs to be made between responding to a burglary call on their radio or writing up a speeding ticket for a housewife that is late to pick up her kid from soccer practice, it might depend on where the cop is with his quota for the month.

These days, while issuing the speeding ticket to the motorist running late to work, the officer will have a much larger incentive to take a peek inside the car to see if there is anything of value that might be construed as something that could be considered the by-product of a crime.

"Is that your laptop computer? It matches the description of one that was just reported stolen in the area. Do you have your receipt?"

Police will "analyze the intentions" of a motorist, determine how nervous the driver or their passengers appear to be, then illegally search their car without a warrant, then demand that the driver sign a waiver releasing the goods to the officer in exchange for not being arrested.

The Comprehensive Crime Control Act of 1984 took civil asset forfeiture to a whole new level by permitting local and federal governments to divide up the confiscated assets between their departments as a way of penalizing people suspected of committing a crime involving the property. In only eight years the authorities kept $3 billion of cash and goods as part of a "crime-fighting strategy".

If a person had the misfortune of getting pulled over for a broken tail light while on their way to buy a used car with cash, they may very well be considered a criminal and end up getting robbed by a band of actual criminals wearing police uniforms.

It used to be that college kids heading over the border to Tijuana from San Diego would be warned to be careful when interacting with the Mexican Federales because they might be targeted and extorted for all the cash in their pocket in exchange for not experiencing a frightening night in a T.J. jail for doing nothing wrong other than looking like an easy mark.

Now they have to worry about the cops on the American side of the border shaking them down as well, but it gets much worse.

Police officers in New York would pull over drunk drivers and seize their cars. The person would be charged criminally for drunk driving, and a civil case would be brought against the property, in this case, the car, for being used to facilitate the drunk driving. The police would then sell the car and keep the money. The way they saw this, the car was an accessory to the crime.

Is this massive conflict of interest becoming more obvious?

It did not take long before police departments realized that they were sitting on a gold mine, so they decided to pass on the robbery calls and instead focus on actively searching out drug dealers driving cars.

They brought in a consultant named Joe David who trained them in the finer points of stop-and-seizure techniques for finding large amounts of cocaine well hidden in cars and trucks on highways. The process was called Desert Snow, and the guy was really great at finding massive amounts of blow in places most cops would not think to check. Soon David and his team had trained an army of cops in his special detective ways in exchange for 25% of the value of the confiscated loot, which put $105,000,000 in his pocket over a five-year period.

Who knew the "finding cocaine business" paid so well?

The cash that was taken from these stops was used to pay for training seminars, equipment, parties, travel to Las Vegas or elsewhere. A Texas prosecutor used confiscated cash to take his wife, office staff, and even a judge to Hawaii for a vacation. And why wouldn't he since there are no penalties for wrongfully keeping someone's cash. All they need to show is that it was in some way drug-related, however they decide to classify that, and the money is theirs.

D.O.J. - The Department of [in]Justice

When the Justice Department got involved in the civil asset forfeiture process back in 1985, they did not really understand the depths of what they had created, as evidenced by the fact that they only netted $27 million that year.

They were really only scratching the surface in those days, but it did not take long for them to think like the crooks that they are supposed to be arresting.

The criminals in the DOJ and there are many, realized that they could steal far more money than they originally thought because there was practically no oversight. When the public made some noise they would just have a couple of politicians enact some law reducing their ability for confiscation then quietly refuse to enforce that law. They were never going to actually shut down that revenue stream. There was simply far too much money at stake to build a dam to stop the river of cash that was flowing right into the DOJ.

This is not about having a few cop cars, some equipment, and a few thousand hours of overtime covered through this theft, and to be clear, it is a form of theft. This is about $4.2 billion dollars coming into the Department of Justice during 2012 alone.[246] Some of this money is from illegal activities, and most of it is not. This is the Department of Justice stealing money from citizens with no remorse and no real oversight. This figure is almost double what it was only two years earlier, and there is no sign of this slowing down anytime soon.

It might be hard to believe that the Department of Justice could find billions of dollars hidden in cars, but the seizures are not limited to drug dealers with cash in their hidden compartments. They take real estate, bank accounts, firearms, Chinese restaurants, motels, sailboats, vacant land, or whatever they can get their hands on. If they think there is even a tangential connection between a person and property, they will snatch it and make the owner figure out how to get it back.

Of course, the real owner will no longer have any money to hire a lawyer to try and get their money back, so this is not going to end well for the victim of this scheme. They do have the right to sue the police department and even collect lawyer fees if they are successful with their suit, but that information is not made available to most people so they assume that there is no point in hiring an attorney for $10,000 in order to help them get their $10,000 back from the police.

When a person does sue the police department for their money back and they win the case, the cash is paid back from taxpayer money, not from the police departments themselves.

People that have fought back against criminal cops stealing their money have, in

---

[246] RT, "Civil Forfeiture Scam Lets Police Collect Billions From Innocent Americans".

some cases, been told by the courts that their money has already gone into the police pension fund and it is not available to them any longer.

The money from working people will be going to finance police officers that are not working. How is that right?

If the rule of law depends on respect for, and fairness by, the police officers, then by keeping this unfair system of random confiscation of assets of the people it must be an intentional way of creating an adverse relationship with the public. When the police look at the average citizen as a pile of money, they become beneath them and are subject to being treated like a second-class citizen.

Bringing down a society happens much faster when the controllers can divide the people into one camp and law enforcement into another. A person that believes that a cop might take everything that they have worked their entire lives for is not going to call 911 when something bad goes wrong in their lives. The rule of law fails to exist under these conditions because there is no trust between the protectors and the protected.

So is this an intentional way to create division?

The answer, of course, is "yes".

This is done by design to divide and conquer the people into much smaller groups while simultaneously sowing fear and doubt in their heads about how the rule of law does not apply equally.

In order to properly summarize how off the rails the civil asset forfeiture fraud has gone, in 2014 law enforcement officers took 50% more property from American citizens than burglars did. The $3.5 billion stolen by burglars pales in comparison to the $5 billion taken by the Treasury and Justice Department.[247]

Who are the real criminals in this scenario?

Bullets For Me, Not For Thee

So much of what helps people prepare for what is coming in the near future depends on one's ability to recognize the changes that are happening, as well as

---

[247] Christopher Ingraham, The Huffington Post, "Law Enforcement Took More Stuff From People Than Burglars Did Last Year".

any unusual disturbances that are out of the ordinary and may be used to alert a person about what the future may hold. Those that are observant will be able to see the moves being made by those in positions of power and can respond accordingly.

As an example, the Department of Homeland Security had issued an open purchase order for 1.6 billion rounds of ammunition in 2013.[248] Some of this purchase order is for hollow-point rounds, forbidden by international law for use in war, as well as bullets, specialized for use by snipers. To put the bullet purchase in perspective in comparison to the six million bullets per month used in Iraq, the 1.6 billion rounds would be enough to sustain a war for over 25 years.

This was not the first major purchase of bullets by DHS. In 2012, the Department of Homeland Security bought 360,000 rounds of hollow point bullets and 1.5 billion traditional rounds.[249] The Department of Homeland Security requested another 450 million rounds in addition to its 1.6 billion order.

The Department of Homeland Security is apparently taking delivery of an undetermined number of the recently retrofitted 2,717 Mine Resistant Protected MRAP vehicles for use in the United States.[250] They are also seeking 62.5 million rounds of .223 Remington ammunition for use with the AR-15 and Ruger Mini-14.

Money spent on military equipment and bullets between 2006-2014:

- Department of Veterans Affairs - $11.7 million.

- Internal Revenue Service - $10.7 million.

- Animal and Plant Inspection Services - $4.8 million.

- Bureau of the Public Debt - $2.8 million.

- National Oceanic and Atmospheric Administration - $1.02 million + 46,000 rounds of hollow-point bullets.

- Food and Drug Administration - $815,000.

- Social Security Administration - $417,000 + 174,000 rounds of hollow-point

[248] Associated Press, "Why Is The Department Of Homeland Security Buying So Many Bullets?".
[249] Reuters, "DHS Under Fire For Buying Another 360,000 Bullets To 'Save Money'".
[250] Civil Dispatch, "DHS Takes First MRAP Vehicles To Be Used On American Soil".

bullets.

- Department of Education - $413,000.

- Smithsonian Institution - $309,000.

- National Institute of Standards and Technology - $262,000.

- Small Business Administration - $76,000.

- Railroad Retirement Board - $44,000.

- Department of Agriculture - 320,000 rounds of hollow-point bullets.

- U.S. Bureau of Reclamation - 41,600 rounds of hollow-point bullets + 10,400 rounds of shotgun shells.

- Department of Justice - 95,000 rounds of 9mm hollow-point bullets + 46,000 rounds of .223 caliber + 4,750 rounds of shotgun shells.

- FBI - 100 million hollow-point bullets.

At least the country can sleep well knowing that the Smithsonian Museum is sitting on an arsenal in case someone tries to steal their T-Rex bones.

It is not an unreasonable question to ask why these agencies feel the need to arm themselves to the teeth, and it also begs the question about who they consider to be the enemy?

One major possibility for causing massive civil unrest has to do with the one aspect of American society that all citizens have in common, and that is the dollar. The outrage that erupts when an unarmed black teenager is shot by police tends to be limited either geographically or due to race, but everyone would be impacted and vocal if there was a bank run.

The scary truth is that what is separating this scenario from crossing over from a possibility to reality is not very much at all. In fact, it is dumb luck that it has not happened already.

PUSHING DOWN THE PLUNGER

The "Invisible Enemy"

Once the building with the rotten foundation has been pre-weakened, the support columns have been identified and rigged with explosives and the co-conspirators have safely fled the crime scene, there is only one thing left to do: wait for the right time to push down the plunger and take this building down.

It is important to consider that in an ideal situation the controlled demolition of the American empire should be made to look like an organic event so that the perpetrators are able to escape blame for what they have done. They plan to ride in on their white horse and play the role of "savior" while everything is coming down, so they will need to pay close attention to not leave their fingerprints on the plunger.

After all, the entire world is watching.

In March of 2020, the plunger was pushed down and the controlled demolition began for the American empire.

An "invisible enemy" that masqueraded as the organic event was needed to take the blame for the transformation of society that the controllers had been laying the groundwork for over the past few decades.

The introduction of the Coronavirus, or COVID-19, was enough to submarine the economy of the United States while simultaneously altering the societal makeup of the country forever.

The only thing that spreads faster than a live and deadly virus is the fear of the virus. In simple terms, the idea of the virus is actually just as disastrous as the virus itself because perception becomes reality once the mainstream corporate media gets involved in shaping the narrative.

Fear sells in America, don't kid yourself.

On the nightly news, the press subscribes to the Rahm Emmanuel philosophy of never letting a good crisis go to waste, so when a massive pandemic hits and shakes the fabric of society, one should never expect the media to do anything other than throw gasoline on the campfire until it turns into a raging inferno.

They do not care about maintaining calm and order; they only care about pushing the narrative they are instructed to promote by their bosses and those running the Council on Foreign Relations and the United Nations.

People foolishly believed that it could not happen in civilized American society, probably because of normalcy bias, but it has, and the public was totally unprepared for what ended up coming their way.

Fanned by a complicit media and government working in concert to stoke fears, the people were the target of a terror campaign that was designed to convince them to hand over their rights in the name of protecting themselves from a virus that has an effective kill rate of a serious seasonal flu. Death statistics were manipulated by classifying anything remotely resembling COVID-19, like the flu or a respiratory illness such as pneumonia, as the virus.

Remarkably, deaths linked to cancer, heart attack, and medical errors magically all but stopped happening during the spring of 2020. Everything was reclassified as a death resulting from the Coronavirus, and the federal government made it financially worth the hospitals' while in the process in order to get those death statistics up to a level that would cause genuine panic over a virus with a dubious fatality rate.

"Right now Medicare has determined that if you have a COVID-19 admission to the hospital you'll get paid $13,000. If that COVID-19 patient goes on a ventilator, you get $39,000; three times as much. Nobody can tell me, after 35 years in the world of medicine, that sometimes those kinds of things [have] impact on what we do." - Dr. Scott Jensen, Minnesota family physician & Republican state senator.

When people are fearful they make poor decisions, and, frankly, if there is one thing that the average American excels at it is making poor decisions when it matters most.

To be fair, it is not all the fault of the decision-making-challenged American public. The mainstream corporate media, one of the most dangerous components of American society, has a system in place to spread lies far and wide that was started under Operation Mockingbird when the CIA fully captured all of the news desks in America. The nightly news has been the mouthpiece of the Central Intelligence Agency for the past six decades and they have their lies down to a fine science.

However, it is worth reiterating that the Smith-Mundt Modernization Act of 2012 legalized propaganda within the United States on Americans. How much of the information the media and government are pumping out about the Coronavirus situation is real and how much is propaganda? It is important to remember that the government would not have gone through the exercise of changing the original Smith-Mundt Act in order to legalize lying unless they intended on doing some lying, so it is reasonable to expect that a percentage of the information being disseminated through the corporate media is propaganda. Unfortunately for "we the people", the government and the media do not have to identify what stories on the nightly news broadcast are fake, so it all becomes a part of the information sausage that is created by stuffing both lies and truth into one disgusting sleeve, twisting it off at the ends, then serving it to the starving public for them to swallow without a thought about the authenticity.

When people are hungry for information, they will gladly eat whatever the government and the media give them.

The curtain has gone up. The show has begun. How it will all end is a mystery for most people, but for those who understand how to follow the breadcrumbs, the plan of where the controllers intend to take society is known. All one needs to know is where to look because they always give these events a dress rehearsal first.

Dark Winter, Crimson Contagion, Lock Step & Event 201

As journalist Whitney Webb described in her article *All Roads Lead To Dark Winter*, simulations during the summer of 2001 of a smallpox attack on the United States thought to be the result of Saddam Hussein created chaos due to an unprepared medical industry. Later in the fictional simulation, mainstream media companies were sent anonymous letters containing the same strain of smallpox and were also threatened with more attacks on the United States if they refused to remove their troops from the Middle East. These simulated threats included anthrax attacks against journalists in America.

When the real anthrax attacks in the United States actually happened a few months later, the blame for that was conveniently placed on Iraq because it fit with the narrative that Iraq was planning on using weapons of mass destruction.

They had been trying to devise an excuse to invade Iraq for many months, so they used them in Dark Winter as the boogieman behind these simulated events.

Journalist Judith Miller, who participated in the Dark Winter simulation as one of those threatened journalists who received a fictional anthrax letter, coincidentally received one of those anthrax-filled letters that were being sent to the media in real life. Her letter was filled with a white powder that turned out to be harmless, unlike all of the other letters that were filled with actual anthrax and led to the deaths of several people.

It was later discovered that the strain of anthrax used in the actual attacks was the same as the one produced by the United States Army's USAMRIID lab at Ft. Detrick, meaning that it did not come from Iraq, making it a coincidence that is impossible to overlook, and yet another in a long list of false flag attacks.

However, the coincidences do not end there. In fact, the similarities between Dark Winter and the October 2019 simulation called Event 201 are many and disturbing.

The idea for Dark Winter in 2001 was designed and scripted by Tara O'Toole and Thomas Inglesby of the Johns Hopkins Center for Health Security, as was the Event 201 scenario in 2019 that was run by Inglesby and the Johns Hopkins Center once again. This is the same organization that was involved in the intentional infection of Guatemalan orphans with syphilis from 1945-1956. Both Johns Hopkins University and the Rockefeller Foundation were sued for $1 billion by the victims for their role in this non-consensual experiment.

What Event 201 simulated in October 2019 was a Coronavirus outbreak that spread from bats to pigs to people, starting in a tightly-packed megacity and spreading through airplane travel all over the world, leading to a severe pandemic where a vaccine would have to be created in order to gain control over the situation.

THE EVENT 201 SCENARIO (WEBSITE):

Event 201 simulates an outbreak of a novel zoonotic coronavirus transmitted from bats to pigs to people that eventually becomes efficiently transmissible from person to person, leading to a severe pandemic. The pathogen and the disease it causes are modeled largely on SARS, but it is more transmissible in the community setting by people with mild symptoms.

The disease starts in pig farms in Brazil, quietly and slowly at first, but then it starts to spread more rapidly in healthcare settings. When it starts to spread efficiently from person to person in the low-income, densely packed neighborhoods of some of the megacities in South America, the epidemic explodes. It is first exported by air travel to Portugal, the United States, and China and then to many other countries. Although at first some countries are able to control it, it continues to spread and be reintroduced, and eventually no country can maintain control.

There is no possibility of a vaccine being available in the first year. There is a fictional antiviral drug that can help the sick but not significantly limit spread of the disease.

Since the whole human population is susceptible, during the initial months of the pandemic, the cumulative number of cases increases exponentially, doubling every week. And as the cases and deaths accumulate, the economic and societal consequences become increasingly severe.

The scenario ends at the 18-month point, with 65 million deaths. The pandemic is beginning to slow due to the decreasing number of susceptible people. The pandemic will continue at some rate until there is an effective vaccine or until 80-90 % of the global population has been exposed. From that point on, it is likely to be an endemic childhood disease.

Wow, it is almost as if they knew exactly what was going to happen before it happened. Even down to the part where they discuss the problem that "disinformation" spreading through social media about possible cures would surely become a danger and would have to be stopped. Information about this event can be found on their website, centerforhealthsecurity.org.

So who was involved in the Event 201 scenario?

Just the globalist-tied Bill & Melinda Gates Foundation, Johns Hopkins Center for Health Security, and the World Economic Forum, as well as the CDC, the Chinese CDC, the CIA, Big Pharma, and the Big Banks. Both the Dark Winter and Event 201 simulations discussed the removal of civil liberties and the possibility of the President enacting the "Insurrection Act" which would allow the military to act as law enforcement, as well as "martial rule" which restricts travel, bans public gatherings, establishes quarantine areas, and the suspension of due process.

Attorney General William Barr is on the record requesting additional emergency powers be granted to him to detain people for an indefinite period of time without the right to a trial.

A few months before Event 201 there was Crimson Contagion, a simulation administered by the Department of Health and Human Services from January to August 2019 that tested the capacity of the U.S. federal government and twelve U.S. states to respond to a severe influenza pandemic originating in China.

The event featured the participation of a dozen states, 87 hospitals, 24 Indian reservations, NGOs, and 19 different federal agencies including the Pentagon and National Security Council that simulated an outbreak of a severe flu virus originating in China and being spread to the United States via air travel.

The results of the simulation showed that the United States was unprepared for the pandemic and that the manufacturing of medical equipment became a problem because so many of the current devices and materials were made overseas. They specifically mentioned that ventilators would be "limited and difficult to restock", that request processes for medical supplies from the government were dysfunctional, and there was inadequate testing to see who had contracted this deadly version of the flu.

Yet another simulation that was used to study how a global pandemic would affect the world in general, and the United States, in particular, was called Lock Step.

In 2010, the Rockefeller Foundation and Global Business Network published a white paper that laid out how governments around the planet would be able to take control of society through a massively publicized pandemic that was set to kill millions of people.

The document was written in 2010 but speaks about an event in 2012 in the past tense for the purpose of their simulation. It is eerily similar to what happened during the Coronavirus insanity during the Spring of 2020.

"In 2012, the pandemic that the world had been anticipating for years finally hit. Unlike 2009s H1N1, this new influenza strain—originating from wild geese—was extremely virulent and deadly. Even the most pandemic-prepared nations were quickly overwhelmed when the virus streaked around the world, infecting nearly 20 percent of the global population and killing 8 million in just seven months, the majority of them healthy young adults. The pandemic also had a deadly effect on

economies: international mobility of both people and goods screeched to a halt, debilitating industries like tourism and breaking global supply chains. Even locally, normally bustling shops and office buildings sat empty for months, devoid of both employees and customers."

This white paper was titled *Scenarios for the Future of Technology and International Development* and it hoped to show how to create "a world of tighter top-down government control and more authoritarian leadership, with limited innovation and growing citizen pushback". It explained how a pandemic could be used to scare the public into accepting a police state, or more specifically, demanding one.

"The United States' initial policy of 'strongly discouraging' citizens from flying proved deadly in its leniency, accelerating the spread of the virus not just within the U.S. but across borders. However, a few countries did fare better—China in particular. The Chinese government's quick imposition and enforcement of mandatory quarantine for all citizens, as well as its instant and near-hermetic sealing off of all borders, saved millions of lives, stopping the spread of the virus far earlier than in other countries and enabling a swifter post-pandemic recovery."

The simulation also praises the authoritarian measures taken by the Chinese government as the blueprint for how to lock down an entire nation of hundreds of millions, if not billions, of people.

The American government pretends to be appalled at the behavior of the Chinese government towards their own citizens, but they are secretly jealous of how much easier things would be for them if they could adopt some of the Chinese principles and get around the human rights organizations, the regulatory agencies, and change the American culture of demanding individual rights and liberty.

Once again the public is faced with a series of very accurate simulations that just so happen to mimic almost exactly the very same components of the official story of the "Coronavirus Plandemic Scare of 2020".

At what point does the public realize that the chances of these things playing out in the same way as the simulation time after time are a mathematical impossibility? Dark Winter, Crimson Contagion, Lock Step, and Event 201 are four events simulating pandemics, then outbreaks and attacks happened just like they were roll played only a few months earlier.

Was Nostradamus running these simulation events? Here is the recap:

- What about the 40+ drills that were happening all around America on the morning of September 11th, 2001 that simulated the events that were actually unfolding at the very same time in real life?

- How about Peter Power announcing on two different occasions on the BBC that he and his team were running drills simulating an attack on two tube stations in London on the morning of July 7th, 2005, when those exact tube stations exploded minutes before they were set to run their drill?

- What about the Boston Marathon Bombing running a drill simulating an explosion at the finish line of the marathon, even going so far as to announce the event in advance on the Boston Globe's Twitter account twice?

Drills are used as a covert way to preposition resources into key areas without arousing suspicion from the general public. They can be used to get people into the right spot, to remove onlookers that might blow the cover of the simulators, warn those in the know about what is about to happen in a particular location, and take control of an area that they plan to use for the real event.

Skeptical Americans that thought that the Coronavirus pandemic seemed fishy were not unhinged conspiracy theorists, as the media would have the public believe, but rather astute critical thinkers armed with the knowledge of a long history of drills simulating events that magically turned live, and the ability to distinguish between a real news event and a manufactured narrative designed to mislead the public for the purpose of changing society.

CDC: Centers for Disease Creation

With billions of dollars in revenue each year from the patents they own on vaccines, the Centers for Disease Control (CDC) just could not manage to get their act together and provide adequate Coronavirus testing kits to the hospitals early and in large enough supply to make a dent in testing the public. When they did finally send test kits out to the hospitals, the kits were tainted with the Coronavirus through either the manufacturing or shipping process, creating false-positive results that were pointed to as the justification for closing down society, along with faulty infection models pushed by Gates Foundation Board Member, Dr. Fauci

Incompetence is par for the course with most government agencies, but oftentimes the mistakes are intentional and designed to create confusion and chaos, while disguised as faulty oversight and mismanagement.

When the narrative being spun is that the Coronavirus is everywhere and that millions of people are going to contract it, then the testing kits are found to be contaminated with the Coronavirus from the start, it does not require a tinfoil hat to make the connection that perhaps this was part of the plan all along to show the rate of infection to be as high as possible by intentionally contaminating the tests to show artificially high rates.

It is almost as if the delays and incompetence were baked into the equation from the start, like intentional failures disguised as typical government mismanagement, in order to allow the problem to grow through the media into a pandemic which would allow for a massive government reaction.

It would not be the first time that the American government, corporate media, and the CDC faked the seriousness of an outbreak in order to cram legislation through Congress to alter society and financially reward the agencies and firms that went along with the scam.

The CDC is not the only leading organization in the Coronavirus plandemic that has massive questions about their integrity and history.

It is worth mentioning that the World Health Organization (WHO), which was referenced as being the leading voice on how to deal with a worldwide pandemic, was accused of intentionally adding sterilants to the tetanus vaccines they distributed in Kenya in 2014. The WHO initially denied the claim before later admitting that their covert sterilization program had gone on for a decade.

The largest source of funding for the World Health Organization comes from the American government, with the second-largest source of funds being the Bill & Melinda Gates Foundation, making them beholden to both entities and anything but the objective and unbiased source of information that they attempt to portray themselves as.

Creating A Police State In A Few Easy Steps

Earlier in the book, there was a mention of a military occupation in the US

(B.C.).

Today, a few years later, the picture is much clearer.

The theory goes that once a disaster or threat of one comes into being in the U.S., martial law will be declared and the Federal Emergency Management Agency's (FEMA's) emergency powers will come into operation, effectively suspending the Constitution and helping the New World Order assume control of America. Truthers have said that FEMA will use 'urban gangs' as auxiliaries to ensure order through racial fear.

Here is some conspiracy evidence to go along with the theory:

- FEMA is a United States government agency tasked with the effective management of major emergencies within the country, including ensuring the continuity of government during a large-scale disaster such as a nuclear war. It provides federal relief to areas affected by natural disasters.

- FEMA was established in 1979 under an executive order by President Jimmy Carter and in 2002 it was finally codified into law and made a component of the Department of Homeland Security.

- Martial law is often associated with the suspension of civil liberties.

- Martial law can only be ordered by the President as commander-in-chief or by Congress.

- Since mid-March, the U.S. military has deployed field hospitals in a few states to provide support during the pandemic.

- On March 18, President Donald Trump, invoking the Defense Production Act to accelerate production of vital medical equipment, said he saw himself as a 'wartime president' in the fight against the coronavirus.

- Two weeks later, Trump said that the government would be deploying thousands of military personnel to certain states to help them deal with the epidemic.

- According to the National Conference of State Legislatures, governors in at least 44 states, the District of Columbia, Puerto Rico, Guam, and the U.S. Virgin Islands have already deployed the Army or the National Guard to respond to the public health crisis.

Such measures are not unique to the United States: many other countries have brought in the military to support government efforts to combat the crisis.

Their goal?

Seamlessly creating the need, and even getting people to want, a Police State.

Bring Out the Race Riots

Yet it became clear that martial law would not be implementable in the name of Coronavirus, because the plandemic was not working anymore.

It was time to take the sheeple's dull eyes and dim minds off the bungled plandemic and show them a shiny new thing to distract them.

Here's an idea! *Maybe start a little race war. We've certainly practiced the scenario once or twice or a thousand times...Let's shoot those who loot, they react and then we can accelerate the passing of gun control legislation to be followed by the abolishment of personal gun ownership and a campaign of gun confiscation.*

Want war?

Create a martyr. It has worked for hundreds of years.

And so George Floyd, martyr of the people, became a homicide victim three times over: First, his livelihood was murdered by the people who executed the Coronavirus plandemic when Minnesota's governor issued a stay-at-home order causing him to lose his job as a bouncer at a restaurant. Then he was suffocated and silenced by the Controllers' armed and dangerous police puppets. Then he died of Covid-19...

Then, pay a group of thugs in the name of #BlackLivesMatter to create anarchy and chaos, purposely destroying private property, setting black against white and white against black.

And so the riots started. The thuggery, the arson, the murder in the name of BlackLivesMatter – the use of urban gangs as auxiliaries to ensure order through racial fear.

Just like it was theorized and roll played. Funny how that happens.

<u>The Terrorist Organization That Wasn't</u>

"The Marxist democrat &^%# that run twitter and faceberg used their social engineering platforms to whip this up and organize these riots. Soros used his subversion NGO shock troops to organize and direct the riots. &^%# burned down and looted their own cities with the encouragement of billionaire &^%&, which will make them poor and cause crime to increase in their shitholes long term. Everyone who is rational will move away and all that will be left will be an economic desert poverty like Compton California, a once thriving crime free city."
– Anonymous

In the years since Donald Trump's election in 2016, a previously almost dormant far-left group has re-emerged — ostensibly in response to a rise in racism and white supremacy. They are called Antifa which stands for Anti-Fascist. The movement first started in Nazi Germany to fight European fascism before the Second World War and reached the US in the 1970s against Neo-Nazism and alt-right groups.

Sic-em Antifa! Sic-em!

We know who the attack dogs are, but who is their master?

Antifa's links to billionaire George Soros have been publicly reported. And Soros' group MoveOn.org organized most of the anti-Trump riots and protests that swept the nation since November 9th, 2016.

"I am going to bring down the United States by funding black hate groups. We'll put them into a mental trap and make them blame white people. The black community is the easiest to manipulate." – George Soros, during an interview with Germany's "Bild" Magazine, September 2014

Whoa! Don't even believe it. This quote is not true. He never said it. How do people know? Because the independent fact-checkers say so! Reuters found no report from a credible source about this alleged exchange. And it has been removed everywhere.

But what about the Democracy Alliance — which has fed upwards of $500 million toward liberal activist groups and candidates since Soros co-founded the group in 2005?

All members of DA are required to give $200,000 a year to recommended activist groups and pay annual dues of $30,000 to fund the DA staff and its meetings.

Democracy Alliance donors have long maintained an air of secrecy, and little is known about most of them. Major Democratic donors who have been identified as members include Soros and Tom Steyer, hedge fund magnate Donald Sussman and technology entrepreneur Tim Gill. Those are the ones that can be proved.

Is Soros the only boss brain behind Black Lives Matter? Of course not. But he does fund the #BLM movement and riots every time the globalists decide they need a new race war started.

Trump blamed Antifa by name for the violence, along with violent mobs, arsonists, and looters. As The President Who Holds The Record For The Most Tweets In The World (not really, but he should), he also tweeted that the US will designate the movement as a terrorist organization. The main problem with that is that, allegedly, Antifa is not an organization but a set of practices, with zero centralized leadership or membership structure.

No one said that The Globalist Billionaires Club is stupid.

Because of this, it remains unclear if it is possible to designate Antifa as a terrorist organization, despite its open Violence Is Good policy:

- The movement sees the use of violence as self-defense and does not consider damaging property as a form of brutality.

- Literature from the Antifa movement encourages followers to pursue lawful protest activity as well as more confrontational acts, according to a 2018 Congressional Research Service report.

- The members do not abstain from involving in direct physical confrontations, also followers monitor the activities of white supremacist groups, publicize online the personal information of perceived enemies, develop self-defense training regimens and compel outside organizations to cancel any speakers or events with "a fascist bent".

So there is an organization that openly practices violent anarchy, arson, and murder, but a loophole in the US Constitution prevents them from being called terrorists.

But wait, are they really just part of creating a Stronger City, authorized by the United Nations?

Strong Cities For Weak People

One thing becomes obvious as a person navigates through American society and that is that the names of groups, organizations, initiatives, and bills that pass through Congress are intentionally misnamed, on purpose, to give the impression that they do one thing while they actually are doing the opposite.

The "Strong Cities" program by the United Nations, is no exception. Anyone willing to dig into the actual purpose of the program will see quite clearly that it will actually weaken the city, and it will also spread beyond the initial locations of New York City, Atlanta, Denver, Minneapolis, Paris, London, Montreal, Beirut, and Oslo.

The first giveaway that this is a fraud is that its goal is to fight violent extremism "in all of its forms and manifestations" in cities around the world, but it is funded by the State Department and the United Nations, two of the biggest perpetrators of violence and extremism on the planet.

How do they plan to prevent violent extremism? By identifying and monitoring people that show signs of being racist, hateful, intolerant, or "extremists".

Seriously.

The United Nations wants to make sure that these major cities are free from hateful people, so to fix this problem they plan to identify and deter potential extremists through the use of "fusion centers", of which there are 78 currently in America, to collect data on the people, use behavioral scientists to analyze that data, review people's social media accounts, compared to information provided by their corporate partners, use facial recognition software, initiate predictive policing like in the movie and book, *Minority Report*, collect personal biometric data, and even something known as behavioral epigenetics which examines a person's life experiences and genetic makeup.

And the United Nations is going to be in charge of this.

Again, what could possibly go wrong?

This will obviously lead to zero tolerance policing and stop-and-frisk practices like it did in New York City with equally disastrous results. And this is the best-case scenario because things will devolve quickly from there.

The public is right to be concerned with the government's anti-extremism programs because they always get turned against the people who step up to criticize the government agencies that are implementing the programs, and this will be no different, except that with a supra-national organization like the United Nations involved it will make everything far worse for the people. It will offer the governing body the opportunity to take nonviolent people and brand them as "extremists" in order to arrest them. The AI pre-crime component of this program is something beyond Orwell's wildest acid trip of how bad society could get, but it shows the direction the government wants to take things and how they view the general public as a bunch of potential criminals.

What this program actually shows the people are the blueprint for tyranny that is coming in the next two decades. When the system is designed from the top-down, with the overall goal of total surveillance of the population so that they can be thrown in cages at will, it does not take a genius to figure out that the framework of the prison is currently being built because they intend on using it. This is not practice. This is the prison planet infrastructure being introduced right in front of everyone with the eyes to see it.

The United Nations' Strong Cities program is the future of the Police State, just rebranded with a catchy name. This is where the militarization of the local police comes into play as well, as the transformation from the police officer in his blue uniform walking his beat morphs into the new black uniforms equipped with helmets, goggles, black face masks, and body armor. Where active shooter drills, false flags, code orange threat assessments, the beating of protesters, and pre-dawn raids for social media posts become the norm.

It will be the crowning achievement of all of the technocratic globalists that dream of having the ability to control the people, especially the ones that do not like what they see happening around them.

The United States - A Second-World Nation

A vision of what the United States might look like after the collapse can be found by examining countries that have experienced the hyperinflation of their currency in a very short period of time. Everybody has heard the stories of people needing a wheelbarrow full of cash in order to buy a loaf of bread, but is that a fate that is relegated to third-world countries exclusively, or is the hyperinflation the trigger that throws a country into third world status?

When Germany experienced this after World War I, they were not thought of as being anything other than a first world country, but that changed once their currency became worthless. It took them over a decade, but they bounced back once they stood up to the banks and refused to pay the penalties that were imposed.

What happens to the United States once the dollar is depegged as the world's reserve currency and the Petrodollar system finally falls apart under the weight of its criminality? What might end up happening is a new type of country that could end up being called a second-world nation? One that is not what it used to be, but not quite Zimbabwe either. A place where the vast majority of people are just treading water and trying to stay alive, but not really focusing on building real wealth. A place that looks like Detroit, Camden, Selma, or Blackwater, Arizona.

It is not just the money that has been sucked out of these places, but the hope as well. That fuels a sense that things will never get better, so why not smoke that crack rock or drink that bottle of Thunderbird with the last of the money they have? The United States as a second world nation will resemble one large Indian reservation, where things are provided but not enough for anyone to really get by on. Or maybe it looks like Brazil or Russia with a huge lower-class and a few ultra-wealthy oligarch types.

The truth of the matter is that had the Petrodollar system not artificially propped up the value of the dollar, the United States would have been a second world country many decades ago if they had attempted their out of control spending without the artificial constraints of the system they had created. The rest of the world has been subsidizing the lifestyle of all Americans for the past forty years, but it is only now that people living in the United States are starting to understand the house of cards that they have been living in. Those that are now awake to this fact are quietly attempting to tiptoe out of the house before the whole thing comes down on their heads.

Austerity For the People, Never For the Government

The government and the media warn that Americans are all living beyond their means so they must tighten their belts if they are to get through these tough times!

It might be smart to make sure that everyone is wearing the same size pants first.

Austerity is defined as a political-economic term referring to policies that aim to reduce government budget deficits through spending cuts, tax increases, or a combination of both. Austerity measures are used by governments that find it difficult to pay their debts.

Austerity is never suggested by the poor, but rather, it is imposed by the rich. The theory states that rather than reinvesting in the economy, they cut funding for social programs. The rich do not need social programs like welfare and public schools, so they make the decision to remove the money that would normally flow to these vital public programs and use it for something that they want, like massive tax cuts for the rich, which are the biggest cause of the problem that they are pretending to care about.

Greece is the test case for how austerity currently operates, and what America can expect once the global banking syndicate gets done with them. Goldman Sachs was the bank behind Greece's austerity push that saw the country strip-mined of all of their natural resources, including legendary parcels of land and islands, in order to pay massive debts that they should not have been allowed to take on in the first place. They were offered these massive loan packages because their membership in the European Union was taken as a stamp of creditworthiness, a membership that has some serious questions surrounding it that, once again, had Goldman Sachs' fingerprints all over it.

Back in 2001 when Greece was applying for membership in the EU, Goldman Sachs created debt swaps that made 2% of Greece's debt magically vanish from their balance sheets of national records.[251] After pricing some of Greece's other debt in yen, dollars, and euros, it created the illusion that their deficit was much smaller than it actually was, and this helped to hide the true nature of how indebted Greece already was, a fact that most certainly would have led to it

[251] John Carney, Business Insider, "Goldman Sachs Shorted Greek Debt After It Arranged Those Shady Swaps".

378

being tossed out of consideration for joining the European Union during their application process.

Instead, their application was approved, in large part because of the financial shimshamery of the Vampire Squid, and Greece was set on a course of self-destruction caused by feeding on the endless amount of cheap debt that is offered to members of the EU. Knowing damn well that Greece could never pay their original debt back, let alone the additional amount that they took on during their decade of debauchery, Goldman Sachs made sure to keep an eye on Greece so that they could sneak back in when things blew up, which they did, and help to orchestrate the fire sale that would most certainly be taking place, especially if they had any say in the matter.

This is what happens to a country when Goldman Sachs captures a government through debt, then sets the rules of debt repayment and orchestrates the looting of a country. These things happened to the country of Greece in order to pay back the debt that the bank and the European Union loaned to them, loans that were made knowing full well that Greece would never be able to handle:

• In Greece, they limited the number of public companies from 6,000 to 2,000.[252]

• They raised the retirement age for benefits while reducing salaries for public workers.

• A limited number of people were eligible for pension payments, and for those that were, they saw huge cuts.

• They massively raised VAT and luxury taxes.

• Lump-sum payments for retirees were cut, and they voted to create a new special tax for high pensions.

• They voted to tax imported cars, and also added an extra tax for "fighting unemployment".

• They increased taxes for those with yearly incomes over 8,000 euros, plus another tax for those with incomes over 12,000 euros.

• Most new government taxes were charged and collected through the electric

---

[252] Ministry Of Finance, "Update Of The Hellenic Stability And Growth Programme".

bill so that people could not avoid paying them.

- Greece was forced to sell off government property at massively discounted prices.

- Education spending was cut by closing or merging schools, and private education was being taxed at 23%.

- New excise taxes were created on such items as coffee and electronic cigarettes, and higher fuel taxes were levied on the people.

- Tourism taxes were created and placed on most hotels.

- New taxes on TV subscriptions, landlines and internet broadband connections were created.

- Increased insurance contributions were approved by citizens voting against their own self-interest.

- Diesel fuel tax for farmers rose from €6 per 1,000 liters to €330 by 2016.

- Income tax for farmers rose from 13% in 2016 to 26% in 2017, to 55% in 2018, and must now be paid in advance.

- Freelancer workers are subject to a gradual increase from 55% to 75% in advanced tax payments for income earned in 2015, but that increased to 100% in 2016.

- In the 14th package of austerity, and certainly not the last, the voters agreed to privatize Greece's PPC electricity utility, the Thessaloniki port, the railroads, and even Athens' international airport.

Mario Draghi, the former Goldman Sachs International Managing Director responsible for the cross-currency derivatives swap that sunk Greece, was installed as the head of the European Central Bank in 2011, so he had a front-row seat to the meltdown that his former company helped to engineer, and he made sure that Goldman was at the table when the Greek assets were heavily discounted then quietly sold to their friends and clients.

While Goldman Sachs made half a billion dollars for concocting this scheme, they do not seem to be in too much of a hurry to hand back their fees so that the people of Greece don't have to pay these outrageous austerity measures.

After all of these cost-cutting efforts and taxation schemes, Greece has had a 57% increase in its debt since the financial crisis began because the focus is on paying back the bondholders instead of helping out the people.[253]

American Austerity

So... what might austerity in America look like?

- A $4/hour minimum wage for jobs, if there are any left.

- Monthly Social Security benefits slashed by 30%.

- The age for qualifying for Medicare will be bumped up by six years.

- Government pensions will pay out a third of what pensioners were told and were expecting, and they will be lucky to get that.

- Gasoline will be $10/gallon and cigarettes will be $15/pack.

- Public schools will be consolidated into fewer buildings, with teachers routinely saddled with 50+ students in a class and reductions to their already small salaries.

- Government agencies and county services that are not already eliminated will be moved to 4-day work weeks with mandatory furloughs.

- A reduction in the police force would mean an increase in crime and a push towards the Orwellian option of privatizing the police departments. Firefighters and emergency services like 911 dispatchers would be cut down as well.

- The cost of airfare would double due to increased airport taxes, as would hotel rooms from local taxes.

- Income tax rates would spike to over 50% for most citizens as taxes increased while services decreased.

- Public prisons would see their funding cut in half, while private prisons would

---

[253] Kimberly Amadeo, The Balance, "Greek Debt Crisis Explained".

multiply.

- Public parks would be privatized due to lack of funds for maintenance and as a method of raising money to cover the cost of the spiraling federal and local debt.

- Homelessness will spike, with up to 10% of Americans living in their cars, on the streets, or in tent cities.

- With no money for housing, mental institutions will simply open their doors and force their patients onto the streets, just like they have been doing on Skid Row for the past 30 years.

- Food prices will skyrocket, as America faces the real problem of starvation on their streets.

- With hope lost and money tight, Americans will give into addiction at an alarming rate, as synthetic drugs like fentanyl enslave large percentages of the population. With no money for treatment, hundreds of thousands will overdose and die, and suicide rates will reach epidemic highs.

- All of this pinned to the fact that the value of the dollar will be worth 70% of what it was before austerity fully kicked in.

Sounds great, doesn't it?

This is clearly a nightmare scenario, but it is a likely one. The banks will refuse to take a haircut on their loan balances and will club into submission anyone that dares to suggest otherwise. The people will be forced to bear the brunt of the pain of austerity, but at least it will be wrapped up in the American flag so that the people feel that they are doing their patriotic duty as the bankers are picking their pockets and digging their graves.

Austerity in the United States will also be the catalyst that allows for unpopular programs to make their way into American life under the false pretense of saving their communities. People are born with an innate moral compass. Ironically, the very thing that makes anarchy work.

Having no money is humiliating, frustrating, and infantilizing. It erodes a person's self-worth in a very particular way. When things get bad, and the city and state are no longer in a position to help out, the people will find themselves making a deal with the devil just in order to stave off starvation and rampant crime. A deal that will come with some very dangerous strings attached.

The Pompeii Society

For those people that have quieted their heads so that they can listen for the alarm, they will be able to position themselves so that not only do they not get financially wiped out, but so they can profit from the coming situation and the misfortune of the others. In a perfect society, everyone would hear the alarm and move to protect themselves, but human nature has been manipulated into not recognizing the signs of impending doom.

Right before the collapse of an empire, there is always a massive inequality in wealth, the rulers seek to control weapons from getting into the hands of the people while they simultaneously stock up for themselves, words and news are suppressed so that the truth about the government and the situation does not get out to the people, whistleblowers are imprisoned by a desperate regime, the law of the land is rewritten then ignored, and the theft of the citizens' wealth by their government begins as they desperately try to stop the loss in value of their currency.

Can anyone honestly look at the American Empire and not see all of these aspects of the collapse happening right now? It only takes a few of these issues to take down an empire but they are all happening at the same time.

Will the people of the American Empire recognize these signs and plan accordingly, or will they be turned to stone as they finally realize, a day late, that the volcano that they have built their homes next to has been rumbling and steaming because it is ready to blow?

Despite warning after warning, the sirens of propaganda have turned people's minds into collective mush and made them participants in an unconscionable, perpetual war and mind screwing propaganda machine.

CLEARING THE DEBRIS

<u>Revelations and Revolt</u>

East Berlin citizens woke up on the 13th of August, 1961, to more than 30 miles of barbed wire barrier through the heart of Berlin. Overnight they were forbidden to pass into West Berlin, and the number of checkpoints in which Westerners could cross the border was drastically reduced. When it became clear that there would be no major action to protest the closing, the tyranny of East German authorities became silently ratified.

So the East German authorities begin building a wall to permanently close off access to the West. The wall, East German authorities declared, would protect their citizens from the dangerous infection of decadent capitalist culture.

For the next 28 years, East Germans worked, cooked dinner, and spent time with family and friends just like West Germans did. Some later claimed they were grateful to their leaders for keeping them safe. But they were also spied on by the Stasi and kept from leaving by the Berlin Wall, the Iron Curtain, armed border guards, and a tightly controlled administration to ensure their civil obedience and economic servitude.

On November 9th, 1989, when the head of the East German Communist Party announced that citizens of the GDR could cross the border whenever they pleased, ecstatic crowds swarmed the wall.

How did this happen?

The communist leaders did not plan perfectly. They planned strategically. And they were well-prepared. They had long prepared police forces and quickly took over the radio station. They believed very much in the power of propaganda, and that if they just could reach the masses by the most efficient means possible then they would be able to convince them to sit back and do nothing, or even welcome a totalitarian state take-over.

What is happening now has happened before: in East Berlin, and the Nazi death camps and Stalin's gulags. The world did not believe it then, and they are not believing it now. And the results will be the same:

Suspension of Individual Rights
Intimidation
Control of the Police
State Propaganda

Public process of "desensitization"
Denunciation of Fellow Citizens
Detention Sites and Camps

All in the name of a New World Order.

Digital Fascism

Digital fascism is real. The first six months of 2020 have proved that most human beings now live in a new kind of totalitarian state – the digital society, which has the following features:

Mass surveillance
Unethical experiments with humans
Social engineering
Forced conformity ("Gleichschaltung")
Propaganda and censorship

"Benevolent" dictatorship
(Predictive) policing
Different valuation of people
Relativity of human rights
Euthanasia for sustainability

The public has long been the subjects of behavioral manipulation and the COVID plandemic has been the biggest experiment of them all. However, the real issue is whether democracy, freedom, and human dignity can survive this new digitally empowered global totalitarianism.

It has been mentioned often: Big Data is necessary to fight terrorism, cyber threats, and climate change. People have felt safe knowing the government is looking after them, but this year everyone has heard it over and over – the vaccines, the microchips, the mass surveillance – all for their own safety against the Big Bad Economy Destroying Virus. They gladly gave up their basic rights to have a job, trading, expression, and privacy in exchange for being locked up while their business, job, mortgage, and pension are sanitized, which is super cop-speak for "assassination".

They use everyone's computers, smartphones, smart TVs, and smart cars to collect and consolidate gigabytes of data just to create a profile of them, their nature, their habits, and preferences. But worse than that, they use these computer experiments called algorithms to find out how people are thinking, and then their behavior can be manipulated.

Then they apply it with catastrophic consequences for us as individuals and for society as a whole.

This might be the last generation who does not get an RFID chip at birth.

Once that becomes an accepted way of life, everyone's money, information, medical history, and everything else will be programmed into this chip. They will not have or need a Social Security Card, Birth Certificate, ID Card, Driver's License, bank accounts, or bank cards because they will irrevocably be part of the machine. The only thing it will not be able to do is to protect them against the flu.

Do people really believe that injecting their children and grandchildren with a tracking vaccine that enables the government to spy on them at any given moment, for any reason, with or without their consent or knowledge is to defend them against the COVID-19 coronavirus?

Or is the public looking forward to the "miracle" vaccine which is apparently at least a year in the making? Like the one people will not WANT to refuse because they are already being brainwashed into believing the flu will kill them without it.

The one they will not BE ABLE to refuse because the stage is already being set for the military and police pawns to be deployed to legally and forcibly make their way into everybody's house and their child's school while holding their freedom as ransom in exchange for getting vaccinated.

Want to get a business bailout?

Better pledge allegiance to the New World Order.

Expect the Expected

People should expect Big Pharma to cram their new medicines down the throats of gullible Americans begging to be saved with experimental vaccines that have not even been tested on mice, brown people in faraway lands (like they normally are), or the military members that often serve as guinea pigs.

Social pressure will be exerted on the nonconformists that endanger the rest of the flock with their noncompliance and reckless behavior until saying "no" to the vaccine is unfathomable in a time of crisis. When an industry pushes the insane theory of "herd immunity", it is not hard to imagine that herd mentality will be too far behind.

The obvious push to put all doctors and nurses on pedestals in 2020 has the look of the lead up to the Middle East wars beginning in 2001 when all service members were elevated in status to a level that was beyond reproach and criticism, even to the point of being allowed to board commercial airplanes first.

One with an understanding of this psychological operation can easily see that when the mandatory vaccination programs are inevitably rolled out throughout the world, it will be much harder for someone to refuse the vaccination from a "hero" nurse or doctor than it would have been just a year earlier.

Nothing about this is accidental. Not the banging of pots and pans for the healthcare workers from patio balconies, not the choreographed Tic Tok videos, and not the hero worship. It is all part of a very well thought out plan to make it virtually impossible to deny a shot from someone of unquestioned authority.

One thing that could absolutely be counted on in the midst of the Coronavirus insanity was a massive overreaction by the American government, not in any way to help the people, of course, but to shore up Wall Street and Big Business. The Federal Reserve handed another blank check to the banks, as they always do in times of crisis, and exactly none of that money found its way to the people that needed it the most.

People were told about another bailout and they did nothing about it like they always do. They stayed inside their homes while the economy was destroyed and the Treasury was looted.

The interesting part will be the sociological studies that will be performed in the aftermath of the crisis. The disproportionate response from the American government will set the stage for how pandemics are handled moving forward, and yet another pillar holding up the fragile American empire will be removed as medical freedoms disappear under the guise of protecting the herd from slaughter.

Why change the plan when the plan always works so well?

Recent history is littered with examples of unfounded fears being ramped up to unimaginable proportions: Bird Flu, Swine Flu, Ebola, SARS, MERS, West Nile Virus...all destined to kill everyone on planet Earth, only to peter out after a few weeks once the media gave up on them for not having a high enough kill rate for their tastes. There will be another, and another after that, and none will end humanity, but the media will give it their best effort to try and sell that potential outcome because nothing puts eyeballs on television news programs quite like the potential of impending death on a planetary scale.

A Viral Victory

How do the fascists compel thousands and millions of people to meekly go inside, give up their lives, and their livelihoods without a squeak?

FEAR is one answer. Military police are being deployed by the thousands to keep the people in check. Women, children, and babies are all subjected to heavily armed men in full combat gear, ready to tear apart families and put them on trucks to quarantine camps or worse. Fear of being grossly neglected and dying alone in hospitals. Fear of starving to death without government blackmail checks. The list goes on.

INDOCTRINATION is another. Both actively by pumping the public full of patronizing nonsense, such as that a 5G city is a "smart city", or passively, by removing any conflicting voices and calling it "conspiracy theories".

With the eruption of the race war, suddenly the public is not "in this together" anymore.

Suddenly, it is every man for himself.

Especially when it comes to deliberately destroying old ladies' shops in the name of Anarchy!

Larken Rose, that "angry white guy with a gun", says it best:

"One common misconception about anarchy is that it means 'every man for himself' or 'survival of the fittest', where everyone has to be selfish and self-sufficient, where there is no real cooperation or organization, and where people all behave like violent, selfish animals."

Except it is the exact opposite.

The violent, selfish animals are the politicians and the banksters and the Military-

Information-Terror cabal. It is the government that gives people no choice. Who steal their money in the name of "tax"; who force them to inject their children with poison as a smokescreen for population control and mass surveillance; and who would not stop at creating a virus, or a terror attack, or a martyr, or an organized riot – all in the name of domination.

Many people believe that they need a ruling class to give commands and enforce rules, through regulation and legislation (and violence if necessary), to dominate people into getting along and cooperating. Because if there is no government to organize them, there can be no structure to society, right?

The question is how does a VERY small group of people control a VERY large group of people?

The answer is fear of the consequence of non-compliance. But, it is also because people are born with an innate moral compass. They want to do good, but they want to do it on their own terms. That is the very essence of being an anarchist, or voluntaryist: believing that all human behavior should be based upon voluntary interaction, not force.

The right question to ask would be "why do people allow themselves to be tyrannized, oppressed, and extorted by a tiny group of people that they didn't even necessarily vote into place"?

Because, according to Rose, *"Most of the victims of legal thuggery and theft see it as necessary and legitimate. People feel morally obligated to obey the politicians' 'laws', any who resist are viewed as 'criminals'" or 'tax-cheats', even by their own friends and neighbors. Most people see government domination as necessary and valid, and so they cooperate with their own victimization."*

Pushing the Reset Button

The first week of June 2020 saw headlines like "Capitalism needs the 'Great Reset' button. COVID-19 is showing the way".

And just like that, a New World Order is on the table, openly, transparently, brought into the open by the Word Economic Forum, endorsed by the International Monetary Fund (IMF).

Founder of the World Economic Forum, Professor Klaus Schwab, declared:

"To improve the state of the world, the World Economic Forum is starting The Great Reset initiative.

We can emerge from this crisis a better world if we act quickly and jointly. To achieve a better outcome, the world must act jointly and swiftly to revamp all aspects of our societies and economies, from education to social contracts and working conditions. Every country, from the United States to China, must participate, and every industry, from oil and gas to tech, must be transformed. In short, we need a 'Great Reset' of capitalism.

One silver lining of the pandemic is that it has shown how quickly we can make radical changes to our lifestyles. Almost instantly, the crisis forced businesses and individuals to abandon practices long claimed to be essential, from frequent air travel to working in an office.

Likewise, populations have overwhelmingly shown a willingness to make sacrifices for the sake of health-care and other essential workers and vulnerable populations, such as the elderly. And many companies have stepped up to support their workers, customers, and local communities, in a shift toward the kind of stakeholder capitalism to which they had previously paid lip service.

Clearly, the will to build a better society does exist. We must use it to secure the Great Reset that we so badly need. That will require stronger and more effective governments, though this does not imply an ideological push for bigger ones. And it will demand private-sector engagement every step of the way."

According to the World Economic Forum, the Great Reset agenda would have three main components:

1. The first would steer the market toward fairer outcomes. To this end, governments should improve coordination (for example, in tax, regulatory, and fiscal policy), upgrade trade arrangements, and create the conditions for a "stakeholder economy". Moreover, governments should implement long-overdue reforms that promote more equitable outcomes. Depending on the country, these may include changes to wealth taxes, the withdrawal of fossil-fuel subsidies, and new rules governing intellectual property, trade, and competition.

2. The second component of a Great Reset agenda would ensure that investments advance shared goals, such as equality and sustainability. Here, the large-scale spending programs that many governments are implementing

represent a major opportunity for progress. The European Commission, for one, has unveiled plans for a €750 billion ($826 billion) recovery fund. The US, China, and Japan also have ambitious economic-stimulus plans.

Rather than using these funds, as well as investments from private entities and pension funds, to fill cracks in the old system, we should use them to create a new one that is more resilient, equitable, and sustainable in the long run. This means, for example, building "green" urban infrastructure and creating incentives for industries to improve their track record on environmental, social, and governance (ESG) metrics.

3. The third and final priority of a Great Reset agenda is to harness the innovations of the Fourth Industrial Revolution to support the public good, especially by addressing health and social challenges. During the COVID-19 crisis, companies, universities, and others have joined forces to develop diagnostics, therapeutics, and possible vaccines; establish testing centers; create mechanisms for tracing infections, and deliver telemedicine. Imagine what could be possible if similar concerted efforts were made in every sector.

Kristalina Georgieva, Managing Director of the IMF confirms their support:

"Governments can put in place public investments—and incentives for private investments—that support low-carbon and climate-resilient growth. Many of these investments can lead to job-rich recovery—think of planting mangroves, land restoration, reforestation or insulating buildings."

Think of the masses and masses of free labor working off their debt in those fields...slavery ring a bell?

"Think of the key sectors for reducing carbon intensity where both the public and private sector can invest. I am particularly keen to take advantage of the low oil prices we see today, to eliminate harmful subsidies and introduce a carbon price that would work as an incentive for future investments.

"We also need to think carefully about how to make sure the jump in growth and profitability in the digital sector leads to benefits that are shared across our societies.

"This is the moment to decide that history will look back on this as the Great Reset, not the Great Reversal. And I want to say—loud and clear—the best memorial we can build to those who have lost their lives in the pandemic is to

build a world that is greener, smarter and fairer."

New World Opportunity

If people really want a world that is greener, smarter, safer, and fairer, they need to break all ties with any government and any organization that wants to organize and control them in any way.

One of the greatest things to come out of the Coronavirus plandemic, is the awareness among tens of millions of people who have finally woken up to the big picture – that their government is not there to help them.

Thank you New World Order. Thank you, Bill Gates, George Soros, Rockefellers, and Rothchilds. Thank you to all the Globalists and Banksters and Elitist Corporate Fraudsters.

People are waking up from the brainwash, the trance, the hypnosis they have been conditioned with for such a long time. If people have not heard it yet, the answer to freeing their minds and their money is to stop.

Stop paying extortion fees.

Stop voting.

Stop paying fines.

Close traditional bank accounts and start a new, and private, life with crypto.

Seeing clearly what is going on is part of liberation at its most basic level. Once people have woken, they can see. And once they can see, they cannot unsee.

The American Empire is falling and it is a good thing. A great thing.

Their "great reset" is a massive opportunity for those who act now. Want greater freedom, peace, and prosperity? It is easy to change the world. But humanity is bound together, connected, in how everyone collectively stands up against enslavement by those who think they are the masters.

Zen Gardner said:

"We have nothing to lose, nothing. We are not just resilient; we are an eternal source within human form.

They, however, have everything to lose. Hence the desperation and rapid deployment of every weapon they can conceive of. So what. It hasn't worked so far and never will."

Here is a simple lesson from the movie *A Bug's Life*:

Hopper: *"Let this be a lesson to all you ants! Ideas are very dangerous things! You are mindless, soil-shoving losers, put on this Earth to serve us!"*

Flik: *"You're wrong, Hopper. Ants are not meant to serve grasshoppers. I've seen these ants do great things, and year after year they somehow manage to pick food for themselves and you. So-so who is the weaker species? Ants don't serve grasshoppers! It's you who need us! We're a lot stronger than you say we are... And you know it, don't you?"*

What needs to be done, right now, is for everyone to wake up and stand up. They will not be alone. As more and more people move toward wakefulness, the easier it becomes for others to do the same. The universe wants humanity to wake up and will guide everyone toward wakefulness if they create the right conditions – until eventually, wakefulness becomes normal for the whole of the human race.

If people are self-reliant they can live completely without fear, so:

• Build a natural immune system so they will not need their vaccines.

• Meditate to take control of their mind and their thoughts.

• Cut loose from government monopoly on their money. Sell un-backed fiat currencies and buy gold, silver, foreign real estate, and crypto. Do not rely on a 401(k) that in return depends on increasingly useless stocks and bonds.

• Become self-reliant by growing their own food.

Do not be afraid of anything except not living. If people can see the bigger picture and find their true inner, unlimited resource and operate from there they have already won.

Larken Rose's *The Most Dangerous Superstition* is without a doubt one of the most challenging and life-changing books a person will ever read. Think of it this way:

"If you value peaceful coexistence, compassion and cooperation, freedom and justice, then teach your children the principle of self-ownership, teach them to respect the rights of every human being, and teach them to recognize and reject the belief in 'authority' for what it is: the most irrational, self-contradictory, antihuman, evil, destructive and dangerous superstition the world has ever known."

Land Of The Free, Home Of The Brave

Freedom means no man has the right to rule another. Not through an election, not through a constitution, or legislation, or education.

Repeat this mantra: "I am not a slave to any man. No one is my master."

This is OUR New World Opportunity:

No more corporate media with their half-century-long track record of lying to the public over and over again.

No more voting, because no more politicians.

No more lobbying industry to push the corporate agenda.

No more military.

No more Federal Reserve. The $26 trillion in debt owed by the American government to the Federal Reserve bank should be wiped away without any additional payments being made.

Money should not be controlled by the government... or the central banks. Nothing should be controlled by the governments and central banks. Begin using private cryptocurrencies such as Bitcoin and Monero.

No more banks.

No more IRS.

No more government indoctrination camps. Rewrite the history books with accurate information, not slanted stories about American heroism and empire-building talking points.

No more government healthcare system. Throw Big Pharma out of the public schools with their forced vaccination programs, psychotropic drugging of children, and the intentional dumbing-down of American society through the use of their products.

No more GMO food and no more Monsanto and other Agra businesses that poison the food supply with their glyphosate and other known carcinogenic pesticides. Take their Board of Directors and C-level executives and put them on trial for their crimes against the people of the world.

No more governmental criminal activity more commonly known as civil asset forfeiture, income tax, property tax, state tax, usage taxes, and licensing fees.

No more National Defense Authorization Act (NDAA), the Patriot Act, NAFTA, and the Five Eyes agreement. They are not in the best interest of the people.

No more United Nations, World Economic Forum, International Monetary Fund.

No more Council on Foreign Relations, the Club of Rome, the Committee of 300, the Bilderberg Group, and other globalist organizations.

No more ridiculous things that play up the stupidity of Americans like Daylight Saving Time, Black Friday, and Columbus Day.

No more killing people, both at home and abroad, especially with drones.

No more torturing people while proclaiming to the world that they are somehow the victims.

No more funding of "intelligence agencies" for spies, regime change operators, blackmail, theft, false flag attacks, and assassination.

No more weaponization of words, the silly push towards 53 different genders, safe spaces, and last-place trophies.

All of this crap has to stop right away in order for the world, in general, and the

American people, in particular, to believe that things are really changing.

It can be done, but it has to happen now.

No. More. American. Idiots.

This must be spoken about out because everyone's grandchildren should be able to live in a beautiful, FREE world with the immunity they were gifted with at birth...not a police world where they are enslaved by debt, have 24/7 surveillance and are forced to inject themselves with poisons so they can travel or work.

Bill Hicks said:

"The world is like a ride in an amusement park, and when you choose to go on it you think it's real because that's how powerful our minds are. The ride goes up and down, around and around, it has thrills and chills, and it's very brightly colored, and it's very loud, and it's fun for a while. Many people have been on the ride a long time, and they begin to wonder, 'Hey, is this real, or is this just a ride'?"

The question for humanity is: "What is your ride?"

While the truth is being massively censored in the media, Facebook, YouTube – but the people still have freedom of thought. The people still own their minds, and that means what they do right now in this diabolical play they have been cast in is really the one thing they cannot control...for now.

Choose an abundant, fearless, and free life – or don't take control of your own life and have the crappiest ride ever.

Now is the time.

About the Authors

<u>Jeff Berwick</u>

Jeff Berwick started The Dollar Vigilante (TDV) in 2010 with his partner, Ed Bugos, and the tagline "Surviving and Prospering, During and After the Dollar Collapse."

During that time, Jeff was asked when he expected the collapse to begin and he responded "By the end of this decade".

The Wuhan coranvirus hoax began almost exactly as predicted, at the very end of 2019 and the US economy was nearly completely destroyed within months.

Since, Jeff has been very active, making almost daily videos which you can see at the following:

YouTube (although not likely to remain up much longer): https://www.youtube.com/TheDollarVigilante

TDV's video website: https://dollarvigilante.tv

Bitchute: https://dollarvigilante.com/bitchute

LBRY: https://dollarvigilante.com/LBRY

Dtube: https://dollarvigilante.com/dtube

Facebook: https://www.facebook.com/DollarVigilante

The Dollar Vigilante also has a newsletter which goes out twice per month as well as alerts and regular updates. It has realtime information on how you can survive and prosper through this collapse at https://dollarvigilante.com/subscribe

The newsletter also has access to the full community of TDV subscribers worldwide. Having a network of like-minded people across the world during a collapse is very important.

TDV stated since its inception that its goal was to help people "during" the collapse... and that is already well underway. We also hope to help people "after" the collapse, which will be coming soon.

Charlie Robinson

Charlie is the author of "The Octopus of Global Control" which is available in paperback at Amazon & BN.com, and in digital formats at his website, as well as being the host of the Macroaggressions podcast on Apple, I Heart Radio, Spotify, YouTube, and Ickonic.com.

He is also the President and Broker of Alter Luxury, a real estate brokerage and interior design firm, and has almost two decades of experience working in Las Vegas real estate.

Website: TheOctopusOfGlobalControl.com

Twitter: @macroaggressio3

Facebook: Facebook.com/theoctopusofglobalcontrol

YouTube: Channel is called Macroaggressions

Printed in Great Britain
by Amazon